LOCAL

A CLUB AND ITS CITY
LIVERPOOL'S SOCIAL HISTORY

Daniel Fieldsend

'Local' Copyright © 2019 by Daniel Fieldsend. All Rights Reserved.
Second Edition.

The right of Daniel Fieldsend to be identified as the author of this work has been asserted by him in accordance with the Copyright, Designs and Patents Act 1988.

All rights reserved. No part of this book may be reproduced in any form or by any electronic or mechanical means including information storage and retrieval systems, without permission in writing from the author. The only exception is by a reviewer, who may quote short excerpts in a review.

Cover designed by Steven Jones (painting by Jules Penlington).

Every effort has been made to trace copyright holders and obtain their permission for the use of copyright material. The author apologises for any errors and omissions and would be grateful if notified (via public forums) of any corrections that should be incorporated in future reprints of editions of this book.

This work is constantly amendable via Amazon.com. For changes, please contact the author.

Printed in the United States of America

First Edition: June 2019
Second Edition: July 2019

Amazon KDP publishing.

ISBN- 9781075605338

For my family.

And for the voices of this red-brick city;
<u>We</u> are Liverpool.

READING LIST

I grew up in the 1990s as a baggy adidas jumper-wearing kid, playing with a flyaway ball inside Tilston Close off the East Lancs. Was Liverpool different to elsewhere? Apparently, but I didn't know why. I hadn't experienced what came before. Because of that, I've had to read the works of some of the best writers who lived through the events covered in this book. My reading list is below and my thanks and admiration goes to the names mentioned:

'I Don't Know What It Is But I Love It'. **Tony Evans**, Penguin. 2015.
'Two Tribes. a City on the Brink'. **Tony Evans**, Bantam Press. 2018.
'John Lennon The Life'. **Philip Norman**, Harper Collins. 2008.
'Jimmy Case: My Autobiography'. **Jimmy Case**, John Blake Publishing. 2015.
'Here We Go Gathering Cups in May'. **Nicky Allt**, Canongate Books. 2008.
'Talking Shankly'. **Tom Darby**, Mainstream Publishing. 1998
'The Ian Callaghan Story'. **Ian Callaghan** and **John Keith**, Quartet. 1975.
'43 Years With The Same Bird'. **Brian Reade**, MacMillan. 2008.
'Ghost On The Wall'. **Derek Dohren**, Mainstream Publishing. 2004.
'Carra: My Autobiography'. **Jamie Carragher**, Bantam Press. 2008.
'Liverpool: A People's History'. **Peter Aughton**, Carnegie. 1990.
'Liverpool FC Heroes'. **Ranghild Lund Ansnes**, Sport Media. 2012.
'The Liverpool FC Family Tree'. **Ken Rogers**, Sport Media. 2011.
'61 Minutes in Munich'. **Howard Gayle** and **Simon Hughes**. De Coubertin Books. 2016.
'Stand Up Pinocchio'. **Phil Thompson.** Trinity Mirror. 2006.
'Joe Fagan: Reluctant Champion'. **Andrew Fagan** and **Mark Platt.** Aurum Press. 2011.
'Mr Liverpool: Ronnie Moran'. **Baldursson** and **Clemente.** Trinity Mirror. 2017.
'In My Blood'. **Gerry Blayney.** Empire Publications. 2014.
'Hillsborough - The Truth'. **Phil Scraton.** Mainstream Publishing. 2016.
'The End – Every Issue'. **Hooton, Jones** and **Potter.** Sabotage Times. 2011.
'The Liverpool Boys are in Town'. **Dave Hewitson.** CreateSpace. 2014.
'Cup Kings: Liverpool 1977'. **Mark Platt.** Bluecoat Press. 2003.
'Supersub'. **David Fairclough** and **Mark Platt.** De Coubertin Books. 2015.
'Anfield Iron' **Tommy Smith.** Bantam Press. 2005.
'Terry Mac: Living For The Moment'. **Terry McDermott.** Trinity Mirror. 2018.
'Liverpool City of Radicals'. **Belchem** and **Biggs.** Liverpool University Press. 2011.
'Liverpool. A City That Dared To Fight'. **Taaffe** and **Mulhearn.** Fortress. 1988.
'Liverpool: The Hurricane Port'. **Andrew Lees.** Mainstream Publishing. 2013.
'Gerrard: My Autobiography'. **Steven Gerrard.** Bantam. 2007.
'My Story'. **Steven Gerrard.** Penguin. 2016.
'Passing Rhythms: Liverpool FC and the Transformation of Football'. **Williams, Long** and **Hopkins.** Berg. 2001.
'Liverpool - Wondrous Place'. **Paul Du Noyer.** Virgin Books. 2007.

ACKNOWLEDGEMENTS

I don't consider this to be an acknowledgements section in the traditional sense. It is more, in my eyes, a collection of truly great names who I will forever be indebted to. The following people are all locals (such is the concept of the book), all Reds, who in speaking with me and offering up their time displayed those great Scouse characteristics of generosity, honesty and charm.

All cities are effectively just bricks and steel, it is the people we encounter who define our experience. Liverpool is blessed with the most charismatic citizens. When we say that we love Liverpool, it is the people and the atmosphere that we speak of.

I don't think he was aware at the time, but Steve Hothersall rejuvenated this project when it was dead in the water, great thanks goes to him. Thank you to Frank Carlyle, George Sephton, Ged Strong, Dave Bilsborrow, Stephen Monaghan and Peter Carney – the history boys. To the players: Jimmy Case, Jamie Carragher, David Fairclough, Howard Gayle, Steve McMahon, John Aldridge, Chris Lawler, Rickie Lambert and Phil Boersma ... you gave up your time and were all so kind, thank you lads.

For talking about culture, politics, distinction and significant moments, nice one to Gary Shaw, Andrew Hudson and Chris Hudson, Brendan Wyatt, Kevin Sampson, George Sephton, Ian Barrigan, Tony Evans, Nicky Allt, Dan Carden MP, Cllr Ian Byrne, Simon Hughes, Paul Moran, Peter Moore, Joe McDonald, John McDonnell MP, Jay McKenna, Gareth Roberts, Andy MacKenzie, Tom Fairclough, Roy Bentham and Dr Joel Rookwood.

To the self-titled Rat Pack: Joe Woods, Day Wilcox and Sean Dever (*très bleus*) and Alan Carr, Sean McAdam and Jack Douglas (*très rogue*) – you've been the rock I've lent upon. Thank you, lads. To Lois O'Brien, *mi amor*, for your love and for keeping me sane and not allowing me to plunge into the despairing inferno that opens up whenever I foolishly think that writing a book is a solid enough idea, ta kid.

And to the exceptional, enchanting and heart-warming fusion of people at Pontville School, you are my extended family. You have time and again given me a loving home (hence my constant boomerangs). I will paraphrase the sentiment from my first book, because it still applies: to the pupils, if you aspire and persevere, you will ultimately succeed – let nothing deter you. To my boys in 4F: fly bravely. Always believe in your ability, because I believe in you.

This book has been fine-tooth combed and scrutinised by a list of friends who I trust above all else and who are among the brightest people I know: Steven

Jones, Mark Graham and his darling mum, Anne. Gareth Flitcroft, Tom Gill, Jake Keating, Lyndsey Robinson and Michael Brennan, thank you so much to all of you. All I can give you is my undying gratitude. Two weeks they read it in, which is all the more impressive given that the during the dividing weekend Liverpool won the European Cup for the sixth time ... Oh, those words ...

The Fieldsend tribe has grown since my last book. Sylvia (mum, you are our universe), Paul (dad, you are a hero to the masses), Rachel (you are goodness personified), Edna (nan, you are my nature), Lily (you are our life), and now Luca and Lydia, the new-born twins (whatever you will be, you will be loved). There are no words for how much I love you all – I'm pathetically devoted to you. Thank you for everything; I have nothing without you and I hope I make you proud.

CONTENTS

1. Wondrous Place – **Billy Fury**: Page 1... *background and context. The Bay of Liverpool; what even is Scouse?*
2. The Fields of Athenry – **The Dubliners**: Page 5... *Africa, the Caribbean, the Welsh, Irish and the nature of settlers.*
3. In My Liverpool Home – **The Spinners**: Page 13... *patriotism, the Blitz, Churchill, living conditions, post-war life, playing outside and becoming footballers.*
4. Face in a Crowd – **Dean Martin**: Page 26... *mythical dockers, culture and the formation of a civic character that stepped upon the Kop.*
5. There's a Place – **The Beatles**: Page 31... *Shankly, the Beatles and teenagers – a message of creative possibility.*
6. When the Ship Comes In – **Bob Dylan**: Page 46... *the famous Kopites of the 1960s. Merseybeat, Panorama, ee-ay-addio and Harold Wilson.*
7. Oliver's Army – **Elvis Costello**: Page 59... *the 1966 victory. The nation and the idea of nationalism. Wools and us: where Liverpool stood.*
8. Life of Riley – **Lightning Seeds**: Page 66... *Saturdays in the Boys Pen and Sunday League football – two vertebrae of civic support.*
9. Come Back (the Story of the Reds) – **The Mighty Wah**!: Page 77... *unfortunate unemployment. Shankly's retirement. Boundary lines and classism. The Scouse web of victorious relationships.*
10. Rotterdam (or Anywhere) – **The Beautiful South**: Page 85... *1976, then 'from Reykjavik to Rome...to Vladikavkaz', Liverpool fans in Europe.*
11. Sound and Vision – **David Bowie**: Page 101... *Thatcherism, the Reds and Norman Tebbit; getting off on Transalpinos. Fashion and Floyd, Scals and Bowie.*
12. Children of the Ghetto – **The Real Thing**: Page 114... *French police and Reds in Paris. Merseyside police and the Granby Uprising of 1981.*
13. Power to the People – **John Lennon**: Page 129... *the death of a hero. The start of the End – terrace lifestyle and fan culture in print, feat. the politicisation of Liverpudlians and the Militants.*
14. English Civil War – **The Clash**: Page 143... *us and them: Town Hall versus Westminster, Liverpool versus Everton, Kopites versus Roman Ultras, Scousers versus the world.*
15. Imagine – **Gino Paoli**: Page 156... *Liverpool in 1985: Heysel and the purging of Militants.*
16. All Together Now – **The Farm**: Page 170... *Reds and Blues at Wembley amidst the Bread-like stereotypes; life as Britain's Buenos Aires – or Britain's Detroit.*
17. Pass It On – **The Coral**: Page 178... *the Merseyside derby then and now. Something to be nourished.*

18. <u>Fearless</u> – **Pink Floyd**: Page 184... *Hillsborough - the day that football stopped. How families fought for justice against a backward establishment.*
19. <u>Heart as big as Liverpool</u> – **Pete Wylie**: Page 219... *miniature biographies of the innocent victims of Hillsborough.*
20. <u>Walkaway</u> – **Cast**: Page 229... *the '90s. The last day of the Kop, the cemented Scouse national image and savouring youthfulness in a tame decade. Cream the club and cream the suits.*
21. <u>Stand By Your Man</u> – **Tammy Wynette**: Page 248... *Fowler, Ferguson, Oasis, the Brit awards, John Prescott and the Dockers' dispute, then Evans/Houllier.*
22. <u>Mersey Paradise</u> – **Stone Roses**: Page 261... *Huyton's finest, the Manchester relationship, the treble and internationalisation. A conflict to Keep things Scouse?*
23. <u>Good Enough</u> – **Dodgy**: Page 271... *The Capital of Culture, a title made for Liverpool. Benitez arrives and Liverpool becomes oh so European.*
24. <u>The Wonder of You</u> – **Elvis Presley**: Page 282... *that fifth European Cup and the sweet taste of relevance. How the continent rebuilt Liverpool.*
25. <u>There She Goes</u> – **The La's**: Page 294... *Reclaiming the Kop, when neoliberalism met globalisation. Coupled with a very local tragedy.*
26. <u>Which Side Are You On?</u> – **Billy Bragg**: Page 303... *a glassy new city with a happy separate economy. Yanks out, the Spirit of Shankly and the socialist bedrock.*
27. <u>Tramp the Dirt Down</u> – **Elvis Costello**: Page 318... *the passing of an old foe.*
28. <u>Live the Dream</u> – **Cast**: Page 321... *a hero from Montevideo, Spion Kop 1906, 77 walkout, a new captain, bus welcomes and Boss Nights – new fan culture.*
29. <u>Newby Street</u> – **Michael Head**: Page 329... *the Kaiser of the Kop and a tide of local appointments. Foodbanks, Brexit, Salah and a club with a social conscience, culminating in Kiev.*
30. <u>Fortune Favours the Bold</u> – **Gerry Cinnamon**: Page 341... *a review of a pivotal season. Operation Unbearable begins.*
31. <u>You'll Never Walk Alone</u> – **Gerry and the Pacemakers**: Page 363... *the centre of the known universe – talking about six.*

Local

WONDROUS PLACE

On the fireplace of his home near Bowring Park are two statues: one of Jesus Christ and one of Bill Shankly. 'Local lads have more feeling and passion and love because we've been brought up with it all,' Chris Lawler, one of them, says: 'I've travelled like, but I've always lived in Liverpool when I can. I moved to Norway coaching for a bit but I still had to live near the water; it must be a Liverpool thing.'

'There used to be a lot of local lads playing because the club scouted tough areas,' continued Jimmy Case from Allerton, the toughest of the lot. 'The players that came in were really hungry for the game, which wasn't so much the case in affluent areas where the kids could play tennis or golf. We just had boxing or footy.'

Howard Gayle stirred his coffee in the Baltic Triangle as seagulls circled overhead: 'When you're brought up here as a socialist then you have a certain way of thinking and a certain dynamic. No other city would have achieved what the Hillsborough families did for example, they kept on going and didn't give up.'

And so continued Steve McMahon of Halewood: 'I don't buy the Sun. It's a Liverpool thing. *Aldo* is a Scouser. I'm a Scouser, and the people who suffered that day, Liverpool and Everton supporters - because it affected all of Merseyside – are united in not buying it.'

'I was brought up in a strong Labour family,' agreed John Aldridge. 'My mum and dad abhorred Thatcher and after the Toxteth Riots we saw how she tried to close our city down. I hated her and everything she stood for.'

Then there was regeneration. If he looked to the left, he would have seen Goodison Park, and slightly to the right there was Anfield. David Fairclough was raised inside a nucleus of fanaticism in Everton Valley. 'I remember when nobody wanted to come to visit Liverpool. It was a place at the far end of the M62 and on the other side was just sea. We were our own little place. Now we're this holiday resort and it's kinda strange for us. You're really proud to come from here. We do see ourselves as our own little republic; we have always had that and it still exists inherently, especially if you're born here.'

Robbie Fowler, who lived his teenage life inside a goldfish bowl, said something similar: 'If you look at a map of where Liverpool is, it's a difficult place to get to. You have the big motorways down the centre of England and Manchester is just off the M6, but Liverpool is on its own. To get to Liverpool you need to actually be wanting to go there, you can't stumble past it. That's something which gets me with Liverpool, if you look at how many tourists are in the city now it's incredible, and that's because they aren't passing through. They all want to be there.'[1]

While Fowler was scoring goals in the '90s, Rickie Lambert was pretending to be him on the astroturf in West Vale. 'I loved my childhood. I know it's a tough place, but when you're a kid you don't realise that, you just get on with it,' he said. After being let go by Blackpool as a teenager he worked in a factory in Skelmersdale before earning a contract with Macclesfield. He got to Liverpool FC through sheer perseverance. 'When I came back it was a completely different city. It was gorgeous. One of the best cities in the country. I couldn't believe it.'

Lastly, from his Mum's house on Knowsley Road where local kids used to peer through the curtains at him after he became professional, Jamie Carragher – a symbol of the times - reflected: 'We go way beyond the norm for cities of our size. They [similar sized cities] just accept they're small and accept the establishment which I don't think Liverpool people do. I think we believe we are the best and we don't take second best from anyone.'

*

There is a feeling that many modern footballers, even locals, are detached from the communities they represent; that their understanding of civic issues are limited; that the only part of a city they actually see is the route from the suburbs to the training ground. I met with the above names and asked them about the city of their birth. Their answers displayed how local footballers remain typically well-rooted to Liverpool and continue to keep their ears to the ground throughout their career. The quotes can be taken as a small ripple of understanding in an

---

[1] Niklas Holmgren podcast, September 2015.

ocean of Scouse identity. My hope for this book is that it forms something of a wave.

There's a general belief that most Scousers share the same principles and aspirations in life, but that isn't exactly true. There are hundreds of thousands of individual stories happening in the city each day, with various hankerings and opinions being formed all of the time. But on political and cultural matters of importance - of *real* importance - it is so often the case that Scousers group together and sing from the same hymn sheet, harmonising word-for-word as if they've heard the song before.

This publication is about the mindset of those people, about their city and about what Liverpool Football Club means to them, told through the eyes of its former players, staff and traditional supporters. The relationship between locals and the club is not exactly unique, but it does draw parallels with a number of other European clubs, such as FC Barcelona and Athletic Bilbao who maintain something of a political substructure.

It has been suggested that because of the collective suffering of the people and the club at tragic events, and because football was an escape during years of deprivation, the two forces became entwined. LFC and their supporters won and lost together... they continue to win and lose together.

The city has evolved over fifty years like nowhere else in Britain. It is now a cosmopolitan European outpost to be enjoyed, where seagulls squawk and tourists mingle and everybody has a certain tenderness for enjoyment. It is once again like Herman Melville described it to be a century ago, where 'visitors find their paradise'.

But Liverpool FC is not rooted in the same way the city is. The club is now something of a global brand, and it needs to be (locals want it to be). With that in mind, I'm aware of the potential limitations of this book. The name in itself is a giveaway... 'Local'. It appears to be dangerously withdrawn, behind the comfort of a drawbridge.

It isn't, and, if anything, I consider it to be an open-armed manual that will assist in the understanding of Liverpool people.

Using football to explain the city was my niche. The sport has shown its ability to hold a mirror up to society time and again. In Liverpool it is often the case that the two reflect together. Today's version of the game can be bright, flashy, loud and brash, but it can, at the same time, also appear a little bit sad and hollow. Indeed, a lot of the modern world is built on uncertain foundations. Local, however, references the roots and values which help to transcend an age of doubt. It touches upon something that can be timeless, provided it is nourished.

There are academic terms for the themes within these pages – like topophilia, glocality and psychogeography. They're fine words which explain our attachment. But they don't describe the feelings involved.

That first can of lager at the Rocket pub bus stop on a far-too-early sunny morning, which hisses and froths beneath the chorus of a vaguely familiar Coral track, on a coach full of the sharpest lads in town who share your sense of place, heading to an irrelevant part of the country for another day of affirmation. *Christ almighty*. The buzz is genuine (you can almost feel it). It transcends the working week - it slows down the passing month. When most other days seem to be laced with confusion and mundanity, being a Liverpudlian gives life a degree of certainty.

Like Plato said of ancient Athens: 'This city is what it is because our citizens are what they are'. It seems that 'locāl' is among the most noble concepts in philosophic history...

But, before you begin, I must mention something else. You really do need to bear this in mind, especially if you're feeling a tad alienated:

The Bay of Liverpool is so difficult to enter, it's undercurrent so volatile, that whenever a large ship arrives a pilot boat has to be sent out first to guide it in safely. I believe there to be a metaphor in there ... 'Scouse', as far as I'm concerned, is as much of a mentality as it is a locality. There are Scandinavians, Irishmen and Ulstermen, Southerners and others from elsewhere who have navigated tough waters and have worked hard to understand that fact. There is also, on that point, a great number of people who live in, and are from Liverpool, who are unfeeling of the city's pulse.

'Scouse' is a set of values and a way of acting, dressing, thinking and voting which guides a lifestyle. It is what you read and what you denounce. It's an incredibly achievable thing to grasp and a visitor with a willing heart will be pulled ashore and anchored if they wish.

For whilst this book unfairly looks to be about an exclusive membership, it isn't. Many of Liverpool's most understanding and dedicated fans and players are from elsewhere.

And while we're at it, 'Wool', its antithesis, is a mentality, a set of values, a way of acting, thinking, voting and dressing too. (For an example, see: 'Paul Nuttall').

Locãl

THE FIELDS OF ATHENRY

His boat moored on a sunny afternoon in the mid-18th century and bobbed gently on the shallow brownish water. His guide offered him a hand and they exchanged pleasantries, before walking uphill away from the bustling docks. Lord Erskine was a politician who considered it his duty to tour the country and write about his findings for the gentry to enjoy. Together over the next hour the two men climbed a steep grass verge (known later as Everton Brow) before stopping to gaze down upon the scene below. It was Liverpool, with its people, boats, luggage and noise. He was taken immediately and wrote that night of its potential:

"If I were capable of painting in words the impression Liverpool made on my imagination, it would form a beautiful picture indeed. I own I was astonished when, after ascending the hill, I was told by my guide – 'All you see spread out beneath you, that immense place which stands like another Venice upon the waters, where there are riches overflowing and everything that can delight a man who wishes to see the prosperity of a great community: all this had been created by the industry of a handful of men.' Well I must have been a stone not to have been affected by such a picture."

Erskine saw intersected docks, tall ships with white sails, enterprise and hustle, set upon glistening summer water. This town was new and exciting and would be defined by its waters, by the River Mersey which emptied out into the Irish Sea and the New World beyond. A school of thought grew from his visit among writers which remains today: that the Mersey is a more pleasing river to look upon than most because its horizon is there to be admired.

To be covered as a 'Venice' type place tends to draw a sense of internal warmth for modern locals, especially those who recognise themselves as being more in-line with elsewhere. Indeed, the city's museum has a quote from 1886 plastered on its wall to remind visitors, and locals, of that fact: 'Liverpool has become a wonder of the world. It is the New York of Europe, a world city rather than merely a British provincial.'

In 1999 the US city chose to twin with Liverpool to help get it 'moving again'. Liverpool had a certain essence which New York retained – John Lennon spoke often of the commonalities between them both. Initially there was a Celticness which marked them out, but over the years their ports welcomed cultures from all over the world, shaping them into hotbeds of life through whose prisms the human condition could be explored.

Paul Du Noyer explained that Liverpool only exists because it is a seaport. Its virtues and vices, its accent and attitude, its insularity and its open-mindedness are all derived from that primary fact. He wrote in 'Wondrous Place':

"As far as Scousers are concerned, Liverpool is not a provincial city, but the Capital of itself. It is deeply insular, yet essentially outward looking: it faces the sea and all the lands beyond, but has turned its back on England. There were local men for whom Sierra Leone was a fact but London was only a rumour. They knew every dive in Buenos Aires but had no idea of the Cotswolds."

Regular inland cities and people from elsewhere would be turned off by such talk – regarding it as conceited and elitist. Yet there remained some truth to the links uniting towns who once harboured trade and dialogue (when Liverpool bid to be the 2008 European Capital of Culture it was supported in its application by agencies in Naples, Marseille, Istanbul, Bremen and Gdansk, campaigning under the collective tag of 'Cities on the Edge'). And there, on that lapping point, begins the gentle thread that unites ports around the world.

Liverpool is like Naples initially, the first port (however tenuously), in that its fashionable people are informed by each other's attire, from head to toe. Much like Rotterdam, it rebuilt itself from the rubble of the Luftwaffe. It has the communal feel of Marseille according to Nicky Allt, and has the marriage of wit and grit which defines Dublin. It studies politics like Livorno, savours music like New Orleans and – similar to the intense phenomena that is Buenos Aires – uses football to explain all of this. Indeed, Scouse appetite for fashion, politics, music, history and culture is displayed through football fandom.

Given that the city has now since exceeded the potential Lord Erskine gave it – with its contributions to culture and the arts – the biggest export from its bustling docks would be football. It'd be taken for granted that the relevance given to an at-times redundant corner of the world was almost always because of the achievements of its main football club. Every time the name 'Liverpool' landed upon the soft pink pages of an Italian gazette or was mentioned inside an American Daily broadsheet, it was usually because of football.

Which leads on to another interesting point. Much like how the city sees a bit of itself in other port cities across the world, Liverpool Football Club could compare its successes to that of other port clubs. The following would make for a fine story:

Glasgow Celtic won Britain's first European Cup in 1967 with a team of local players from communities shaped by the fortunes of the Clyde. They were defeated in 1970 by Feyenoord of Rotterdam, a club whose city had suffered in the war. Ernst Happel, the Feyenoord manager in 1970, later won the trophy with Hamburger SV in 1983. Hamburg, another dock town, hosted mass unemployment and unrest for fifteen years prior to the victory, as port trade declined. In the late 1980's Porto was equally underfunded by the Portuguese state. Their team, FC Porto, reacted to reginal oppression by winning the European Cup in '87. In 1992 it was FC Barcelona's turn, from the repressed region of Catalonia. And in 1993 Olympique Marseille became the first French team to win the European Cup during a period of degeneration, with the French government having prioritised trade from Le Havre in the north at the time.

Marginal success was also had on the periphery. IFK Gothenburg, whose city pours out into the North Sea, won two UEFA Cups in the 1980's, being the only Nordic club to taste success in Europe. And when Diego Maradona told the Neapolitan masses 'I want to be the idol of the poor children of Naples, because they are like I was in Buenos Aires,' he inspired them to win 1989's UEFA Cup.

Cities kissed by water reclaimed their sense of difference and were afforded a degree of self-confidence through the successes of their striving clubs. All of which sounds familiar, because from 1965-1990 Liverpool FC were the cream of the entrepôts.

*

Laura Brown, when referencing the 1980s, wrote that Liverpool developed its own sense of exceptionalism because it 'didn't want to be defined by the story being written for it,'[i] - a fair point. But there were more historic roots that allowed such sentiments to grow.

It would see itself as a city-state because of its history. The first purpose-built prison, library, cast iron building, blind school, deaf school, transatlantic ship, office block, public baths, wash-house, radio broadcast, NSPCC and RSPCA societies, as well as trivial start-ups like goal nets, chess clubs and crossword puzzles, all came from Liverpool. The American Civil War ended there when the Shenandoah's white sails arrived after weeks of sorry travel, surrendering itself in the Mersey, consequently resulting in the abolition of slavery.

It is forgotten now, but Confederate failure in the Civil War upset capitalists in Liverpool. The city's wealth, beauty and status – with its Victorian and Georgian homes – had been cemented by the blood of slaves. Between 1741 and 1810, just under 1,000,000 people were taken on Liverpool ships and triangulated across the world (though few reached Liverpool, it must be said), being forced to live cruel, inhumane lives. It wasn't until 1999 that the city apologised for its role in slavery.

Capitalists made a fortune and transformed the town. Money came in from the Mersey, through a treacherous Liverpool Bay. P.J. Waller noted how by 1840 Liverpool had sixteen docks. But by 1900 it had forty docks that covered some 1600 acres, with '35.5 miles of lineal quay space'.[2] For wealthy visitors, Liverpool's dock warehouses were as monumentally breath-taking to gaze upon as the pyramids in Egypt.

The labour that built those megastructures came from immigrants: Irish, Scots and Welshmen. Liverpool was acquiring monikers galore throughout the 1800s and was known as the 'Capital of North Wales', as well as a Venice, New York and Dublin type place. There were some 40,000 Welsh settlers in 1860 who spoke no English whatsoever, who began building thousands of small homes for cheap. By 1900 there were 80,000 Welsh using Liverpool as a venue to maintain their culture and language.

In the 20th century the city became more Celtic-minded, especially following the Potato Famine when Irish people flocked and settled in the nearest place that wasn't Ireland: the streets near Liverpool's docks. The scale of immigration was incredible. It was estimated some 2 million people passed through Liverpool in a decade. Most moved on, to Boston, New York, Chicago and elsewhere, but enough stayed to create a distinctive local culture. Troughton wrote how the Irish formed 'the local manners of the town, which have always been distinguished from those of other Lancashire towns, by a peculiar hospitality, activity and sprightliness.'[3]

---

[2] Liverpool: A city that dared to fight. (1988), Taaffe and Mulhearn.
[3] Scouse: A Social and Cultural History. (2012), Tony Crowley.

Living conditions which the Irish suffered created a fertile environment for radicalism to take root. They were hated by English landlords and, in return, the Irish hated them back. That distaste for capitalists carried through generations and the bourgeois lived in fear of a revolution.

Probably a product of such republican thinking himself, the Militant politician Tony Mulhearn wrote in the 1980s about how hostility to the English was carried on into second and third generation of Liverpool Irish. He explained: 'They considered themselves as more Irish than English,' and regarded that identification as a factor in the temperament of the impending labour movements to come. Leon Trotsky had commented that 'a temper runs through the veins of the working-class', especially, he felt, those who carried Scottish, Welsh and Irish blood. Liverpool, geographically exposed to the incoming world, harboured all three.

They came with their beliefs and rubbed shoulders with Liverpool's orthodox population, causing instant friction. Frank Carlyle is a historian from Gerard Gardens. He describes the slow alterations that took place: 'The Irish came over to work on the docks and elements of sectarianism came in almost instantly. This originally was a non-Catholic city. After the Famine, the Irish were starving so they left the country to escape it. There was a huge influx into Liverpool in 1847. Some of them were diseased. Scotland Road was the area where most settled because the Catholic church St Anthony was there. They celebrated everything: communions, deaths... a wake went on for weeks. They also carried effigies and the non-Catholics didn't like this, so sectarianism kicked off in around 1851.'

Part of original English population was a capitalist named John Houlding. Born on Tenterden Street, Houlding was a member of the Orange Order, a Freemason and a staunch Conservative. His money was made through public houses, such as the Sandon Pub in Anfield where in 1892 he founded Liverpool Football Club – Everton FC had played there beforehand. If a certain Gaelic temperament would come to influence the attitudes of the people of the city, and indeed supporters of his new club, it was a nature that was foreign to him.

His football team however quickly gained the support of many in the city. When Liverpool won its first league title in 1901, the players arrived at Central Station to find thousands of fans celebrating. It didn't matter to them that the players were not from Liverpool (it was a seafaring town where people came and went daily), no, the team belonged to the crowd and they had won in the name of the city and that was all that mattered.

There grew an irony that football's overwhelming importance to the city helped phase out the religious divides that Houlding lived through. By the 1960s, people knew each other's religions as well as their team colours. In the 1990s when Rickie Lambert was growing up, nobody cared. 'It didn't come into it,' he reflects. 'My mum was a Protestant and my dad was a Catholic. Neither were really big religious people and it never got pushed onto me. You find out if somebody is a Red or a Blue first. The biggest divide in our family was that my mum liked the Royal Family and my dad hated them.'

Tony Evans once wrote that if Scouse is a stew, then so too is the identity.[ii] There were Irish, Chinese, Caribbeans, Africans, Italians, Welsh and Scandinavians settling in the one place. The Irish lived around Scotland Road; the Welsh were based off Stanley Road; the Jewish community lived in Allerton and built a synagogue off Queen's Drive. The Chinese resided around Pitt Street, while Liverpool's black population from West Africa and the Caribbean settled in the south end.[4]

Integration was an issue for a long time, just like it was in Belfast and Glasgow. In 1909, Protestants lined Juvenal Street with swords to stop the Catholics from marching. But in the end, a sense of unity among the people usually emerged whenever a common enemy appeared.

The 1911 transport strike just two years later backed up that point, when dockers, railway workers and sailors united throughout the summer - despite their religions – to fight unemployment and casual employment, in what would prove to be one of the first major acts of trade unionism and working-class solidarity in British history. 85,000 people gathered on St George's steps and chanted against the government. Winston Churchill, Home Secretary, sent 3,500 troops in against his own people and positioned gunboats on the Mersey. 400 were injured and two people died. This act of radicalism, according to Professor Phil Redmond, forever set Liverpool apart as a colony and not a mere province: "Its own 'People's Republic', never again to be part of England."[5]

1911 was to be a huge year for the city. Liverpool was well and truly in the national eye between 4th March and the 1st April when members of the upper-class came from London and France to admire the works of Gauguin, Picasso, Matisse,

---

[4] Seeds of diversification would be seen in football. Wayne Rooney and Robbie Fowler could have opted to play for Ireland. Aldridge did. Howard Gayle could have picked Sierra Leone. Ross Barkley, Nigeria. Kevin Nolan, The Netherlands, and so on.

[5] Liverpool: City of Radicals. (2011), Belchem and Biggs.

Locăl

Vlaminck, van Gogh, Derain, Rouault, Cezanne, Denis and Signac. Their paintings were housed at the Walker Art Gallery alongside British works for the first time, together, in history. Virginia Woolf wrote how shocking it was for this exhibition to appear in Liverpool before London. It was perhaps all the more shocking given the nature of Liverpool at the time; a city bubbling with radicalism and a desire for revolution.

By 1921 and the partition of Ireland, the nature of Liverpool had been changed completely.[6] It had a number of Irish nationalist councillors and even an MP, T.P. O'Connor. Richard Sadleir from Cork became the city's first Mayor and Sinn Fein won the Exchange seat in 1918. As recently as the 1960s the area sweeping from the top of Everton down to the Mersey was considered by many to be Catholic territory. The other side of Everton was Orange land. Tony Evans from Scotland Road wrote in 2013: 'Particularly in the North End – bounded by Tithebarn Street, Great Homer Street, Boundary Street and the river – the city became a different country.'

A different country indeed, but not exactly Ireland East. There were other ingredients mixed together in a stew of communities that created an accent so rare that in certain streets around the Mersey it was almost indistinguishable. The character of Heathcliff in Wuthering Heights was described as a dirty boy from the docks who was as good as dumb, and who only spoke a version of 'non-discernible gibberish'. They debate in the book whether he speaks Creole or Gaelic, but in fact he was speaking an early version of both: he was talking with a Scouse tongue. That was in 1848.

James Picton wrote in 1888 about his friend, the Liverpool born Prime Minister William Gladstone's accent: "There is no man who has not contracted in his early life some mannerism of accent, tone or dialect derived from his surroundings, of which he can never entirely rid himself." And nor should he. But Gladstone would not have considered his tongue to be 'Scouse', and Heathcliff sounded nothing like the modern local.

The term was used to slur children born on Mann Island – a coalescence of pubs, beggars, drunks and prostitutes. Young women with no money would leave their babies on Mann Island in the hope that they'd be adopted by wealthy members of the upper-class. Sailors who passed through the city came to adopt

---

[6] So wrote Tony Evans in 'Two Tribes', a fantastic piece of work.

the term as a way of tarnishing Liverpool people at sea. Over time, Scousers adopted it as a badge of honour.

There are so many varying interpretations of where the term originated, but the outcome is always the same: 'Scouse' was a put-down that was eventually worn with pride.

The novelist Kevin Sampson believes that the modern Liverpudlian is identifiable through clothing and attitude, but the accent is: 'The point of the arrow when it comes to being Scouse. It is as sharp and intimidating as it can be.' In itself the accent provides a barrier. If two Scousers wish not to be understood, they can allow that to be the case (subtitles were provided to US viewers whenever Jamie Carragher spoke on the 'Being Liverpool' documentary), which is a nod to the Welsh and Irish history of the place.

Nowadays Liverpool is the one city besides Dublin where St Patrick's day is best celebrated. Catholics from Northern Ireland who have taken up residence in the city, either full-time or for university, are free to celebrate without fear. Yet despite that, although Liverpool has been spiced with Irish influence, it is its own place altogether. In 2008, Bono of U2 presented Paul McCartney with an MTV lifetime achievement award at a ceremony at the Echo Arena. The Irish rock star took ownership over the Beatles as an Irish band in his speech, claiming them to have been diverted to Liverpool from 'Bubbling Dublin' by the famine. He was booed vociferously by the crowd.

The Beatles could only have been created in Liverpool and influenced by the docks, by the incoming trade and buzz of enterprise. Paul and John were taught music by Lord Woodbine, a Scouse-Trinidadian bohemian black artist from Liverpool 8. Cork, Dublin, Kerry and Galway: Ireland had not created the Beatles and nor would it. Only Liverpool's cake-mix of people would shape the band, who adapted black music for white Americans.

Bono, in his likely unintended ignorance, failed to recognise that Liverpool was its own place and for local residents, the Beatles – and everything else that came from Liverpool - belonged to Liverpool.

Local

IN MY LIVERPOOL HOME

As the sweat dripped down his forehead and onto his baking uniform, the team's captain, Joe Fagan, shook hands with his Egyptian opponents, patted his victorious comrades on the back, guzzled down water from his flask and began thinking about returning home. It was 1945. The lad from Litherland, who had grown up off Scotland Road's grey streets and volunteered for the Royal Navy, found himself playing in exhibition matches under a hot Egyptian sun.

Fagan may have come out Celtic-thinking Liverpool, but like all Scousers he was quick and willing to fight for his country when a real and dangerous foe emerged. In the face of a common enemy, patriotism was a natural response. Liverpudlians battled proudly against the Axis powers to protect the old folk back home. Thousands joined the King's Regiment to fight under Arabian, Libyan and radiant suns in far foreign lands. Was there any other alternative?

Liverpool FC was the first club to respond to the call for arms, enlisting 20 players into the 9th King's Battalion of the Territorial Army, as well as their manager George Kay and his assistant Jack Rouse. Arthur Riley and Dirk Kemp were made sergeants. Willie Fagan became trench mortar expert; Jack Balmer learned to drive tanks and Bob Paisley rode into Rome on one.

Joe Fagan, who was raised by an Irish father and a Scouse mother, volunteered as a telegraphist for the Royal Navy despite having no appetite for the sea (he joked often about being sick on the Seacombe ferry). He worked on a minesweeping flotilla off the coast of North Africa – the edge of the earth for somebody of his background. His father had been a bookie's runner and young Joe grew up streetwise. He was hard, too, known amongst his colleagues for being a knock-out boxer.

Also based in a dry region that seemed to British soldiers like a scene from another planet, was Tom Saunders from West Derby, a future schoolmaster and Liverpool FC employee, who'd first volunteered for the Territorial Army aged 16.

Navy men and soldiers positioned in Africa prayed each day for nuggets of optimism, for news to come in explaining that the war was soon to be over. They were exhausted by the heat and thirst and longed to return home, back to the morning dew on green fields, to gardens, vegetables and certainty. But home didn't look like it used to anymore, at least not where they were from.

Liverpool had been battered. Winston Churchill started making regular visits to the city from 1943 onwards because of its key military position, and he frequented the Western Approaches Command bunker[7] - a secret bomb-proof chamber under Exchange Flags - where, alongside Royal Navy, RAF and Marine forces, he monitored incoming attacks from the west. It was from here that the Battle of the Atlantic victory was coordinated.

Locals tried their best not to think too much about their own mortality and sang ditties about notorious Nazis, like Goering and Himmler. In their parlours they turned Adolf Hitler into something less than the maliciously evil man he actually was.

Hitler wasn't a psychopath. He didn't have a mental illness and, as Fritz Redlich wrote, to afford him one would excuse him of his paranoia and delusions: 'He knew what he was doing and he chose to do it with pride and enthusiasm.' When Hitler attacked Liverpool during the Blitz - a place he'd visited in the past and by all accounts enjoyed (his brother Alois lived on Upper Stanhope Street in 1912) - he did so without any recoil or hesitation.

Britain was supposed to be in retreat, as proven by events at Dunkirk, and his expansionist campaign was succeeding. So, when the RAF executed a surprise hit-and-run on Berlin, something Goering boasted could never happen, Hitler reacted furiously, pouring hell onto Britain's major cities.

Liverpool was the worst hit port and would be the second-most bombed British city during the Blitz, targeted over 80 times by the Luftwaffe. More than 3,000 local people died: 2,736 in Liverpool, 454 in Birkenhead and 424 in Bootle. The Customs House, the Cotton Exchange, the Rotunda Theatre and Lewis's department store were nearly destroyed; 190,000 homes were damaged. Each morning, various cargo ships from Canada and the United States lay sunk in the

---

[7] Not the Storrington Avenue pub - he wasn't that brave.

Mersey. Were it not for the Home Guard setting fires in the fields of North Wales to deter incoming German bombers, Liverpool would have been completely levelled.

A number of the bombs intended for Bootle missed their target and landed in nearby Crosby. The coastal town, famous for being the birthplace of Titanic deserter J. Ismay, was also home to Ronnie Moran. Born in 1934, Moran would become the most consistent character in the establishment of Liverpool FC as a 'Bastion of Invincibility'. His father, Joe, fought in the First World War and was a binman for the rest of his life, picking up rubbish and taking it to the other end of the borough by horse and cart. Ronnie would sit at the front as a boy and go with his dad as he worked.

When Luftwaffe bombs destroyed Merseyside's coast, causing the evacuation of local children, 7-year-old Ronnie stayed behind. He hid under the stairs with the rest of his family as beachside sirens blazed outside. When the Bryant and May match factory in Bootle exploded, the Morans' and other families in Crosby peered out of their shelters to see the night sky ablaze.

Locals lived in total darkness, their windows boarded up, besieged by sirens most nights. Throughout the whole of May 1941, Liverpool was on fire. Priests prayed against the apocalypse. People looking down from Ormskirk to the north and from the coast of North Wales in the distance saw Liverpool's red sky aglow for a month.

Rationing placed communities closer together as families 'lent' bacon, ham, sugar, jam and butter to each other. Eggs from countrified villages like Maghull and Lydiate became secret commodities.

But the 'single worst civilian incident of the war' according to Churchill, had happened in Liverpool on 29th November 1940 in Edge Hill. Following 8 hours of bombing, a parachute mine fell onto Ernest Brown Junior College at 2am where 300 people were hiding. They'd fled there from factories and local houses. A furnace exploded, scalding everybody beneath with boiling water. So horrific was the outcome that lime powder was scattered over body parts and the basement was sealed.

"I see the damage done by the enemy attacks," Churchill reflected of Liverpudlians, "but I also see the spirit of an unconquered people." Bruised and beaten, they would suffer countless times in future years, but that spirit of unconquerable fortitude would inevitably come to define them.

*

Daniel Fieldsend

During the war, Liverpool FC kept fans happy with novelty football matches, aimed at sustaining attendances. The Reds beat Preston 2-0 in August 1940. It was Tom Finney's debut and Liverpool had Stan Cullis playing as a guest centre-half. But as the political landscape shifted daily the government, worried by the threat of the Luftwaffe, banned the assembling of large crowds.

It didn't stop Liverpool manager George Kay from signing a World Champion in 1943 though. Joe Louis visited Anfield and Kay is said to have asked for his autograph on a folded piece of paper. After Louis signed it, Kay revealed that it to be a playing contract for Liverpool FC.

By late 1943 people started to sense some optimism. Churchill addressed the nation with a speech that began: "After the war". The Beveridge Report was being spoken about, which promised to create a welfare state and a National Health Service, and people were finally allowed to predict what the future would look like. Once the fighting was over, Churchill voted against the report in Parliament and, eventually, in 1945, the Labour party were elected.

Politics in Liverpool had always been locally spiced. Trade unions were well organised and outside the docks they spoke for the grievances of ordinary folk. Labour after the war capitalised on the decline in religious voting which allowed for a number of big, outspoken local characters to step out of the shadows of union halls and into the public arena, campaigning for workers' rights and better living conditions.

Bessie Braddock between 1945 and 1970 became as recognisable a woman in Liverpool as the Queen. A former communist, 'Battling Bessie' served the Liverpool Exchange seat for 25 years, once telling the Tories in Parliament how she'd be willing to "Take a machine gun to the lot of them." Braddock was of the same ilk as Eleanor Rathbone – another battling Liverpool lady with radical ideas. She took her experiences of Liverpool's streets to Westminster, working tirelessly for social reform.

Braddock also pushed for Liverpool's slums to be made safe. With buildings along the docks still smouldering, people lived in fear of structural collapses. But for kids, oblivious to any alternative, a playground was being reshaped every day. Houses that were decimated became 'ollers', 'hollows' or 'empties' for their enjoyment. The council slowly began demolishing all of the other damaged buildings, levelling over the ground and covering it, creating makeshift football and cricket pitches for children in between the remaining terraced blocks.

'Empties' became a feature of Liverpool's scenery for thirty years. Chris Lawler, Ian Callaghan and Tommy Smith honed their skills on them before and after school each day. Even when David Fairclough was a boy in the 1960s, they were still a part of the landscape. On the side of the houses enclosing Fairclough's 'empty' was graffiti – one end had 'Everton' painted on it and the other had 'Liverpool'. Summer evenings were accompanied by the sounds of children's laughter and the constant thud of a ball against a wall. For people looking back who were raised on those smouldering streets, there was a purity that they recall with fondness.

Ronnie Moran developed his technique on his 'empty' and was subsequently picked up by Bootle Boys in 1948, before being recommended to Liverpool FC by his postman, who convinced club chairman T.V. Williams to come take a look at the lad. Chris Lawler had a similar story, although he was picked up by Liverpool Schoolboys. He reminisces about those halcyon days: 'I was always out on the street playing. You don't see kids playing out any more, we were never in the house. We'd thumb a lift off lorries and all kinds.'

Although he was slightly younger, David Fairclough lived outside all day as well: 'There was nothing else to do. Houses were so small you didn't spend time at home.' The children who played outside organised themselves like kids do, discovering for themselves who the local neighbourhood leaders were – the spiky kids with rolled up sleeves who nobody dared say 'no' to.

Ian Callaghan joined a 'street league' that had been established by such boys. Matches took place between groups of kids from various parts of Liverpool. 'We organised them ourselves, but it all ran like clockwork. Those games were hard, competitive affairs because neighbourhood pride was at stake,' he wrote.

At home with no disposable income to waste, mothers cut their children's hair, while fathers were tasked with mending broken shoes caused by playing too much football. Mary Callaghan, Ian's mother, told John Keith about her son's life as a boy:

> *"A few yards from our house was a bottling store and at lunchtime the men who worked there would have a game of football in the street. If Ian ever disappeared, I knew where to find him ... he'd be kicking a ball around with the men, and this was before he'd started school. I'll never forget on one of the occasions I went to collect him after he'd slipped away to have a game with the workmen. "That boy of yours will be a footballer when he grows up," one man said. He's been proven right, of course."*

Daniel Fieldsend

The Football League restarted in 1946 and Billy Liddell was finally able to take on the First Division. He played left-wing, ahead of Bob Paisley at left-half. Their captain was Matt Busby. Rattles that had been used as air raid warnings were painted red and brought to matches by boisterous supporters.

As 1950 approached, young families tried to put the war behind them and move on with their lives. Ronnie Moran started training twice a week for Liverpool. He served an apprenticeship with Mersey Docks and Harbour Company as an electrician at the same time and listened each morning to the sharp mickey taking that began on the overhead railway, continuing throughout the day.

It was in this environment that he further saw the importance of both hard work and the need to be passionate about one's vocation. Jobs were difficult to come by, so to be working on the docks had great value. Years later Moran described his appreciation of how hard the fans who attended matches had worked to be there. In the 1994 'Last Day of the Kop' match programme, he wrote: 'I stood on the Kop as a lad and the place was packed with humourists and enthusiasts; the right mix for football. Those fans worked hard during the week and demanded the same effort from the players they supported.' As a player, he rewarded them as best he could.

*

Old Scotland Road was far from utopia. It was tough. Policemen patrolled its dim lights in groups. There was a transparent refusal to accept authority for most who lived cramped within it - the community was self-governed. But it was also a mesmerisingly warm and buzzing place for those who knew it and understood how to live there.

Women chatted in the wash houses of a morning and carried on their talks in the street as their children played around, taking turns to put pots of tea on for everybody else. When the sun fell slowly behind a terraced row the kids came home for food. People had little, but they had each other. Gathered around wooden tables in the low-lit ale houses at night, they played cards and sang folk songs and gambled and smoked.

But life was not as romantic as reflection suggests. There were thieves and all manner of rogues who had to be sorted out internally, and in the winter, conditions got so bad that if it rained people stepped over buckets on the stairs, and if it was frosty then nobody could flush the outhouse deposits.

Locāl

Why does any of this matter? Because Scotland Road teetered on the edge of poverty. If Britain were to move on, then the old places and the old ways of living had to be left behind. The Slum Clearance Act of the 1950s and '60s put an end to that grubby age of coterie, effectively ending a piece of civic history by relocating core groups of people (and historic Scouse identity) to a wider catchment area, picking them up and putting them down in spacious new towns.

It had been done in New York around the Cross Bronx Highway; massive demolitions blew away houses and communities, as well as small businesses, established family links and networks of communication. Local folk legends came to a close as people were forced to move to new, foreign districts. In Liverpool it was *au revoir* to Scotland Road, the Foster's House, Paddy's Market, Sailor's Home and the world-famous pubs. Everton's bright cramped lights which welcomed seamen home at night died before the glow was even faint. A folk song rang out of the pubs before they shut forever:

"We'll miss the Mary Ellens,
And me dad'll miss the docks,
An Gran'll miss the washhouse,
Where she washed me Granddad's socks,
Don't want to go to Kirkby,
Or Skelmersdale or Speke,
Don't want to go, from all we know,
On Back Buchanan Street."

Locals had no understanding of the things they lived without. There was little complaint from the five women who shared one stove to feed their families, and the four kids who shared a bed at night knew better than to say anything. They just lived among the damp and vermin because nothing else had ever been imagined.

The Slum Clearance Act proposed that people should have access to light, gardens, space and clean running water. Houses were built over three years to begin with, dividing people up and sending them across the boroughs. The Liverpool Echo revealed the impact of the project. Skelmersdale (population 6,216) welcomed 48,000 Scousers. 18,000 went to Widnes; 19,000 to Halewood; 6,000 to Cantril Farm; 3,500 to Formby and 30,000 to Kirkby. Homelessness had been so bad beforehand that the Echo ran a headline suggesting ships on the Mersey could 'be turned into homes'.

The act plotted future Liverpool players about a bigger-than-before city, like seedlings in a map of soil. Civic identity expanded instantly. The Lawler family moved from Scotland Road to Norris Green; the Faircloughs from Everton to Cantril Farm. Halewood raised the McMahons, while Kirkby was home to Phil Thompson, Terry McDermott and Phil Boersma.

Areas that traditionally retained sectarian beliefs were broken up, too. Many Catholic families from around the docks moved to towns and shared streets with Protestants. With forced integration and increased wealth and living standards, tensions wavered.

In the Kirkby that Phil Thompson grew up in, a scattering of Orangemen marched on their day and the Catholics on theirs, but violence was hardly prevalent. People had different ambitions than before and came to care for the places they lived.[8] Steve Rotheram from Northwood explained to Keith Roberts that Scouse identity was prouder by the 1960s, which helped overwrite any predetermined bigotry: 'Through the Beatles and the Merseybeat era, with the accent being an easy identifier, when you went abroad you became a 'Scouser'. It didn't matter if you were Catholic, Protestant or anything else.'[9]

David Fairclough had been happy in Everton, minding cars on Robson Street for fellers on their way to the match. From the top of Major Lester schoolyard he could see the Mersey and feel its air. But he found in Cantril Farm a desire from rehoused people to form a new community: 'You see old images of women stood at the door talking to other people and you don't get that now, but that's what it was like. The fact that you're all living in each other's pockets fostered a respect.'

New shops and department stores popped up in the mid-1950s where slums once stood, birthing a consumerist society. Tuebrook survived more or less intact, while West Derby was the setting for new council flats. Speke on the outskirts hosted grand experiments of housing schemes. Softly spoken and always smiling, Chris Lawler remembers life in Norris Green at the time: 'The neighbours all raised each other's kids. I was one of fifteen. There were eleven lads.' He thinks his dad wanted his own football team. After the war, replenishing the population was actively encouraged. Lawler is of the first generation of baby boomers.

They grew up in shorts and dresses and climbed and fell and returned home only for food. There were new comforts to enjoy in the '50s, if they wanted them. Days out to the beach, to Southport and Crosby for jam butty picnics and ice-

---

[8] There was one occasion however in 1958 when Cardinal John Heenan was stoned by a mob of Protestant youths after leaving the home of a sick Catholic in Scotland Road.

[9] Liverpool Sectarianism: The Rise and Demise. (2017), Keith Daniel Roberts.

cream were had. If it had been a good week then dads would take the kids to the picture house to watch a show, and they'd all cheer together whenever a character going on a boat to America mentioned the name 'Liverpool'.

Terry McDermott remembers going on holiday to New Brighton and taking the Royal Iris to get there. 'It only took 10 minutes but it was exciting. We'd take a few bottles of water and some sauce butties and we were as happy as could be,' he reminisced in his autobiography.

Parents living on a particular road decided among themselves to host 'play street' days, banning traffic and supplying children with old toys to keep them occupied. David Fairclough laments how 'you're more likely to see a '*No Ball Games*' sign nowadays,' than see children freely enjoying themselves.

'I was a quiet lad from a big family,' Chris Lawler said. 'Being one of the youngest they were always on top of me all of the time. The older siblings helped raise the younger ones in our family. We were all close.' Lawler would disappear for days on end as a kid playing cricket and football. 'I used to bring medals home every week and my mum and dad didn't even know where I'd been.'

In those carefree days the 'Scallywag' (a young male, typically, with an almost Huck Finn indifference) was born. They ran over railway lines, climbed onto roofs, sneaked into places they shouldn't, pinched wood from empties and swam in manky canal water, doing their best every day to avoid the grip of a patrolling bobby. Peter Stockley wrote about his rascal childhood: 'We learned our skills from older lads who had done it all before us. The docks, warehouses and canals became our playground which we trespassed on and plundered almost every day from the age of six.'[10]

Terry McDermott had lived in a two-bedroom tenement in Scotland Road, modelled on the *Karl Marx Stadt* blocks from socialist Vienna, before his family moved to Kirkby in 1957. He ran around with holes in his socks and with cardboard covering the gaps in his shoes because his family were that skint. He'd freely admit to being a bit of a Scallywag as a child, climbing up an unfinished 15-storey block of flats and swinging down the balconies from one to the other. If his hand slipped, he'd have died. David Fairclough was always cautious with such affairs: 'My mother always told me not to get into trouble because I'd be blamed for being the red haired one. I wasn't exactly a goody-goody, I took risks, but I

---

[10] The Scallywags - Memories of a Rascal's 1950's Childhood. (2016), Stockley.

was brought up to remember that I'd probably be the one to be caught out,' he said.

Tommy Smith's upbringing was tougher than most. He was born in the month Adolf Hitler committed suicide and, while other families were being rehomed, his Scotland Road house remained. Other kids always tried to fight with him growing up. They came to know him for his fists first and his feet later. He had his first straightener when a lad jumped the queue for the swimming baths around the corner from St John's School in 1952. Smith tried to intervene but was headbutted for his troubles. He got up and battered the lad. So frequent were incidents from then on he'd end up having his teeth removed by a local dentist known as 'Baker the Butcher'.

When he was fifteen, Smith's father died. After the funeral, the procession went back to his house on Lambeth Road and Tommy watched on as the priest, Father Songhurst, got blind drunk before falling over on his way home. It was an embarrassing display. He swore he'd never go to church again after that: the image stayed with him. Eventually Tommy and his mum moved in with his nan. They were so poor that the council paid his mother £1 a week for his food. He had a void in his life, at the most confusing age, the size of a father and an absent faith.

Anfield would fill that for him and he'd sneak in to watch Billy Liddell and his other heroes play. Indeed, the single most common activity that all lads of Smith's age and era enjoyed was going to watch football.

Ronnie Moran, Jimmy Melia and Gerry Byrne were of a generation who thought little of attending matches at both Anfield and Goodison Park, depending on who was playing that weekend. But the city was not without its partisan edge. 'All of my family were Reds and I learnt the difference between being a Liverpudlian and an Evertonian very early on,' Chris Lawler recalled. One day when he was playing football in Ellergreen around the corner his mate Vinny asked him if he fancied going to watch Everton's reserves that afternoon. 'We walked all the way to Goodison from Norris Green and once I came home my brothers and dad – who'd been listening to the wireless for their coupon - asked where I'd been. When I told them, you'd have thought I'd killed somebody. They all went '*What*?!' and threw me out the house again. As a kid I didn't know the difference.'

There were varying degrees of fanaticism, even then. Back in 1947 the Post reported on Liverpool fans who'd cycled to Blackburn to watch the Reds play in an away game because there had been a transport shortage. This was in the month when poverty was so severe that books were burnt in Bootle for warmth. Ian Callaghan was not of that level of devotion. He played himself and got more enjoyment from that, plus his father was away at sea a lot of the time and it was typically a father's duty to take his son to games.

There was one occasion however when his entire neighbourhood travelled to Wembley to watch his mate, Willie Carlin, play for England Schoolboys. Carlin was a few years older but played alongside Callaghan for Caryl Gardens' street team. 'What Willie had achieved made me ambitious and I wanted to follow in his footsteps,' said Callaghan. He did so, the following year, representing Liverpool Schoolboys at Penny Lane.

When Callaghan eventually left school, he became a trainee French polisher before starting an apprenticeship as a central heating engineer. It was at this point that Willie Carlin influenced his life again. He'd joined Blackburn as an apprentice before signing for Liverpool in 1958. It was he who negotiated with Liverpool and told them that they really needed to sign the fifteen-year-old Callaghan. They sent one of their trainers to take a look at the lad and he was so taken by him, he instantly invited him to play for the club's B and C teams. From this point Callaghan was converted by the whisky-enthusiast Tom Moore, a local headteacher who coached at the club part-time, from wing-half to outside-right.

Chris Lawler was a real talent, too. When he was 15 years-of-age he captained England Schoolboys at a packed-out Wembley against West Germany. People in Norris Green became aware of him and kept an eye out for him. They admired him because he was one of them: a white working-class lad from a big family. But Norris Green wasn't always the most welcoming of places.

The Slum Clearance Act had achieved many things, enhancing basic human needs and eradicating religious divides, but it failed to conquer the genuine racism which existed in the city, brought to the surface whenever ethnic families were forced to move to predominantly white areas. Howard Gayle's family were put in temporary accommodation in Norris Green in the early 1960s while their house in Liverpool 8 was being renovated. Once they got settled, they received news from their friends in the south end of the city that their home had actually, unbeknown to them, been demolished.

Gayle would be racially abused throughout his entire childhood in Norris Green. White fathers denied him entry into their homes despite him playing outside with their sons: *"Don't let that lazy Nigger in!"* he recalls them saying in his autobiography. Racism was not endemic in Norris Green, he says, but was deep-rooted enough to be threatening.

Daniel Fieldsend

He reflects of his childhood: 'The difficulty for me and my family is that we were shipped up to a very white area on our own and we had to deal with the trials and tribulations of society. Most of it I didn't understand because I was only young. My parents didn't prepare me for it. I suppose they were trying to get us through that period of my education as uneventful as possible.' His father was a strict disciplinarian from Africa who had a different view of racism. He'd grown up in Sierra Leone believing that the streets of Europe were paved with gold.

'My father was probably wary – nobody talked about racism on the scale that Martin Luther King did in America. There wasn't anybody in the UK like that. Our parents tried to play the racism down, although it was horrific and they were suffering from it too. There wasn't a complaint box; you couldn't go to the police or council about it, so you had to endure it and deal with it on a daily basis of how it come.' Gayle had to literally fight other youngsters to change their perceptions.

*

The Coronation of Queen Elizabeth II in June 1953 marked the beginning of the television age. Neighbours in Liverpool gathered in whatever house owned a TV and crowded around to watch her ascend the throne. There had been months of build-up for the event. Central Library ran a competition for primary school children, asking them to write an essay about the new Queen for a book token. Paul McCartney of Allerton, aged 10, came out victorious. There were hundreds of streets displaying flags and buntings, especially off Park Road, where mums gathered to combine their supplies to feed the neighbours.

Was this not supposed to be the city of radical Celtic difference? When asked if he was part of the occasion, Lawler smiled: 'Nah, we weren't interested.' For him, he says, only football mattered.

On the day Elizabeth II ascended the throne, Ronnie Moran and the rest of the Liverpool squad headed to the United States for the first time (Moran's first time abroad), embarking on the Queen Mary from Southampton to New York. They were so unknown nationally at the time that the squad was mistaken for a fishing club in grey suits.

By 1957 Liverpool FC were still lingering in the Second Division. Moran married Joyce who he'd known since childhood. After the wedding service he left to go and play Barnsley at Anfield. The Reds won 2-1 and Moran got changed back into his wedding suit after the game, returning to a hero's welcome at the after-party. Nine months later his daughter was born. By then the couple were living in Broadgreen, where LFC owned ten houses for staff to live in. All of the players –

including future colleague Geoff Twentyman – met up each morning and got the bus to Anfield together. They were free to live normal lives and the fans left them to it.

Dave Bilsborrow from Bootle remembers seeing players around the city – some of them even got the bus with him to the match. 'I recall Dixie Dean getting the ferry over from Birkenhead,' he says. 'Liverpool's players used to play golf at Bootle course after training and they'd have a few glasses of beer in the Park Hotel. You could just go and have a chat with them and ask them if they wanted a round.' The old man sighed thinking back, if only the innocence lasted.

All the while, despite the return of competitive football and advances in the lives of the post-war generation, the government struggled to pay off its war debt. Liverpool was poor – everywhere was – but it was about to get poorer. Britain sold off its empire and the city's port became less significant overnight. Something that had been Liverpool's lifeblood, that had shaped its identity and the attitude of its people, was about to dry up.

Daniel Fieldsend

FACE IN A CROWD

It is 1955. Over the water, amongst the clouds above Birkenhead, the sun lies low, white and blinding. As another huge ship comes in to harbour, Terry Moore gets his papers together ready to inspect the load. He is a freight clerk and will be until the time comes that his job is gone. He'll then be forced to invest in pubs, taking over an ale house on Dryden Street, before owning the Gay Cavalier in Garston.

In this environment his son Peter observes quick wit, social confidence and charisma. The old-school dockers who he encountered were quick workers who handled every type of cargo, and they rubbed together a sharpness of thought and tongue that seemed to spread out across the rest of Liverpool, typifying each encounter and upping the pace of conversations and humour.

Working behind the bar as a boy, Peter Moore soaked in that 'core Liverpudlian mindset and personality,' he says. He calls it a gregariousness: 'We lack a filter and are not reserved.' This strength of being was attained at sea, he reckons. 'We say what we think; we see situations and react to them. We wear our heart on our sleeve as a city, and that's ingrained into our DNA as far as I'm concerned. Those are the raw attributes of a Liverpudlian, then you have to polish them and be intrigued about things, be inquisitive and if you add all that up together... that core sense of being a Scouser is a sense of self-confidence and a sense of liking people.'

Is that forthright nature genuinely a consequence of the city's maritime history, though? 'Well you got forced integration and you got forced assimilation – there were so many people coming through who decided to stay – which you historically had here and Boston, in Marseille as well and so forth. We're port cities. Ships used to unload right there at the Pier Head and the Albert Dock,' he said, pointing down at them from his office window.

/ Local

For Moore, something crystallised at the waves. That was why Malcolm Lowry wrote in 1947 that Liverpool's main street was not Lord Street, Church Street or Bold Street, but the Mersey itself which led out to sea. Everything the city was – its very existence - was because of the water. The people of the city bought into the myth of it all, of themselves and their starboard identity and they distanced themselves from nearby cultural backwaters.

While Manchester, the nearest big city, could centre itself around Canal Street, Liverpool was informed by Alabama, Nigeria, Ireland, Suriname, South Carolina and the West Indies. Wherever its ships could harbour, a gleam of knowledge was attained. It was a constant flow of trade and culture. 'Everyone had a story about an uncle who came back from Buenos Aires with a monkey,' jokes Peter Carney who now runs tours in the city. The sight of a monkey above a piano was not uncommon in many ale houses. TJ Hughes department store in the 1950s had a chimpanzee in their grotto next to Father Christmas.

From the 1900s up until the arrival of Bill Shankly in 1959 and his charismatic input, the docks formed Liverpool's self-fabled character. Work was not guaranteed; men had to arrive at the pen at 7am on drizzly mornings and hope that they'd be tapped on the shoulder for a day's labour. It was a fragile existence, dependent upon whether the bosses deemed a face to fit.

Being turned away was embarrassing and many men would go to the pubs along the Dock Road to scheme a way of earning money for the day. They had to be creative, which inadvertently helped contribute towards forming the modern Scouse character.

Simon Hughes from Crosby describes the role of the docks: 'It's down to working patterns. In this city they were the main source of income for a lot of people and there were not any consistent shifts there, so people would have to turn up most days and stand outside the gates. If they didn't get work, they would walk away, so this contributed toward a sense of irreverence and not really knowing if they were coming or going, so they had to act with imagination.'

He continues: 'It also contributed toward a sense of rebellion, with capitalism being such a powerful force, people were underpaid and they didn't have any legal employment rights so they had to think creatively about where money was coming from. Manchester and other mill towns had shift work but Liverpool didn't on the docks. Alongside this, the tides of the Mersey were unpredictable; lives were very transient which created a consciousness of being different to the rest of the country. Not many other seaports had this culture, which later passed on from generation to generation. With music you have the sounds of the communities which came here from the Caribbean and West Africa. People looked outwardly towards the sea.'

From the docks with its wondrous cargo and tales of travel came a certain tenderness for stories and invention. Shaped by the lives of people who worked there, who formed the character of the town, Liverpool from the 1950s birthed writers, musicians, artists, actors, sportspeople and comedians. Phil Thompson, David Fairclough and Ian Callaghan, who'd personify that new sense of belief, all had fathers who worked away at sea.

Dan Carden, whose dad was a docker and who himself is now the Member of Parliament for Walton, absorbed the atmosphere of the waterfront as a boy and acknowledges now that, as well fostering creativity, the docks sustained intelligence and community: 'You've got the fact that immigration comes in to the city and we've had people arrive from all over the world. It became a melting pot of cultures which created a coalescence of music and literature and history, originally from all across the world but now found in one place.'[11]

George Orwell had been drawn to that intelligence in 1936 when he travelled to Liverpool to meet a docker called George Garrett who lived off Park Road. The works of Garrett – a writer who'd been homeless in Argentina, had been a POW in the First World War, had lived in New York at a time of cultural change, and who was blacklisted as a communist upon returning home - specifically his essays on 'The Tempest' and Joseph Conrad's novel 'The Nigger of the Narcissus', influenced Orwell. He allowed Garrett to massage his social conscience as the Scouser advised him to volunteer in the Spanish Civil War to fight fascism. The unlikely pair remained friends, Orwell an Etonian and Garrett a man of labour, going shopping together in the day before discussing Dostoyevsky and Ibsen at night.

In many ways Garrett represented the story of old Liverpool. He fought for the underdog, campaigned for social change, had great intelligence despite his means (he sold his bedsheets on one occasion to feed his family) and was shaped by the water. A stowaway in 1912, he later sailed upon the *Mauritania* and became a night watchman on Bootle's Docks during the Blitz, before dying in 1966.

---

[11] Indeed, in Carden's maiden speech (which was followed by a Tory whose mother passed through Liverpool via Jamaica), he told MP's about Liverpool's black community (UK's oldest), Chinese community (Europe's oldest) and Abdullah Quilliam Mosque (Britain's first). Their legacies stem from the water.

Local

Dave Bilsborrow came later. He's a socialist and a former docker who lived it, loved it and misses it. He remembers the mickey taking between cramped groups of lads of a Monday morning; the canteen with tiny windows which never opened; the ceilings dripping from rain and condensation: 'If you got a sarnie you put the plate upside down. You could smell the weather and the sweat. There would be arguments going on everywhere, about 30 or 40 lads, between mates who worked and drank together, and it would be heated about football, but then they'd go out of the canteen, laugh it off and get to work.'

On Saturday mornings in the 1950s the fellers would work a half-day until 12 noon: 'Then we'd all go the match. It would be a scramble. We'd get the bus from Bank Hall and there would be loads already lined up ready to take us, 20 or 30 buses.' Tickets were not guaranteed at Anfield or Goodison which contributed toward making the match an 'event'. Excitement built waiting to get in, with kick-off signalling a release of tension from a tough week.

Workers from all over came together on the steps of Anfield's terraces. 'The crowd was so good because everyone was of a similar mindset,' Bilsborrow recollects. 'All Scousers, working in similar jobs like factories and docks and even on the timber yard, which stretched for miles up Seaforth. One feller I went the match with could have told you what timber it was blind, by the smell of it.'

The port of Liverpool employed some 30,000 men. "*Come back when you're 21,*" bosses would shout down to the older fellers in the pen. If they got in, they'd work from 8am until 7pm with only 1-hour break. They were overworked and underpaid but there was a sense of solidarity. If one man went on strike, they all did. Unionism encompassed it all: 'There used to be working-class Scouse values,' remembers Bilsborrow. 'Dockers and warehouse guys, we all stuck together. We supported nurses; you name it. I stood on the picket line outside Walton Hospital. That spirit carried through to Robbie Fowler on the pitch who was one of the last.'

If Fowler was last, Ronnie Moran was one of the first. He'd been riding the Dockers' Umbrella just a few years earlier. Everton did everything to sign him but he chose to play for the less famous Liverpool team. But his career was interrupted when he was sent away on national conscription, to fine-tune his personal standards which'd enable him to one day become club captain.

A lad from the south end of the city wanted to be conscripted too, but was two years too late. He was raised on seafaring stories – all young Liverpool lads were – and he decided to enlist at the Pier Head with his mate Nigel Walley, dreaming of the exotic world. But John Lennon's aunt Mimi blocked the venture and brought him back down to earth.

He would have to stay in Liverpool at the end of the 1950s. He'd have to meet Paul McCartney at the Woolton fête and create something special. Ronnie Moran, who'd go running on fields around Crosby, would have to return home from service as a tougher feller than before and impress Bill Shankly with his standards. Lennon and Moran would have to unwittingly stay and fuse together a period of cultural emancipation. There were happenings in place which were about to put Liverpool the city and Liverpool the club on a trajectory nobody expected. A spark was set to be lit. But it wasn't a little spark. It was an almighty, unseen before, society-changing explosion.

Local

THERE'S A PLACE

He got back into the car. It had started to rain. His face told the story. 'I've done the right thing, haven't I Ness?', he asked. When the Shankly family arrived in Liverpool, the club and its city were in such a state that they harboured grains of doubt.

Back in 1951, Liverpool's board had invited Bill Shankly, then of lowly Carlisle, to apply for their vacant manager's job. When he discovered that they instead gave the post to Don Welsh, Shankly asked: *'Is he in the Masons?'*. Eight years later, Leeds United were sounding Shankly out from Huddersfield for their vacant post. He was settled in Yorkshire; Ness was happy, Barbara was in a good school and of a Sunday he enjoyed a kick-about with the locals. Shankly held ambitions for Huddersfield to be the "greatest football team of all time" and targeted Brian Clough from Middlesbrough and Ian St John from Motherwell to join Dennis Law at his young squad, but the board refused to spend.

Late in the afternoon on the 17th October 1959, two men approached an increasingly disillusioned Shankly. Huddersfield had just beaten Cardiff City and the men, who'd been sat in the stands watching the Scotsman inspire and orchestrate his team, were impressed. They introduced themselves as T.V Williams, chairman, and Harry Latham, director, of Liverpool Football Club, and asked him if he'd be willing to manage their squad. In Shankly they saw somebody who'd give the club new life.

Saturday afternoons at Anfield in the late '50s were marked by a grey disposition. 30,000 flat-capped men turned up to games, only to return home disgruntled and upset after another abject performance. Their team had been in the Second Division since 1954, far too long for a club of such stature. They were the joke of Merseyside; Evertonians rejoiced.

Daniel Fieldsend

The importance of city's dockside trading centre in the late-50s was diminishing by the day, too, as Liverpool slipped dangerously into insignificance. A physical symbol of this decline was the demolition of the Dockers Umbrella in 1958 – a great feat of engineering in its day - which, upon opening in 1893, had been another 'World First'.

Local politicians knew they were in trouble. It was obvious to them. Boats that used to come in from all over the empire ceased to anchor. Local shipowners complained to Downing Street about the process of decolonisation. It lightened their pockets, so they withdrew their finance and invested elsewhere, signalling the downturn of Liverpool's fortunes.

Advances in train and air travel also meant that the days of famed cruise liners leaving from Liverpool to North America were all but dead. The *Carinthi* and *Franconia* only attracted a few hundred passengers *en* route to Canada in 1958.[12] Manchester developed its inland airport and Liverpool did not. Having an open, sea facing geography was now just windy and pointless. Cunard, who had been operating out of Liverpool since 1840 delivering mail to the empire, began drawing up plans to relocate to London, ending a significant historic relationship with their hometown.

Peter Carney believes though that as port residents, Scousers had it ingrained in them to deal with such outcomes; work was never guaranteed after all: 'This place is a social dynamic' he said. 'It never settles or is still, it's always moving. It adapts naturally to change.' A good number of Scousers kept their jobs as stevedores, chandlers and crane operators, while many more found work on ships as deckhands and stewards.

The remaining dockers defended their jobs through militant trade unionism. To disable them, they were portrayed as workshy by the media, with the Herald writing: "They have been adopting [a method of] overcrowding a stand requiring only a small number of men, taking care to keep well behind the [other] dockers." Other articles at the time tried to cause national alarm by linking Liverpool's docks to extreme politics.

Over the pond, Americans were terrified of the spread of communism: the 'Red Scare' dominated news articles for more than a decade. In the same approach used by right-wing papers contemporarily, turning readers against

---

[12] On 24th November 1964, the *Sylvania* headed sadly for Boston as the last ever Cunard ship to set sail from Liverpool, ending a historic relationship.

immigrants, 'communists' had been the dehumanised focus of the day: "They have tried to create unrest in Liverpool by suggesting to the docker that he is being exploited over the question of payment for late work," so stated the Herald on another occasion. It had always been in the interest of profiteers to turn the heads of working-class readers.

Shankly knew all about Liverpool's economic heyday when its dockland had thrived and he empathised with the stark demise. 'He had himself experienced economic decline in Glenbuck,' wrote Tom Darby. 'When the coal and mill owners were done with you, off they went, leaving communities scraping for a living until those communities lost their souls and died.'

It was embedded in Shankly to believe in the power of the community. 'When he took over, Liverpool was the people's club,' says Nicky Allt. 'Everton tried to take that tag later but Liverpool was always the people's club.' Part of the lure for Shankly was the idea of harnessing the crowd and he, perhaps unconsciously, perhaps not, used their social uncertainty and desire to escape that as a tool to cajole, motivate and inspire them. Did anybody believe that the image he cultivated for himself was by accident? It was all by design and 'his crowd' quickly became emphatic.

Following his arrival - between late 1959 and the end of 1961 - ripples of change began to happen in wider Liverpool. A new movement emerged from the clubs and pubs. Culture and artistry spilled out from local venues and into the national focus. By the end of the decade, the forlorn image Liverpool held was replaced by one of creativity and confidence, acclaimed across the world as a place of imagination.

*

It began in the pubs. The Duke of Wellington introduced the 'Beer House Act' in 1830 to encourage the consumption of alcohol rather than diseased water. The act gave permission for any householder to purchase a licence, enabling them to sell ale from their home. Seemingly overnight, 20,000 such houses appeared in Liverpool. Over the coming century pubs would become central to working-class identity.[13]

---

[13] As fans eventually toured Europe in later years, their banners – white writing on a red background – paid tribute to their local pub. The Kingfisher, Eden Vale, Leatherbottle, Oak Tree Huyton. Even the legendary Grafton Ballroom would get a mention with a nod to those 'grab a granny' nights.

By the 1950s romance painted a glowing image of its drinking culture, with memories of smoke-filled Liverpool ale houses crammed with singing men and women; with regulars playing instruments and setting the tone.

In truth some brewers preferred their pubs to be mostly silent, while others banned singing altogether. A music licence was needed in the city-centre. Some public houses along Queen's Drive were more like bourgeois roadhouses for discourse than typical pubs in the post-war years, so wrote Michael Brocken.[14] Locals however saw singing as a way of biting their thumb at the establishment and did so gleefully. There were few record players, so the ambience came from within, from the regular dwellers of warmly-lit parlours who began sing-a-longs.

Renowned Manchester based journalist Geoffrey Moorhouse visited Liverpool in 1960 to sample the rumoured changes taking place. He stood on the Kop, frequented the city's pubs and, upon returning home, wrote: "Liverpool has an air which Manchester lacks. A swagger and a sense of adventure. It is in the nature of a seaport to be more dashing than any inland clearing house, of course."[15] Moorhouse acknowledged the new generation coming through, who cared more for youthfulness and enjoyment than rigid social constraints. Football and music were becoming the primary points of their identification.[16]

George Sephton of Long Lane watched the changes taking place. In the mid-50s 'Cunard Yanks' came home from America with new records, introducing fast-paced rock and roll by the likes of Chuck Berry and Little Richard to white British children whose ears had only ever heard folk, classical and war-time tunes. 'Because it is a sea port you have a mixture of people arriving from all over the world,' Sephton said. 'I'm old enough to remember the first 7-inch vinyls appearing. I'm talking about the late 40's or 50's here. Men who worked at sea would go to America and hear music in the clubs and bars and bring the records home which locals listened to.' Somebody who was influenced by the social happenings at the time, Gerry Marsden, recalled: 'There was always somebody in every family in the Merchant Navy bringing music back with them. The first record I heard was Elvis Presley and Hound Dog,' which motivated him to become a pop star. He wasn't alone. Beat City, a documentary in 1963, estimated that

---

[14] Other Voices: Hidden Histories of Liverpool's Popular Music Scenes. (2016), M Brocken.

[15] Britain in the '60s: the other England. (1960), G Moorehouse.

[16] They were intertwined: the people's club at Anfield attracted those anti-establishment singing types according to Allt.

Liverpool was home to some 300 bands and cited unemployment as an enabler for the stat.

Chris Lawler recalls it all: 'In the early-60's it used to be jazz music for half of the night, and then the groups would come on.' On Boxing Day 1960, Liverpool beat Rotherham in a Second Division game. Things were slowly starting to look up for the Reds. Kopites were telling their Evertonian mates about how this Shankly fellow - a year into his tenure - was overruling the directors and doing things his own way.

That night, Litherland Town Hall hosted local bands the Deltones and the Searchers. On a sign outside they presented another band: 'Direct from Hamburg – The Beatles'. When they came out with their strange hair and leather clothes, everybody in attendance assumed they were German. When Paul McCartney screamed the opening lines of 'Long Tall Sally' down the microphone, the crowd looked at each other and smiled. Fantastic, exciting, possessing an aura and destined for great things, but German and probably soon to disappear back home.

'It was that evening that we really came out of our shell and let go,' John Lennon recalled years later. 'We stood there being cheered for the first time. This was when we began to think that we were good. Up to Hamburg we'd thought we were *okay*, but not good enough. It was only back in Liverpool that we realised the difference and saw what happened to us while everyone else was playing Cliff Richard shit.'[iii] That night had almost never happened. George Harrison had been deported from Germany and Paul McCartney arrested. After the Litherland gig the group cemented a hardcore local following.

Chris Lawler had his foot in both camps as a teenager. He remembers the early days of the Beatles at a time when he was an amateur at Liverpool: 'Well you know Ringo Starr? He went on to marry a Liverpool girl called Maureen Cox who was from my grandmother's side. Her father used to ask for tickets off me for a Saturday and he asked me one day if I wanted anything off the Beatles like an autograph? I said *"Nah, you're alright."* Imagine the money it would go for now?'

Bill Shankly arrived at a musical city, perceived by many to be sneered upon by a *"You've never had it so good"* MacMillan government. The docks had declined, militant unionism was on the rise, bomb craters were still played in and rag-and-bone men were a present feature in neighbourhood slums, but Shankly was excited. Influenced by the writings of Robbie Burns, he saw it all as socialist potential.

Having stepped into a backroom environment that had been governed for seventy years by Conservatives, he promised his players success, provided they didn't 'overeat or lose their accents'. He offered Liverpool's left-leaning fans a distillation of the theory through football:

> "The socialism I believe in is not really politics. It is a way of living. It is humanity. I believe the only way to live and to be truly successful is by collective effort, with everyone working for each other, everyone helping each other, and having a share of the rewards at the end of the day. That might be asking a lot, but it's the way I see football and the way I see life."

*

A letter fell on Tommy Smith's mat one day asking him to meet the Liverpool manager with a view of joining the club's ground staff. He swallowed his butterflies on the morning of the meeting and went to his regular barbershop, before putting on his fancy jeans and getting the bus to Anfield with his mother. 'We've heard he's a good player,' Shankly began, 'and we'd like to put the lad in our B or C team...' Ms Smith replied instantly: 'You've never won the cup have you Mr Shankly?' he shook his head and began to talk, but before he could, she told him: 'You will when you play our Tommy.'

Smith painted the back of the Kop three times during his apprenticeship. He drained both goalmouths and gave the dressing rooms a lick of paint. In Shankly, a straight-talking tough-guy, he had a male role model, something that had been missing for years. 'I think he felt sorry for me and mum,' Smith later said.

In truth Shankly was conscious of the qualities young players brought to the team, their exuberance and desire (coupled with the fact that the board were not big spenders), and he looked to nurture talent whenever possible. Ian Callaghan was training with the club and working as an engineer at the time, a good job for a lad his age, but he aspired for more and asked Shankly after training once if he'd mind talking to his parents about him possibly becoming professional.

One Sunday afternoon a few weeks later a black Ford Corsair pulled up outside Caryl Gardens. All of the local kids stopped playing and came to look. When they saw the Scot get out, they shouted: '*Shankly is going to Ian's house!*' In front of Callaghan's parents, Shankly swore he'd look after their son and 'give him plenty to eat'. It was enough to convince them.

Early in 1960 Callaghan made his Liverpool debut, replacing his hero Billy Liddell. He'd casually gotten the bus to Anfield at 1pm that day, time enough for a 3pm kick off, and deputised in front of 40,000 fans. After the match, all four sides of the stadium rose to applaud him, including the referee who ran over and shook his hand.

Outside of football the youngster spent a great number of hours in the basement of a coffee house on Bold Street. It would come to be developed into a social venue where a core group of Liverpool and Everton players, as well as local entertainers, would gather to talk. The Beatles would be there from time to time, as well as Jimmy Tarbuck who'd been to school with John Lennon. Tarbuck was mates with Jimmy Melia too because their dads worked together in the betting industry.[17] Tarbuck, a would-be advocate of Thatcher in the 1980s, told John Keith in 1976:

"It was in the late 1950s when I first met Ian Callaghan, but even before that I remember him playing for Liverpool Schoolboys. I really got to know him in those coffee house days. We were just kids then, swapping stories and having a bit of a laugh. Of course, we didn't know what was ahead of us. I was playing gigs at local clubs and Liverpool were just emerging from the Second Division. The success that followed later, both in entertainment and in football, was a surprise. We had no idea what was coming."

Happenings were at play. George Sephton had been in the same school as Paul McCartney and George Harrison: The Liverpool Institute for Boys. One wet break he stumbled upon them practising guitars together in the science room and stood watching.[18] Sephton says: 'I'm old enough to remember what life was like before the Beatles came on the scene and the music we had to listen to. What McCartney has done since for the city is just incredible.'

Bob Spritz wrote of the instant cultural impact the Beatles made in Liverpool: 'A whole new chapter of musical prophecy was being written. No one, not even Elvis, had that great of an impact all at once.' They had clear personalities and fashions which shook up the cultural standing of the time and revolutionised the national music experience.

Bill Shankly likewise was stirring things up with his own distinct approach to management. Jimmy Melia from Newsham Street remembers life before he came along: 'In those days, the team would be picked by the directors on the Tuesday or Wednesday night and would be announced in the Liverpool Echo, so most of the

---

[17] 'Tarby' forgot his roots as far as many Scousers are concerned once success beckoned.

[18] The school closed in 1985 and became a dilapidated building, until a sentimental McCartney reopened it in 1996 as LIPA.

players would rush to buy the paper to see what team was going to be playing.'[iv] Shankly insisted upon taking full control of team affairs and redefined the role of the 'manager'.

Melia makes for an interesting discussion regarding local footballers at the time. He had scored on his debut at the Kop end years before in a Second Division game as Liverpool beat Nottingham Forest 5-2. It was the best way to introduce himself. The Liverpool crowd had a reputation for being demanding of local footballers, bordering on overtly-critical. This toxicity had been part of the reason why Joe Fagan, as a 17-year-old, turned down both the Reds and Everton and considered offers from Manchester City and Manchester United instead. He knew the reputation the Anfield crowd had. 'There was a feeling at the time that if a youngster joined his local side, the fans would not think as much of him as an outsider,' he stated. Jack Balmer from West Derby had always been the object of vitriol if the Reds had not performed well.

Phil Boersma made his debut under Shankly years later in the late-60s but remembers it still being the case then: 'If I did something and it went just wide, they'd (the crowd) be like *"fucking hell!"*, but if it was somebody Liverpool had bought, they'd say: *"At least he's having a go"*. The Kop in those days expected it from local lads,' Boersma continues. 'It has totally shifted now. The local players have the fans behind them. As a teenager back then you didn't really think about representing the city.'

Ian Callaghan played with a certain honesty and devotion that somehow transcended criticism. 'I could hardly believe it,' he said after replacing Billy Liddell. 'It was like a dream.'

*

Before the 1960s, America possessed something Britain did not: teenagers. They were shown on films enjoying themselves, drinking cola and driving cars. Socialising together and being free. In Britain a child was expected to leave school and become a doe-eyed version of their parents, job, clothes and all. A giddy resistance seemed to take place in Liverpool in the early '60s.

The city had always been ambitious. It had floated dreamily for so long in the Atlantic with its fortunes coming in from the west. Bill Shankly tapped into that enthusiasm and held his own ambitions, for Liverpool FC to conquer the North Sea, Black Sea, Baltic and Mediterranean. He portrayed a Napoleon complex and the press lapped it up.

Liverpool's teenagers looked to what he said, and to what the Beatles did, and were fed a message that anything was possible. An explosion of talent emerged from this point. Simon Hughes said of the phenomena of the early '60s: 'I don't believe it was always there before then, that belief. Let's face it, post-war Liverpool was battered. Shankly's arrival gave people a sense of being better; he unleashed it in the way he was. He thought he was the best at everything whilst also embracing the best Scouse characteristic of being humble too. There can't be big-heads in the city.'

Club captain Ronnie Moran was the one to keep Liverpool FC grounded as they stood on the threshold of change. 'Big-headed bastard' would be his insult for anybody he deemed to be getting ahead of themselves, which'd become a catchphrase of his in the future. He drove a yellow Morris Minor and proudly told the staff how cheap it was. 'He didn't have them same high standards which he had for teammates at home though,' his son Paul remembers. 'It wasn't a case of *"my family is better than yours,"* he was fundamentally humble.'

Moran took notice of a new coach at the club who'd been recommended by Rochdale (and future Everton) manager Harry Catterick back in '58. Joe Fagan arrived as a trainer initially but quickly took on an all-encompassing role, solving issues, building relationships and laying down the foundations for future success.

The Litherland man was somebody Shankly admired, having tried to sign him for Grimsby Town towards the end of his playing career. He was an organiser, was astute and knowledgeable about cohesion, and became an essential cog in the silverware to come. Roy Evans, then just an amateur player, believed him to be the most important person at the club. 'It was Fagan who held it all together,' he told Derek Dohren. 'While Shankly motivated and Paisley was tactically astute, nothing would have worked without Fagan. He was the one to reason any spats within the playing and coaching staff. He'd ensure that harmony was always maintained.'

'I knew the Fagans like,' Paul Moran says, thinking back to his boyhood, 'but you wouldn't come home of a Saturday and expect dad to say we're going out for a meal with them. The Boot Room (which Moran would join after his retirement) weren't all that close.' Shankly's men were colleagues more than anything else, focussed on working together for the betterment of Liverpool FC. He'd gathered them initially – Reuben Bennett, Joe Fagan and Bob Paisley – and told them his expectations for the club and how he planned to operate, assuring them that their jobs would be safe, provided they were loyal. He needn't have worried.

Daniel Fieldsend

The Boot Room became a council of football knowledge whom players sought approval from. Howard Gayle would later state that what made Liverpool achieve success was the collective mentality of the backroom staff. They'd tell players 'we're watching you', placing the fear of God in them. Any grievances could not be singled against Shankly or later Paisley individually, as lone operators, but would be against the 'staff' as a collective. It was a form of socialism in itself. Tottenham was Bill Nicholson and Wolves was Stan Cullis, but Liverpool was a union, and no single player, no matter how disgruntled, could topple a union.

*

Remembering his visit to Marseille as an adolescent, Nicky Allt from Kirkby wrote: 'The rougher the setting, the warmer the people'. Liverpool in the 1960s was like that. Although films based in the city at the time, like *Playground* and *These Dangerous Years*, made the city seem, to an outsider, like the setting of a lawless Wild West showdown, where sharp knuckles and violence triumphed over diplomacy, the truth was very much on the contrary. 'You have to be a comedian to come from Liverpool,' Ken Dodd told black-and-white cameras in his early days. 'We tell gags about our own particular characters and there is a great sense of fun to be had.' Ian Callaghan would agree, telling John Keith: 'It has been said many times, yet it is no less true. They are friendly and warm people and the history of Liverpool as a seaport made it a melting pot of many races and cultures. This gives the city a very personal identity.'

The city centre had an abundance of characters, like Effin Nellie who ran the pubs; Lizzie Christian who sold fruit in Williamson Square; Jack Jones the unionist and Stan the Harpist. Every neighbourhood and community had larger than life personalities who'd suffered but could find joy in life whenever possible. They guided and shaped the nature of the Ken Dodds, Jackie Hamiltons and Eddie Flanagans of the city, as well as the witty John Lennon's and affable Ian Callaghans. Part of the subsequent attraction of the Beatles was their transparent normality. Geniality over the coming decades remained an irrefutable trait of the city. Peter Moore talks about the surprising warm welcome outsiders have: 'I visit with family from the States and they say: "*Everybody says hello,*" and "*Everybody calls you love,*" and "*Everybody acts like they know you.*" It confuses them. That is part of the core fibre of being a Liverpudlian...'

*

In January 1962 Z Cars aired for the first time. It was filmed at Kirkby police station and was based on the Panda Cars that had been introduced to the town – a far cry from the days when police walked the beat and blew their whistles at criminals. Following the Clearance Act, Kirkby bubbled with a certain rascality. The kids who'd lived in Liverpool's slums had spent their days smashing the windows of derelict houses for fun. Upon moving to Kirkby, they continued the sport, but discovered that these were new houses with people living inside them and the sport was no longer acceptable. A ditty emerged to a familiar tune, describing the supposed roughness of the town:

"Way out in Kirkby, the kids they wear clogs;
There's eight million children and ten million dogs;
They play tick with hatchets, I tell you no lie;
And they call you a 'cissy' if you've more than one eye."

It was exaggerated of course (who wore clogs?) but gangs of dogs were an actual feature. On Cherryfield Drive and Bewley, outsiders had to be careful not to antagonise them. Phil Thompson would stress that the town he grew up in was not actually as rough as its perception later allowed: 'It was a tough place but I hated people knocking it,' he said. He and his mates were content enough playing on St Joseph's field with a plastic Fido ball.[19]

Despite there being 30,000 people unemployed in Liverpool in 1962, with 35 men going for the same job at any time, the Kop was packed to the rafters. A sense of excitement and optimism had returned for the fans. 50,000 were in attendance when the Reds clinched promotion to the First Division against Southampton with five games left to play. Regulars on the Kop sang all afternoon until they were hoarse.

Police waiting on Breck Road for fans to spill out after the game were confused when two hours later hardly anybody had left. '*We want Shankly. We want Shankly!*' the crowd sang, refusing to depart until their manager appeared. When he stepped out into the directors' box with T.V. Williams they roared in delight, oblivious to the April rain. '*We want the Reds. We want the Reds!*' they continued. But Liverpool's squad were still in the bath celebrating their achievement. When they were told that the fans refused to leave, they came out in various stages of undress. There was pandemonium. The police had to go into the crowd to rescue Ian St John and Ron Yeats who'd been swallowed up by joyous limbs. A number of Scallywags ran onto the pitch with glee, among them Terry McDermott.

---

[19] The LFC Family Tree: Sport Media, 2011.

The Albert Pub was packed to the rafters on an occasion when nobody wanted to step beyond its threshold and head home, savouring a moment in time. But fans had little idea of what was to come. On Monday morning, T.V. Williams received telegrams from local politicians thanking Liverpool for adding to the city's skyline of emerging talent. When directors presented each other with silver cigarette cases in celebration, Shankly asked, *"you're not satisfied with that are you?"* He wanted to build a dynasty.

The following season was one of vocal expression at Anfield. George Sephton remembers the first PA system being introduced: 'You would hear both sides of the vinyl played before the game. That's when they started playing the Top 10. A guy called Stuart Bateman came to an arrangement with a record shop in Everton to play the charts before the game.'[20] The singing that followed was a combination of things, including Liverpool FC doing well, the Beatles hitting the scene and the invention of Merseybeat. The place was full of local bands, coupled with the good crowds and the vocal nature of the Kop. I just think the fact we were associated with people like the Beatles rejuvenated everything and gave it all a life of its own. When I started working at Anfield I followed on.'

1963's 'Beat City' documentary explored the roots of musical expression in Liverpool, citing the Spinners playing folk songs at Gregson's Well pub as proof music being 'a natural feature of the Liverpool scene, spanning from sea shanties'. It seemed that singing came from the sea, to the pubs, to the bands, then to the match. The documentary also suggested that folk music was embraced by the political left and that in the Coffee House pub in Wavertree it was accompanied by Marxist discourse.

The presence of singing in Liverpool ale houses tended to originate closer to the Dock Road before filtering out towards the suburbs, where Labour clubs and Legions had grown in membership. 'There is definitely an Irish tradition of music-making mixed in there as well,' George Sephton added. Nicky Allt agreed. 'The Irishness has a large part to play in it. Other clubs don't have the tune-base to create songs. You have a lot of musical people who follow Liverpool, and Glasgow Celtic too.'

Ian Callaghan wrote about the atmosphere differing between Liverpool and Everton at the time: 'Anfield is like the Cavern while Goodison is like the Philharmonic Hall,' he said. Callaghan explained that people's perceptions about

---

[20] Bateman got them from NEMS, a store owned by the Epstein family.

the two atmospheres, he felt, was because Anfield's crowd were close knit, whereas Goodison's were not. 'I don't know why this is because we're talking about people from the same city. Perhaps I'm a bit biased towards Liverpool, but then the neutral observers who go to both grounds notice the contrast so it must be true.'

Stan Boardman from Morley Street told a joke about it: he said that fellers got their ashes scattered on the Kop, but they didn't do the same thing at Everton. Policy at Goodison, he said, was to stuff fans and put them in the stands. 'They did it to a feller a few weeks back and he got off at half-time,' Boardman laughed.

Allt has his beliefs about the difference in atmospheres, linking Everton and Rangers together, and Liverpool and Celtic: 'Songs come from the people. Everton were the wealthiest football club in the country because of the Moore's family and the Littlewoods pools. So Shanks was in charge of the singing people's club.'

Shankly convinced supporters that they were part of a movement, more than just being followers of a team. He fostered a feeling that being a Red was a cultural belonging, igniting the flames of fanaticism beyond which English football was accustomed to at the time. His savviness drew attention to the Kop crowd, creating something of a national celebrity of it. 'It was a perfect relationship between him and the city's football supporters. He provided that can-do attitude by making impossible-seeming things quite possible actually,' said Simon Hughes. It fed into a process of sorts.

It would, however, be unfair to suggest that Everton fans were not cut from the same cloth. 'They had a good atmosphere back then too,' says Dave Bilsborrow. 'They did all their own songs as well. I don't know what happened though; they kind of got in the shadow and it demoralised them.' When Everton won the Football League in 1963, with stars like Alex Young and Brian Labone, their atmosphere was tremendous and the Echo reported: "If the Pier Head pigeons were disturbed by the sound I would not be surprised." Evertonians simply focussed on their team and likewise with Liverpudlians.

On November 2nd 1963, 'You'll Never Walk Alone' was played at Anfield for the first time. Fans arrived at the matches early because tickets were sold on the gate, so they listened eagerly to the charts to pass the time, singing along to the hits they knew. Stuart Bateman played Gerry and the Pacemakers' record as the final song before kick-off that day, with it being Number 1 in the charts. It stayed there for four weeks. By the time 'You'll Never Walk Alone' disappeared out of the top 10 eight weeks later, fans knew it word for word and demanded it remain a feature. *"Where's our song?! Where's our song,"* Gerry Marsden nostalgically recalled them chanting.

Marsden had heard the song in between performances, having watched Carousel one rainy afternoon, and he argued with Brian Epstein and George Martin to allow his band to release it. They were sceptical. It was too slow for the time and had already been covered by Frank Sinatra without any great success. But Marsden got his way and the track cemented itself with Liverpool FC and the city during moments of despair and victory. 'Liverpool is very much a community city and a community football club. The lyrics are perfect. It's very Scouse,' he reflected.[v]

There is, however, an alternative theory regarding the emergence of the club's hymn; that it was only released by Marsden because fans had already drawn his attention to it. At the start of '63, Gerry and the Pacemakers were known for their hits 'I Like It' and 'How Do You Do It'. After a guttering loss to Leicester City away in the cup, a collection of smart-arse fans began singing *'When you walk through a storm hold your head up high,'* as a tongue in cheek response to the performance. It was sung again against Birmingham, then Aston Villa, then Sheffield Wednesday. The proprietors of the rumour believe that Marsden copied them and they sang it with gusto in the charts because it was already their song. *Chicken or egg?*

By the end of 1963 the Beatles had gone from being the Litherland Town Hall backing group to the biggest band in England with songs like 'Please Please Me', 'From Me to You', and 'I Want to Hold Your Hand'. In the coming months they'd be doing shows in Versailles and Paris. 'It all happened so quickly' wrote Ian Callaghan. 'Suddenly Merseyside was the "in" place. Wherever you went, people wanted to talk to you, and I must admit it gave me a lot of self-confidence.'

Ronnie Moran captained the club that year and a 19-year-old Chris Lawler finally made his debut. 'Well it was a good time,' he remembers. 'I loved the Beatles. The music was superb and the bands were special. If you look in the Kop, they're all wearing collar and ties because after a match they'd go straight into town. And we players were right after them. We'd go the same pubs and bars as them. There used to be a club called the Tiger and we'd go there with the Everton players too.'

It was an age of golden optimism, when the sun shone brighter and the air felt cleaner. A raw and uncouth Freddie Starr did acts in the Sandon of a Saturday afternoon after matches, despite being a Blue. Everybody went to town after games, young and old, comfortable and poor. 'There'd be businessmen and we'd all chat together, even with barristers in top hats, and nobody thought they were bigger or better than anyone,' Dave Bilsborrow remembers. Tommy Smith made his debut and walked the streets for hours afterwards on a cloud. Everybody had been infected with Shankly's natural enthusiasm, for everything, for life and for the simple greenness of the game. He loved the people and they felt it, declaring their love for him in return. Life was building up and up. In 1964 Shankly gave fans their best moment to date.

Daniel Fieldsend

WHEN THE SHIP COMES IN

On the 13th August, 1964, upstairs at Walton Prison - 'Landing 2' - were 10-foot gallows. There, with a white hood over his head, Peter Allen waited, numb and exhausted. At 8:01am the warden thumbed his signal, the executioner opened the floor and Allen's body fell, squirming until it stopped. The warden checked his watch. 8:03pm. He was the last man to receive the death penalty in Britain.

A lot seemed to happen that year. In September, the arts cinema Hope Hall was taken over by a group of poets and playwrights who scrimped their pennies together and turned it into the Everyman Theatre. Roger McGough recalled: 'Before the Everyman opened up in the mid-60s there was the Playhouse, which had an older audience. It was regarded as elitist – the actors came up from London, did the shows and then went back on the next train. The Everyman was different. The actors came and stayed in Liverpool. They put on proletarian, socially conscious stuff.'[vi]

It was a ground-breaking venue with a political edge that kickstarted the careers of Bill Nighy, Julie Walters and Pete Postlethwaite (the latter two lived together in town for six years). Steven Spielberg would later call Postlethwaite 'the best actor in the world,' yet the man himself acclaimed the Everyman to be 'the best space in the world' where he learnt his trade.

The following month on a mild October evening, a crowd of people gathered outside the Huyton Suite to offer their support for the incoming visitor. News cameras from across the country were in attendance, with British Pathé recording that: 'The crowd won't admit the possibility of any there being any other Prime Minister in the next 24 hours, except Harold Wilson.' As his car arrived, locals began singing *'For he's a jolly good fellow, and so say all of us*!' In London later that night, several hundred young people gathered at Trafalgar Square to celebrate a Labour victory in the fountains.

Politically and culturally – resurging together, like they so often do - a movement was happening.

Harold Wilson was a former Head Boy at Wirral Grammar School. He was a one-time MP for Ormskirk and, since 1950, had been MP for Huyton. Earlier, when he was elected Labour leader in 1963, Wilson tapped in to the changes in British society of the mid-60s. Popular culture was fresh and exciting and he saw no harm in being associated with it all. The public were hazily beginning to recognise their position in a globalised world - no longer part of an empire - and cared more for civil rights than before. Popular music, both at home and in the US, became a medium for it all.

Wilson's department rode the wave of new culture. In March that year he met the Beatles and made sure that his friends working in the tabloids splashed the image of them – the four of them laughing, him bunched in the middle – on the front of their papers. He'd later write about the meeting in his memoires as a moment of devised acclaim (they would go on to moan about him as the 'Taxman'). Wilson's Labour targeted the same social groups as the Beatles: the lower classes and an uncompromising younger generation.

It had been 14 years since Labour, the local party for many wards in Liverpool since 1955, had won an election. Preceding all of which, it had also been 17 years since Liverpool FC had won the First Division title. An outpouring of delight roared out of Anfield on the 18th April 1964 as Liverpool beat Arsenal to become champions of England. *'Ee ay addio, we have won the league!'* the fans sang. David Fairclough bounced about outside the Kop with his friends waiting for '3/4 time' when they could enter. As soon as the exit gates opened, they 'legged in to join the carnival.'

Liverpool as a city was a firm focus of national interest at the time and local festivals of unpretentious emotion, in music and sport, were heavily in vogue, hence why BBC Panorama decided to film the Reds' league championship victory over Arsenal. BBC started the programme by asking young fans outside the ground why indeed they were able to intimidate opposing players? "Because we've got big mouths," a cheeky lad replied.

Stood in front of the Kop with a microphone in hand, John Morgan – BBC's reporter – asked the fans to sing for the cameras. They laughed off his request and told him where to go. He waited some ten minutes before beginning his recording... "The desire to win was an agonised one. They would be the champions of England and they wanted their own people to see them become so..." without pausing, he described the scenes poetically: "They don't behave like any other football crowd here, especially not at one end of Anfield ground: on the Kop."

The footage (still available) panned to the swaying masses of support who beamed and sang *'She loves you, yeah yeah yeah! And with a love like that, you know you should be glad.'* Moving across the young faces and the occasional older docker, who was probably no more than 30 years of age, the footage captured the essence of a moment. "The music the crowd sings is the music Liverpool has sent echoing across the world," said Morgan.

He then eloquated one of the best summaries of Liverpool people *en masse* ever spoken:

"It used to be thought that Welsh international rugby crowds were the most musical and passionate in the world, but I've never seen anything like this Liverpool crowd. On the field here the gay and inventive ferocity they show is quite stunning. The Duke of Wellington before the Battle of Waterloo said of his own troops: 'I don't know what they do to the enemy, but by God they frighten me.' I'm sure some of the players here in this match this afternoon are feeling the same way."

And he continued, as the crowd sang '*Anyone Who Had a Heart*':

"An anthropologist studying this Kop crowd would be introduced into as rich and mystifying example of popular culture as any South Sea island. The arrhythmic sway is an elaborate and organised ritual. The 28,000 people on the Kop itself begin singing together. They seem to know intuitively when to begin [and] seem mysteriously to be in touch with one another. With 'Wacker' the spirit of Scouse."

His words tailed off into a statement applicable forevermore ... "On Merseyside, football is the consuming passion. It is hard to convince anybody to talk about anything else."

A number believed that to be a slant, but it was true. The swinging 60s of hippies and beatniks that London, Amsterdam and San Francisco experienced bypassed Liverpool. Granted, the city may have encountered a newfound freedom – though one much less flamboyant than elsewhere – but football was still very much the primary release for the casual worker.

Local

Back-to-back houses had been torn down, families relocated, people were without work, yet despite the uncertainty of the times, Anfield and Goodison remained stable points of communion and working-class solidarity. They became locations of worship because – coupled with the success of the clubs - they welcomed a congregation of people who didn't really know where else to go.

Panorama's visit to Anfield was part of a series of documentaries introduced by Richard Dimbleby titled: 'Liverpool – the most talked about city in Europe'. The title undersold things: Liverpool was the most talked about city in the world at that point, especially in 1964. American beat-poet Allen Ginsberg declared then that: 'Liverpool is the centre of the known universe'. In the 12 months before BBC filmed, from April 1963 – April 1964, Liverpool groups had posted 12 Number 1 hits, while television shows began to focus on homemade Liverpool comedians. What BBC captured at Anfield was nothing more than an outpouring of civic pride at its most climatic point.

A few weeks later, eleven years after touring America for the first time (and being mistaken for fishermen), Liverpool FC were again on the ferry to the United States; this time so famous that they were guests on the Ed Sullivan show. For three consecutive Sundays in February that year the Beatles caused a sensation, paving the way for LFC by opening and closing each show. They sang 'I Want to Hold Your Hand' to a staggering 73 million viewers – a record – and prompted journalists to assert it as the biggest moment in US music history to date.

Peter Moore believes their performances were of cheek and young bravado, which despite their teenage audience, was still fresher, more exuberant and newer to American eyes. 'There is no filter there. They're not thinking "*oh we shouldn't say that*" they just said what popped into their heads and people loved it. Before that period everything was staged and there was decorum and people were worried about stepping out of line. In the US there was also the Vietnam War and when the Beatles landed in the States something happened. It was fresh and uniquely from this city. There is no other city - go anywhere in the UK - there is nowhere like this that could have produced that.'

Gerry Marsden took the credit for getting Liverpool's squad on the Ed Sullivan show. 'Soccer' was not popular, but all things 'Liverpool' was, and the Americans were happy to see more Liverpool people in the flesh: 'We were in New York doing the show,' Marsden said, 'and the Liverpool team were there too playing teams. So I said to Ed "there's a soccer team here from Liverpool. Get them on stage and they'll sing 'You'll Never Walk Alone' with me." We did it, and afterwards coming off Bill Shankly said to me, "Gerry son, I have given you a football team, but you have given us a song.'" Although Marsden's statement may seem based in romance, Shankly did choose the song as his eighth and final track on 'Desert Island Discs' in 1965.[vii]

It became a firm favourite for Chris Lawler and Tommy Smith who were best mates in the team. Matt Busby had been sounding them out for Manchester United, aware they were two of the finest young players in the country who were not getting much game time. They went and informed Shankly, who promised them a reshuffle. With Gerry Byrne from the south end of Liverpool and Ron Yeats, they'd form Liverpool's backline for the rest of the '60s. 'Ronnie Moran was coming to the end of his career,' Lawler remembers, 'so Shanks shifted Gerry Byrne to left-back and put me in at right-back. Every time I saw Ronnie he'd joke and say *"you ended my career."'*

On that America trip, the two young Scousers behaved mischievously. Lawler shuffled back into his armchair to reminisce: 'I was only 21 or something, Smithy was 20. We played ten games and we went all over the place, but it was all done on the cheap. We'd fly at 6am and meals were part of a budget which we'd be given for the day. Me and Smithy would go and have a cheap breakfast and save our money up for other stuff, you know? I remember we played a church team in one game and afterwards the Monsignor asked us how things were going? I told him we were starving. The next morning, he was downstairs with an envelope for $100, a lot of money back then, and told us it would help us to eat. He must have known I was a good Catholic lad.'

During their time in New York, the pair larked about avenues, gazing upwards in amazement at the size of everything: 'We'd train of a Tuesday afternoon but were free to do what we wanted. We'd throw our bags into the room then go and have a little tour. One day we went on a walk and were looking in music shops, and Tommy wanted to go over the road to another one. Anyway, a police car pulled us over and arrested us. They put us in with a load of criminals in the back. *"What's going on?"* I asked them. They wanted to know where we were from and told us we were crazy for just crossing the road however we wanted. They nicked us for jaywalking. But the copper was sound and he drove us around the block before dropping us off on the corner.' They'd been shitting themselves, Lawler says. Shankly never found out.

*

A 2015 report explained how there were some 200 Spion Kops worldwide, from Strasbourg to Breda, Linfield to Paris. It failed to credit where the infamy of the title originated. For Liverpudlians, there is but only one Spion Kop, with the rest all standing as tributes. Anfield's had always been, and continues to be, the most famous body of supporters in world sport.

The name came from South Africa to begin with. Outside Ladysmith (Durban) in the 1890s, a massive mound of land cast shadows for miles. It was soon to be the scene of human brutality. Churchill, believing in his own youthful invincibility, went there as a journalist, and, going down the spioenkop hill during the Boer War, reported: "Corpses lay here and there. Many of the wounds were of a horrible nature. The splinters and fragments of the shells had torn and mutilated them. The shallow trenches were choked with dead and wounded." Gandhi was there too as a medic going up the hill, forging an understanding of Britishness. The Battle for Spion Kop in the Boer War of 1899-1902 was to have great historic military significance.

It would have equal cultural significance, too. The British Army at the hill was made up of a core body from the Second Battalion of Lancashire Fusiliers, a county of which Liverpool belonged. Scousers returned home from the war in a disparate world of thought, shaped by the horrors of what they'd witnessed in South Africa.

While they were away, their Liverpool FC side won its first two league titles and constructed a new 132-tier stand on Breck Road, casting shadows for miles around. It was steep and roofless and took in some 20,000 people. Veterans of the war who stood upon it in 1906 compared it almost immediately to the Spion Kop of the Boer War.

It soared and looked like its Ladysmith namesake, and the roars in pursuit of victory that accompanied it were just as warlike. Amid the bustle of feverish match-day discourse, the newly appointed Sports Editor of the Post and Echo, Ernest Edwards, heard the comparison and put it into print, receiving credit for the terming of Liverpool's new terrace as the Spion Kop – as forever it would be known.

There were stands elsewhere in the country (Arsenal already had one), and there were lively people in other cities, too. But Liverpool and the Spion Kop seemed livelier and more spontaneously emotional, with more diverse types of people and more varied displays of fanatic behaviour, than elsewhere, prompting reporters and anthropologists to flock and see it – to stand upon it and feel the breeze sweep backwards, followed by the collective howl of support.

In 1932, four years after it was topped with a roof and extended to welcome 30,000 fans, the Liverpool Echo sent a reporter to the Kop. He was taken aback by its steep banks, its bright fresh opening from Breck Road, it's demographic and their relationship with Elisha Scott, the goalkeeper. If this was not the first exploration of working-class fan culture in British history, it was one of them. He wrote:

> "They had commentaries on all phases of play and from their unequalled view they reckoned they saw thing that people in other parts could not hope to see. Two women were there, one in chocolate brown and the other in a beret. Two swarthy sons of Ireland came beside me. They had come to see the MA of goalkeepers, Elisha Scott. One wore a black velvet beret and a film face that suggested a Valentino. He was plainly of Basque extraction and was silent.
>
> Where I had expected slashing attacks on players, I found praise and kindness. The kind way they talked of players on the Kop astonished me. These were embittered partisans. They were an object lesson to me...Their sportsmanship; they treated the players encouragingly and in a sporting manner. This spectator is matchless."[21]

Irish fans would travel over on cattle boats, spending twelve hours in the company of cow manure on lapping waves, just to come to Liverpool, to visit family and stand on the Kop. The article mentions them, and it mentions women too, which is important as the two groups so often get overlooked when discussions on the formation of Kopite values are discussed.

Matt Busby understood the Kop. He'd represented the club after the war and fondly remembered the smoke from pipes rising up from its legion of fans. As manager of Manchester United he said: "The deafening roar that accompanies every attacking move carries sufficient volume to cause all but the most experienced of defences to panic. I know this is true because I have played at Anfield – for and against – and I know which side I'd rather be on."

In the 1960s, the Kop was shaped by the presence of various groups of mates – of varying ages – who proudly settled into a 'spec' of their own. The age paradigm would prove to be an important one. At other grounds, younger more boisterous fans settled behind the goal and ousted the older, war-veteran and industrial-worker type fans. At Anfield the older Kopites remained and sought to educate younger fans on the values they'd maintained. 'Fellers used to say *"Oi, give it a rest"* if anyone got on the team's back,' Dave Billsborrow remembers. 'I

---

[21] 'Passing Rhythms' – John Williams et al, 2001.

never shouted horrible things, only encouragement. I remember a big red-haired feller calling players names. Anyway, someone must have sorted him cos' he didn't do it ever again.'

Those 'old working-class Scouse values' which Bilsborrow describes rubbed together with the youth culture of pop music to create a fusion worthy of celebration. But it could, at the same time, be an equally cruel and harsh beast. Arthur Hopcraft, a writer of great repute, described that nasty topophilic combination of metal, wood and people at Liverpool best in 1968:

> "There is no more chilling sound in the game than one of the long howls of animosity which the Liverpool crowd can drill into the ears of a visiting threat to their club's supremacy ... Anfield can give voice to collective vindictiveness in a way that no other English crowd can match. The Liverpool crowd is consistently the [most] obscene. The Kop sometimes achieves a unison with four-letter words which drums in the head like a [hit] in the ear from a mallet. On a wet day, with the steam and the cigarette smoke hanging grey and yellow in the air, and the derision exploding in wicked humour out of this gloomy cavern, the Kop has all the menace of a hysteric's nightmare."

It became a tedious national debate, where exactly collective fandom and chanting originated. Singing had always been present whenever crowds of people gathered, no matter what the occasion was. Liverpudlians were supposed to have sung 'You Made Me Love You (I Didn't Want to Do It)' as early as 1913. Newcastle fans sung 'Blaydon Races' at the 1924 FA Cup final, while West Ham retained 'I'm Forever Blowing Bubbles' from the '30s. Throughout the 1950s Liverpool fans sang 'The Happy Wanderer' whenever they won away, motivating Hopcraft, whose job it was to commentate on such matters, to conclude in 1971:

> "It was created in Liverpool, where the city character, with its pervading harshness of waterfront life and bitterly combative Irish exile content, was given a sudden flowering of arrogant expression with the simultaneous rise of its pop musicians and its leading football teams."[viii]

Self-awareness prompted Liverpool fans in the '70s and '80s to chant affirmatively at opponents '*You got your education from the Kop*', from which there was no viable comeback.

'When you saw the red stand of the Kop coming up Oakfield Road it was exciting. You knew you were going there to sing,' Bilsborrow said. The atmosphere inside was non-stop and spontaneous. '*Ee-aye-addio*' stood as the plinth for most songs, with the words changing to suit the occasion. If visiting fans tried to join in, the Kop's collective 'fuck-offs' would morph into an: '*Ee-aye-addio, sing your own songs,*' or '*ee-aye-addio, the parrots are here again.*'

In the 1960s, home advantage was significant and the Kop felt it was their duty to influence change in every game. David Fairclough has his recollections of peak working-class tribalism: 'My dad was a big Liverpool fan and back then the support was different. The passion and fervour that was around in the '60's seemed to kick on at that time. Everton were successful, so were Liverpool. They had Alan Ball and Labone... Alex Young too. Both teams had their great stars and it was an age when television began to take more of a part in the game. Liverpool football fans picked up the baton in terms of fandom, more than Manchester.'

*

By 1965 Anfield had been redeveloped. Shankly trialled an all-red European kit against Anderlecht in '64, which stuck. Fans were finishing work and turning up at Anfield at 5pm to secure entry to European games. A fascination with visitors from the continent slowly replaced previously held sentiments in the twenty years following the war.[22] Mersey music was on top, so was its politics, so were its teams. In 1965 Liverpool looked set to conquer.

Bob Dylan came to England on his pilgrimaged UK tour on the 1st May that year. His first performance was in Sheffield, where the audience sat on the floor at the front and sang along to his folk repertoire. The next day he came to Liverpool to play the Odeon on London Road. He saw masses of people on his way to the show, all along Lime Street and up Ranelagh Street and Mount Pleasant. When he finally got to the theatre the singing had been going for some time. As he appeared on stage, young people were on the seats in a huddled throng, swaying to keep their balance. "*Ee ay addio, we have won the cup!*" they sang over and over at the top of their voices. Dylan must have thought the place was mad.

More than the league, the FA Cup had been the trophy that all Liverpool fans longed to win. It retained the most domestic value and credibility. Evertonians had mocked Reds for thirty years, "*the Liverbirds would fly away if you lot ever won it.*"

I

---

[22] To an extent, patriotism lingered. Against Bayern Munich and Inter Milan the Kop still chanted '*Ee-aye-addio, we won the War!*' Was it was a boast of self-achievement or national pride?

Local

Throughout that month of May half of the city wore red rosettes as Blues watched on. Bunting covered pub windows for the first time since the Coronation.

So electrified had the atmosphere been and so scarce were tickets for the final that, before the game, a group of Liverpool fans pinched a steamroller off a building site in London with the intention of gaining entry. 'If young kids did that today, they'd all get ten years jail time,' jokes Nicky Allt. 'If that happened in Kiev it would have started a war, making news in New York and all over!'

Back home the city still had 80,000 homes unfit for purpose. Two thirds of town needed redeveloping, prompting the government to propose the biggest housing programme of its kind in history. Thousands of Scousers watched on, gradually slipping out of work.

Fans, however, believed that their football clubs belonged to them – it had been embedded into the fabric of their identity – and while the steamroller was an anecdote, it was also an example of the lengths that Liverpool supporters were willing go to in order to support their team.

They had an underdog mentality, which they channelled into a strength. Leeds United and Inter Milan, two much bigger clubs, had been the anticipated talk of Merseyside. Both would be faced in the same pivotal week. Shankly had been invited onto Desert Island Discs the weekend before the final and when Roy Plomley asked his castaway what luxury item he'd like to take onto the island, Shanks replied: 'I'd take Liverpool Football Club, so I can continue my job in creating the greatest football club of all time.'

He then told T.V Williams to organise a meal for the Friday night before the game. In attendance would be the reserves, a score of youth players, and Liverpool's 1950 losing FA Cup final team who he wanted to be a part of the occasion - Shankly wanted to build a family club. That night he took his team to the London Palladium to watch Ken Dodd perform. Doddy knew they'd be coming and asked the team to stand up for applause. He then began reeling off his fast-paced gags:

> "Don Revie has had Leeds doing special training this week. They've been dribbling in and out of dustbins. Lads, the dustbins won 2-1... Liverpool are going to win in Europe too. I'll tell you the best way to score in Europe: down by the canals in Amsterdam... Leeds star Jim Storrie has been appointed as Britain's Davis Cup coach: he knows how 'not' to put the ball into the net..."

Daniel Fieldsend

Liverpool won the FA Cup on Saturday and, afterwards, Bill Shankly cried. British Movietone News covered the homecoming, showing locals on top of the rooftops of Castle Street, climbing up to catch a glimpse of the cup. They reported: "One can only guess how many thousands were there. One hundred? Two hundred? Half a million? Never before has a winning team had such a fantastic welcome."

Reports confirmed Liverpool's homecoming parade to be around 60% of the population of the city. At the Town Hall, BMN's commentary continued: "It is an incredible scene. Hundreds of thousands of singing, shouting, swinging, swaying people crammed from wall to wall. No success story ever had a finale like this, outshining any homecoming by any victorious team ever before."

Ian Callaghan stood at the front of the bus looking out for familiar faces in the crowd; Caryl Gardens had emptied out to see their local hero. That night when he got home, he and the rest of the squad could hardly sleep. They were full of adrenalin after a long unseen before parade, plus they were thinking about their next game: Inter Milan at Anfield in the semi-final of the European Cup.

Before the Italians came to town, Chris Lawler married his fiancée Geraldine. He was duty-bound however to return to travel with Liverpool after his ceremony in West Derby, and was made to share a room with Tommy Smith, his mate, in the Norbreck Hotel on his wedding night. When Lawler came into the room, Smith pushed his bed up against the wall and said to the groom: "Don't you fucking come near me!"

The buzz of winning the FA Cup lingered for a long time. 'We were still walking on air when we took on the Italians,' Callaghan wrote. The Reds had travelled to Blackpool the day before the game and when they got back to Anfield on the morning of the match, Inter's players were already there, doing press-ups in the corridor of the Main Stand: Luis Suarez (the original), Facchetti and Mazzola - famous names who flexed and jumped and squatted in an attempt to intimidate Liverpool's young squad.

'That overawed me a little,' said Callaghan, 'but when we stepped out onto the pitch it was forgotten.' 55,000 fans were already in the ground hours before kick-off. A ten-year-old Phil Thompson was there and remembers the deafening chant that rang all around: *'Ee-ay-addio, we've won the cup.'*

Only Manchester United had brought famous names like Helenio Herrera to Britain before (the Argentine was widely regarded as the best manager in the world at the time). As steam rose from every corner of the ground, floodlights caught a hold of them, turning Anfield into a cauldron. A scattering of Italian supporters stood together in the Main Stand. When their presence became known, the population of the stadium pointed and sang '*Go back to Italy*' to the tune of Santa Lucia. 'The noise was deafening when we went out onto the pitch,' said Callaghan. 'I dread to think how it affected the Italians.'

Bill Shankly was feeling emotional. Earlier that day, ground staff had discovered club chairman Jimmy McInnes, whose office was next to the Boot Room, hanging in a turnstile booth in the Kemlyn Road. Nobody was sure why he killed himself or why he had chosen to do so in such a way on such a night. But his suicide affected the mood of the staff.

A distant Bill Shankly stood in the changing room and listened to the noise outside. Things had been simmering for hours and he planned to use the crowd to lift his players. As he began to explain his requirements for the game, he heard booing and whistling which landed like a bomb all at once. Internazionale had gone out onto the pitch early to do stretches. In an instant he decided to frighten them further.

The hissing that the Italians encountered turned once again to euphoria when Gerry Byrne and Gordon Milne were spotted coming out of the tunnel holding the FA Cup. Shankly had no idea that the Anfield crowd could make such a noise. The Italians knew the enormity of Liverpool Football Club in an instant. Stephen Kelly wrote: "Grown men alongside me were in tears, 25,000 of us packed in like sardines, swaying one way then another, all on our tip-toes trying to catch a glimpse."

From the first whistle Liverpool stuffed the world champions with the match finishing 3-1. It was to be one of Anfield's greatest nights. But although they won the battle, they would go on to lose the war. A week later Liverpool were cheated in Italy by goals that should not have stood. They also had a perfectly fine St John goal ruled out. Inter won 3-0 and their fans inside the San Siro set fire to cushions, frisbeeing them at the small collection of Liverpool supporters who'd travelled over.

Tommy Smith saw a red mist. Angry at being cheated, then furious after a bottle smashed at his feet, he saw the referee in front of him walking off the pitch: "I kicked him hard in the back of the legs," he wrote. "Strange thing is, he didn't turn around and just kept walking. That didn't just tell me something, it told me a lot."

Despite the outcome, this was the occasion when Liverpool's obsession with the European Cup began. Chris Lawler recalls the era. 'Everything was fresh with new success and the crowds were getting better and Liverpool was gaining more support. I still get goosebumps when I think about the fans singing.'

The biggest shame of 1965 is that Liverpool could have become the first British club to win the European Cup. They deserved to get to the final and Shankly deserved to win it. In Smith's biography he wrote: "I think he saw it as a watershed for the club, a vindication of everything he had done since arriving at what was then a middling Second Division club with a ramshackle set-up and ground."

It was a blessing that, back on that rainy day in 1959, Nessie had reassured her husband that he'd chosen to do the right thing.

Local

OLIVER'S ARMY

Bob Dylan came back to Liverpool in 1966 for his world tour. His agent took him down to Dublin Street off the Dock Road to shoot some publicity photos, but while they were there they were swarmed by a gang of grubby-faced local children who saw the camera and realised Dylan was famous. The kids had been playing out, recreating that day's FA Cup final, pretending to be Everton, the winners. After his set that evening Dylan went to the Raz on Seel Street where girls pinned either blue or red rosettes on him and spoke to him faster than he was accustomed.

All night Everton fans sang for the cup and Liverpool supporters sang for the league. Once again, Dylan thought the place was mad. This was a music town, like New York and Memphis, he thought, but there was something else seemingly more important that the folk singer hadn't encountered anywhere else. A sport, football, was the capstone of Liverpool life.

That summer was perhaps the highest point in the city's post-war golden age before living conditions declined. Between 1966 and 1977 a global economic recession hit Liverpool hard and 350 factories either closed down or were relocated elsewhere. Although there was not one significant moment which ended it all - that idyllic era of Liverpool in vogue – it seemed that its fashion slipped away with every passing day as 1970 loomed.[23]

National pride, something Liverpool still felt keenly, had been at its zenith back in the summer of 1966. Never mind Dylan and his rosettes, the World Cup

---

[23] In those years the city continued to decorate itself; Paddy's Wigwam was completed in 1967; the Radio City tower (though it wasn't named as such) was completed in '69, and in '71 the Kingsway Tunnel was completed - to be paid for by locals forevermore.

was coming to Liverpool, that once radical outpost on the corner of western Britain.

Where did the city see itself at the time, as Lancashire? England? Something more or something less? Did its seafaring outlook separate it from the distant fields beyond Ditton and Whiston? Where did the allegiance of the people lie? In 1907 Ramsay Muir had written that Liverpool was: 'Not English, like London, nor Lancashire, like Manchester'. Did that mean the fervour of patriotism would bypass the port?

On the contrary, the World Cup was embraced. The overall answer to what the tournament meant to Liverpool varied from community to community, taking on different meanings in the Afro-Caribbean households of Granby and the Irish streets of Scotland Road, than the traditional homes of Woolton and Aigburth. There were buntings, flowers and street parties again. Around Harlow Street, houses were decorated in the colour of the residents' historic nation; mostly England, some for Switzerland and Italy.

Stanley Rous the FIFA president had announced before the tournament began, way back on the 6th January, that Goodison Park would host all three matches of reigning champions Brazil, sending locals into a frenzy to secure tickets. A makeshift office was set up on Cases Street for the sale. It wasn't supposed to open until Monday, but people began gathering on Saturday morning for tickets costing £1 10 shillings.

Dagens Nyheter, a Swedish newspaper, reported from Goodison Park following Brazil's match against Bulgaria: 'This is the football city of England - not stiff and serious London where you can hardly tell there is a World Cup competition going on. I don't think I have ever heard a football crowd enjoy themselves as they did here.'[ix]

With racism still very much prominent in Liverpool, members of the black community seldom went to football matches. They avoided Anfield and Goodison Park because of the racist comments made to players. They knew of William 'Dixie' Dean who was of dark complexion, who had once hit a fan for calling him a 'black bastard'[24] but Dean was not a black man. 'Dixie', rather, was a word that had carried over as a slur term on boats from Alabama and South Carolina where the US's black population was concentrated. Liverpool 8 felt ostracised from

---

[24] As mentioned in "Dixie Dean: The Official Biography of a Goalscoring Legend" by Nick Walsh, 1977.

football games in north Liverpool and only a brave handful chose to attend, but when Brazil arrived – a team made up of various ethnicities such as *indígena*, *pretos* and *pardos* – they had to get involved. Pele was a symbol of pride.

Howard Gayle remembers them coming. Plenty of residents in the Granby ward associated more with them and Portugal, who had an African-born star in Eusebio, than they did with England's squad. "To be honest we were cheering for Brazil. There weren't that many black role models in football so it had to be Brazil," Wally Brown, a community leader from Liverpool 8, told the BBC in 2016.[x]

Every single African team had boycotted the competition due to FIFA's decision to admit South Africa and its apartheid regime into their body. Sierra Leone, Gayle's father's nation, had only gained independence five years earlier and probably wouldn't have qualified anyway. Gayle would turn down an MBE as a man because of Britain's bloody desire to colonise Africa. As a footballer he'd reflect: 'I didn't even consider myself English so why should I be proud of representing England?' That sentiment was to become more common in Liverpool over the years.

*

Questions that abounded beforehand as to where the city fitted into the national picture were asked for obvious reasons. At times Liverpool had stood at the forefront of Britain's ambitions, chest out and proud, but had at other times slumped willingly into the shadows, awkward and unwanted. There'd been moments in the city's history when Liverpool lashed out against its country, in something of a crisis of adolescence.

Back in 1812, Spencer Perceval, the Tory Prime Minister, had been shot dead by a Liverpool resident. In 1856, a Liverpool fairground included a firing range for locals to shoot at effigies of the Queen and Prince Albert. One manifestation of difference seemed to follow another.

In 1956 there had been a genuine worry that the city could become its own little Ulster – all of the figurative ammunition was there - but that didn't happen. It was the port of the British Empire, with cargo from all over the New World arriving every day, yet the people still chose to call those streets of great importance around the port: 'Town', tying it somewhere loosely between international and provincial. Many local politicians felt that Britain needed Liverpool more than it needed them. Their home had been dubbed Ireland East and the Capital of North Wales, but, as Du Noyer wrote, it mostly believed it was the capital of itself.

Was that a limitation? Perhaps, but because of that self-belief there blossomed a sense of expectant achievement. The Royal Liver building didn't just get a clock in 1910, it got the biggest mechanical clock in the world, and the architects and company men toasted that fact by using it as a grand table the evening before it was hoisted into infamy. It was a statement and a point.

Because of its own remarkableness Liverpool had never really given any regard to the towns beyond its borders, either. Roger McGough from Litherland once said: "If you take the East Lancs road out towards Manchester, it is not long before our tribe quite suddenly ends. There is no transition. The accent, loyalties, the sense of belonging stop abruptly."

His tribe... What was norm became obvious in the face of extraordinary difference. Something interesting happened when local, longstanding Scouse families were thrust by the Slum Clearance act from all they knew into new, quagmire towns.

A unique terminology was created. Scousers silently regarded, scrutinised, and formed opinions on the new people they lived close to. The word 'Woolyback' began to be used more often to define them. It would prevail as a successful slur for generations. The Liverpool Echo debated the emergence of the term. It had, they wrote, originated from two possibilities:

A) From scab workers who were brought into the city from surrounding towns to manually unload ships. They'd been asked to carry woollen bales on their backs, hence the association with outsiders. Or:

B) The men prior to World War 2 who delivered coal into Liverpool from mines, who wore sheep-wool fleeces on their backs. They looked comical to locals and, like the scab workers, were also outsiders.

Either way, it referred to somebody strange, a visitor, and was used to identify people from the periphery, from Prescot, Runcorn, St Helens, Widnes et cetera. Labelling them as such them allowed Scousers to detach themselves from the region beyond they were used to, and therefore wider England beyond that.

The lines, however, became blurred. 'Woolybacks' dressed and acted differently and over time it mattered not if a person was from Runcorn or Rwanda, if they fitted the visual criteria and acted differently, they could be called a Wool.

Testimony comes from Jamie Carragher who, when asked to identify who the biggest Wool at Liverpool was, replied laughing: 'Didi Hamann definitely. He was the scruffiest bastard you've ever seen in your life. But he wasn't trying, he wasn't too bothered how he looked. He'd have holes in his trainees.' Hamann was from the obscure Bavarian town of Waldsassen, not Widnes.

'Who was the biggest Wool?' Carragher continued to ponder. 'Scouse-wise I'd say Jay Spearing. He had a funny accent. Djibril Cisse used to come in with outrageous gear too, he could have done with going into Wade Smith (shop) at the time.'

Scousers in 1966 having moved to the edges of an ever-expanding city found themselves with neighbours who retained polar opposite beliefs to them, as well as a sense of humour and dress sense which was deemed to fall short.

In response, they disregarded them. On the Kop (and at Goodison Park) local fans chanted in the '70s: *'There's a Wooly over there, over there. And he's wearing brown Airware* (or 'baggy flares'). *With a 3-star jumper halfway up his back, he's a fucking Woolyback, Woolyback.'*

Isolationist? Not exactly. The Guardian wrote how Liverpudlians have: "Long had a tendency to look down upon – pity, even – those who were not born or raised within it, and its inhabitants' greatest disdain has seemed at times to be reserved for those who live and work just beyond its boundaries." The Liverpool identity was sweeping outwards and would have continued to do so, had it not met inevitable resistance. The Woolyback emerged as an almost comical antithesis figure to assist in the construction of a Scouser's sense of self. As Jean-Paul Sartre said of human identity: "You are what you are not". They were always going to appear at some point.

There was also another way of determining what was Scouse and Wool. A scholarly paper by Philip Boland looked into 'sonic geography', a branch of science exploring speech and the various identities attached to accents. Through sonic geography, locals positioned people with softer twangs, like those from Crosby, Wallasey and Woolton, in a different dimension to those from 'core', grittier locations, such as Fazakerley and Wavertree.[25] Instantly, according to Boland, a Scouser could authenticate an opinion on another person by the sound of their voice.

---

[25] Sonic Geography, Place and Race in The Formation of Local Identity: Liverpool and Scousers. Bolad, 2010.

Daniel Fieldsend

Simon Hughes sees Scouse validation as a strength, despite it being dismissed as self-righteous by outsiders. He notes how it all began with dockside trading: 'Insularity is a difficult thing to define because I think Liverpool people are great travellers and we are intrigued by Europe. Wherever you go you bump into somebody from Liverpool, which I think is connected to the history of the port. We're interested in the rest of the world more than we are with our own country. There are a lot of misconceptions about Liverpool and I'm willing to just be myself but I won't doctor my behaviour to the norms they expect. Large parts of middle-England are Tory hotbeds and I'm not going to meet them halfway.'

Instead of reaching out to those with different identities in the 1960s and 1970s, Scousers massaged their own symmetry and constructed the core beliefs that went into creating, what Laura Brown called, 'Scouse exceptionalism'.

Simon Hughes touched upon the belief, albeit genuine, that Liverpool was (is) better received by people in other shores than it is by its own land. Because of that interpretation, England's 1966 aged into something less than it actually was, and was seen certainly as being less of an achievement than Everton's FA Cup win of that summer and Liverpool's league title triumph, especially for younger generations who did not live through it all. Jamie Carragher wrote in his biography:

> "For my family, the most important event at Wembley that year was Everton winning the FA Cup... That's how we've been brought up to feel, and playing for my country didn't change that ... 'God Save the Queen' doesn't get my blood pumping ... Our nation is divided, not only in terms of prosperity but by different regional outlooks. For some of us, civic pride overpowers nationality... If you're born near Wembley it's a more natural aspiration to play there. On the streets of Liverpool, we have a different view."

Romanticising isolationism isn't healthy for any marketing team, anywhere, but it exists to varying degrees. Being republican-minded would develop as a part of that. Chris Lawler, when asked if he was patriotic growing up, replied: 'Nah, there was a street party for the Coronation I think but we weren't interested. My ambition was always to play for Liverpool. England was just a secondary thing, you know? Same mentality as Carragher.'

Between 1966 and 2006 various governments became the architects of Liverpool's heightened sense of separation. By 2008 it reached the point whereby fans voted England as their "4th most hated team" on LFCTV, with one fan outside of Anfield telling Liverpool's channel: "I would rather Liverpool won a throw-in than England won the World Cup." Jamie Carragher acknowledges the roles of political figures in dismantling Liverpool's patriotism but believes that, at the end of the day, civic pride just outweighed everything else, turning isolation into a form apathy:

'In regards to '66, my dad only ever spoke about Everton winning the FA Cup; it was never about England. He's never once mentioned Bobby Moore lifting the World Cup. I don't know what it is. It's been there even before Margaret Thatcher and the Conservatives [that mentality]. Our passion for our football clubs overrides everything else.'

And with what was to come - the riots of 1981, Militantism, Thatcherism, Heysel, Hillsborough, the Dockers' Dispute, misconceptions, stereotypes and a bereft feeling of being totally misunderstood - by the end of it all travelling Liverpool fans singing *'You can shove your Royal Family up your arse'* to Glasgow Rangers supporters in a 2008 pre-season friendly was seen as totally normal, expected behaviour.

Daniel Fieldsend

THE LIFE OF RILEY

In the early 1970s everything was brown. The walls; the carpet; the furniture; dad's slacks and his bottles of ale. The fizzing '60s spilled into a sorry unexpected hangover. There were blackouts reminiscent of the Blitz but without the heroism. Ted Heath battled the unions. Irish Republicans threatened everyone and the army fired back at them. Ethnic tension was normalised by TV characters like Alf Garnett; the bigoted, Tory, racist, cockney who BBC writers believed spoke for the working classes. Unfortunately, he probably did. His stereotyping of Scousers as thieving and idle slowly embedded itself into the English psyche for generations to come.

The decade had five official states of emergency, two property booms and two oil crises. Telephones, computers and new forms of technology were merely shrugged at. TV's had 3 channels. Food was boring. Pubs shut at 10pm. Across the nation, football terraces were known for their misogynist, sexist, racist, homophobic and violent dispositions. They were little more than microcosms of society in general.

In Liverpool it was impossible to find a street without a boardered-up house. Warehouses stood abandoned and landmarks were soot-black. A number of proud Georgian homes on Mount Pleasant were bulldozed to make way for a grey, depressing, multi-story car park. City planners nodded to each other when New Hall Place was built; an ugly brutalist tribute to a grim era.

In the early months of 1970 Freddie Mercury lived above the Dovedale Towers pub on Penny Lane. His band took their logo from the Queen Insurance Buildings on Dale Street. A few years later, they had risen to the Cavern Club, fulfilling a dream of Mercury's. Then it closed, was filled with rubble and sealed like a tomb. Youthful optimism got trapped inside. Arthur Dooley put a statue outside the entrance which seemed to resemble Death itself. When a tribute to the Beatles was proposed to the council, they turned it down replying: "Why should we put a statue up to four drug addicts," another trick missed. Self-doubt reigned supreme beneath a blanket of a sorry mood.

Anfield seemed to be the only spot on the map which stood alone, bright and joyful. While England was depressed, Liverpool FC were mustard. From 1973 the Reds won 11 titles and finished outside the top two only once in 19 seasons. 'We were unstoppable,' said Tommy Smith.

It was the presence of two distinctively Scouse institutions in particular (synonymous with the times), in this period of despondency, that had a tangible effect on Liverpool FC, influencing the continental successes to come. The Boys' Pen - an ear-piercing block of screeching kids which fanned the passions of Phil Thompson, Terry McDermott and David Fairclough - and the amateur leagues which blooded the likes of Jimmy Case, John Aldridge and Howard Gayle.

Saturdays

'[The boys] found themselves eager to take a place in this demented but partly secure society. They were glad to touch the brown backs of the fence that hemmed in the terror and made it governable.'
William Golding.

Lord of the Flies was released in 1954. It was about the flaws in human nature and the primitive ways in which boys thought. They, marooned together on an island, were always more of a threat to each other than anything else. Its inspiration could genuinely have been Liverpool's Boys' Pen, so graduates of the cage would later say. There, on fresh Saturday mornings, gangs of youngsters from across the city met and created an environment where intimidation ruled.

The original Boys' Pen emerged in the 1920s. It was in the Kemyln Road stand but lacked the barbed wire, mesh enclosure and animalism which typified its Kop evolution. Bad behaviour was infrequent. In February 1938 Leeds United came to Anfield and the kids in the section threw fruit onto the pitch - the club received its first warning. One year later in February '39 fruit was once again thrown onto the pitch, this time directed at Wolverhampton Wanderers players. The club received its second warning and the FA threatened to close the section down.

After the Second World War the enclosure relocated to where the Main and Kop stands met, high in the eastern corner of the ground on Lake Street. It was a cold, windy block compared to a Soviet Gulag, where poor youngsters packed in for warmth. In the queue outside the turnstile, some urchins threatened new faces: 'Money or your life?'

Or did they? Accounts vary. In the '50s and '60s the Pen was said to be more jovial and carefree, but in the '70s reports describe it as being harsher and at times dangerous (was this not just reflective of society in general?). Older kids in later years squeezed in with their knees bent double, stubble hidden. Newcomers walked up the concrete stairs, ignoring the shouts from behind. At the top was a white wall and beyond it, green and empty, was Anfield's turf. It was tradition to get into the Pen early, allowing oneself enough time to escape.

Getting out of the it was part of an apprenticeship for younger fans. If they escaped into the Kop, they were adults. Phil Thompson recalled the process, writing in his autobiography: "I was desperate to stand on there. The earlier you got in, the easier it was because there were fewer stewards around. We used to call them guards. I was a good climber and nifty on foot so I was a prolific escapee."

Howard Gayle was aware of the hellish potential of the Pen and wrote in his book: "Kids who stood in there were tough. Fighting and swearing were commonplace. There were gangs from all different areas of the city. I went with lads from Norris Green. Then there were gangs from Dingle, Halewood, Speke, Scotland Road and Kirkby. Although the obvious enemy was whoever Liverpool were playing, there were times inside the pen when lads would have a scrap to claim their own territory."

At times indeed. History always has a tendency to sensationalise events. Many youngsters turned up, watched the game and went home without encountering any *aggro* whatsoever. They saw the occasion as another part of their young liberation.

Most of the kids inside the Pen, whether they were civilised or otherwise, had progressed there from being 'three-quarter time' Reds: boys who stood outside the Kop having a kick-about, listening to the crowd for updates, waiting for the 70th minute when they could surge in through the big red doors that opened up.

After the game they'd walk home alongside adults, ear-wigging on their opinions and acting like they'd been there all along. As football changed in the 21st century, children would be deprived of any such match-day experience, excluded by both the demand for, and cost of, attending matches. Instead of receiving an education from the Kop, they got one from Sky Sports in pubs.

'Pennites' in the '70s however had a much different experience. Reports describe thieving, with pockets sliced and money taken, and bangers dropped into hoods around Bonfire night. Those who only went in there because their dads dropped them off stepped out after the game as young Western heroes, braver than before.

Throughout the season the Kop almost always acted as a big brother of sorts, keeping the urchins in check. If a kid criticised the team, they'd be bollocked for their naïve understanding of the game. If a kid jumped, the Kop would catch them. If the Boys' Pen began singing, an embarrassed Kop would out-sing them to drown out the soprano screeching. When they were hungry, Kopites passed food through the meshed fence, as if to animals in a zoo.

Against Everton in November 1970, with Liverpool 2-0 down, Pennites began chanting *'No Surrender'*, forcing Kopites to join in, collectively rallying a statement of defiance. Liverpool went on to win 3-2. Chris Lawler got the winner and Anfield erupted to its loudest best. 'I felt the noise hit me,' he recalled.

Given the brawling schoolyard nature of the Pen, described by Arthur Hopcraft as a 'biting monster', it is little wonder the less deranged tried to escape it early. Getting out required inventiveness. An hour until kick-off, the pre-match entertainment began. One method was to climb up onto the girders at the back, high above the crowd. If attempted early enough, before the policeman took his post, then it was possible to scurry up a drain pipe, onto a ledge and down into the Kop.

As kick-off approached and the Kop began to fill, a decoy fight would take place in the pen, allowing the first brave kids to make an ascent. They'd climb to the rafters, wait, take a deep breath, close their eyes and then jump down bravely into the scores of chanting Kopites below.

But over time such processes became boring. The youngsters grew up and tired of the Pen, and it simply became cooler to stand on the Kop with mates, where the only real danger was the sight of a feller rolling up an Echo newspaper.

From the Kop the young men became part of a synergy, linking supporters to the achievements of the players. After making his debut Phil Thompson reflected: "When I looked up at the Pen during matches it always felt strange. That was where it all started for me."

One season toward the end of the 1970s, fans entered Anfield and noticed that the Pen was gone – no explanation given. An institution had been demolished. From being three-quarter time urchins to becoming Pennites, before advancing onto the Kop and then joining the away day scene, youngsters in the '60s and '70s received an education in the values and devotion required to be a Liverpool supporter – something that was unfortunately going to be consigned to history over time.

Sundays

Underneath the shadow of Anfield and Goodison Park, on a block of green land between Queens Drive and Utting Avenue, hundreds of lads turned up on Sunday mornings to play football. There were fifteen pitches leading all the way up to Walton Hall Park as a roulette of families braved the weather, standing watching wholesome semi-structured football. 'That's the nature of the city,' says David Fairclough. 'The game keeps us all together and it drives our lives.'

Walton Hall Park was one of many venues operating to create the impression that everybody played football of a weekend. There was Sefton and Stanley Park too, and the Joe Stone, Wavertree, Long Lane Rec and Barnfield Drive Recs, where on occasions Bill Shankly was known to saunter over for a tribal fix. Densely populated areas like Speke, Huyton and Kirkby had a great number of teams playing on local fields as well.

The Zingari League had been around since 1895 and had historic importance, while the Business Houses League was massively populated with twelve divisions playing on a Saturday morning and eight of a Sunday. Squads were hard and skilful and matches were always intense. Lobster, Fantail, Seymour, Dingle Rail, Almithak, Nicosia and the Oyster all won the National Cup. So high was the standard in Liverpool that the FA made regulations limiting the number of Scouse teams, so amateur sides from elsewhere in the country had a chance to win too.

Kirkby had some of the most talented teams. The town was a coalescence of lads playing the game and improving together, with little else otherwise to do. Schools like St Kevin's had around five hundred boys attending at any one time. There were three teams for every year group. To be the captain of the firsts, you had to be talented.

Terry McDermott played for Kirkby Boys in the early '70s. His teammates were Jimmy Redfern who signed for Bolton Wanderers; John McLaughlin who was signed by Liverpool; Gerry Farrell who joined Wolves; Kenny Swain who got scouted by Chelsea, and Dennis Mortimer who'd go on to captain Aston Villa.

Peter Carney played alongside Mike Marsh, who was the youngest and most outstanding player in the league. 'He was a little whipper-snapper who was brilliant as a kid,' said Carney. 'He was bought by Liverpool from Kirkby Town.' Marsh was signed on the strength of Phil Thompson's word, who'd kept his ear to the ground. Carney's cousin Terry Darracott went on to play for Everton.

What made the standard in both Kirkby and the wider city so good? Carney believes it is linked to economics: 'It's out of the daily grind, football. The poor working-class of this city viewed the game as a release. There are more footballers who come out of here than anywhere else in the country, and London is twenty times bigger. It's in the DNA. A good midwife can tell if it's a boy or if it's a Scouse boy by counting the balls. A Scouser is born with two in the sack and one at the feet.'[26]

In amateur circles, most players knew each other and a select number of players became legends. The Fantail had a lad named John O'Leary who was described by Bobby Charlton in his autobiography as: 'The finest player to have never turned professional'. He built up such an aura that there'd be whispers before a match that he was playing. Once, a team of London dockers came up from Camden to the Delco on Moorgate Lane and couldn't believe his talent, making him an even bigger myth down south afterwards.

Pub teams were also talented. Because they were sponsored, a huge spread would be awaiting players and their muddy post-mortem conversation after matches, fostering a sense of community. The Eagle and Child in Huyton was one of the most notorious ale houses in the country. It took courage to go in there, but even more courage to play against them. Wingers had a torrid time at away matches, avoiding angry Dobermans on the side lines.

Phil Thompson coached the Falcon pub on Bewley Drive because his brothers and mates all drank there, training them on the Windy Arbour fields in Northwood. They'd get up of a Sunday morning – still pissed from the night before – with Thompson exhausted from Saturday's match. He often had arguments with other Newtown League managers but insists: 'There was a bond struck spending time on the touchlines of Kirkby.'

The north end of Liverpool had robust teams and the south had huge crowds. Crocky Legion were a fine side, managed by the affectionately titled 'Fat Harold'. Canada Dock, Sandon Dock and the other dock teams were always in the top

---

[26] The Telegraph found that between 1992 and 2011 there had been 62 Liverpool-born players in England's first division. Birmingham came second with 55.

division too. John Durnin was signed by Liverpool from Waterloo Dock for a few hundred pounds in the '80s.

It was possible then for the most outstanding players to forge a career in the game, rising from the Sunday leagues to semi-professional and eventually fully-professional football. The Blue Union groomed Jimmy Case and John Aldridge, while Howard Gayle joined the Bedford, before all three eventually made their way to Liverpool.

*

Jimmy Case grew up near Mather Avenue in a terraced council house. His dad, one of twenty-two (including half-siblings), taught him how to fish and hunt for ferrets. They'd fatten turkeys up in their shed and sell them at Christmas for a few bob. People did what they had to. Allerton was close-knit and playing for local team, the Blue Union, was a badge of honour within the community. They were the hardest and most skilful team in a strong league. 'I was sixteen coming up against thirty-year-olds. If you were picked for them it meant you weren't a bad player. The coaches would say things like *"Make your first tackle count"* or *"You have to earn the right to play."'* It set him up for life at Liverpool.

His neighbourhood had a communal feel with the shops on Allerton Road being family owned. Hargreaves, Alldays', Joughin, Clegg's. From Penny Lane roundabout up to Allerton library, everything was familiar and Case began to get recognised. He moved to South Liverpool FC and played at Holly Park, combining the few quid he made there with his electrician apprenticeship. Getting a trade was essential in the '70s – more important than amateur football. One night at Holly Park when the rain fell hard, Case gathered the ball to take a corner. A man in a flat cap walked past and asked the cold, mud-soaked teenager if he'd like a trial at Liverpool? *"Fuck off will you*?!" Case replied, assuming the feller was taking the piss.

Tom Saunders persisted, though, and Liverpool offered him a formal trial. When Saunders told Case that Bill Shankly wanted to sign him, the youngster said *no*. 'My mates and brothers thought I was mad, but in truth I wasn't sure if I was good enough and I remembered what my dad had told me about getting a trade. By signing for Liverpool, I would have given up two years of apprenticeship at Evans.'

A solution was had: he'd split his time between the club and his apprenticeship, becoming the only semi-professional player at Melwood, costing an insignificant fee of £500. That sum would be all the most incredible given that

Case would eventually win Liverpool's first three European Cups and be named as the 'Best Young Play in Europe' in 1977, before the likes of van Basten, Ronaldo, Maldini and Messi won the title.[27]

Case's daily routine throughout that period entailed him clocking on at Evans at 8am, driving to Anfield an hour later, getting changed and jumping the coach to Melwood; training and studying Tommy Smith's aura; having lunch and then going back to Evans from 2pm to 5pm. Of a Tuesday he'd train with the schoolboys in the evenings and of a Wednesday night he'd go to Old Swan Tech college until 7pm. 'It was hectic but I was loving it,' he said.

David Fairclough remembers training alongside Case of a Thursday night while he was still working his apprenticeship. 'He'd turn up with his denim jeans, bomber jacket and bag over his shoulder, looking hard even back then. He stood out from the crowd,' he wrote. They'd played against each other as boys: Major Lester versus Springwood. But Case's exterior was polished by a tough Blue Union upbringing.

*

John Aldridge followed in his footsteps, literally. 'I was at the Blue Union when I was sixteen. Jimmy played for The Blue and the Woody's just like me, and he played for Cheshire Lines a few times and South Liverpool, so we were very similar. He was an electrician by trade and I was a toolmaker so there were loads of similarities.'

Aldridge was well regarded in schoolboy football, but was not ready for the big time until years later. When he was fourteen he played against a lad at SFX school who was the best player in the city at that age, a little midfielder called Sammy Lee. Despite Aldo being a striker and scoring 3 goals that afternoon, Lee scored 4 from a deeper position. 'I thought he'd go on to play for the schoolboys and then Liverpool. I doubt he thought the same of me.'

Like Case, Aldridge believes there were intangibles developed in amateur football which supported him in his professional career. Specifically, tough love. 'The Sunday league in those days was really tough. Defenders would kick you and I was punched in the back of the head a couple of times. People tried to snap you so you'd learn to see it coming and down the line it toughens you up.'

Aldridge would go on, after Liverpool, to become the first non-Basque footballer to play for Real Sociedad. Initially he was spat at in the streets of San

---

[27] But despite his ability, he still never received an England cap.

Sebastian, vilified for being the person who replaced a tradition. But abuse was something he'd encountered ever since his first few games as a semi-pro. He continued to score goals and before long was adored in the Basque country. 'They say that I worked and acted like a Basque person and it's lovely how they portray me. They're very similar to Scousers in that they stand up to their own principles, morals and standards.' He found during his Blue Union upbringing that nothing endears a footballer to people like work-rate.

*

Four months, the judge decided; four months for biting a policeman. At 18-years of age Howard Gayle had already been to court eight times before. He was lost, stealing from factories and pinching cars to drive to away games in. Always an outsider in Norris Green, Gayle looked toward petty criminality as a means of fitting in.

A lifeline was thrown to him in the form of amateur football during the 1970s. He'd grown up soaking in the sights and sounds of Sefton Park as a boy whenever his family visited the south end. Every pitch was taken up with matches on a Sunday morning. "[It all] dripped into my consciousness," he wrote, "educating me about the game and what it meant to the people of Liverpool… Matches were noisy with instructions being shouted by players and spectators. Everyone present had something to say."

Timepiece, the only all-black team in the Liverpool leagues, rescued him. When they played home matches, racism was infrequent because of the presence of hundreds of spectators from the black community on the side-lines. Away from home it was a different matter. From his autobiography:

"Gradually, I became familiar with the unprecedented and harsh world of Sunday league football in Liverpool – a place where only the toughest or those with rapier wit survived; where insulting words like 'nigger' and 'coon' were a part of the vocabulary used by parents as well as players, especially when you were facing teams from Scotland Road or Warbreck – two of the toughest inner-city areas where attitudes were entrenched and a peculiar Celtic insularity survived."

Gayle played for the Bedford, too, who were coached by Eric Dunlop. He lived in Gateacre and knew John Bennison, the youth coach at Liverpool. Dunlop nagged Bennison to take a look at Gayle who, at the time, was embarrassing defenders in the league with his skill and confidence. He was eventually invited to Melwood with hundreds of other amateurs on a Thursday night and scored from

30-yards to impress Bennison and Tom Saunders on the sideline. His career progressed from there.

Jimmy Case and John Aldridge had played in the same south end leagues as Gayle. Teams contained a collection of players who could play football, but also rough up opponents. It took a streetwise nature and a quick tongue to be successful. Ian Barrigan is head of local recruitment at Liverpool academy. It is his job to tap into the pool of talent in the city. He believes, fundamentally, that the game just overwhelms civic consciousness, inspiring so many to play it.

'My dad was in the army so I've lived all over. Let's be honest, there is only one sport in Liverpool. I don't know anywhere else like it. There is boxing, but even boxers are invested in football. There is no rugby here, no cricket, no basketball. If you go to London or Birmingham, they have different things like speedway. Here, everybody has to play football. How many people do you know who aren't into footy? If you meet a Scouse feller who isn't interested in the game, you think there's something wrong with him. The standard is huge. When I was away across the country in school aged 9 or 10, I was the best player. I'd come back here and have to play in goal.'

Liverpool's non-league game benefitted from that standard. There remains a mutuality and a respect from professionals for local lower-league sides. When Ronnie Moran was suffering with Alzheimer's, his son Paul would take him to watch matches at local clubs, such as Marine and Lairds. At Bootle FC they bumped into Jamie Carragher and had a chat. Taking Ronnie to lower league games lifted the veil of his illness temporarily for Paul, giving him his father back. 'He used to watch matches and say *"Look at the left-back creeping out of position"* and this was within the last four or five years of his life. And he'd be right; the other team would capitalise on the space behind every time,' Paul remembers.

Back in 1973 pleasure in life centred around football for a deprived class and generation of younger people. They'd work tedious jobs throughout the week; have a pint of a Friday once the pay package came in. Do the pools. Place a bet. Go to the match of a Saturday. Release the tensions and anxieties of an uncertain existence. Play on a Sunday morning in one of the city's famous amateur leagues, and then do it all again.

The abounding hope for them came from Liverpool and Everton. Shankly's second great team had just missed out on the league but were going for the FA Cup against Newcastle. Shanks placed a letter in the Echo the week of the game telling fans that if they needed sorting out for tickets, write to him and he'd see what he could do. 200 people replied and 200 people got tickets, every single letter returned to them was signed off with *'Best Wishes, B Shankly'*.

Before the game striker Malcolm MacDonald said outright that Newcastle were going to win. Afterwards Phil Thompson, in his first ever interview, asked reporters: *'What about that fucking Supermac now?'* - nearby directors spat out their drinks. Liverpool had emulated the side of '65 by winning the FA Cup. Two supporters jumped over the Wembley hoardings after the game and kissed Shankly's feet. A banner in the stands read: 'You Say God. We Say Shankly'. All around rang *'Ee-ay-addio, we've won the cup'*.

But Shankly was getting tired. It was difficult maintaining his aura. On the steps of St George's Hall the following day he stood in front of 100,000 fans, one hand in his pocket, one in the air. He declared: 'Since I came here to Liverpool, and to Anfield, I have drummed it into our players *time and again* that they are privileged to play for you. And if they didn't believe me, they believe me now.' His heart pounded as they serenaded him in return.

On a quiet afternoon later that summer he was sat in 30 Bellefield with Nessie watching the World Cup, in a distant realm of thought. A few kids knocked on his door and asked him if he fancied a kick-about. *'Later,'* he told them. He was tiring – not physically, his health was perfect – but mentally. He told Nessie how drained he was and that he was thinking of calling it a day. She reassured him like she'd always done. For Liverpool fans, the day that would be as poignant as Kennedy's assassination was on the horizon.

Local

COME BACK
(THE STORY OF THE REDS)

P eter kept his mates at Tate and Lyle updated about his boy. Clocking on of a Monday morning, they'd ask *'How's Terry doing?'* and he'd say *'Fine'*. He'd tell them how he got on for Bury at the weekend, how he'd moved down there and was doing well. A camaraderie was fostered at the factory in those years - a siege mentality between the workers. Redundancies were commonplace. By the time Peter's lad had moved to Newcastle United, the closeness between his mates at work was cemented by the uncertainty of their futures.

A month before Christmas 1974, the number of workers let go by Tate and Lyle reached 600 for the year. That same month Peter McDermott's son was bought by Liverpool. Dad and lad went to meet new manager Bob Paisley to sign the contract – two lifelong Reds in a state of euphoria. "My dad knew he couldn't change in front of his workmates," wrote Terry McDermott. "Inside he would have been elated, but outside he was his normal, humble hard-working self."

The number of unemployed workers city-wide seemed to rise each year whenever statistics were released. In 1974 there had been 2,280 people made redundant by Mersey Docks and Harbour Company. 1,902 were let go at Cammell Laird. People were forced into unemployment all over the city, from companies who, to work for, had been a rite of passage for generations. British Leyland let 3,700 workers go over the course of the year. Dunlop released 2,600 at the same time and a further 2,400 were gone from Plessley's.

Families continued to live in relative poverty inside a glass bowl city that was so frequently misreported upon. "Liverpool factory workers have threatened to strike in protest of Mr Shankly's retirement," the Guardian wrote - a fabrication. Jobs were hard to come by and - despite the age-old quote being taken out of context over the years – football was certainly not more important than life or death. The narrative of Liverpool as a strike-happy place was sustained by a farcical media force.

Inside Liverpool's city centre, unemployment reached 30%. The place emptied out. Population fell by 160,000 between 1965 and 1975, a phenomenal figure. Businesses stopped investing; workers moved elsewhere. A city whose infrastructure had inspired New York and Shanghai was reduced to being little more than a byword for deprivation in a single generation. The Albert Dock and Canning Dock were put up for sale, only to become overgrown wastelands – relics to the past.

While the media had indeed opted to sensationalise the event, it was true that Bill Shankly's retirement had winded the people of Liverpool. 'Mr Manchester' Tony Wilson took to the corner of London Road on 12th July to break the news to locals for Granada. He encountered responses ranging from bemused to frightening.

"*You're having me on aren't ya?*" A youngster questioned him... "*Who said?*" A group of young men reassured their friend: "*Nah, he's kidding you up.*" More young faces appeared, "*I don't believe it,*" smirking nervously, as if they were the brunt of a joke.
An old woman then told Wilson: "*You're going to have me crying.*"

A young supporter from Halewood, Stephen Monaghan, cycled home from school for lunch. When he heard the news, he couldn't stop crying. Back at school during assembly he started whistling Amazing Grace in tribute to Shankly; the rest of the school joined in.

Shanks was a divine figure who assured Liverpudlians that life was not all grey, that Anfield was a place of escape and possibility. Under his guidance, anything could be achieved. The uncertainty of casual labour and bleak living conditions was made bearable by the sense of 'more' Shankly gave people. Young and old were able to overlook their predicaments for a short period whenever Liverpool played.

That degree of attachment was all intended, at least on Shankly's behalf. "It's not a club," he wrote in his authorised biography, "it's an institution. I wanted to bring the crowd closer to the club. People have their ashes scattered here. One family came when it was frosty and the groundsman dug a hole in the goal at the

Kop end. Not only do they support Liverpool when they're alive, they do it when they're dead. That's how close people were brought to the club. There's no hypocrisy about it. This is why Liverpool are so great."

But change is the only constant in life. Nessie had only been taken on two days out by her husband in 14 years: once to the theatre and once to a garden fete in Southport. In public Shankly poetically explained that retiring was 'like being taken to the electric chair'. Behind closed doors he expressed a different sentiment to his wife.

Prior to his arrival in 1959, the Kop had maintained an awkward relationship with local players. Upon his retirement, Liverpool supporters had developed an appetite for their own – an affection and avidity for them. A new station called Radio City capitalised on that affection with a show called 'Scully', narrated by Alan Bleasdale, about a local schoolboy who daydreamed about playing for Liverpool, who fantasised about players and lived life with a mischievous gaiety. Every lad in the city saw a bit of himself in Scully, whether they were from Aigburth or Aintree.

The understanding of locality became official on 1st April 1974 when the government created the Merseyside borough. Boundaries were drawn up around Knowsley, St Helens, Sefton, Wirral and Liverpool. Chester and Ellesmere Port were out - Southport sneaked in (their local council requested to be accepted as part of Merseyside). Further alterations took place in Parliament over the coming months, with Skelmersdale being removed from the area.

But this was it, an official dividing line. The act detached Merseyside from its historic neighbours. On one side was Lancashire, established in 1182. Over the water on the other side was Cheshire, an even older county, having been recognised in the Domesday book in 980 AD.

Despite the rich history of both counties, Merseysiders had developed their own identity and welcomed the independence. They believed themselves to have little in common with the likes of Blackburn, Burnley and Chorley and were happy for the solitude. Simon Hughes comments that historic notions of class played in to the mental divide. 'There is a British mentality of "*you should know your place,*"' he says. 'If you look at the rural areas and the mill towns mentioned, they were class defined. In Liverpool things were different. We didn't accept our lot.' Now there was a county recognising local difference.

The drawn lines became a point of mickey taking, especially concerning Bootle, Huyton and Kirkby – hotbeds of Scouse life which now found themselves on the other side of the bridge. But that's all it was: a wind-up. No fan on the Kop ceased to believe that Phil Thompson was a Liverpool man because Southdene was now situated outside new lines. Kirkby had always been a Liverpool experiment. 'I hated people knocking the place,' he said. 'I was very proud of the fact I was from Kirkby and I think a lot of people are like that.'

In 1974 at the pinnacle of local awareness, with Scully and Merseyside and Liverpool FC on people's tongues, there was a spider's web of relationships between lads from various parts of the city slowly forming the base for potential glory at the club.

Jimmy Case explains firstly that the management team and scouts at Liverpool looked in local parks for players, and that 'the lads that came in were really hungry for the game.' There is a small irony given the seafaring history of the city, that Liverpool didn't look to recruit Dutch players like Ipswich or Argentines like Tottenham, but instead remained insular, mistrusting even Southerners, creating something of an inward phenomenon.

It is here that 'Local', in many senses, actually begins. Joe Fagan moved from Litherland to Anfield to be nearer the club when he joined in '58. He'd walk up Arkles Lane every morning before work under a quilt of relative anonymity. Later when his name was etched across Europe as a man of success, he continued to live in a three-bedroom house within walking distance of the stadium, even allowing fans to park their cars up his drive on matchdays.

Fagan founded the 'Boot Room', which was both an institution and a mentality. It was a cubby-hole escape from the bedlam of the changing room (territory of the players, typically), and would sit there with other staff members to mull over the day's events. He once allowed a local works team from Guinness to use the facilities at the stadium and as a thanks their manager Paul Orr (who'd go on to become Lord Mayor of Liverpool) offered the club crates of the black stuff in return, stored inside the Boot Room. The presence of alcohol and pots of tea, as well as calendars with ladies on gave a homely, albeit masculine, feel to the room.[28]

Roy Evans from Bootle joined the cast in 1975, becoming the youngest professional coach in the country.[29] He quickly began to view Fagan as the top

---

[28] Nude calendars are the reason why all photographs of the room are taken from the same angle.

[29] Chairman John Smith prophesied: 'One day he will be our manager.'

Local

man at the club, as the glue who held things together. Evans had been the golden boy of Merseyside football when he was 16, playing for England Boys alongside Trevor Brooking, Peter Shilton, Frank Lampard Snr, Brian Kidd and Joe Royle. His ability caused such a stir that the Mayor of Bootle, Joe Morley, put on a special reception at the Town Hall to celebrate him. Evans' place in the England squad had initially been given to him by another Liverpool man, Tom Saunders.

Saunders, from West Derby, was head of England Schoolboys and a former schoolmaster at Olive Mount in Wavertree. He came to Liverpool in 1968 and was tasked with developing the club's youth sides. A headteacher by trade, he was as comfortable mingling with directors at the club as he was with youngsters and had a natural ability to make everybody feel at ease.

One of his first recommendations to the board was to appoint South Liverpool manager John Bennison as a youth coach. Bennison, from Toxteth, combined his duties at Holly Park with an unofficial role as a scout, recommending talented youngsters to Liverpool for their A, B and C squads. One lad on Bennison's conveyor belt was a skinny midfielder called Phil Thompson. He also brought in Sammy Lee who in 1993 would eventually fulfil the arc and takeover Bennison's role coaching the reserves.[30]

Ronnie Moran from Crosby would sometimes watch Liverpool's youth sides train of a weeknight. He liked Thompson's leadership skills and his desire to win. 'I remember his first [session] with us when he arrived with a batch of other kids. Sometimes you can instantly spot players who are going to make it all the way to the top. You could see it in him straight away. His attitude was right, he was positive. He was the Liverpool prototype. When things went against him, his heart took over,' Moran said.[xi]

There was a mutuality there: the coal shed at the end of Thompson's garden in Kirkby was updated with Liverpool's squad each season, but the lad could never scrub out Moran's name, even after the full-back had retired. When Joe Fagan started coaching the first team, Moran took over the reserves and converted Thompson to a central defender. Thompson was only 15 and didn't drive, so Moran would drop him off after training by the Crown pub on the East Lancs where he'd get the bus home.

---

[30] And when they were both gone, far into the distant future, Thompson himself started coaching the reserves. He brought through a young striker called Robbie Fowler, and so it went on...

During his apprenticeship, he'd clean the boots of Callaghan, Smith and Lawler and scrub the bath with ajax afterwards. Whenever Shankly saw him he'd say: 'You must have told a lot of lies as a boy', but he was loving it.

There had been a brief spell when Thompson had stood on the Kop cheering on the team, before going to Melwood to train with them the next morning. By 1973/74 he'd grown in authority at the club and was challenging Tommy Smith for the central defence position. He took Smith's number 4 shirt for a game at Highbury at the start of the campaign and the defender was so angry that he picked up his bag and got a train home on his own. It was his club.

Thompson's influence began to extend off the pitch. When Bob Paisley decided that he wanted to sign Terry McDermott, he got his fellow Kirkby-ite Thompson to write him letters and call him to let him know. McDermott thought it was a wind up.

Within that web of characters there were genuine friendships. Tommy Smith was Roy Evans' best man at his wedding, 'only so I wouldn't look too bad on my wedding photos,' he joked. Lawler too said of Smith before he passed away: 'We're mates for life.' Ian Callaghan met his future wife (and future Miss Liverpool) Linda Foulder through Evans: they bumped into her whilst out shopping for records in town one afternoon and Evans introduced them.

That was the old guard. The younger Scousers in the team were also good mates who made for even better drinking partners. They were regulars in the Beehive and the Croc. They drank in the Liver in Crosby some afternoons too. Those who lived in West Derby went to the Jolly Miller after training. Trouble was rare because of their regularity, although Thompson once managed to get them all banned from the Hen and Chickens in Kirkby.

McDermott was with Thompson in the Toad Hall in Ainsdale when he met his future wife Carole. He bumped into her again in Ibiza when he was holidaying with Peter Reid. They started dating and he'd convince her to pick up his brother Robert, his dad and himself and take them to the Quarry Green for a Sunday session, the lucky girl.

The Quarry Green working man's club in Kirkby was a decent sized windowless venue with its old regulars who'd bet on the horses. Terry's brother Peter was a singer and master of ceremonies there, so Liverpool players were able to stay behind for 3am lock-ins. Rival players also went, with Peter Reid and Bryan Robson both frequenting the club with McDermott in later years. 'The locals loved it. They'd play snooker with them,' recalled McDermott. All the while Liverpool FC were winning league titles and continental trophies with ease.

The troupe of locals stayed close, arranging the dressing room accordingly. 'Over the other side of the room were the foreigners,' says Jimmy Case. 'The English, Welsh, Scots and Irish. Don't get me wrong, we got on brilliantly, but it wasn't surprising there was a special bond among the players born and bred in Liverpool. We knew more than anyone what it meant to pull on the red shirt and the commitment that [was] needed to keep our supporters happy.'

Case believes that because of his upbringing he could never pull out of a tackle, even knowing he would be hurt: 'Because I was representing them and they were my people. I cannot think of another club where that bond exists to such an extent as it does at Liverpool.'

With so many big characters in the team however, tensions often flared. Jimmy Case, who used to call Tommy Smith 'dad', was the only player brave enough to go toe-to-toe with Ronnie Moran in training, once clashing shins with him in a 50-50 tackle. Moran bounced up and squared up to Case: 'You're not playing fucking alehouse football now you know!' he shouted. Case just walked away.

Howard Gayle recalled in his biography how Bill Shankly had told him to use his pace, to knock the ball past defenders and run onto it. He states that Tommy Smith had recently lost his captaincy and resented the fact, but still had an 'awesome ferocious presence'. It disappointed Gayle then to find that each time he tried to knock the ball past Smith, he'd receive a kick and racist comments on the way past.

One true friend to Gayle was a fellow south-end youngster, Sammy Lee. 'He's still a good friend of mine today,' he reflects. 'Sammy and his family were great, they showed me a hospitality and a friendship which was not something I'd been used to. I was used to people telling me I couldn't come in the house, but the Lee family were brilliant. You won't hear many people saying a bad word about Sammy and that's because of his family and his upbringing.'

Lee was from the Bullring which overlooked town. He was always out with his local mates and would get up early to help them set up a stall at Greaty Market at 6am on matchdays. Despite only being 5 ft 2 he was constantly in motion. His old man was a butcher who'd prepare a steak for Gayle before matches. The pair would carpool together, with Lee picking Gayle up on Allerton Road. They'd go on holidays together, too. Of all the Scouse players at the club at the time, Gayle believed Lee to be the most fanatical Red. 'He loved the club then and still loves the club now.'

David Fairclough describes the bond the players felt to each other and to the fans: 'You can't put a value on it,' he says. 'It's not a burden, you realise you're a part of something special when you play for Liverpool as a local.'

Jimmy Case agrees. He says they're like a band of brothers. 'I think when you have that situation, you are a family. It's a strange thing to try and explain but once you've played with them, and even now when we all walk in together after matches and do functions in the legends' lounge, there will be certain players who come in who haven't been there for a while and it's like meeting your brother again. It's as if we all belong together. We'd never let each other down.'

And the fans were a part of that brotherhood too, all working for the same cause. Case says: 'In the old days when we were up against it, there were times when your passing was off or something like that, the crowd elsewhere might have groaned, but that was the time when the Kop started shouting your name. They knew you needed help and they gave it to you. The bond is like that, they gave us a lift when we needed it and we treated them with trips to Wembley.'

Before the very big trophies were to be won Liverpool signed another local, David Johnson from Garston. He'd played for Everton but was a Red and even had a beloved nephew called Ian 'St John' Johnson. Shankly had tried to sign him four times before Bobby Robson eventually allowed him to leave Ipswich. Johnson had stood at the Town Hall years earlier, listening to Shankly's Chairman Mao speech, despite being an Everton player at the time. Now he was with his boyhood club, with local teammates who were about to conquer Europe together.

And after they did so, when Terry McDermott was named as the Football Writers Play of the Year and invited to the Savoy in London, what did they choose to do? They went to the Quarry Green instead for a pint. It was an inward phenomenon...

Locăl

ROTTERDAM (OR ANYWHERE)

From their autobiographies:

Tommy Smith: 'The Olympic Stadium in Rome boasted a capacity of 60,000 and it was estimated that some 50,000 of the supporters that night were Liverpool fans. How on earth they managed to get tickets I don't know... It was like a home game.'

Terry McDermott: 'There wasn't much money about because the of era. The fans weren't bothered. They would have sold anything to get to Rome. On the trains, some of them were sleeping wherever they could to make the long journey more bearable, even on top of the baggage racks. When we saw the fans, we just knew we couldn't let them down. I'm, convinced that was the inspiration for us to win the European Cup.'

Ian Callaghan: 'Our fans must have travelled straight from Wembley to get to Rome. I remember going out onto the pitch before the game and it was just a sea of red, [it was] absolutely amazing to see the amount of fans that were in the stadium to cheer us on.'

David Johnson: 'We'd had such fantastic support home and away during the league programme, as well as at Wembley, and we knew that following a team home and away wasn't cheap, so when we went away we were wondering how many supporters would be in the stadium cheering us on. We asked a press guy, and we were told about five or six thousand, so you can imagine the players' amazement. You've never seen so many flags, banners and scarves. You could see it in [the players] faces that they weren't going to lose.'[31]

Phil Thompson: 'As soon as we entered the tunnel area a wall of noise swept over us. Then we caught our first glimpse of the terraces. Red and white chequered flags were everywhere. Liverpool's travelling army exploded when they saw the players. It was the kind of deafening roar that made the hairs stand up on the back of your neck. As a Scouser I was so proud. The German supporters were just taking photos of our massive travelling army.'

*

At the start of 1976 Jimmy McGovern sat down with his brother and helped him create a C.V. "It was this litany," he said, "Birds Eye, Bendix, Leyland, every one of them read 'reason for leaving': factory closed, factory closed, factory closed." Midway through that year 66,000 people were jobless. Citing significant under-reporting, Liverpool City Council determined that the actual number of locals unemployed was beyond 150,000.[32]

Around Vauxhall and Bootle some families were so necessitous that if tragedy struck and a relative died, a representative from the street would knock on doors asking for donations to help with funeral costs.

As history has shown, where there's a poor economy, there is civil unrest. Colin Jordan, a shameless neo-Nazi opportunist, sought to take advantage of the situation by joining forces with the National Front. Together they spent the summer inciting trouble in Britain's major cities. They marched through Leeds and Bradford to begin with before setting their eyes on Liverpool. Arriving at the Pier Head in June however, the right-wing group were met by Liverpool's Young Black Panthers and 400 other anti-fascists. Jordan and the NF were forced to flee for their lives, protected by police Land Rovers.

Brendan Wyatt (of Transalpino clothing) grew up in Kirkdale: 'I can't recall anyone having a job at the time. Nobody had careers and nobody went to university. The only outlet was football and we were fucking brilliant at it, Liverpool and Everton.'

---

[31] 'What's up Doc?' The Liverpool Way, 2006.

[32] A number equivalent to the combined populations of Anguilla, Gibraltar, San Marino and Monaco.

Local

Jimmy Case was firmly established in Liverpool's first team by this time. He reflects: 'We all knew there was hardship because it was all around us, especially us lads who lived locally. I looked at all my mates. They had problems just getting a job. The players were aware of it because we were amongst it, and we appreciated the efforts that fans went to.'

Bob Paisley had taken over from Bill Shankly the previous year but had failed to win any silverware in his first season, uncharacteristic for Liverpool. There was talk in the press that he could be replaced, with Dave Mackay at Derby County and the young coach Bobby Robson who'd done well at Ipswich Town fancied. It was little more than baited speculation. Shankly reiterated to Liverpool's board once again the dangers of hiring "outsiders".

Paisley quashed all speculation through his own endeavours in 1976, winning a league and UEFA Cup double. The pilgrimage to Wolves – who had to win the game to stay up (Liverpool had to win it to clinch the title) – remains, for many fans, the greatest domestic Scouse away day.

'We must have had between 40,000 and 50,000 people at that game' says Nicky Allt, 'and that was mostly just Scousers. It was a hardcore support because we didn't have a worldwide fanbase that we have now. Back then Liverpool would have a mass following to away games of virtually 95% locals.'

Among the crowd of fans seeking entry was Phil Thompson's brother Owen and his gang of mates. They were without tickets, but had been reassured by Phil that he'd sort them out. He asked Bob Paisley if he could sneak a small group of family members in through the changing rooms, convincing him that nobody would notice. When Paisley opened the doors for them, fifty people charged into the ground, cheering and thanking Liverpool's manager on their way past. Returning to the changing rooms, a flustered Paisley asked Thompson: 'Bloody hell man, how many relatives have you got?!'

Fans were dispersed by police to less populated sections of the ground that night, hence the now-famous images of youngsters sat around the perimeter of the pitch. 5,000 Liverpudlians were unable to gain entry and stayed outside, grilling anybody who left for updates, listening intently to the noise of crowd and banging loudly on the stands whenever Liverpool scored.

The Reds won the title thanks to a 3-1 victory. David Fairclough remembers the game; he recalls the devoted demographic in attendance too. 'When we clinched the title at Wolves I couldn't believe the passion of the young people who ran onto the pitch, it was unbelievable. That was raw and football now is far too sanitised. It's sad to see young lads who would follow Liverpool to the ends of the earth struggle for tickets.'

Terry McDermott recalled the determination fans had to enjoy themselves, despite the difficulties of their everyday life. 'There was a real buzz going back on the coach,' he wrote in his autobiography. 'There were fans on the motorway celebrating and when we later got stuck in a traffic jam on the M6, some of them got out of the cars and started playing an impromptu game of football.'

There was a feel that Paisley's young squad - with emerging talents like McDermott and Phil Neal, who had outgrown the Central Reserves League - were now ready to establish themselves as the best team in Europe. The composed manner in which they overcame Barcelona that season (an experienced side containing Johan Cruyff and Johan Neeskens) in the semi-finals of the UEFA Cup inspired belief in the city that Liverpool could soon win the elusive European Cup.

Barcelona had been a venue of political turmoil at the time. General Franco had died a few months earlier and when the Catalans tried to march for autonomy, they were beaten viciously by the Spanish Civil Guard. The city was placed under lockdown. As it had been for generations, the Nou Camp became an arena for banned Catalan discourse. Locals so desperately longed for Barça to win the UEFA Cup and reclaim their pride and status. When Liverpool beat them, Los Cules – Barça's fans – stood and saluted the Reds before angrily scorning their own team.

The following morning, *Diario AS* described Kevin Keegan as the "best player on the continent" and linked him with Real Madrid. Liverpool's squad was water-tight, though. Everything was just falling into place. Tommy Smith, set to retire at the end of the upcoming season, echoed the sentiments of the fans: 'I'll help Liverpool win the European Cup next season and retain the league title.' He was 32. Ian Callaghan was 34.[33]

*

Liverpool FC's rise in European competition contrasted the relationship between the city's port and the continent. In 1955 when the European Cup was born - as LFC languished in the Second Division - Mersey Docks had 16,085 employees. By 1977 that number was down to 6,402. Britain's accession into the common market five years earlier placed Liverpool on the wrong side of the

---

[33] Quote sourced from: 'Cup Kings, Liverpool 1977' by Mark Platt.

country. With trading streams decreasing each year, football provided Scousers with the only real opportunity to go abroad.

A small number of fans had travelled to Liverpool's first continental game in Iceland back in 1965. Alan Brown told Janet Goodwin: 'None of us had ever flown before. We expected them to look like Eskimos, we couldn't believe it when they looked the same as us.'

With the city remaining in relative poverty, the majority of Liverpool's support base couldn't afford to fly to matches. But that same year a small number made the trip to Milan to watch the team lose, most recognisably a fellow in corduroy pants wearing an armour and lance made out of red cardboard, known as the 'Red Knight'.

In 1966 Granada Television followed 120 fans from Speke airport to Budapest. The nation was attracted to happenings in Liverpool at the time, prompting Granada to introduce the programme by saying: "There they are, the finest supporters in the world." On the flight Ben Hendry, a recognisable musical fan, walked down the aisle with his guitar singing *'We're a happy bunch'*. The innocence allows the footage to remain endearing. After the game against Honved, the fans and players went out to a nightclub together. Ron Yeats was filmed twisting with a local. 'I was looking forward to the goulash,' a Kopite reflected to cameras, 'so we got a taxi across town, but it wasn't a patch on my mam's Scouse.'

Such games were attended by older fans who had decent enough incomes and could book flights from Jet Set Travel in Precinct Square. It wasn't until the mid-70s that a younger generation joined in. Stephen Monaghan delayed his exams so he could go to Bruges in 1976. 'It seems close now but it was a million miles away then for people here who'd never been abroad before,' he said. Monaghan has done over 100 European away trips since and his anecdotes provide a picture of what travel was like back in the '70s for young Scousers.

His stories can be viewed as a jigsaw piece, showing Liverpool's place in a European-map puzzle. Tales of travel, of youngsters in big fresh cities which required an adventure to reach, are amplified in their exhilaration by the meagreness of their domestic optimism. Liverpool was a limited place, but Europe had infinite possibility. Monaghan and his like-minded colleagues were given a real-world schooling: 'We used to sing *'You got your education from the Kop'* at other teams, but I for one certainly got my understanding of life through being a Liverpool fan. Of course, it was great winning trophies, but meeting people around the world is what life is about.'

Daniel Fieldsend

In Bruges, 1976, he recalls getting the boat from Dover to Ostend. 'All of the fans got off the boat, one hundred of us. It was 3am and the bars were all shut. We found one open but all the lights were red. I didn't drink at the time and I didn't realise where I was. All I got told by others was to keep a hand on my wallet. There were all these ladies walking around. One sat on my knee and I instantly put my hand in my pocket to protect my ticket. That was my introduction to being socially aware. The next morning, we were on our way to the match. It was a hot sunny day and I was dead thirsty so I knocked on this house with my mate and we asked for a glass of water. The woman invited us in and brought us coffee – back home we didn't have proper coffee, it was like oil Camp Coffee – and she brought us a croissant too, and we were like *"this must be what they put their bacon sarnies on."* It was all new.'

The youngsters returning home were part of a cultured few. The following year when Monaghan developed photographs of the Alps that he'd taken *en*-route to Zurich, his friends and family were in disbelief. At the start of 1977 there were 46,000 kids aged between 16 and 24 unemployed (52% of the city). None of them thought they'd ever see such a wonder.

Brendan Wyatt's father had been a seaman. He'd sit him on his lap and talk about Hong Kong, Buenos Aires and Singapore, before saying: *"You'll never get a chance to see these places."* Wyatt became determined to prove him wrong. 'A lot of the opportunity to see them came through Liverpool FC, because as a port city it has always been ingrained in us to travel.'

There were young kids across the city who, all at the same time, came to see the club as a passport. Nicky Allt shared Wyatt's sense of wanderlust. 'I recognise us looking outwards. I wanted to join the Merchant Navy but that was dying out when I was leaving school, so Liverpool FC became my way of seeing the world. It's not just that I wanted to go and watch football, I wanted to see cities like Munich, Paris and Rome. But I didn't want to just see these places on my own, I wanted to be with my mates and have adventures. Liverpool ruined my job prospects and relationships because they were that good in Europe. I became addicted, but it was worth it.'

Peter Carney, like Allt, grew up in Kirkby longing to travel. He believes that the rise of football gave the people a confidence that was in danger of waning. 'Being a port means there is a tradition of travelling. It isn't a hindrance, it's a pleasure. My dad's generation all went to sea. That's what I wanted to do as a kid. There were a million people who went to the New World from Liverpool. That's thirty people a day for 100 years. If you think of it as a dynamic, then that pool of

Locāl

consciousness about travel and moving, about bettering yourself through immigration, those ripples remain over time. Football in the '70s and '80s became key to it, but those skills were already there about making friends with strangers with no money in your pocket.

Young Scousers with little finance adopted a pirate mentality, determined to sail the seas and travel the world, ignoring the economic constraints imposed upon them. From Jennese Esche of Luxembourg and Stromsgodset Iderettsforening, through to Oulun Palloseura and Alania Vladikavkaz, they'd dedicate themselves toward following the club anywhere.

*

Liverpool's 1976/77 European Cup campaign began with Belfast side Crusaders. Because of the conflict in Northern Ireland at the time, coupled with an unexpected descent of heavy fog, Liverpool were delayed from flying and almost missed the game, an outcome that would have prompted UEFA to eliminate them from the competition. The squad began their preparations for the match in a hotel in Speke and waited for the fog to clear, which it did an hour later, giving them time to take the short trip over the Irish Sea to secure victory.

It was a place that, at the time, seemed so close yet in truth was so far away. 'My mates wanted me to go,' says Monaghan. 'I was up for it but my mam wouldn't have it because of the Troubles - Mrs Mono ruled the house. I was gutted not to go. My mates went and it was fine.'[34]

Sectarian violence in Liverpool had all but disappeared following the displacement of communities in the 1960s. Beforehand, Liverpool had been the city with a Nationalist Party of Ireland MP, but civic pride grew in place of division. Scholars refer to an incident in 1939 as proof of this, when a republican teenager named Brendan Behan was arrested in Everton for plotting to blow up ships on the docks. He angered Liverpool's Irish community so much that they tried to attack him, demanding that the intervening authorities "*string the bastard up*".

---

[34] News reports in the 1970s barely focused on the happenings in distant lands. For example, in 1977 Switzerland had its biggest post-war crime in Seewen. In France Albert Spaggiari went into hiding after committing 'the heist of the century'. And there was instability in Rome as the Radical Party (*Partito Radicale*) fought with the state, throwing Molotovs at police. Liverpool's 1977 campaign cut directly through the centre of an unsettled continent, yet nobody knew and no harm became of them.

Daniel Fieldsend

In 1976, the famous Liverpool Football Club were treated to a hero's welcome in Belfast. Crusaders fans stood and cheered for them before, during and after the game, with a reception being put on for the club at Seaview stadium. Local Reds sang 'Poor Scouser Tommy' with the brave Kopites who'd travelled over, walking them back to the docks from the club house after the game.

Liverpool's next fixture in Turkey was one of organisational mayhem. After the plane landed on the edge of a cliff, the team were followed around the streets of Trabzon by angry looking locals. They made their way to the hotel which Tommy Smith joked to the press was so small he was able to shit, shower and shave all at the same time. His comments were a nod to Phil Thompson, who'd quite literally shit himself at dinner, such was the standard of food. Only one fan made the journey, a lad called Twed who etched his name into folklore that night with his unfathomable logistic planning and devotion to the cause.

Against Saint Étienne in the quarter-finals Paisley's team truly arrived. Despite losing the previous year's final to FC Bayern, *Les Verts* were considered favourites to win the cup. They'd been French champions for three consecutive seasons. Their green shirts and style of play had captured the affection of neutrals watching on the continent. Kopites were anxious.

On 2nd March '77, early in the afternoon, just shy of 1,000 Reds set off from the centre of town to deep central France. European travel was new for many of them and passports were regarded as an after-thought. By the time they reached Portsmouth, the floors of the various would-be legendary Crown Coaches had been washed sticky by empty bottles of ale, while body odour clung heavily to the seats: it was far from the glamour of the continent they'd anticipated.

On the ferry to Le Havre that evening, a large group of fans tried to sleep under the drone of the boat's engines. Others hit the bar. Others threw-up, jelly legged. When dawn finally broke, all of the hunger and grogginess eroded and they rejoiced as France came into view in the distance. *'Liverpool, Liverpool, Liverpool!'* It was 6am.

In those years a younger generation of fans, abroad for the first time, had their heads turned towards the fashion worn by continentals. At a pitstop in Lyon young supporters acknowledged the fine attire of the locals: their cream shorts and yacht pumps. Many of the Scousers were still wearing flares and big collar shirts, but that was soon to change.

Saint-Étienne was a manufacturing town on the road between middle-class getaways, Lyon and Toulouse. It was a tough, working-class place where football

Local

success was the main source of pride for locals. *Les Verts,* as they were called, were the most successful team in French history when they played Liverpool, with 9 league titles to their name (they dominated the region. By contrast, neighbours Olympique Lyonnais were a small insignificant lower-league team with no trophies at all).

Like Liverpool, Saint-Étienne had a declining population and economic unrest. England was in the midst of an ongoing bread strike at the time. The irony was not wasted on Scousers when the French threw bread at them with rocks inside before the game kicked off. Just when things began to look hostile, the local fans began singing *'Ava Saint Étienne'* slowly and passionately. Stephen Monaghan stood and soaked it all in: 'It was haunting; it just reverberated around the ground.'

Liverpool lost the game, but Reds took comfort in their situation. *'We'll support you ever more'* they serenaded Paisley's men afterwards. One Kopite realised that *'Allez les verts'* – the words of the home crowd – meant 'Come on the greens', and found Liverpool's alternative. 'We took a song from them that night, from Europe, with *'Allez les rouge''*, says Monaghan. 'We sang it up and down the country and nobody else in England could do that. It still carries on today on our travels.' Fans were beginning to separate themselves from domestic rivals with a continental outlook.

It became customary in later years for travelling Reds to bring back fragrances or a gift for their partners from their travels. In 1977 when Crown Coaches stopped off in Rouen for food, Scousers filled up on freshly baked bread as a gift for loved ones. The coach home reeked of an overpowering combination of barm-cakes, ale, sweat and piss by the time it returned to England (all travel is glamorous in retrospect).

Phil Thompson had gotten injured in between the games and would be out for the season.[35] Tommy Smith had been approached by Wigan Athletic to be their player-manager, but instead stepped up from the reserves to fill the void. 'He's one of the best players in the country still,' Paisley said of him. In his pre-match press conference, Liverpool's manager was questioned about the invasion of St Étienne fans who'd been arriving in Liverpool for days. 6,000 *Saintés* were estimated to be in search of tickets. They filled every hotel, with a good number of

---

[35] He overstretched playing against Newcastle, then made things worse by going immediately to watch John Conteh fight at the Liverpool Stadium, followed by a night out with Terry McDermott at Flintlocks nightclub.

them sleeping on the streets. 'There's going to be some atmosphere out there,' Paisley told the Echo - little did he realise.

On the eve of the match, the French visitors took over the city. They drank all night inside the Crown Hotel and left ale soaked green scarves on the floor of Lime Street. Early in the morning, Liverpool fans awoke with a belly of excitement. David Fairclough rose from his boyhood bed at 7am. He looked out across the grassy verge at the back of his small council house in Cantril Farm like he'd always done, before heading down to have breakfast with his mum. Throughout its most successful era Liverpool FC had been an institution built on routine, yet on this day there were changes.

For the first time the players warmed up at Anfield rather than Melwood. They headed to the Adelphi rather than their usual Holiday Inn base. Fairclough and the team went for a walk around town, up to Leece Street and back for the first time, noting the number of green-clad invaders on the way. This was the first mass gathering of European away fans in the city's history.

Everything felt unprecedented. Almost as soon as the players got back to the hotel, they were told to gather their belongings and travel to Anfield, because thousands of supporters were already there and the roads would soon be gridlocked. It was 4:30pm.

Early darts from work took place all day. Kids bunked off from school at lunch. Everybody wanted to guarantee entry for the big occasion and ditched their commitments early, getting the bus, cycling or jogging to Anfield from all corners of the city. Liverpool were considered underdogs for the game, a tag they'd go on to wear well. The turnstiles couldn't click quick enough as fans bounced up and down in the queues. Charles Corver, the Dutch referee, felt the excitement and blew his whistle to start the game six minutes early. Anfield erupted.

Toilet paper decorated the mouth of the Kop, hiding the ball whenever it went into the mound. Flags were visible in every stand; a flare was set off in the opening minutes which sucked the light around it, pronouncing itself bright red against a pitch-black Kop. Silhouettes could be seen on top of the Kemlyn Road stand, rocking back and forth. 'There was so much passion emanating from all four sides it was almost frightening,' said Fairclough.

Whenever the ball went up the other third of the pitch, the players took turns to glance at the happenings in the stands. Only Ian Callaghan and Tommy Smith had encountered anything like this, against Inter Milan in '65. 'After Keegan scored, I tried to keep my balance but I felt the floor beneath me bounce up and down,' said Phil McGreal of West Derby.

The roar accompanying David Fairclough's run to goal that night was more primal than anything ever heard at the final furlong of Aintree, even for Red Rum who'd go on to win his third Grand National the following month. A young Gerard Houllier was in the Kemlyn Road that night with a few mates, watching, listening and falling in love with it all. He insists that after the match, the name 'Fairclough' became as famous in France as it was in Britain. Liverpool had needed to win by two clear goals and, thanks to the ginger substitute's late strike, the match ended 3-1.

A few months earlier the young striker would get the 12C bus to training. Now he was an overnight star. But he had no choice other than to remain grounded. After the game, he stepped out into the clear night with his father and drove home. He watched Sportsnight with both parents, had a cup of tea and went to bed, closing the curtains on the grassy verge behind.

Liverpool's victory that night acted as a pillar of support for the city. '*We shall not be moved*' trailed from the masses walking downhill towards Bootle and Vauxhall, as renditions of '*In my Liverpool home*' boomed out of the Albert pub. That week, central government published a white paper document titled 'Policy for Inner Cities', dangling the fact that: "Unemployment is particularly severe in Liverpool," more so than elsewhere. The report recognised how one in four people in the Vauxhall district were without work. They'd wake up to giro rationing and Job Centre queues, but that night they dreamt of Rome.

By April, and despite still having to play FC Zurich in the semi-finals, Liverpool fans were preparing for Italy. All month Kopites sang: '*We're the greatest team in Europe and we're going to Italy.*' Success was pre-empted. Fans began pawning washing machines, record collections, cars and jewellery to afford to travel to Rome. They took up odd jobs painting whitework, mowing lawns, delivering papers and collecting glasses. Some older fans cashed in on life insurance. Shankly once said that Liverpool fans would rather 'go to the match than have shoes on their feet' (referring to a brief conversation he had with a young Stephen Monaghan). Never had that statement been truer than in the days and weeks before Rome.

The semi-finals came and went. Tommy Smith called it an anti-climax and told the press that the Swiss players were little more than a 'bunch of amateurs.' Few fans travelled to the game and those who did were mostly impressed by the sight of the Swiss Alps from their carriage windows. A banner taken summed up the fixture: *'Zurich – Zur Out'* it read. The Reds won 6-1 overall. With absolute confirmation of the impending fixture to come, the city poised itself for its first European Cup final.

*

'We're on our way to Roma, on the 25th of May,
All the Kopites will be singing
Vatican bells will be ringing
Liverpool FC will be swinging
When we win the European Cup.'

In the month of the final Sophia Loren starred in a film set in Rome called 'A Special Day'. It wasn't about Liverpool, but it could have been. *En* route to the Eternal City were 30,000 Kopites carrying little more than a bag of sandwiches and a change of socks. With an apple as a toothbrush, they resembled a legion of young naïve Tom Sawyers'. Those with homemade banners had a makeshift blanket for the 5-day journey – including the purely coincidental standard which read: 'Tommy Smith Is Prettier Than Sophia Loren' (it is unknown whether she saw it).

The Scouse armada set off by coach, train and plane... they hitched in the back of transit vans and bunked from Dover through the continent. At Manchester airport, a spontaneous and loud conga stretched from the longue to check-in: *'If you're all scared of flying clap your hands'*, they chanted. Only a small percentage of locals had been abroad before; everything was alien to them. By far the most difficult form of travel – for the most determined of fans - was the football special, a rattily old train. Phil Thompson described it in his autobiography:

> *"Fans told me later that most of the trains had no running water and no working toilets. People were sleeping in the luggage racks. Some Scousers even managed to get from Lime street to Rome's Termini Station without buying a ticket. That takes some doing, but Scousers are the best in the world when it comes to improvisation."*

Poet Dave Kirby captured the excitement of that sunny month better than anybody in the pre-eminent book 'Here We Go Gathering Cups in May'. He described the feeling of pride fans felt as they stood waiting at the Park Brow in Kirkby, decked out in red, with cars going past beeping them, and the bus drivers letting all Rome-bound passengers ride for free. Stephen Monaghan felt that the fans travelling to Italy were backed by everybody in the city. 'My boss in work gave me £20 which was a lot of money then, I was only on about £5 a week. I ended up losing my wallet with my money in and the rest of the lads had a whip-round for me.'

Kirby writes how before leaving Liverpool, every ale house in town was full of people sharing an unexplainable excitement. 'Fellas were getting off buses and punching the air,' he wrote, hugging and shaking hands in celebration with complete strangers. At Lime Street the fans felt liberated for their endeavours, especially when they finally got on the train: *'We're going to Italy, tell me mah, me mah'*. There were lads with coal in the back pocket of their trousers, a tradition from the war which meant they'd have a safe return home, given to them by their nans, encapsulating the unity and enormity of the whole occasion. On the train, every carriage was standing room only. British Rail stated that the journey would be a dry one, but everybody was drinking and singing and passing each other biscuits and crisps.

It was like living a dream, until the initial six-hour buzz settled down and people deflated from their highs. The carriages began to appear dismal. At midnight, fans tried to kip on luggage racks, draped in flags to cure the cold, but could hardly catch any sleep. At Ostend the following morning things got worse. The train was scolded by the rising sun. There was no food or drink or running water, and the toilets were blocked by what Kirby describes poetically as 'a pan-full of King Edwards... The bogs were starting to smell like Widnes.' Desperate measures forced a gang of mates to wash themselves with a warm bottle of Kia Ora.

After days of hardship, reaching Rome felt like stepping into heaven for the rag-arse youngsters. Hysterically, they bathed in the city's fountains before slumping in the shade, hungry and confused about being abroad. Many headed for the Colosseum. Frank Carlyle, of Italian heritage, had spent his youth fantasising about Rome. 'When I told my mates that I wanted to see the Colosseum they thought it was a strip club,' he says. They'd never encountered a world beyond grey-skied Liverpool.

June Titherington in 'Reykjavik to Rome' told the writer that she had to explain to a contingent of outraged Scouse lads that the Colosseum hadn't actually been damaged by the Germans in the war. By mid-afternoon the ancient structure was bedecked in red banners. Most fans were unsure how to behave there, treading with caution, until one Scallywag sent a shout of *'Kopites are gobshites'* echoing around the ancient gladiatorial structure, setting the tone for the afternoon.

Daniel Fieldsend

Homemade tapestries were a feature of Rome as local met continental. 'We Came We Saw We Conquered' and 'Pope Paisley' lined the route to the Vatican, as statues of emperors looked back at bedsheets saying 'Super Reds' and 'Liverpool Are Magic'.

Scouse eyes, used to seeing the backs of dole queues and run-down housing estates, gazed lovingly up at the architecture of Bramante, Bernini and Michelangelo - their horizons broadened purely because of an emotional attachment to their city's football team.

Older fans were emotional. Fellers in their 50's had fought against the Italians in the war. The only Germans they'd ever met had been enemies. They'd supported a bog-standard Second Division team upon returning home and now found themselves back in a supposedly settled continent, cheering on Liverpool who were set to become the greatest team in the world. In just 30 years the world had changed more than at any point in history.

The entrance to the Olympic Stadium looked like a neoclassical oil painting. A white marble path led to its entrance, lined with stone pine trees and sculptures. The whole scene was contrasted by thousands of marching Kopites with red and white chequered flags – a symbol of the occasion and an eternal reference to 'Europe' for a soon-to-be cultured fanbase. Sunshine reflected up like a mirage creating an eternal portrait of a moment in time.

*

The final whistle blew. Liverpool had won 3-1. Back home tens of thousands of people poured out onto the streets. Most were crying. Tommy Smith and Ian Callaghan sought each other out, thoughtfully remembering 1965, Shankly and Inter Milan.

Everybody tried to savour the moment in their own unique way. Liverpool's squad contained a core group of traditionally working-class men who intermingled and empathised with the fans, appreciating the devotion they had for the team despite their financial situation. When the final whistle blew and Liverpool became champions of Europe, fans and players saw no alternative but to celebrate together. Word got out that the squad were staying at Holiday Inn Aurelia, so the Scousers went to join them.

Tommy Smith sat off in the corner of the after-party with his wife drinking Peroni. Bertie Vogts and Jupp Heynkes were there dissecting Anglo culture. Jimmy Case was sat with his brothers. Paul Moran was on Joey Jones' shoulders. They were surrounded by Reds shaking hands, laughing and getting photographs with the cup. Initially there were suits and dignitaries in the room but after a few hours they formed a minority, wedged among 300 flag-clad fans. 'It added to the whole atmosphere of the night,' said Case. 'After all, what we had just done was for them and we couldn't have done it without them.'

To the bemusement of future generations, a number of school-age Kopites bunked flights home without money or passports. On-board plane etiquette was an unknown concept, hence why a collection of fans patrolled the aisles and had a whip-round for the pilot to say thanks. Back home, an itinerary was in place for Liverpool's squad: they'd land at 5pm and slowly make their way to St George's Hall with the cup via Hunter Street. They had no idea of the numbers waiting for them; locals had been congregating at Wellington's Column since 12pm.

Jimmy Case likened the response that greeted the team to the old newsreel footage of the Beatles landing in America. There had been fans at Speke airport waiting in the morning and the line of supporters carried on all the way into town. 'As we reached the fire station on the corner of Bryant & May all of the engines were outside and they let their sirens off as we went past in tribute. That went right through me. I'm not that emotional, but that did me. It's then that you realise that this is what the people of the city had been waiting for and how much it meant,' he said.

Fans climbed to the top of traffic lights and perched in trees. They sat on top of roofs, just to catch a glimpse of the silver cup. Several times the bus came to a standstill on Queens Drive, causing desperate players to knock at the doors of (Evertonian) households when they needed the toilet. Everton Brow bottle-necked into Scotland Road and the crowds got denser. Public displays of affection for the Reds were commonplace, but this was on a different level. The Daily Post, Liverpool's more serious newspaper, called it "The Greatest Sporting Reception This Country Has Ever Seen", even better than the parade of '65.

On the littered streets that night were several copies of the Liverpool Echo. Michael Charters' coverage would prove to be historic:

"On an unforgettable night in Rome, a night to live forever as the highlight of a thousand sporting memories, this magnificent team completed the greatest season in the history of any English club by adding the European Cup to their League championship... Through all of this the magnificent Liverpool fans, a sea of red and white at one end of the ground with others bunched in patchwork quilt fashion throughout the stands, roared their team to victory. They were never quiet; they gave their all in a vital part of the triumph to dominate the off-field scenes as much as their team did on

the field... Did the Liverbirds take wing when Tommy Smith in his last game (his 600th) for the club before retiring tomorrow after a distinguished 16 years at Anfield, score a goal which, in effect, won the cup for Liverpool? If they didn't, they should have done... You can get no higher than this in football."

Paisley and the squad were greeted on the steps of St George's Hall by Lord Mayor Paul Orr, the same man who'd gifted crates of Guinness to Joe Fagan years earlier. Bill Shankly was there too. As the crowd bubbled in anticipation, Shanks sensed a moment to step forth like he'd done on so many occasions before, but Roy Evans held him back. It was Paisley's moment. Emlyn Hughes was on the right side of tipsy. He took the mic and chanted: "*Liverpool are magic, Everton are tragic, na na na na!*". He'd have his house windows smashed as a consequence by Evertonians but always maintained that it was worth it.

The symbiosis between Reds and 'The Reds' had proved to be so successful, mostly, because of the mundanity of working life. Patriotism that summer tethered uncertainly around a Silver Jubilee; in politics the Tories were making gains on Callaghan's Labour: although in opposition, Thatcher slithered towards power, dining with Jimmy Carter in the day whilst being tutored by Laurence Olivier at night. But the city had the club. Dave Kirby explained better than anybody what it meant to be a Scouser supporting Liverpool FC in May '77. He wrote:

"They represented who we were, our city, hopes, dreams and fantasies. They were how most of us got through a working week, our escape route from the dole queues, building sites, factories, mundane offices, domestic shit, wedge troubles or family grief. We needed them, and they needed us... We existed for each other, and together on one beautiful spring night we made history."[36]

---

[36] From 'Here we go gathering cups in May' book.

Local

SOUND AND VISION

The day Margaret Thatcher won her majority, ousting James Callaghan's Labour, something seismic occurred. All day television cameras followed her; from her home in Chelsea to the Conservative headquarters, to Buckingham Palace where she met the Queen, to Whitehall where she telephoned her cabinet. At every stop she was greeted by a crowd of cheering supporters. The whole occasion - the build-up and sense of celebrity - had an air of a cup final day to it.

Presenting herself as a woman of compassion, she quoted St Francis of Assisi to the awaiting press outside 10 Downing Street: "Where there is discord," she began, "may we bring harmony. Where there is error, may we bring truth. Where there is doubt, may we bring faith. And where there is despair, may we bring hope." By the end of her tenure she'd delivered each point in the opposing order. Despair triumphed over hope, truth was hidden, doubt reigned and discord smouldered in inner-city communities.

Of Liverpool's eight seats that day, five went to Labour. The Tories took Garston and Wavertree, and the Liberals took Edge Hill. Locals were gutted but were optimistic that she'd bend to the unions – Liverpool was a red, union city (blurring into purple in the suburbs). By the time Thatcherism concluded in 1990, blue would be totally removed from the political map of Liverpool and the city's cultural isolation would be secured: a legacy of her governance.

Howard Gayle was on LFC's books at the time. He recognised that Thatcher targeted his city from the first day of her tenure. 'She came for the docks here which have always had strong unions,' he said. Her speeches – all televised – exploited Labour's inability to negotiate the Winter of Discontent. In Liverpool during that period, gravediggers had gone on strike. The local council considered informing families that they had to make their own arrangements for burying dead relatives. 'Labour Isn't Working' stated Thatcher's posters, accompanied by an image of a long queue of people heading into an unemployment office. Her election was inevitable.

Maria Eagle – who'd go on to become MP for Garston and Halewood – was a schoolgirl at Formby High School at the time. Although she was residing up the road, Eagle saw the city's distant blaze. 'Liverpool was going through a genteel decline, but the Conservatives came in, shut down the little industry there was left and turned it into a catastrophic crash.' Why? Because Liverpool represented everything Thatcher disliked, according to Eagle: 'A lot of working-class people who looked out for each other, a lot of solidarity, and a great feeling of specialness that led to a pride she didn't understand and didn't believe in.' For the new Prime Minister there was no such thing as society.[xii]

Thatcherism began at a perilous time. Howard Gayle had been in and out of prison in the mid-70s. He was known on Liverpool's terraces as a dedicated supporter who nicked cars to drive to away games in. When he made his club debut at Maine Road (a stadium he'd once been chucked out of for fighting in), he realised the fortune of his situation: 'It kinda reached me at a really critical time in my life because the only other offerings for me would have been to live a life of crime. There were no jobs; no real potential for future development. Football saved me; it got me out of jail.'

It was in this period that Bill Bryson, the American darling of idyllic-England literature, passed through Liverpool. He wrote about the festival of litter which greeted him at the station: crisp packets and carrier bags piercing the 'bland and neglected landscape'. He stayed at the Adelphi Hotel, frequented the Philharmonic pub and wrote about how charming it was that Liverpudlians didn't want to bid for the next Olympics. His tone was condescending. He wrote: 'The factories may be gone, there may be no work [and] the city may be pathetically dependant on football for its sense of destiny…'

In that last line Bryson provided surface detail without bridging an understanding. Indeed, it was because of the fact that there was no work that the people of Liverpool depended on football. It got Gayle out of a life of petty crime; it got the hopeless through the week. Liverpool and Everton supporters were aware of their plight and the players were aware of their duty. Historian Frank Carlyle and footballer Jimmy Case explain:

Carlyle: 'Liverpool Football Club was the saviour of those depressive times. Politically we were left in the wilderness. It was the club that got us away from the deprivation and unemployment. Everything went away simply because the

Reds were such a fantastic team. The love of Liverpool for the ordinary people was a saviour. Not only were we delighted for ourselves, but it took us out of our depression... Make no mistake about it, they saved us.'

And Case: 'People were either on the dole or in a low paid job and they came to matches to escape that. I understood the fans. If you're winning games and trophies that's the best thing you can do for them.'

Economically, given their route into the game and the nature of football at the time, footballers were not detached from society, but, rather, were given a 'working-class-hero' status. Case again explains his position: 'I was going to be an electrician but in the end I was probably only on twice as much as a footballer. We as a group of players were aware of how hard things were for fans.'

In 1979 the city had both the best football team in Europe and the highest rate of juvenile crime for any major European city, too. Politicians viewed Liverpool as a mausoleum of an imperialist past. Bryson saw the bad – forgivably easy to do – but as a one-day-tourist was unable to get a sense of the formidable good: the enduring spirit of the people. Eager to paint a fairer image of the city, Liverpool Council began planning a sculpture to the words of Swiss thinker Carl Jung, crediting the city as the pool of life.

Although he only dreamt of his visit back in 1927, Jung saw Liverpool's 1970s future (perhaps) and how life – and the people of the city – punctured the darkness of the times. He dreamt:

> *"I found myself in a dark, sooty city. It was night, and winter, and dark, and raining. I was in Liverpool. With a number of Swiss, I walked through the dark streets. The various quarters of the city were arranged radically around a square... Everything was extremely unpleasant, black and opaque – just as I felt then. But I had a vision of unearthly beauty, and that was why I was able to live at all. Liverpool is the pool of life. 'Liver' is the seat of life, that makes to live."*

It read like a premonition of Thatcherism: the beauty of people daring to live vivid lives despite the darkness of the era. After his dream, Jung came across a stone which he felt had cosmic significance. He cherished it for the rest of his life. In 1976 Bootle-born poet Peter O'Halligan travelled to Basel to buy the stone. O'Halligan believed that a fruit warehouse on Mathew Street was the location of Jung's dream and thus placed a sculpture of the Swiss psychoanalyst there, carved out of the 'cosmic' stone.

Jung's story and the substance surrounding it displays the depth of culture within Liverpool at the time, overlooked by writers and politicians. Locals remained artistic, noteworthy and passionate. Although they were trodden underfoot, they continued to prosper in specific areas, like seeds without sunlight. Liverpool FC were two-time champions of Europe. They started the season looking for a third consecutive European triumph, just like the great Ajax and Bayern Munich sides before them.

Backed by the devotion of their supporters, Liverpool's players were inspired to achieve new success. And likewise, Liverpool's fans - taken to new lands by the club - had their horizons broadened beyond the slim grey potential of dole queues and apprentice schemes.

It was at this point, because of travel and their liberated lifestyles, that Scousers became fully aware of their place in the world and the unique nature of their character. They came to recognise their identity – left-wing (for the most part), hard, street-wise, funny – for what it was, and they dressed it in an arrangement of European trends, so that wherever they went they could be recognised beyond their accents.

*

That was May '79. In September Liverpool headed into the unknown, to the Soviet Union, during the blanketed Cold War. Few people had heard of Dinamo Tbilisi, their European Cup opponents. Fewer knew anything about Georgia. The Liverpool Echo blagged that they did however and produced a report for fans describing Tbilisi as: *"The Florida of Russia, where the sun shines and the people are friendly"*. They'd not expected many people to travel there. Stephen Monaghan and his mates went over and took heed of the report, opting to wear Lacoste t-shirts and sandals. 'When we landed, the doors opened and the air hit us. It was like -20 degrees. The Russian soldiers were stood there with their hats on with their guns and they were looking at us confused. We ran straight into the building it was so cold.'

Upon arriving, 100-plus Liverpool fans were greeted by a line of schoolchildren who handed them a flower each. 'They were portrayed back then as the enemy from behind the Iron Curtain, but that wasn't the case.' Monaghan had packed ham sarnies and a change of clothing for the trip, but nothing else.

Fans were advised not to leave their hotel rooms for anything, other than for the match, so naturally they ignored this advice and explored the city. 'It was so drab and dreary. The people were so miserable. They themselves couldn't believe what they were seeing with us. There we were, twenty young aliens wearing adidas. We stood out.'

Monaghan and his mates heard a noise on the road behind them. They turned in time to see the Liverpool team coach drive past – players saluting as they went by. 'Then,' Monaghan recalls, 'as we got closer, we saw thousands of people queuing up for this building. We assumed they were queuing to get in to the stadium. But they were going in and coming out with bread. It was a foodbank. It was so sad, there were *thousands* of them.'

Although nothing back home compared to the poverty witnessed in Georgia, locals in Liverpool were marching against closures at the Meccano plant and Dunlop's that week. Liverpool's 'claimant count' had risen to 11.7% that year (it would peak at 21.1% in 1986) whereas the Great British average had fallen to 5.4%. Life on Merseyside was twice as difficult as elsewhere in the first year of Thatcher's leadership.

The city had always been the antithesis of conformity though, typified in this era more than at any other time. The people were poor, but they'd decided that they weren't going to appear impoverished. In fact, as life became more wearisome, their appearances became more ostentatious. 'I think that's the Liverpool manifestation of it,' says Kevin Sampson, 'people were immaculate and very specific about what they were wearing, which is why I've always had beef with the term 'Casuals' which came later... there was nothing casual about it.' The fashion stood up against Thatcher's neoliberal paradigm shift which had caused massive unemployment.

1979 was not the origin of this resistance however. Brendan Wyatt – who now retails fashion – says this came earlier: 'Go back to the '50s and '60s when you see the black and white images of the Kop. They're all well dressed with suits and ties on despite only being young lads. What you've got to remember is that all their *arl* fellers were either working on the docks or going to sea. They were the original Cunard Yanks who were bringing back all the vinyl as well as suits which couldn't be gotten here. They influenced the Beatles too who'd gotten suits from their uncles who'd travelled to New York.'

Wyatt's chain 'Transalpino' is named after an era. It is a nod to the Scousers who used Transalpino student tickets to travel across Europe in the late 1970s/early 1980s, identifying new fashions and bringing them back to the city to be sold.[37] The change in style which separated Liverpool people from those around them began in 1976 with the dismissing of flares, sequin shirts and long hair – still worn everywhere else – spiralling from there.

Tony Evans in 'Two Tribes' cites the genesis of it all as a moment of chance early in the summer of 1976, when a parked lorry was liberated of its belongings outside the Salvation Army hostel on Scotland Road. It was a typical happening – there was nothing but vacant wasteland facing the hostel so drivers parked and slept there, with their luggage was often stolen – but the goods inside this particular lorry were to have a cultural impact. They were t-shirts: three striped adidas tees with round necks, sold on the black market by locals in Scotland Road.

Whatever came out of 'Scottie' usually caught on in the north end of Liverpool, then wider Merseyside, once residents were seen at the match wearing new styles. Youngsters at Anfield had vacated the now-lame Kop and set up camp in the boisterous Anfield Road end of the stadium, where they could bait visitors and display their vociferousness. A different lifestyle was to be had on the Anny Road away from the older, often out-of-town and typically unfashionable Kopites (who, according to Road Enders, were "gobshites"). Likewise, Kopites distanced themselves from this new mob, regarding them as bad apples. But the mob was organised, and the Road End became a catwalk of trends.

Kevin Sampson remembers when the Reds had won the league at Wolves in 1976 and how the subsequent pitch invasion was little more than 'a mass of flaring denim'. But then at the Charity Shield two months later something had happened: 'It was the long hot summer; there was an invasion of ladybirds it was that hot. I was sat on the grass bank at Wembley enjoying the sun and eating my butties. It was like a Spaghetti Western with heat haze, when all of a sudden ten or eleven lads came over Wembley Way with short side-parted hair and adidas t-shirts on with a round neck. It was clearly a uniform and they all identified with each other. That for me was the start of it and I kept an eye on those same faces at away games, always desperate to see what they were wearing.'

The group were Scottie Roaders and the hair was a tribute to, firstly Nick Nolte, then David Bowie whose *Low* album had amplified the look. It was called a

---

[37] Transalpino was a student travel shop on Myrtle Parade which did discount travel for under 26-year-olds. It was set up by the Janonne family in the 1950s to transfer migrant workers to Europe and back. It sold tickets at universities with discount. The tickets could be doctored, with the initial destination reading 'Calais' but the actual destination being Vienna, or Munich, or Zurich.

'wedge' – quiff swept across the side of the face, ear on show - and had been in Vogue magazine in 1974. Bryan Ferry played the Liverpool Empire during the course of 76/77 and his wedge secured the style as a staple part of the look.

Donna Summer's 'I Feel Love' was the ever-present song in nightclubs from May 1977 onwards as Reds headed into town after every win to celebrate with a catwalk of trends. 'It clicked; all of a sudden everyone was talking about fashion,' says Stephen Monaghan. 'In a pre-season tour in July I got a pair of tight jeans from Amsterdam and a small collar shirt from the Army Navy shop in town which completed the look. Then in Liverpool it became an epidemic and everybody bought the same stuff which gave us our own little army.' Lois jeans from Spain (with a bull on the back pocket) became the replacement of yesteryear's flares, and that was that: visible difference.

Going up and down the country Liverpool fans stood out. Sampson says: 'You'd go to places like Stoke and it'd be the hinterland of ridiculous fashion. They'd have legs like tents.' With wedged hair and straight legged jeans, the young legion of Reds (self-titled as 'Scals') would be wolf-whistled and called puffs by three-star clad locals. 'There was a hardcore of young Liverpool kids who just wanted to dress and look different to the rest,' Nicky Allt concludes.

They relished trips to London to show the Cockneys a *real* movement. 'In our pomp we loved going there. At Chelsea they were all bone-heads; flying jackets et cetera,' says Monaghan, 'and our identity was so recognisable. It was the first time since the Beatles haircuts that people could call out what a Scouser looked like without knowing.'

But while t-shirts and hair were important, footwear was crucial. Adidas Samba shoes came first. They were durable and kids could kick a ball in them, climb walls and run away from threats. Kevin Sampson saved up for a pair of them but by the time he got them, everybody on the terraces had moved on to Stan Smiths. 'In terms of it being a reaction to circumstance, what I loved about it was it was completely self-labelled and self-regulated,' he said. 'There would be a group of lads whose faces you knew, they were a bit older and always looked great, and whatever they were wearing we all wanted to wear the same. It was uncool to go over and ask them where they got their clothes from, so you had to scout the shops to find them.' Independent retailers like Mann's, Neal's Corner and Jonathan Silver capitalised on the scene.

Prior to 1977, training shoes were considered sportswear. They were for tennis and athletics, not casual streetwear. Jesse Owens raised the profile of adidas shoes in 1936, running in the Munich Olympics in a white pair. Gola and

Converse built on the idea of a 'training shoe' in the '50s and by the mid-1970s they were part of the Brooklyn hip-hop uniform.

Every few months at parties and on the terraces in Liverpool, there was a new style of footwear to contend with, from Pods and Kickers through to Trimm Trabs.[38] The city's zest for new styles coincided perfectly with consistent continental travel. The Zurich game in '76 and then the Saint Etienne match and final in Rome in '77 had given a buzz for lads who fancied more of the same. They wanted to look good, they wanted to travel around Europe, and they wanted to do it for free. Because they couldn't (and shouldn't) have afforded to, they incarnated the wisdom of John Lennon who believed: *'There are no problems, only solutions.'*

The answer was to fund their excursions by bringing back clothes from Europe to sell at home. In Austria and Switzerland shoes were displayed in pairs, the very idea of half-inching being totally alien to shop owners there, so they took them to sell. David Fairclough knew what was going on: 'Liverpool fans were the first ones to do it, the way the lads went to Germany and elsewhere. They weren't hooligans. Not to condone it, but it was more about the fun element back then.'

It created a black market built on clothing; brands like Lacoste, Fila, Sergio Tacchini – then Ellesse and Kappa in later years – showed people that you'd either been abroad or knew somebody who had. Competition became so intense that many Scals wouldn't dare be seen in a pair of trainers that could be bought in Liverpool.

For adidas wearers, there was something about the names on shoes from distant places that took them away from the bleak uncertainty of Thatcher's England. They went to games with München, Malmo, Stockholm, Zurich, Koln, Amsterdam and elsewhere on their feet. It was liberating for them, and it gave them an identity at a time when such notions were under threat.

'We were going on trains up and down the country and it was like a catwalk,' says Stephen Monaghan. The sight left domesticated supporters who'd not experienced the continent aghast. But being a Scal was not limited to appearance alone. There was a walk, an attitude, a politics and a taste in music that mixed the palette rouge. It was all about being part of a scene.

---

[38] There was: Inega, Rizzy, Kios, Farah, Ben Sherman, Fred Perry, Second Image, Yankee, Boston, TRX 10, Gansgear, Barney Shield House, Puma Cabana, Rossini, Foothold, ZX500, Palermo, Corsica… and so on…

Local

They'd go to Scarlet's Bar and show off their new gear. At Checkmates on Wood Street and Cagney's off London Road they'd hear the latest Bowie songs. 'One of my growing-up rituals was going there,' says Sampson. 'The lads who went there were at the heart of Liverpool's away support.'

Quadrophenia had been released in 1978 and it birthed a re-emergence of Mods. There were Punks at the time too, as youngsters sought an identity. The alternative was to be a Square or a Straight, which in effect symbolised absolutely nothing. Scals were match lads who were different.

At Eric's they watched the the Undertones and Elvis Costello play. Identity became multi-pronged. The Beatles had been dismissed as 'uncool' years before, because they were mainstream and commercial 'and that wasn't us' says Sampson. The Clash and the Jam stood in their place. Scals also – later on – became incredibly taken by the progressive and psychedelic music of Pink Floyd. Brendan Wyatt would go on to see the band fifteen times. 'I've worked all over Europe following their tours, they're the number one.' Kevin Sampson agrees: 'Pink Floyd were off-the-wall popular in Liverpool. They could play 365 nights in the city and sell out every night. Even Roger Waters acknowledges that symbiosis between them and the city.'

Waters grew up in Surrey as an Arsenal supporter, but he was, and remained, a dyed-through red activist – even creating an opera about the early days of the French Revolution. In 1971 he released the song *'Fearless'*, backed by a hypnotising sample of audio taken from the Kop. It bemused Floyd fans – why Liverpool? - so World Soccer magazine attempted to clarify: "It was his admiration for the people of Liverpool, for their notorious left-wing allegiance, that inspired him to blend the sound of them singing on the Spion Kop with his band's experimental music, regardless of his affiliation to Arsenal."[xiii]

World Soccer wrote that the fame of Liverpool's fans, rather than Everton's, and their devotion to socialism matched the anti-establishment theme of the song. For Scals it was all so perfect. *'Fearless* was of its time,' says Wyatt. 'Beatlemania was only a decade before and it was all still fresh and they were amazed by Liverpool.'

Scals were going against the grain, especially in comparison to fans elsewhere, and adopted their own subculture of music and identity. 'Is it a Gaelic thing?' Sampson ponders. 'Gerry Cinnamon is the current embodiment of it now. There must be a music scene in Newcastle or Birmingham but it can't be anywhere near as intense as it is in Liverpool. There isn't that same desire to embrace or go to lengths to support music like we do here.'

Daniel Fieldsend

As the Scally look became recognisable it was taken on elsewhere by fans at other clubs, so Scousers altered it to remain different. They'd continue to do so forevermore. Jamie Carragher throughout his career in the late-90s and 2000s – in an age of mass-media consumption – kept his ear to the ground and continued to dress in a working-class, typically Scouse, style. 'Liverpool is the fashion capital of Britain. We started it all in the 70's and 80's and if you're going to take direction from anyone there's no doubt it'd be us,' he said.

Continental travel had birthed it. 'What people were doing was saying *"We look like this because we support the best team in the world and go to the best places in the world,"*' says Kev Sampson. 'It was a form of civic pride in who you were and who you represented.' ... Stephen Monaghan agrees and concludes: 'Between 1977 and 1979 we were like no other crowd in England. We just stood out.'

*

There remained a constant irony that Liverpool was better understood by foreign sources than it is by its own land. French correspondents *So Foot* wrote the following of 1981 when Liverpool FC drew FC Bayern:

'April 22: In Munich, the semi-finals. Liverpool is dying in the midst of a national crisis. The Northern Soul is no longer dancing because Maggie has recently come to power, sounding the end of the welfare state recess. The mythical Kop is a legend, already respected around the world, but legends do not give you work. However, the club has a golden team and is hated by fans of all of, "those cursed" clubs, as Philippe Broussard will write in 'Génération'. The Scousers like to differentiate themselves from their counterparts in the "South", having been attributed with inventing the casual look...'

The French paper knew of Liverpool's desire to disassociate itself from *le Sud*. As trains trudged from Edge Hill into Lime Street in 1981 graffiti on the side of a shed read *'Fuck Off All Cockneys'*. It'd remain there for ten years. It conveyed a vivid sense of how the city 'felt besieged and persecuted by the metropolitan power located in the south,' Alexei Sayle told the Guardian.

So Foot referred to fashion as an important factor in Liverpool's trip to Munich in '81. Indeed, when the draw was announced Scals rejoiced: they'd be able to return with a collection of new adidas Grand Prix trainers, as worn recently by Ilie 'Nasty' Năstase.

The most promising aspect of the tie however was its potential to reclaim civic pride. The European Cup had gone to Nottingham Forest in the previous two seasons, led by Brian Clough who snubbed invites into the Boot Room and claimed he could walk on the River Trent (a demeanour contrasting that of Bob Paisley).

The Bayern match was to be all the more significant in the south end of the city, in Liverpool 8. Granby's own Howard Gayle was about to become a beacon of pride for a disenfranchised community. If things were bad in Liverpool with unemployment and uncertainty, they were far worse inside Granby.

Joblessness had risen by 120% in the Liverpool city region between 1974 and 1981, yet in Granby it had risen by 350% in that same period, an astronomical figure. A report by Lord Gifford and Wally Brown found that 70% of young black men were without work.

'Toxteth' (so-called by people who often mean Granby) had often felt like its own place – a microcosm - inside a city which too had considered its own difference. What was about to happen there in the summer of 1981 was part of a specific sequence of events.

The day before the Bayern home tie – a 0-0 stalemate which Gayle watched from the Kop – 31-year-old Edge Hill MP David Alton, known as *'the baby of the house'* - told Commons: "There are forces at work in the city of Liverpool which are praying on the disadvantages of our young people." He called unemployment "a ticking timebomb within inner-city communities" and wrote a letter to Margaret Thatcher warning her of the fact. Alton paraphrased the letter and published it in the Times on the 18th April in an attempt to drive home his message. He knew how precarious things were becoming. Thatcher didn't respond.

She was busy. No sooner had Alton made his case, riots broke out in Brixton. They ignited after locals and police tried to escort Michael Bailey, a black youngster who had been stabbed, to hospital. A lack of trust in both parties was rife. The real antecedents of the riots were social and economic problems: high unemployment, low prospects, poor housing and overtly aggressive police tactics. Indeed, in the six days prior to the riots, just shy of 1,000 people had been stopped and searched in a manipulation of the 'Sus law' from the 1800s.

In Liverpool 8 the same social conditions applied. Police openly challenged Afro-Caribbean youngsters to *'do a Brixton'* as they exploited the Sus law, looking down from the Metropolitan Cathedral with binoculars at potential targets. The police would then go 'gardening', according to locals, planting evidence on potential car thieves.

Gayle lived in Liverpool 8 by this point having moved out of Norris Green. He was well aware of the happenings within his community and was worried. Yet while tensions bubbled in his hometown, his professional career was taking off.

Outside the ground in Munich, Bayern supporters were given leaflets with directions to Paris on - the location of the final. Joe Fagan intercepted a number and passed them around Liverpool's dressing room. The players were fired up in an instant. Early on in the game Kenny Dalglish got injured. Waiting to go on with 75,000 fans watching him – with many in the Bayern end shouting racist abuse - Gayle was doubly motivated.

He'd been a key figure in Roy Evans' reserve team: an environment where mickey-taking and jibes were part of a toughening-up process. He'd been a key figure, too, for Timepiece, playing on muddy pitches as a talented teenager just a few years earlier. In Munich his pace and directness put Bayern on the backfoot and helped Liverpool secure passage to the final.

'Sometimes I think Howard doesn't realise how big that game was,' says Nicky Allt who was at the Olympic Stadium and heard the monkey noises from Bayern's crowd. 'He ran the legs off the German defenders.' Scousers needed the club to be successful in 1981 more than any year before.

Tony Lane had been a prophet of the most Orwellian standards, having written in 1977:

"Unemployment will continue to rise and housing conditions in the public sector will worsen. Young people, already disaffected, will turn increasingly to theft and destruction of public property. Old religious antipathies will revive, the black community will be scapegoated. Riots will occasionally break-out, shops looted and buildings fired. Repression will escalate to the point where the working class, failed by its own organisations, will be cowed into submission."

Incredibly, Lane also recognised the potential of football in pacifying tensions:

"... If none of this development takes place then we must all pray, along with the Chief Constable— albeit for different reasons, that the Reds at Anfield continue to win all the leagues and all the cups lest energies be directed elsewhere."

In Munich, Gayle tried. He sprinted and dribbled and gave everything, but it wasn't enough. In Paris, in the final, the rest of Liverpool's squad tried. But

Local

tensions had grown to a point back home whereby even football couldn't distract people any more. Liverpool's relationship with its nation – how it was viewed and how it felt - was about to change forever.

Daniel Fieldsend

CHILDREN OF THE GHETTO

L'été 1981.

One is mostly grey, with a seagull dominated Pier Head, and the other handsomely azure with a white yachted Vieux Port, but there is a link between Liverpool and Marseille. Most dock cities have a history of self-reliance. Barcelona, Bastia, Palermo, Genoa, Bilbao, Naples, Rotterdam, Hamburg and (half of) Glasgow have all prioritised civic pride over national duty at some point. Because of their history of maritime exploits, of commerce and trade, they regarded themselves as miniature republics, more storied, cultured and significant than nearby inland folk.

Liverpool and Marseille share that. The French national anthem, *La Marseillaise*, is named after the people of Marseille who marched toward Paris in 1795, spurred on by patriotism. Yet generations later whenever the anthem is played in public, the modern Marseillais boo it. They're disliked by the French, with their accents, fashions and attitude defining them as different. Locals tell the story of when Napoleon turned the cannons at Fort Saint-Jean, which look out to sea, inland at the riotous locals below (shades of Churchill's gunboats in 1911). And when France came to trade more with mainland Europe in the 20th century, it was Le Havre that benefitted from its geography, plunging Marseille – on the wrong side of the country – into miserable economic decline.

In the summer of 1981, cars were overturned and buildings scorched in the working-class *banlieues* of Marseille as young people of various ethnic backgrounds organised themselves to stand up against poor urban policy programmes and heavy-handed policing. The uprising would reach Lyon and Paris, too, as street battles with police (called *rodéos*) took place. Molotovs were thrown and CS gas was returned. In Liverpool that summer, it'd be a much similar picture.

France's *'National'* police had a reputation for hard-handedness. They're still regarded as violent, especially against ethnic groups (interventions from Human Rights Watch and Amnesty International are common), and have an ability to escalate issues from minor tensions into full-blown riots. *Le Monde* referred in 2018 to a deep-rooted worry that revolution could spring up at any time, as if the climate of 1789 still defined France. This, they felt, is the reason why *'National'* police act truculently.

Scousers would encounter organised militia-styled policing twice within a couple of weeks in 1981, at the hands of both Parisian and then Merseyside forces. Everything to come would be in response to the frustrating climate of the time. Howard Gayle highlighted the absence of a Martin Luther King-style figure in Britain from 1960 onwards, which in many senses allowed racism to go on unchallenged. But the language and sentiment of the Atlantan preacher travelled to a city that had always found inspiration from the west. His line: "A riot is the language of the unheard," would prove to be of outstanding significance in Liverpool.

*

The summer began with the 'People's March for Jobs' on the 2nd of May. 280 locals set off by foot from the steps of the Anglican Cathedral to London. Bishop David Sheppard had transformed the role of the church, from pacifists to an institution with a voice of dissidence. Alongside union leaders, he gave a speech on the cathedral's steps about the inhumanity of modern-day suffering, before saying a prayer and wishing them well on their journey.

Along the route thousands of people joined in at various points. They slept in town halls and community centres where support for the cause was absolute. When they finally reached London on the 31st of May, media attention was huge. 150,000 people joined a rally at the capital on the day of their arrival. Sadly, however, the government failed to recognise any of their grievances and every single Tory MP refused to meet representatives of the march.

A documentary captured the emotions of the marchers throughout that month. Everybody interviewed, from Liverpool to Luton, felt subjugated by the government of the time and believed that they could overthrow it, maintaining that ordinary people had the power to triumph against the interests of Thatcherism. They were wrong.

Those interests were defined as Monetarist. She believed that the government should control the circulation of money; raise taxes and interest rates; cut public expenditure and pursue overseas trade. She followed a doctrine set out by American economist Milton Friedman who said to anybody who listened that inflation was like alcoholism and 'had to be suffered'. A sad irony is that thousands of working-class (and lower) people were driven to drink by Friedman and Thatcher's Monetarist policies.

On her team of advisors was the economic professor Patrick Minford. He worked at the University of Liverpool and reported to Downing Street on what was happening within the 'Liverpool Model'. They looked at the responses to cuts in Liverpool as if it were an experiment - at least that's how it felt to the locals who graffitied their feelings on the walls of Minford's department for all to see. Liverpool University's campus was wedged between Toxteth and town. Its two chancellors in 1981 sustained an agenda of buying up many of Toxteth's old Georgian houses and renting them out to students, which over time contributed toward unwilling gentrification. It felt for people in Granby that they'd been neglected from every possible syllabus.

By midway through the year, national unemployment was close to three million. People were so malnourished that rickets returned – a Victorian disease. Political scientist Brian Jacobs labelled the negative effects of global economic change on cities in America as 'The Liverpool Syndrome'. It was sad. Many Scousers had relocated to London for work as labourers. When the Reds reached the European Cup final in Paris, they joked '*at least we're half-way there*'.

Those who'd missed out on Rome in 1977 were determined to ensure that they'd be there for the next big occasion. The following season when Liverpool reached the final at Wembley – hardly exotic, Liverpool always went there – it only served to fuel a determination to have a bigger, more eye-catching foreign adventure. The opportunity arose in Paris.

One route of many to the French capital was to get the ferry to Dieppe, followed by a train to Saint Lazare station. Waiting at Dieppe however were French riot police who set water cannons on the Liverpool supporters as soon as their ferry docked. When the police tried to herd them up, Reds replied with laughter and sheep noises.

National police would continue to be a constant presence in Paris, attempting to resolve unsettled bar tabs and minor disputes with forceful arrests. The Liverpool Echo had been correct in their predictions a week earlier, writing: "They're not all Inspector Clouseaus, especially the riot police who still bear the scars of their clash with Leeds fans when they rioted in the Parc des Princes stadium."

Local

France's Lille-supporting Prime Minister Pierre Mauroy was worried about hooliganism (his view would be justified a week later as England fans fought with Swiss supporters at the border) and wanted to tackle any encounters early. He was surprised to find, though, that Real Madrid and Liverpool supporters had no interest in fighting. Rather, they preferred to swap hats and have photographs taken together on the *rues* of the Moulin Rouge: travelling Scals in particular were much more interested in the fashions displayed inside Paris's boutique shops - Lacoste in particular – than they were in fighting.

For them, just being in Paris was victory enough given domestic circumstances. 'Here we go' was amended to: '*On the dole, in Paree, drinking wine*', a chant used as a two-fingered salute to the government. Daring to follow Liverpool abroad was seen, for many fans, as a form of political resistance.

Youngsters had turned up at Lime Street station with a number of photos for a 48-hour passport, and nothing else. Everything was done on the cheap. Kevin Sampson remembers: 'We had nowhere to stay or sleep in Paris so we just stayed out. At that age it was brilliant. The clubs there were like nothing we'd ever seen before. You'd go into these cellars and they'd have on Senegalese or Nigerian highlife music and we all got into it. There was a scene going on and everyone was having a drink so we embraced it. I'd say you went with maybe £25 on these trips and you'd do it on that.'

Tickets – a lack of which – would prove to be the only antagonist of small scenes of trouble. John Smith and Peter Robinson appealed to UEFA to move the final to an alternative stadium once they saw who the other semi-finalists were (Milan, Bayern and Real Madrid). LFC were fortunate that Real Madrid triumphed and that, because of the culture of Spanish football, they didn't take their full allocation of fans.

Liverpool on the other hand, who were allocated 15,000 seats, had almost 40,000 supporters making the trip (thousands of Evertonians went with their Kopite mates, wearing Harrington jackets to blend in). Nicky Allt and his group spent the day scheming a way into the stadium. They arrived there several hours early and found the riot police ready and waiting. 'They tried to chase us, but we turned and chased them into the ground. They thought we were looking for violence, we weren't! Once we were inside the stadium we dispersed into every corner and hid until kick off.' Some hid in the toilets, others crouched in the stands. Allt recalls peering up and seeing 'lads running out of the ground with the riot police's helmets and shields,' in a bizarre Benny Hill-style twist of events.

Outside the ground as kick-off approached the riot police lost control. Many fans didn't have their tickets checked, others were knocked to the ground. The police were instructed to let off tear gas, an act that confused fans more than anything. George Sephton had been flown over to work as a 'familiar voice' in case trouble flared up, but the police were so disorganised that they pointed a gun at him as he tried to enter the stadium.

After the game, once Liverpool had won the cup (beating Real Madrid 1-0), the police took a step back, either believing that there'd be no violence because Liverpool were victorious, or just stopped caring altogether.

*

The following year Aston Villa won the cup and afterwards panicked when it was stolen from the Fox Inn pub near Tamworth. Colin Gibson took it in, having got his inspiration from Phil Thompson, who'd taken it into the Falcon a year earlier, where it remained safe and sound. Thompson likes to tell his story:

'We won it of a Wednesday night. On Thursday we did a trip around the city and I'm seeing everybody: all my family, all my mates. The lads were saying to me *'get back The Falcon, get back the Falcon'*. We came down Queens Drive and turned up Utting Avenue and I could see Anfield in the horizon. This is where everybody from the north of Liverpool came – it was packed. I got off the bus at Anfield and carried the European Cup in a red velvet bag which I put in the back of my Ford Capri. Then I drove through the crowds and headed straight to the Falcon. When I got there, the pub was absolutely packed. I walked in with the cup under my arm and everybody stopped to look. There were no mobile phones back then so people formed a queue for the payphone to tell their families to get down there. One of the lads came up to me and asked "Tommo, can I go first?" *First for what*, I asked? Well we filled it up with ale; he put about 8 pints in it and lifted it up to fill his boots. Next thing, it was an absolute tsunami – he was soaked.

'After that we all just got photographs with it but there were that many people that I'd have been there til 5am, so I said to them "come back tomorrow at 11am and we'll get more photos." Anyway, I got home and my phone rang the next morning at 9am: it was Peter Robinson. He says 'Hello Phil, I've got the world's press here and they want to know where the European Cup is, do you happen to know where it is?' I looked across the room at my sideboard – still drunk - and saw five European Cups moving. I said: 'Yes Peter, it's safe with me,' but he wanted me to bring it down straight away. I thought *shit* because I'd promised to take it back to the Falcon for 11am. The photographers were so angry when I eventually turned up late at Anfield with the cup. I didn't say a word to them. And can I add, by the way, that Stevie didn't take it to Huyton after he won it!'

*

Back in 1974 everybody was too preoccupied with the retirement of Bill Shankly to notice a report that had been published, titled 'Crime in the City', investigating the causes of an upsurge in crime in Liverpool. The Lord Mayor, civic and church leaders and voluntary sector workers were all part of the investigative body. They found that poor housing, a lack of youth clubs, poor educative facilities, poor relations with the police and a 'lack of worthwhile employment opportunities' were the main factors in the rise of city-wide crime.

The police in particular were viewed with distrust in many of Liverpool's communities. Kenneth Oxford had arrived from Northumbria after the report was published and quickly became head of the force. It was under his tenure in 1979 that Panorama investigated the death of a local man, Jimmy Kelly. Initially arrested for being drunk and disorderly, witnesses told investigators that they saw Kelly being assaulted by police officers. He died in custody and Harold Wilson – local MP – was outraged, calling for a public enquiry. The police airbrushed events and discredited witnesses, stating that Kelly 'somersaulted' onto his own head. Margaret Simey protested against what she believed to be a cover up. She requested another inquiry, but the Thatcher-led government declined.

One of the first acts following Thatcher's appointment as Prime Minister had been to issue a 45% pay rise to the police. They'd go on to act with impunity, according to the political left, who'd dub them "Thatcher's boot boys" because of their role in the miners' strike, the printers' dispute at Wapping, the poll tax riots and all other disputes to come. By the time of the Brixton riots a clear 'us and them' divide was considered to be in place.

Local police had a particular prejudice against Afro-Caribbean communities, as displayed by a 1978 feature by BBC's Listener magazine, in which Martin Young spent time interviewing Liverpool's police force. Kenneth Oxford would deny, then later paraphrase, the following body of text which emerged from the feature in an attempt to show what police were 'up against':

"...the problem of half-castes in Liverpool: many are the products of liaisons between black seamen and white prostitutes in Liverpool 8, the red-light district. Naturally, they do not grow up with any kind of recognisable home life. Worse still, after they have done the round of homes and institutions, they gradually realise they are nothing. The Negroes will not accept them

as blacks, and whites just assume they are coloureds. As a result, the half-caste community of Merseyside – or, more particularly, Liverpool – is well outside recognised society."

Crime in Liverpool 8 was on par with other parts of the city, yet the area was viewed as being more lawless and ungovernable. Local press in the 1950s had referred to it as 'the jungle' – an animalistic place.[39] And why? It referred to a problem within Liverpool's own self-perception. When working-class white youngsters committed crime, it was so often construed as cheeky and adopted into folklore (*"at stealing from lorries I was adept"*). Yet when Liverpool's black and mixed-race community stole, they were afforded a harsher glare, depicted as having flaws in their make-up and ghettoised.

Crime had always been a consequence of a poor economy. If Liverpool 8 had more crime, it was because it had more unemployment. The complaints and difficulties of black unemployed people were brushed aside, many felt, because whites were struggling too.

The history of all of Toxteth, including Park Road, was a magnified history of Liverpool itself. In the early 1800s it was known as 'Sailortown' and by the 1840s was home to grand Georgian and Victorian houses where wealthy shipowners lived. Following the Second World War, they relocated after the docks took a battering, slowly continuing to abandon Toxteth over the coming 40 years. Liverpool's dockside significance decreased and the grand houses, rather than being demolished, became flats for multiple families, from which Liverpool 8 took on a more working-class identity.

By the 1950s it mimicked a bazaar, according to Howard Gayle, with its Muslim butchers and Arab, Pakistani and Bangladeshi mini-markets selling exotic fruits, unusual vegetables and red-hot spices. With Simon Hughes, Gayle describes the setting beautifully:

"West Indian mommas sat on the doorsteps of old dilapidated buildings where their husbands, wearing Panama hats, smoked hash, watching the days go by. There were faces of every creed and colour, while accents and dialects were also diverse...The atmosphere spawned an exciting nightlife.

---

[39] Evening Express on Jan 11th 1955 "Lord Derby visits the Jungle and feels proud". The report went on to say "Lord Derby went into Liverpool's 'Jungle' last night to listen to Negro spirituals and Calypsos and to give his blessing to the work of Stanley House in Upper Parliament St."

From the seaward end of Parliament Street towards Smithdown Road on the way to Wavertree, it always seemed like there was somewhere to go. By the docks, the alehouses overflowed and ladies of the night hung around offering sexual favours to testosterone-filled partygoers and seamen who were passing through Liverpool en route to Asia or West Africa."

The area brimmed with culture: Calypso, jazz, R&B and acapella music came out of its many clubs, such as the Palm Cove, the Nigerian, Somali Club, Pink Flamingo, Silver Sands, Dutch Eddies, the 101, the 68, the Polish, the Sierra Leone Club and Lynda's. Blacks and whites from across the world frequented this collection of drinking parlours, creating a multicultural experience.

Arthur Dooley's sculpture of 'Black Christ' unveiled in 1969 defined the area. Princes Park Methodist Church had set aside £200 to have the lettering on their façade redone. They contacted Dooley, who provided them with a £3,000 sculpture and charged them £200. When it was unveiled, it caused a sensation. The Daily Mirror described it as: "Christ the resurrection looking a bit like a West Indian and a bit like a Red Indian." In fact, the sculpture was modelled on the face of a local man - whose heritage was a mix of European, Caribbean, Native American and Chinese – and represented multiple continents. Dooley saw it as the face of Liverpool's history.

Granby had always represented 'port Liverpool'. In 1934 the novelist JB Priestley visited a school there and said it had given him "a glimpse of the world of the future", declaring that: "The various races may have largely intermarried," and that: "All the faces of mankind were there, wonderfully mixed," stating how much he loved it.

Granby Triangle was the centre of it all, with its wide streets of terraces intended for Victorian artisans. People shopped there, but also went for a social. It'd take an hour to get to the end of the street as they stopped to mingle. Few people from the community were employed inside town and no black people ever found work on the docks, so they seldom ventured into the city centre. Issues were sorted out internally, according to Gayle, and Granby became self-reliant. It was necessitous to be so. Of the 22,000 staff working for Liverpool Council in 1981, 169 were black or mixed race. There was obvious unspoken segregation.

Few residents had attended football matches because of the normalised racial language used, until Gayle played for Liverpool and inspired a process of self-reflection. Howard's brothers would fight with any fan who used racist terminology toward any player. In a match against Coventry City, a Liverpool fan abused Garry Thompson and was quickly dealt with by Gayle's brothers; "I don't mean you and Howie!" he'd said, attempting to excuse himself. 'Gayle did a lot to erode racism,' says Brendan Wyatt. 'It's at a point now that we'd never dream of singing what Millwall were singing against Everton.'[40]

But it wasn't just in shops that the community lacked representation. In July 1981 there wasn't one single BME solicitor, councillor or barrister working in Liverpool. There was nowhere to turn, especially when the police upped the rate of stop-and-searches. Under constant surveillance, policemen called locals 'monkeys' and 'mongrels' and gardened evidence on them.

It was harassment, bullying and intimidation. They'd wait outside Stanley House of a weeknight and Sus random youngsters who walked by. Rather than being protected, locals were made to feel like occupied citizens. Official resistance was futile: 1,631 complaints had been made against officers in recent years but only two disciplines were sanctioned. No jobs were lost.

A new generation of youngsters were unwilling to overlook their treatment like their fathers and grandfathers had done. They were born and bred in Britain, were aware of their rights and were not prepared to bow down to the prevailing mentality of colonialism. In a Panorama programme from 1985 a young poet approached the camera and summed up why the uprising in Granby occurred:

> *"You wonder why we up-rise,*
> *Economically destabilised,*
> *People dehumanised,*
> *Youth criminalised,*
> *Mentally vandalised,*
> *Housing ghettoised,*
> *Politically unrecognised,*
> *And you wonder why we up-rise?"*

The poet was Leroy Cooper and it was his arrest on the 3rd July 1981 that caused the pot to boil over.

*

It was a Friday night. He was in a youth club on Selborne Street when word spread that a lad had been arrested over an alleged theft of a bike. 'They're at it again,' people were saying. By the time he got to the scene, a crowd had gathered around the incident. Three police vans arrived. Twenty coppers were there. Locals

---

[40] *'I'd rather be a Paki than a Scouse'* 27th January 2019, Millwall vs Everton, FA Cup.

surrounded the van and pulled the lad free. In the raucous that followed, Leroy Cooper was arrested. He'd return to Liverpool 8 six weeks later, by which time it resembled a war-zone, and although he never threw a punch or charged at police, his name would be synonymous with the events to come.

As the police vans departed under a shower of bricks, fifty people gathered and decided to show further resistance. In came the Panda cars – which typically meant dispersal – but the crowd stayed and bricked them. Then came the Black Marias and they too were bricked. Those involved reckoned that if they fled, they'd be done for, so it was time to stand up.

Howard Gayle believes that the truest narrative of why the riots occurred was because of years and years of mistreatment by the police. With no jobs, no purpose and no optimism, they rioted because they felt they had nothing to lose.

By the following afternoon hundreds of locals were out and ready to fight. They set up base on Crown Street not far from the Royal William pub, where barricades where made and the streetlights smashed. The myth that Britain was socially cohesive was being broken by the minute. Locals gathered up bricks and scaffolding poles. An anonymous call was made about a stolen vehicle, luring the police back to Granby.

By midnight they'd set up barricades and were in control of the battle. White youths from as far as Kirkdale and Bootle, as well as from Vauxhall and Wavertree, joined the action because they suffered their own forms of social oppression and wanted to prop up the momentum. The Sun newspaper ran with the headline "White Riot" on Sunday morning in response.

As a football fan, Kevin Sampson was well aware of the severity of police brutality in general. 'They knew they could hit you and they'd continually remind you of that fact. There was a level of experience that everybody had with them, and then there was a level of experience on top of that which the mixed-race community had with them. It was seen as us-and-them.' Sampson made the journey over from Birkenhead to Liverpool 8, guided by the glow of flames in front of the cathedral.

As the police came around the top of Upper Parliament Street, they entered a warzone. Many of them were untrained for such circumstances and had no knowledge of how to control the situation. A local 18-year-old rioter commented: "What was scary was the police standing there with these batons, and then banging the batons on their shields, as if it was a war. I suppose that's the way they had to try and intimidate people to get them off the streets. But I think it did the opposite. I think people started saying: 'Look, that's a gang, and we're a gang.'"[xiv]

Back-and-forth battles took place on Saturday night with missiles thrown in what was, according to one local resident, an almost carnival-like atmosphere. On Sunday though things were different. Scorched paper drifted through the air like confetti. Traffic lights went from green to red and back again without any cars in sight. Shops were looted and buildings burnt.

But it had been organised. When the geriatric building caught fire, the rioters stopped what they were doing to evacuate the building. They went no further than Upper Parliament street, even after police lines had withdrawn, as if blocked by an invisible barrier – a historic draw-bridge defining where they felt they belonged.

Kenneth Oxford composed himself. He puffed out his chest and told reporters "They won't beat me". Hundreds of policemen were shipped in from neighbouring counties to be caught on camera beating their riot shields and making antagonising shouts ('*come on you black bastards*'). Brendan Wyatt saw it on television: 'It wasn't acceptable. People understood more about what was going on after that.'

Howard Gayle was desperate to be involved in it all. He wanted to stand up for his community, but his brothers persuaded him otherwise, reminding him that Liverpool 8 needed its role models more than ever. If the press photographed him fighting with police, it would be the end of his Liverpool career.

Although they were more organised than the night before, the police force was still unable to stop the rioters. Against the ropes with nowhere to turn, Oxford decided to give the order. Despite not having government permission, he told his coppers to fire CS gas for the first time on British mainland. It was the second time in a matter of weeks that some Scousers had encountered it. It worked, and the rioters dispersed, but its use was contentious.

By law CS gas was only permitted to flush out armed gunmen, and was not to be used on an outdoors crowd. Oxford stated afterwards that any civilians hit were the 'unintended victims of a ricocheting canister'. Phil Robins, a footballer for Southport FC, had been hit unintentionally in the chest and back from a few yards, according to Oxford's stance.

Things settled down enough for the media to stop caring, but throughout the rest of July there were pockets of behaviour that went unreported. The mere sight of police cars patrolling Granby was enough to rile locals.

Liverpool Labour called for the resignation of Kenneth Oxford but it wasn't to come (he'd eventually be knighted). Conservative Home Secretary William Whitelaw saw it all as politics. He dismissed Labour's view of events: "They will almost certainly seek to blame high unemployment for the unrest, and to demand major changes in the government's economic policies." Government supporters by contrast, he said, would "suggest a response concentrated on law and order issues." What Whitelaw did raise in Commons, however, was the belief of Liverpool's two churches: that the root cause of the unrest was a feeling of alienation among the young.

A few days later Thatcher made an ill-advised trip to Liverpool. A hostile crowd pelted her black Jaguar with tomatoes and eggs as she arrived. Derek Worlock and a representative of David Sheppard met with her. She asked: 'Why is there such hatred for the police?', both men stressed the need for compassion, only for her to reply: 'I find that word so condescending'.

A collection of city officials were rounded up that evening at Town Hall by Thatcher and given a dressing down, lambasted for having failed to deal with the disturbances. A local black community leader, Delroy Burris, interrupted her midflow. 'Yo Maggie,' he said, dropping the titles, 'we're not here about jobs and unemployment, we're here about the race issue.' But Thatcher stared him down and said she was not concerned about the colour of people's skin, condemning the rioters as criminals.

She then met with Kenneth Oxford and, rather than questioning his use of CS gas as many hoped, listened as he requested a water cannon for future use. He would go on to argue elsewhere that the 'true Liverpudlian' possessed a 'turbulent character' that was 'proportionately tougher [and] more violent', a factor he linked to historic migration.

Thatcher's press secretary Bernard Ingham, in the aftermath of it all, had been chauffeured around the wide burnt-out streets of Liverpool 8. 'I formed the strong opinion then,' he said, 'that the government was being put to the test by people who wished to bring it down.' Ingham would retain a dislike for the people of Liverpool which he later displayed in a cards-down 1996 letter about the Hillsborough disaster.

From the distant comfort of Whitehall, Sir Geoffrey Howe began formulating an idea. He decided that Liverpool's 'concentration of hopelessness' was 'self-inflicted' with its 'record of industrial strife'. In papers released in 2011 by the 30-year-rule it became public knowledge that Howe, as well as the Industry Secretary Sir Keith Joseph and Thatcher's Downing Street advisers, Sir John Hoskyns and

Sir Robin Ibbs, believed Liverpool to be 'the hardest nut to crack'. Howe wrote that money invested in the city was equivalent to "*pumping water uphill*" and pondered: "Should we not go rather for 'managed decline'?"

That term – managed decline – would embed itself in the minds of locals 30 years later as a token of Tory compassionless. It referred to the end of a lifecycle of something, and although it was used in business, it also denoted the quality of life somebody with a terminal illness received. Members of the government were considering the financial oblivion of Liverpool, with little apparent concern for the implications that would have on the people left behind.

Howe was writing to Thatcher about the city, and about Michael Heseltine too, the Environment Secretary, who called for funds to be made available to regenerate Liverpool instead. Howe warned Thatcher against "over-committing scarce resources to Liverpool" and told her to keep an eye on Heseltine.

He was a danger to her. Heseltine was the darling of Conservative supporters - particularly ladies - with his long golden hair and his passionate speeches, and he strived for 'Common Sense' politics, loathing the 'Nasty Party' tag to come. At a cabinet meeting a few weeks earlier he'd asked for £100m a year to be invested in Liverpool. He was given £15m instead and was warned against making the sum public knowledge.

Heseltine then appointed himself as the 'Minister for Merseyside' and set up the Merseyside Task Force, making weekly visits to the city to rebuild its crumbling infrastructure. He wanted to create media-grabbing events to change public perceptions. 'The Mersey got to me,' he wrote. 'It was enormously significant in the history of our country and I felt a debt to that river.'

Residents in Liverpool 8 saw cosmetic improvements to begin with and small developments to housing, followed by a garden festival which they couldn't get jobs working on nor afford to attend, but no great overall change. Any suggestion that Heseltine improved their neighbourhood would be contentious. The biggest change in Liverpool 8 would eventually be the appointment of an ethnic minority police officer who patrolled the beat and got to know members of the community.

Throughout it all, Liverpool FC had a raw, talented youngster with emotional conflictions. Did the club assist Gayle? 'No, I was never supported by them with issues surrounding race,' he says. The extent of the club's involvement in 1981 was for Bob Paisley to tell him to move out of Toxteth and live in another district. 'They expected players to be able to sort themselves out and look after themselves, which I think was part of the management trying to figure out who you were as a player. I tried to say *"here I am, I'm a young black kid off the streets of Liverpool 8 and all I want to be is a footballer"* but you had to be yourself through your own ability and fit in to the model that they had.'

By the 10th July there had been riots in Manchester, Birmingham, London, Leicester, Preston, Blackburn, Sheffield, Newcastle, Luton, Wolverhampton, Stockport and Chester. Yet, as Frank Carlyle says: 'Every time riots are mentioned it's Liverpool.'

Robbie Fowler, in the first few pages of his autobiography, bemoaned the image his area retained for years afterwards, despite there having never been any newsworthy issues before:

"Toxteth is somehow portrayed as being the bogey-man of the inner cities because of the riots but the God's honest truth is, it really wasn't that bad for me. I remember it being a safe enough place to grow up. It wasn't a no-go area by any means, there was serious unemployment... nobody had any money, and there was some unrest because of the poverty. But if you live there, you're used to it."

A narrative of the rioters as instigators – rather than as fighting back – painted it as Beirut, Sarajevo or Detroit: a place to be avoid at all cost. Later that summer, following the marriage of Charles and Diana and the Disneyfication of public mood, any ounce of sympathy or desire to find solutions melted into a longing to point blame.

The riots would be the first episode in a series of events in which Thatcher presented herself as a rival to Liverpool. John Aldridge was playing for Newport County at the time – they'd paid South Liverpool £3,500 for him the season before – and formulated an opinion from a distance: 'She tried to close our city down after the riots,' he said. 'Only for Michael Heseltine, we would've been in a much poorer way. She always hated Liverpool because we stand up for ourselves. We won't be bullied and we won't let people tell us what to do.'

Liverpool's capacity to defend itself was because of the spirit of its inhabitants. Howard Gayle says: 'I think Liverpool is unique in itself because the people here are survivors – that's one thing that's in our DNA. We can go anywhere and do whatever it takes to survive, and that will never change.'

Kevin Sampson sees that manifestation elsewhere: 'There is a thread through the attitude of the city which ties in with our fan culture. There is an anti-authority spontaneity to Liverpool people which I see as something worth celebrating; it's something I'm proud to have even a tenuous association with.'

Daniel Fieldsend

A number of days after the riots, Howard Gayle was back with his community marching against Kenneth Oxford. Brendan Wyatt clocked him there wearing an adidas hoodie on a sunny day. 'A few weeks earlier he'd been playing against Bayern Munich, but there he was making a point.'

And while Gayle now recognises great changes in Granby, there are certain things which have not improved: 'I think in modern-day Liverpool our young people still aspire for jobs and education and want access to a level playing field. Take construction, this is a city full of cranes and sites but youngsters from Granby don't have any trade or apprenticeships or worthwhile jobs where they can provide themselves as positive role models for the future.'

Despite the image L8 retained nationally, it continued to be a vibrantly cultured place after 1981 with a coalescence of residents from across the world aspiring for betterment. That sense of belief helped to rebuild the area over time. When years of dust finally settled, Granby won a Turner Art prize for its communal restoration of Beaconsfield St, Cairns St, Jermyn St and Ducie St, and was featured in the New York Times as a Harlem-come-good type of place. Fitting, deserving, yet not mentioned enough.

Locãl

POWER TO THE PEOPLE

On the drizzly morning of December 8th 1980, John Lennon did a photoshoot for Rolling Stone magazine. Later that afternoon he was confronted by a fan who requested his autograph. He obliged and then went with Yoko to a studio to record the forgettable 'Walking on Thin Ice' single. At around 10pm they returned home to the Dakota building, physically exhausted. As they stepped out onto 72nd Street, the same fan from earlier, Mark Chapman, pulled out a gun – said *'Lennon'* - and shot him four times in the chest. John Lennon stumbled a few steps towards his building and then collapsed and died. He was 40-years-old.

From midnight as word spread, crowds gathered outside the Dakota building and sang renditions of 'Imagine' and 'Give Peace a Chance' until morning light appeared. In Liverpool, locals went to work oblivious to what had happened.

That was until a special edition of the Liverpool Echo came out. Late in the afternoon, people walking past a vender in Williamson Square stopped in shock and stared at the headline: 'JOHN LENNON SHOT DEAD'.

'They've killed Lennon' people whispered... *'the Americans'*... On the car park where the Cavern Club once stood an unofficial congregation appeared. Everybody felt like they knew him, even if he had "left and never came back".

A week later Sam Leach, the former Beatles promoter, organised a service at St George's plateau which, according to him, just shy of 25,000 turned up to. Messages of sympathy poured in from across the world from stars and fans alike. Liverpool had an awakening – the Beatles were still important, valuable and precious.

Many in the city had been complacent towards the band in the 1970s, believing that they'd always be there – somewhere in the distance. Scousers had learnt to survive without them, but a reaffirmation occurred following Lennon's death of how much he, and they, actually meant.

His music had matured in line with the character of Liverpool, from his pop origins into becoming an artist with a catalogue of protest songs tailored toward social justice, which seemed to mirror his hometowns response to its own economic decline. His recordings – 'Power to the People', 'Working-class Hero', 'Give Peace a Chance' and 'Imagine' - deviated away from the mainstream, which suited Scousers, and his public persona became an extreme projection of far-left ideology in the years before his assassination. It was an attitude more radically Scouse than his 1960s self had been.

But if his loss in 1980 had left Liverpool sad, another unexpected death the following year left the city distraught. When Bill Shankly died on the 29th September 1981, Merseyside was in pain. While Lennon came from the city and left for elsewhere, Shankly ran opposite. He found the city and loved it. It became his home and Liverpudlians became his people. 'Although I'm a Scot, I'd be proud to be called a Scouser,' he said, and: 'I wanted to bring happiness to the people of Liverpool.'

His affection ran so deep that when he flirted with the idea of returning to football in 1976, he wouldn't consider jobs beyond driving distance of West Derby, opting instead to advise coaches at Tranmere and Wrexham. It hurt him that football carried on without him – the game had been his life – and felt he should have been offered a place on Liverpool's board. But Manchester United had offered Matt Busby such a role and in the summer of '74 they'd been relegated, which factored into Liverpool's reluctance.

Despite those wasted years between 74-81, Shankly's belief in a people faced with doubtful grey lives propped up a legacy that would endure for generations. He'd been in Paris watching the Reds back in July and mingled with fans, telling them his predictions for the game – there'd been no sign of an ill man. His heart attack (the first one he survived and joked with nurses about, the second one the following day killed him) was most unexpected and further winded a city smouldering from a summer of riots.

On the day of Shankly's funeral, masses of people from all over Liverpool came to pay their respects. They lined Canning Street to welcome the procession to the Anglican Cathedral and politely clapped as Bob Paisley, Ian St John and Tom Finney walked in alongside Nessie and the Shankly family.

Locāl

Jock Stein, Ronnie Moran and Joe Fagan were already inside sat at the front. A congregation of Liverpool fans were also allowed to attend, having received tickets from the club earlier in the week. 'They are the ordinary people who Shankly cherished like family,' said Eddie Hemmings, covering the event for BBC Merseyside.

Shankly had his ashes scattered at Anfield so he could join the legions of Kopites who 'support the club in death, too'. Training was cancelled at both Melwood and Bellefield (Everton had given him a home in his later years). Matt Busby was so distraught according to reports that he locked himself away for two days. At the Labour Party conference that week, members stood in a minute's silence for a man who'd always championed socialism. Deputy Mayor James Ross summed it all up: 'With his death, something irreplaceable has gone out of the life of the city.'

For all the enjoyment that would be had over the course the next ten years – because Liverpool didn't wallow for a decade – the 1980s would host a collection of tragedies unlike any other period in civic history.

*

There was talk of Shankly's legacy midway through the 1981/82 season. Many on the Kop asserted how recent performances had been below the standards of Shanks' teams – that players weren't fighting for the shirt. A spark had disappeared from Anfield and the fear-factor looked to be gone.

Despite not yet being 30, injuries had caught up with Phil Thompson and he struggled to keep his place in the team. Souness had taken his captaincy and he was soon phased out of the club. Over the coming 18 months Terry McDermott, Jimmy Case, David Johnson and David Fairclough would be moved on too, leaving Sammy Lee as the sole Scouse representative of the mid-1980s.

By December, Liverpool had lost five games and were 12th in the league (they had only lost eleven games at home throughout the entire 1970s). There was anger in the air. Following a defeat to Manchester City, the Kop forgot itself and threw a bottle at City's goalkeeper Joe Corrigan.[41] The respect of keepers had always been paramount in Kopite traditions - something was clearly wrong.

Joe Fagan, assistant manager, gathered the team unexpectedly without Paisley being present and gave them a dressing down, placing the blame for Liverpool's

---

[41] It couldn't have hurt too much; Corrigan was goalkeeper coach at Melwood from 1994 to 2004.

sliding performances at their feet. He told them in no uncertain terms that the onus was on them to change the club's fortunes and that the supporters deserved better.

For a core group of fans however, although the loss in form hurt them, winning was not what defined their existence. They were Liverpool supporters and, in general, football supporters, and, as such, were part of a group with a distinct culture and set of norms and practices. They didn't maintain their lifestyle in the vain hope that their team would win matches.

Their identity was defined by happenings on the terraces more than happenings on the pitch. It was a counter-culture, refined by a group of like-minded lads. And, like all lifestyles, had a readership-in-wait.

It was in early 1981 that 'The End' magazine came into being. Peter Hooton was a youth worker from Cantril Farm with musical inclinations. He'd been in Paris following the Clash that summer and sat in on interviews with the band. When he got home, he noticed a punk fanzine with an anti-royal theme (Charles and Diana were portrayed on the front vampires) for sale in Probe Record shop on Button Street. There were hundreds of similar grassroots fanzines at the time, made by and sold to 'student types'.

Hooton's mate Phil Jones was producing a mod one called 'Time for Action'. Jones was a bricklayer who had Steve Rotheram as his collaborator on the paper. Hooton asked if they could combine football and music together to create a niche fanzine. Jones bought into the idea and agreed, starting the beginning of 'The End'.

It had an attitude. It was working-class; it was satirical and took the piss out of everybody. Fans from Leeds, London, Sheffield, Derby and elsewhere wrote in about their hooligan movements and fashions, only for 'The End' to reply with comical disdain. It targeted committed fans: away supporters and connoisseurs of fan culture. Everyday characters were written about: bullshitters, gamblers and no-mate types. The humour interlaced in each feature intended to show that life wasn't all bleak, and that football fans were not all nihilistic bone-heads like the press made them out to be. In itself – as a chronicle of a movement – 'The End' showed how imaginative people were in Liverpool during a politically, socially and artistically creative era.

It was embraced because of its relevance, with copies bought at the Anny Road and Bullens Road ends. Readers longed to see what had been deemed as 'in' fashion or 'out'. Celebrities could be put out of fashion, with 'famous' Scousers like Stan Boardman and Jimmy Tarbuck being permanently deemed 'out' for professionalising the local character.

What the fanzine did most successfully was collate acceptable norms: what not to wear, how not to act, what not to say - a particularly Scouse thing to do. Fashions that were 'in' were put in the 'out' column to confuse leeches. Paul Du Noyer said it had the cockiness of people who knew their scene, as opposed to pundits who were merely second guessing. He was right. At a time when groups of fans across the country had no idea that they shared similarities, 'The End' broke down barriers. Acting as a chamber of sorts, fan groups could have their reputations enhanced or discredited, particularly the latter if they were seen wearing dodgy attire.

The magazine recruited famous admirers for its dry mockery, including the popular Heswall-born DJ, John Peel. 'From a football point of view, it was right. From a musical point of view, it was right, and from a political point of view it was right. It represented everything – not that I am – but everything I wanted to be,' said Peel in a documentary.

The End's biggest achievement was to paint Liverpool in a more high-spirited and enjoyable light than other media sources did, as a city which still enjoyed life. By contrast, people in Britain (who had no cause to, yet had been deterred from visiting) were led to believe that Liverpool was an area plunged in a pessimistic and continuously bleak despondency.

TV shows constantly referenced the doldrums, such as Brookside (circa 1982), Boys from the Blackstuff (circa 1982) and Bread (circa 1986), while theatre shows sustained the theme with Our Day Out (circa 1977) and Blood Brothers (circa 1983), turning poverty into an entertainment genre. Playwrights would argue that they merely held a mirror up to society, but the reflection wasn't pretty.

Willy Russell had good intentions, by all accounts, and made Margaret Thatcher the most important character in his plays without ever mentioning her. Mickey and Edward in 'Blood Brothers' had different lives, aspirations, encounters, experiences and outcomes because of the effects of Thatcherism. Russell's work showed how a lack of opportunity would eventually turn talent into anger (think Howard Gayle in the years before LFC signed him).

Whatever the intentions of the creators – either raising awareness or lining their pockets - their shows would have a damaging long-term effect, as Peter Moore explains: 'People still have a view of what a Scouser is, which is not complimentary, and those shows fed into that stereotype. They're funny, but still paint us as in a certain light.'

The most famous show nationally was 'Boys from the Blackstuff'. Written by Alan Bleasdale, it centred around five unemployed road workers looking for a job. The accents were fake, the characters always shouted and aggression was a constant undertone (Harry Enfield sat taking notes), but beneath the sensationalism was a strong critique of British society at the time: "Nobody on the dole counts," one character, Dixie, said in episode one, setting the tone.

Bleasdale used his characters to explain Liverpool life through dialogue form. For example, he used Snowy, a supposed communist agitator, to say:

"The police started the Toxteth riots... Be warned, the way things are going with this government – swing to the right, tax relief for the rich, redundancies for the poor, mass unemployment, poverty, containment of freedom, starving the unions – it's all heading for one thing: a fascist dictatorship."

Bleasdale also used the dying old-time docker George Malone to say: "I watched my first ship come in [at the Albert Dock]. They say that memories live longer than dreams, but my dreams of long ago still give me hope and faith in my class. I can't believe that there is no hope - I can't!"

In a scene that depicted community and collectivism, Chrissie, one of the central characters, took George around a dry and overgrown brown-looking Albert Dock in 1983 to reminisce before he died. The old man spoke about women cleaning the steps, corner shops, children playing out, Atlee, Liddell, Dean and Nye Bevan. "Saturday afternoon and nobody here," he observed, "...once upon a time Chrissie... it'd be payday Saturday, there'd be hundreds coming along here. Repairmen, scalers, dockers, the Mary Ellens who'd clean out big liners, and then those great big cart horses."

One of the most important characters in the show was Yosser (Yozzer) Hughes.[42] Portrayed as assertive, emotional and desperate for work (*'I can do that'*), followed everywhere by his three children, Hughes' sanity deteriorated as the show progressed. He struggled to find employment to feed his children and attempted suicide after social services took them away. Throughout the show he headbutted objects – viewed as an act of control in a world where he had little. And he stated his name often, something that was intended by Bleasdale to

---

[42] Hughes was featured on the front of The End volume 9 saying 'I could write that'.

demonstrate to viewers the uncertainty Hughes had as a man, having lost his sense of masculinity as the traditional role of a 'breadwinner' was taken away by a profit-seeking state.

Liverpool was filled with Hughes-type characters in the mid-80s who struggled for their dignity in the most dishonest of times. In the final scene, three of the main characters stood and watched as the old Tate and Lyle factory was demolished before them. It was supposed to symbolise a requiem for the failed working-class dream.

Yet for all the powerful themes in the show, Boys from the Blackstuff aged into a catchphrase - *'Gis a job'* - and become a stick to beat the city with, as travelling football fans from elsewhere in the country coined the deriding chant: *'Sign on, sign on, with a pen, in your head, cos' you'll never get a job'*. It mocked a sad fact: between 1972 and 1982, 83,000 jobs were lost on Liverpool's docks, as manufacturing shrank by 52%.

*

Mid-way through 1982/83 the Daily Post reported that Joe Fagan was set to take over from Bob Paisley in the coming season. Fagan was closed off to the idea initially – the thought of following on from two club legends was daunting - until he realised that a new manager would come in and upset the applecart, overwriting all of Shankly and Paisley's methods and recruiting his own staff and players. Fagan took the job purely to keep his colleagues in work.

There was an unemployment league in Liverpool at the time. It was the brainchild of the City Council and was supposed to give jobless locals some degree of purpose in life. Ran by Dickie Johnson, a former Tranmere Rovers goalkeeper, every participant had to show their UB40 card before joining a team to prove they were without work – even the referees were on the dole.

'Our kid was in the league,' says Brendan Wyatt. 'They used to play on a Wednesday afternoon. This wasn't 5-a-side, it was 11 vs 11 and there was a queue to put teams in, which shows how bad things were.' There were two leagues of teams and an unofficial piece of etiquette was to shake hands after a match and say to the opponent: *'I hope I don't see you soon'*.

Such initiatives from an outside perspective fed into the narrative of Liverpool being one entire jobless blob, carried by the rest of the nation. But many people were still employed. They worked on building sites or as joiners. There were butchers, drivers, fitters, public sector workers, council employees... plenty of others took Norman Tebbit's advice and followed work down to London, Bournemouth and Jersey.

There was also, despite it all, a prevailing sense of fun to be had. Alan Bleasdale wrote that Liverpool was sinking like the Titanic but the people were still dancing on the deck.

'The State opened in 1982 and you *had* to go there of a Thursday night,' remembers Kevin Sampson. It cost 1p to get into the club, which had marble floors and Grecian columns – juxtaposed by homemade 8% proof cider. 'You're coming out of the Eric's scene and then into Gatsby's, where there was the Genesis corner, where lads just sat there having weed, from which the scene of Groundpig appeared.' So much was going on.

'But the inescapable fact,' Sampson says, 'is that from 1982 to 1986 I was forced to sign on. I wanted to do so much but had so little means of doing it. The trainers I lusted after from Wade Smith were out of reach. It was either buy them or miss the match, or not go out at all. How could I make that giro go as far as possible? That was the issue.'

Wade Smith's was a training shoe shop on Slater Street named after its owner, Robert. He'd worked for adidas in the early 1980s and, after the German sportswear manufacturers showed a lack of foresight in selling shoes in Liverpool, capitalised. It was difficult to buy decent trainers at the time – few retailers stocked them – and he was aware of the great difficulties locals went to in bringing back shoes from Europe, having bumped into a group of Scallies at Ostend with bags full of attire. All Liverpool needed was a domestic retailer, so he opened a shop.

He spoke to the BBC in the early 2000s, surrounded by Prada and Gucci clothes (the very idea of such brands being found in 1980 unimaginable) about his story. 'What caused all this was Liverpool fans travelling around Europe,' he said, 'and they picked up on things you couldn't have in the UK. They were buying them at a lower cost in Germany and that created a cult back home, because there were 5,000 fans who could get them, but 50,000 Merseyside kids without access to them. And that's what created the boom.'

Of his Slater Street store, he said: 'We planned to sell 26,000 in the first year, but we sold 110,000. In our second year we did a quarter of a million. It was like winning the lottery.' Pairs of Münchens, Trimm Trabs, Grand Slams and Forest Hills sold out in a matter of hours. People were styled by fashions from Austria,

Denmark, Spain, Italy, France and Holland. Cagoules and Ellesse ski-wear flew off the shelves.

The look exploded. Sampson wrote about it for 'The Face' and before long it had spread beyond Manchester down towards London. The Mail on Sunday and New Society began writing about training shoe clad youngsters who went to football matches and called them 'Casuals'... 'There were two seasons when us, Everton and Tranmere were the only football fans who were dressing that way,' Sampson says. 'It was because of us going to places like Zurich and bringing back trainers that it emerged.' Now it was in danger of becoming a national look.

As Sheffield, Derby and elsewhere tried to catch up, 'The End' magazine continued to take the mickey out of them. Fashion had always been a constant theme in the magazine. As too had humour (*'The Great Bus Journeys of the World – The 30A to Netherton'*). It satirised things as random as elbows, Jack Charlton's head, holidays in Kirkby and leather jackets. Increasingly, with every volume, the standard of writing improved; as too did the content. But the subject which gained more and more attention as the mag evolved over the years was politics.

In the beginning, it had been limited to being 'in' alongside 'ordinary trains' and 'snooker', with 'Mark Thatcher' being out. In volume one, The End nobly attempted to explain why the riots of 1981 began – a topic other publications skimmed over. Yet by the mid-1980s it had cemented its stance against Conservatism in partisan style and was reinforcing that position with every paper.

Alan Bleasdale talked to the writers about Blackstuff, saying: "It might open some people's eyes, but will it open the government's pockets? She'll say it's lies and shite, you know? Next year we're going to have an election and we'll have another five years of that twat. She'll walk it. She'll increase her majority. Thatcher's going to get to 1990 and if we haven't all been blown up then there's going to be a revolution."

As the mag evolved, Pete Wylie would talk less to them about music and more about corruption at political level, while Alexei Sayle would reference the poison of the ruling class. In 1983 The End would tell readers about Reds and Blues in the Wine Lodge singing *'Arthur Scargill, we'll support you ever more'* together. It would denounce the Sun as a daily collection of lies (before the ultimate lie) and publish poems from a republican standing. Did any other city have such an all-encompassing literature on its culture like Liverpool had with The End?

Daniel Fieldsend

By 1984, the writers were interviewing Militant figures such as Terry Fields and Derek Hatton. 'Neil Kinnock has political amnesia,' Fields told them, while Derek Hatton cited an unchanging fact: 'When you think that five millionaires own 95% of the press, we're not surprised that there is a campaign against us.'

Described as 'maggots' within the Labour Party by Neil Kinnock, Militant Tendency had done what all maggots do – they fed upon something already dead. Labour in the early 1980s was bankrupt of ideas and organisation.

Liverpool had an adventurous nature and an impulsive, rebellious spirit which had been created by the ebb and flow of its waters. Militant tapped directly into that. Andrew Lees introduced the climate of the times best:

"Liverpool was on the wrong side of the country. The uneven geography of England was widening and the city-island had become a beacon for everything the English feared: class revolution, squalor and poverty, and a threat to the rising political challenge of the middle-class. The creation of Red Merseyside, with its monstrous Eastern-bloc civic-centres run by men with northern accents, drinking pints of Cain's and calling one another 'brother', was the anathema to the Conservatives and much of the rest of England."

Lees wrote that Mrs Thatcher's corner-shop mentality of snobbishness, thriftiness, self-interest and narrow-mindedness clashed with the Liverpool character. Derek Hatton had witnessed first-hand the dangers of squalor and neglect in the early 1970s whilst working as a fireman. On one occasion he was called out to a house in Bedford Street South where fifteen Irishmen were living in one room, surrounded by excrement in every corner. He saw the effects of poor housing and became determined to rid the problem. His opportunity came when he was employed as a director of community schemes within the Labour Party in the late-70s. From there his Trotskyism matured.

Originally, Militant had been known as the Revolutionary Socialist League, a Leninist group that had been around since the 1950s. They'd meet at underground venues and sing *The Internationale* – that French socialist anthem. In 1974, Militant Tendency was found by reports to be a 'party within a party' which ought to be quashed before it grew. In Liverpool however, they gained popularity. Early 1980 saw the London media write apprehensively about the dangers of a Militant takeover of Labour, but in Liverpool there was no such paranoia. Eventually Liverpool Labour adopted Militant policies for the city, spearheaded by the George Lansbury slogan of the 1920s: 'It's better to break the law than break the poor'.

The basis for Militant's recent rhetoric began in 1978. 'Inner City Partnership' (a government plan) looked set to offer £48m towards the construction of new houses in Liverpool. But in 1979 when the Tories were elected, the plan was scrapped and public spending cuts were introduced. It was a betrayal, socialists believed, which justified the perception that Thatcher did not care about Liverpool. The riots of 1981 had only added to that belief.

In the 1983 local elections Liverpool was buzzing with political discourse. Match-lads were talking about cuts; women on the bus were discussing housing. Soon there would be mass demonstration after mass demonstration. Militant had tapped into a mood and a desire. 'It seemed that everybody between the age of 16 and 25 around ours were, if not involved, supportive of them, and there was a great sense of fighting back – of not taking any more shit,' says Tony Evans from Scottie. 'Even the boys who went the game supported what was happening. Everybody wanted to beat Thatcher.'

But the lines were blurred. Was the city voting for traditional Labour or for Militant?[43] Whose flag would fly over Town Hall? It was difficult to discern.

Upon being elected to represent the council, one of Militant's first acts was to chisel the name of Sir Trevor Jones from his Liberal office door. They abolished the position of Lord Mayor and replaced it with a role of 'Chairman'. They immediately cancelled the 1,200 redundancies planned by the Conservative-Liberal administration and froze council rents, launching a progressive house-building programme in their first week which targeted the city's most deprived neighbourhoods.

From day-one it seemed they opposed all of the demands of central government, exactly as they promised. Many people were charmed by, and believed in, what Militant said: that Liverpool was still a great city which deserved national respect. Slums were torn down; new leisure centres and nurseries were built and apprenticeships were created.

A week later in the 1983 general election, Thatcher secured the most decisive Tory victory of all time. She swept Michael Foot, the Liberals and the SDP away as the majority of Britain got behind her, soaring from a 44 majority to one of 144. Liverpool people on the other hand sent out a clear statement. By voting Militant Labour, they marked the city out as antipathetic to the rest of the country, going

---

[43] Terry Fields would argue in The End that Militant was the most traditional form of Labour.

as far left and as far away from the mainstream as possible, toward an almost Bolshevik solution. Labour took 23 of the 33 wards in the city.

Terry Fields' campaign to win the Broadgreen seat was described by his Liberal rival as being 'unlike anything I've seen in the country, even in by-elections'. Fields was an ex-firefighter and was backed financially by the Fire Brigades' Union. He was Militant's key man on the shop floor. In the months before the election, he campaigned hard: at a local bin depot 200 workers waited to hear him at 7am; he appeared at ten factory-gate and canteen meetings; he stood on street corners with a microphone and, with his team, knocked on every door in the constituency.

Two weeks before the election he spoke at the Railwaymen Club in Kensington to workers in overalls at 5pm. Tony Benn took to the stage to introduce him, saying to the crowd: 'Once confidence flows back into the working-class in Britain then no power on earth can stop us.' The atmosphere was electric, with thunderous applause and whistles. Fields shared the stage with Derek Hatton and Pat Phoenix (better known as Elsie Tanner in Coronation Street). There was a growing momentum around it all.

A few days later Fields addressed hundreds more on a plateau in Old Swan alongside Arthur Scargill. 'The atmosphere was like that of a football match,' wrote Peter Taaffe and Tony Mulhearn, 'with workers standing with their arms raised high in sheer class determination.'

Town Hall on the other hand, despite the outside support, became a venue for manic management. Meetings lasted minutes as policies were pushed through with spending largely ignored. Hatton joked that everybody just wanted to get to the match. Consultations on housing matters were dismissed as unnecessary bourgeois exercises, so wrote Lees.

Militant opted to build five thousand low-rise, low-cost council houses in seventeen priority areas. The idea would provide jobs in the private building sector and create decent accommodation for the poor. A plot on Everton Brow became the darling of the initiative and Militant propaganda (if it could be called such) announced incredible views of the river, with sunsets each night and open grassy parkland.

They spent from a purse that the Tory government clutched on to, which riled the gentlemen of Westminster. Militant were ordered to reduce their spending budget, thus making all building plans unlikely. Faced with a debt from the previous Liberals, the Labour council attempted to claw back £30 million of the £100 million they believed had been stolen by cuts in rate-support grants. 'If the government want cuts, they should make them themselves' was the idea. It was 'us-and-them' politics.

In December 1983, 20,000 people demonstrated in support of the council's stance. Militant pressed ahead with their urban regeneration project, building 1,000 new homes with front and back gardens.

Peter Carney recalls it all: 'I knew Dereck Hatton as a council official in Kirkby and he was brilliant back then. What they were doing here as Militant was brave, protecting the houses and facing off with the witch. To me, that was the right and proper way to do it. There was no two ways about it, Liverpool was flying in the face of the rest of the country. The fact they elected a Labour council, which came from the grassroots, showed balls because nobody was standing up for themselves.

'Liverpool council were getting called for all kinds elsewhere in the country but capitalism was in collapse. I remember Militant knocking down the tenements - Sydney Gardens and Gerard Gardens - but they were dead right to do so. They'd served their purpose those buildings. They were getting replaced with houses with a garden. Militant were trying to make it a better place for the people of Liverpool,' said Carney.

With the comfort of retrospect, commentators argue that Militant adopted the easy solution of spending money which didn't exist. Others see them as an extreme solution to extreme times.

Under the previous Con-Lib alliance, there had been no social houses built for four years, between 1979 and 1983. Something had to be done, surely? Existing social houses had the highest rent costs outside of London in the country, squeezing living conditions for locals. Thatcher had also lowered the rate support grant which Scousers relied upon and cut down on public sector spending. Even Militant's most fierce critic, Neil Kinnock, conceded that they offered the impression of: 'Standing up for Liverpool against the barbarian invaders from Westminster'. Militant understood the mentality of the city and tapped into it.

At the start of it all, Liverpool City Council were part of a borrowing coalition with Birmingham, Sheffield and Lambeth, but one by one they dropped out and imposed central government cuts. In every single sense the city began to find itself all alone.

Simon Hughes was just a boy, but he'd be shaped by it all. 'Liverpool defined itself as being another place in the '80's because we were the only city led by

Militants that put lines in the sand. There were opportunities for other councils in the country to challenge Thatcher but none of them had the courage. It was a battle that had to happen because God knows what would have happened to this city otherwise. There comes a point where people have bills to pay and families to feed; they couldn't have said *"well everything is going to be okay in ten years' time."* There had to be a stand. Liverpool was in the press all of the time during the '80's and it was the most defining time in the city's history.'

The climate of 1911 had returned to Liverpool. It was a standoff between a council and its government – them and us, syntax and semantics, Scousers versus the world - and nobody knew how things were going to end.

Locāl

ENGLISH CIVIL WAR

War Is Peace

Had George Orwell's 1984 come true? Was Liverpool to be the setting for some dystopian present? The conflict with central government continued. Nobody was certain if Militant were going to follow through with their promises – *politicians always break their promises*. Surely what 10 Downing Street demanded had to be complied with? Budget Day loomed and workers around Moorfields speculated but nobody really knew. It was on the 19th of March when Militant eventually made the announcement: they were going to follow through with their pledges; they were going to ignore Downing Street; they were going to break the law.

It would become a battle of wills. Militant maintained throughout that they understood the state of the city and couldn't in good conscience implement the government's cuts. They also realised that they were pioneers for the whole movement. In fifty years, the Militant Tendency had never been so popular. There had been 50,000 people marching in support of them a month earlier. They had to keep the electorate behind them.

Mulhearn made the point that such physical demonstrations of support showed true political backing. There'd been a 62% turnout in the local elections, meaning Militant were duty-bound to stand up against the government. Half an eye was also kept on the potential for civil unrest if they failed to proceed. The riots had only been a few years earlier – more broken promises could create an unmanageable situation, they felt.

1,000 homes were built in the first month of Militant's office, turning Liverpool into the largest public works project in Britain. 4,000 more homes were in the pipeline and 16,000 private sector jobs were about to be created. Hatton told the press that they'd not been elected to carry out the 'draconian cuts' proposed by the Tory party. It was a refusal which consigned Liverpool to the political wilderness. 'Ken Livingston had talked big but backed off, so had David Blunkett, but we drew a line in the sand,' says Tony Evans.

The following day, council representatives were on the phone with Liverpool and Everton FC officials. The city was about to experience its first ever all-Merseyside Wembley final that weekend. The buzz was tangible. Stalls in Greaty and Kirkby market made a roaring trade by selling blue-and-white and red-and-white chequered flags. Long Lane and Queen's Drive began to look like Mardi Gras was arriving: wide vast roads brimming with colour. Kerbs and bollards were painted in club colours for the first time in years.

A former Everton midfielder who grew up in Sparrow Hall told me: 'Half of the street would be blue and the other half would be red. The city – because of how Thatcher treated it – had a sense of backing each other up. Football was our lifeline, it's what kept us together, united.' He and everybody else made arrangements for a weekend in London.

For City Council, the big problem related to a proposal surrounding bus celebrations. To put on a unified front, it had been suggested that the winners of the trophy went first and a second bus with the losers on went behind. Howard Kendall flat-out refused to consider the idea, leaving the council dumbfounded. After an hour or so of brainstorming it was decided that both Everton and Liverpool would share the buses together: nobody had to go last.

This was supposed to be the most defining game of the season. Liverpool fans had cheered for Everton in the semi-finals, hoping they'd overcome Aston Villa and join them in the final. The Reds had been in a mini-crisis beforehand, going months without the injured Dalglish and Souness. 'We're not as good as we'd like to be,' Joe Fagan admitted to the press, himself desperate to win some silverware and shake off the legacies of the managers who'd came before him.

Howard Kendall had been Everton manager since 1981. He was equally desperate to win the cup – or any silverware: Everton had been 16th in the table at Christmas – only 13,000 fans had turned up to watch them play Coventry on New Year's Eve. His job was under scrutiny. Both camps longed for a trophy to take away any pressure.

On the train down to London on the day of the final fans handed out badges which declared *'I Support Liverpool City Council'*. It was all set up to be an occasion for Scousers to present their city in a positive light. That sentiment was shared with cameramen from Granada Studios who followed fans down and documented their experience.

One older fan told cameras early on in the documentary: 'I think if we do go down there and give a good account of ourselves and show that we are human beings and not scroungers like they think we are, then it can create jobs, because the eyes of the world are on us down there. People seeing Liverpool and Everton supporters together will think *'they can't all be bad."*

The programme was called 'Home and Away' and showed a deserted Liverpool with only the women left behind, and a London full of boisterous Scouse males. It captured the fun to be had in-between, with Reds and Blues on the coach together playing cards and singing neutral songs: *'Here we go, here we go, here we go,',* *'Wild Rover'* and *'When I'm sixty-four'*. In both cities the men and women were filmed breaking into constant renditions of *'In my Liverpool Home'* - that much forgotten chorus of civic pride.

A variety of issues associated with Liverpool at the time came through on camera, with unemployment and the role of football proving to be central themes. One fan said: 'It doesn't matter if it's a Conservative government or Labour or SDP, this place would still get knocked. But Wembley is ours and nobody can take that from us. We've got a full weekend of letting off everything that has built up, and if we didn't have it to let off, I'd say God help [Thatcher].'

Another fan, Graham Edgerton, told cameras: 'The people: that's the beauty of Liverpool. They make it tick over. There's no point me having a mansion somewhere and I can't get on. I'd rather live where I do now and have the people.' One lad stated how he'd very much like to run onto the pitch and show his arse to the Queen Mother. Another, Steve Waldron, lamented the fact he was no longer a child and found himself burdened with responsibilities.

There was a regular reference to masculinity throughout the documentary, something Alan Bleasdale had captured in *BFTBS*: 'It has its strains being out of work: what man wants to be kept by a woman?' asked a feller in his 40's. The wives and girlfriends get further mentions: 'I told her I'd marry her when Everton got into Europe. That was three kids ago!' a Blue joked.

The women were filmed at Flames Disco, attended, it seemed, by just one gender. In a London pub the men stood on tables singing together. A couple of younger lads chatted to some southern girls. One of them, they discovered, worked for the dole; everybody booed her.

Fans at Wembley stood together on the 25th March in a sea of red and blue. The players realised that a special occasion had occurred and, despite the game finishing 0-0, joined the moment of unity. Alan Kennedy and John Bailey tied their scarves together and walked a lap of the pitch, side by side. The two teams walked behind them, chatting to each other. The 100,000 people in attendance sang '*Merseyside, Merseyside*' in one loud voice. At a time when Liverpool was known for TV-poverty, unemployment, rioting and Militantism, this was a display of solidarity for the nation to see and hear.

'That did it for me,' a supporter in his late-40s told Granada. 'We let every fan in the country know who we are then... Now it's back to the doldrums and looking for a job, which is the hardest thing in the world for me.' The documentary ended at night with fans getting off the coach, saying '*Ta mate*' to the driver before returning to uncertainty.

On the 29th March there was a co-ordinated strike and demonstration in Liverpool: one of the largest citywide general strikes in British history. All forms of workers marched on Town Hall: firefighters, post officers, printers, mechanics, builders, seamen, dockers, hospital workers, civil servants, office staff, transport workers and shipbuilders, with many more descending upon Castle Street individually.

A representative from the Yorkshire Miners Association stood on the balcony where Shankly had back in '65 and addressed the crowd, but the mood was much different. He told them: 'The miners are in the same position as Liverpool's council, and in both cases if we stay united, they can't defeat us.' Terry Fields followed him and referenced the 1921 movement in Poplar in which councillors were jailed. His rhetoric of resilience went down well: '*Labour council, Labour council, we'll support you ever more*,' people chanted.

It felt for many that Liverpool was out on its own, but that wasn't completely true. On 12th April Thatcher was reminded of the spectre of the city on a visit to Indonesia. The Post wrote:

> "*Dissident students taunted Mrs Thatcher with a defiant cry when she visited Bandung University...* 'Liverpool, Liverpool'*, they chanted in unison, adding the only sour note to an otherwise rapturous welcome for the British Prime Minister. No one quite knew whether the chant had a football connection, or if news of Liverpool City Council's defiant stand against Mrs Thatcher's government really had travelled halfway around the world to dog her footsteps.*"

Peter Taaffe and Tony Mulhearn pondered whether the rationale behind the chant was so simple that Thatcher was British and so were Liverpool FC, a popular football team? Or was it the case, they asked, that the much-reported struggle of Liverpool's City Council had reached this distant colony of the former Dutch empire? Either way, it appeared that the city was receiving support in some capacity. "It is little wonder then that Thatcher 'personally and politically detested the Militant Liverpool leaders," the pair wrote.

*

An opportunity to put Liverpool in a more positive light to a wider catchment of people – specifically business investors – was had on the 2nd May with the opening of the International Garden Festival, set to be the biggest event in Britain since the aptly named 'Festival of Britain' in 1951.

It was Michael Heseltine's baby but was met with resistance both in Whitehall (from people who couldn't see the point investing in a lost-cause-town), and locally too. 'I remember people shouting at me on the street saying *"give us jobs not trees,"'* Heseltine said. The Queen opened events on a sun-kissed morning as City Council looked to capitalise. 'We're not opposed to tourism' Hatton told the press.

A vast number of locals boycotted the festival, viewing it as a rug over a hole. They saw it as 200 acres of reclaimed land with cute Victorian ladies and John Lennon statues, born out of a summer of riots, but with no opportunity for the people of Liverpool 8 to work there. 'We were having none of it,' remembers Tony Evans. 'Everyone was saying *"they're planting trees when we need houses."'*

Margaret Thatcher came up to take a ride on a novelty train, seemingly oblivious to her role in its creation. For many locals it was pointless. But for others it was a refreshingly nice thing to have at a time when nice things were uncommon. Over the next six months the festival would exceed its target of 3 million visitors.

Blue Peter came up. As too did Worzel Gummidge. The months were as sunny as Heseltine had predicted. For a city with such obvious negativity surrounding it, it was strange to have something pleasant for once. The Cast Iron Shore was no longer a rubbish dump, but instead had a centrepiece in the middle of it, donated by the Japanese government. There were giant jam jars, daily performances and a (terrifying) large teddy bear. Complimenting all of which – that mood of trying to reclaim optimism - Liverpool FC were flying in European competition and continued to be a beacon of light for everybody (some things don't change).

*

Liverpool's European Cup semi-final against Dinamo Bucharest had been lively, with Graeme Souness breaking their captain's jaw in an off-the-ball encounter. The other fixture between Roma and Dundee United however was unexplainable chaos. With the final set to be played at Roma's Stadio Olimpico, the local supporters would allow for no alternative other than a Roma victory. Tony Evans wrote about club officials bribing the referee 100 million lira for the game. Roma sought to antagonise Dundee United's fans and staff in every possible way. Before the game, a banner lined *Curva Sud* which read 'God Hates Dundee United'. Afterwards Roma's staff surrounded the United bench and spat at their coaches. A bust-up followed and the police intervened – all this despite Roma having won the game. What would happen if they lost?

When tickets came on sale for the final, 8,000 people in Rome ambushed the ticket office. A riot ensued: helicopters circled and tear gas was discharged. 12 people were seriously injured. It was a totally different story in Liverpool where, reluctantly, 9,000 Liverpool supporters slowly bought tickets for the game – a combination of relative poverty and anxiety deterring them. LFC bought the 7,000 leftover tickets to deny Roma supporters the opportunity to get their hands on them. It cost the club £30,000 but was a decision that would save lives.

The Eternal City was a tense place to be. Pope John Paul was recovering from an assassination attempt, while Mirella Gregori and Emanuela Orlandi – two fifteen-year-old girls - had been abducted, causing local panic. It was all supposed to be linked.

Seven years earlier Rome had been full of Liverpool supporters who'd been welcomed enthusiastically. That seemed like a lifetime ago. This was now an invasion as far as the locals were concerned. A city built by generals on the strength of its army, it had a deep-rooted sense of superiority. "Great empires are not maintained by timidity," said Tacitus during his rule. The Romans wouldn't allow Liverpudlians to invade freely: 'We were under attack from the minute we got there,' says Tony Evans.

Back in the 1920s and '30s, Roman strength had been portrayed through fascism. Whilst working at the University of Rome in 1925, Mussolini's right-hand man Giovanni Gentile wrote: "Fascism before all else is a total conception of life". Mussolini elevated the city and its people to uphold his belief in the strength of the doctrine in the '20s, and his blackshirts occupied Rome in the '30s, turning it into a base for his movement.

Even after 1952 when it became illegal to resuscitate Mussolini's image, many Romans refused to waver in their support for him. Proclaiming admiration for him was not considered heretical, but was seen as a sign of courageous thinking. By 1984 when Liverpool visited, swathes of Romans held on tight to the achievements of '*Il Duce*', and of fascism, and the Empire, allowing them to overlook their dire economy and malign in a sinking part of Southern Italy. Football had grown to become a vehicle encapsulating all three.

There had been 8 teams in Rome in the 1920s. They collectively weakened the chances of Rome having one great club to power the city's status, prompting Italo Foschi – a representative of the National Fascist Party - to come up with a solution. In July 1927 three of the clubs (Alba, Fortitudo and Roman) merged together, birthing AS Roma. The club was based in the working-class neighbourhood of Testaccio and immediately presented itself as the team of the people. Lazio wore blue, they were for the region. Roma took the colours of the city.

Supporters from Northern-Italy called Roma fans *Fogna* – 'sewer people'. In 1984 locals were desperate for the club to win and reaffirm their sense of self. Brian Reade wrote about his visit to the city, telling of how in Genoa there had been signs saying 'Forza Liverpool' and, at Livorno, the train station had been decked out in Liverpool flags. Reade acknowledged that it was more to do with how parochial Italian fandom is, rather than there being genuine backing for the Reds. Everybody wanted Roma to lose, and Roma knew this.

Liverpool arrived as one of the greatest names in Europe, supported by a devoted fanbase who had strong leftist inclinations. Was conflict in Rome – a fascist hotbed - inevitable on political grounds?

Perhaps not. Scousers were driven into the city by Lazio supporting taxi drivers and were served enthusiastically by Lazio supporting waiters who shouted 'Forza Liverpool' at collections of fans. If conflict was to be based on political differences, then why would Lazio supporters – with deeper neo-fascist inclinations than Roma – be so welcoming?

Tension was built on fear, pride, status and incursion. Roma didn't want any team coming and taking *their* trophy, Liverpool or otherwise. 'They'd already won the European Cup as far as they were concerned,' says Tony Evans. Anxiety was whipped up by the local press who led with the headline: 'The Barbarians Are Coming'.[44] Despite the Reds having gone decades participating in Europe without

---

[44] In 2018 *Il Tempo* wrote that Liverpool and Lazio fans were going to team up and fight with Roma *Ultras*. They ran the headline 'Help!' and had a picture of the Beatles with weapons in their hands. They also wrote that Liverpool supporters were to blame for the clash outside Anfield in the previous leg. None of it was true.

any recognisable incurrence of violence, the article stated how the English were hooligans and Liverpool would be no different.

Liverpool FC's chief executive Peter Robinson had travelled to Rome as soon as the tie was announced in an attempt to defuse potentialities. He understood the situation. 'Unfortunately,' he said, 'British fans are acquiring a bad reputation abroad and the Italians are extremely volatile. We are certain our supporters will not let us down and we want to ensure they have an enjoyable visit.'

There had been a wave of incidents of British supporters in Europe fighting and acting antisocially. Rangers rioted in Barcelona in 1972, receiving a two-year ban. Tottenham were barred in '74 after fights in Rotterdam; West Ham supporters did the same in Madrid. Leeds United received a four-year ban in 1975; Manchester United were made to play matches 125 miles away from home after fighting with St Etienne supporters in 1977. England's FA was fined after fights in Turin. In 1982 Aston Villa fans rioted in Anderlecht and Manchester United supporters attacked police in Valencia. In 1983, thirty Spurs fans were arrested in Holland and in '84, a few months before Liverpool got to Rome, there was mass-trouble between Spurs and Anderlecht.

Liverpool supporters were no angels, shoplifting on the continent and bunking on trains to get to matches, but they arrived in Rome shouldering Britain's reputation for mindless thuggery. The barbarians, as far as locals were concerned, had arrived.

Stephen Monaghan had been tasked with organising the trip over for his group of mates. 'There was going to be fifty of us, fifty of Liverpool's finest,' he says, bracing himself to recall the story. 'There were lads from Huyton, Kirkby, Halewood, Scotland Road, areas of Liverpool where all our mates were from. We all met at the Leatherbottle in Halewood and set off from Manchester to Rome, Friday to Friday with the game in between.'

They were supposed to be staying in Ostia, home of the rich and famous, but the group somehow ended up in Ladispoli – a 'one horse town with one hotel and one road,' says Monaghan, with a housing estate nearby and one bar called the International. The group reluctantly based themselves there, prompting locals to believe they'd been invaded. 'Within a couple of hours of us being there our lads had been chased by a gang of Italians. Throughout the rest of the day there were skirmishes going off everywhere. We were supposed to be there for a week! A gang came again and were trying to smash the bar up, then this copper turned up with a gun demanding to know who was in charge.'

Locāl

The policeman was called Angelo. He asked Monaghan how long his group intended to be in town for. When he found out it was for a full week he negotiated with the local Romans. 'All of the young lads who wanted to fight us then came into the bar; it was surreal. The skirmishes stopped and we we're all shaking hands. One of the main lads, Carlos, became friends with us and he invited me to his mums house the following day. I went with my mate Philly and we bought her a bunch of flowers. We got into his convertible and were saying to each other "we've bought flowers for our own grave here."'

But the welcome Monaghan and Phil received was far from hostile. 'She gave us kisses. She'd cooked us spaghetti, a steak and a salad, with a big bottle of vino. That week we had the time of our lives. We organised a football match against them and they were all dead skilful. We got beat but there was a bigger picture.' The travelling Reds had shown themselves to be humble visitors, not threatening barbarians. Stripping aside the supposed differences, the Romans and Scousers found common ground and got along.

But inside the city centre there was no opportunity for communication and things remained hostile. Tony Evans describes the burgundy and yellow flags that flew everywhere, high above the hills of the capital. He remembers Fiat cars driving alongside Liverpool coaches, with fans stood up inside the moving vehicles launching bricks at the windows. The streets were lined with balloons, as if it were Chinese New Year: this was supposed to be Roma's moment. 'We were the party-poopers,' says Evans, 'and they didn't want us there.'

As scooters zoomed down cobbled *Vias,* back-passengers sat with scarves around their faces, with one arm around the driver and another holding large Roma flags. Liverpool fans received a heavy police escort all the way from the airport to an abandoned funfair. At first Kopites assumed that the police regarded them as potential trouble-causers, bottling them away for safe keeping, but found out later that it was the other way around.

The Mayor of Rome, Ugo Vetre, had been quoted in the press welcoming Liverpudlians: "We wish to make this a great occasion…in a spirit of sportsmanship and goodwill." Local newspaper *Il Messagero* said there would be: 'Peace, love [and] songs'. Yet within a few hours of arrival talk had already circled about small groups of Kopites being slashed and hospitalised. *Romanistas* on scooters were going past and stabbing people in the arse, so Reds were saying.

Buttock-stabbing had been how Gladiators displayed supreme skill in duelling. Locals believed that wounding a rival in the arse was considered to be total humiliation, known as *'punicate'*. In actuality, for Kopites over there, it seemed more akin to shithousery, done so the perpetrator could avoid being charged with a fatal crime. There were no fights between large groups, just unprovoked and cowardly attacks. Roma's many *Ultra* groups began to congregate outside the abandoned funfair, picking off Liverpool supporters who left to explore the city.

A few hours before kick-off things grew eerily quiet. The Roma followers left their stations and headed to the Olimpico – their focus shifting towards intimidating Liverpool's team. A wall of armed policemen awaited Kopites as they arrived. German Shepherds snapped and growled at them and tickets went unchecked. "You sensed immediately they were expecting trouble, but seemed as fearful of their notorious home ground '*Tifosi*' compatriots as they were of us, and whatever reputation we had acquired," stated David Pye.

Tony Evans clocked how the Liverpool fans had anything that could be deemed a weapon taken from them, but were not ejected as this was an accepted part of the Italian game at the time. On the other side he noticed how the Roma fans were pouring into the stadium unchecked.

Inside the ground, *Ultras* hit Liverpool's section with missiles throughout. When Reds reacted, they were beaten back.

George Sephton had been brought to Rome by the club and, for the second time at a European final, had a firearm pointed at him. 'Peter Robinson insisted that because of the trouble we had in Paris that I'd go as part of the team on the coach. They all wandered off onto the pitch and I stood in the dressing room talking to Tom Saunders. A UEFA official collared me and me asked where I was going and if I had a pass. I said "no, your lot screwed up and nearly got me shot in Paris, so the club put me on the coach." Anyway, he told me I must go. I refused and Tom gave me a ticket while this lunatic wondered off. He came back with a policeman who pointed a gun at me and told me to get out.' Tension was rife.

Lazio fans had warned Scousers about Roma. They painted them as poor and described them as being from the housing projects. They were unemployed and right-wing youths, so said the *Irriducibili*. They attributed a term to them and a claim that they were all from outside the city: '*Burini*', meaning 'peasant'. It was a back-and-forth insult; *Romanisiti* belittled Lazio fans with the term and *Irriducibili* used it back at them – the Roman 'Wools' of the time.

Inside the ground Liverpool's squad arrived early. The Roma supporters were already there. Ronnie Moran instructed the team to go for a stretch. As they came out of the tunnel there was an almighty thud and roar as 60,000 *Ultras* bounced.

Local

Dalglish, Hansen, Lee – indeed most of the players would go on to say it was one of the most frightening moments of their lives. They were deep inside the cauldron. Sammy Lee said he wanted to come out, do a few stretches on the pitch and quickly get back into the changing rooms. Souness had other ideas.

The Scottish captain was made of sterner stuff. He told the team in no uncertain terms that they were going to look the beast deep in the eye, leading them slowly around the perimeter of the pitch as missiles rained down from shirtless Romans *Ultras,* who beat their chest and climbed towards them. Souness' nonchalance, unphased by the anger coming his way, inspired the rest of the squad to perform.

In the tunnel before kick-off, Roma's players tried to get into Liverpool's heads, keeping them waiting for ten minutes. When they finally appeared, the rhythmic clinking of their boots on the hard ground brought on a second impromptu sing-along from Liverpool: *"I don't know what it is but I love it, I don't know what it is but I want it to stay..."* They'd soaked up everything Rome had to offer and just sang, blasé. It disarmed a world-class Roma side.

Joe Fagan's team talk had also been carefree. Referring to everybody as 'lad' he said:
'Don't give free kicks away outside the box - you know how good they are at falling down.
'We are not going man to man mark Falcao, but the nearest man pick him up quick.
'We shall respect them but we are going to win here.
'Let them do all the worrying about us.
'Same formation that brought us to the final.
'All the best lads - let's do em,' ... Smoking Joe, Litherland's finest.

Three hours later, Fagan had made history. When Alan Kennedy scored the penalty kick to win the game, there was a deep and ancient primal groan of agony and anger. The Roma fans began burning their scarves and flags; they were beyond angry. 'I've never felt rage like it,' says Tony Evans. Nobody considered a Liverpool win. Souness ran to Joe Fagan and the two men embraced; it had been a long year.

Outside the ground the city was furious. It seemed as though Kopites had been set up by the police and *Carabinieri,* being kept inside the Olimpico until Roma's *Ultras* were in position. 'By now armed with baseball bats, clubs, chair legs, pool cues, chains and knives, a pitched battle ensued in the narrow streets of the ancient capital,' wrote Tony Evans. They had stashed weapons in their cars, indicating that no matter the outcome, this was going to happen. *Ultras* set bins on fire and threw them at Liverpudlians. They lashed bricks and bottles and moved in like a scene from the Warriors, trapping Reds and stabbing them in the backside. Scousers would have been done for, were it not for the arrival of sky-blue *Irriducibilis* who fought with and distracted Roma's mob.

Plenty of Liverpool fans fought back - many others fled. Leaving the city became the primary objective. Nobody felt like celebrating. At *Ponte Duca D'Aosta* there were stabbings galore. When Liverpool fans turned to the police for help, they were teargassed and beaten. George Sharp from Halewood was stabbed in the kidneys and almost bled to death. When his 16-year-old son Ian pleaded with police for help, he was truncheoned in the eye. Were it not for the actions of one decent policeman who put George in an ambulance, he'd have died on the banks of the Tiber.

Liverpool fans ran to their coaches. Policemen stood and watched. The windows on most vehicles were already smashed. Reds lay on top of each other in the aisles as missiles continued to rain down throughout the city.

90 fans were hospitalised that night. Hundreds more went home unchecked. The Roman press were disgusted by events. *Il Messagero* claimed there had been an organised attempt to hunt down the English, writing: "The gravest aspect is that the English did nothing to provoke the violence." Further north in Milan the *Corriere della Serra* wrote: "The Roman louts did not demonstrate calm and self-control which are typical British characteristics," condemning it as unjustifiable violence.

Back home there was hardly any coverage whatsoever. At a time when hooliganism was flavour of the month for the British press, nobody was interested in what had happened to Liverpool supporters in Rome. Only Brian Glanville wrote: "Hundreds of thugs chased Liverpool supporters through the streets beating, stabbing and kicking." Tony Evans acknowledges the bitter taste a lack of coverage left: 'We felt if it had of been anybody else, the press and politicians would have rallied around to condemn the Romans,' he said.

George Sharp returned home a week later. The Roman authorities paid for his flight. It had been hell. The Liverpool fans who limped across the runway at Speke airport said they hoped to never see another Italian again. 12 months later Liverpool played Juventus at Heysel.

*

In the meantime, the Tories had taken a battering of sorts. Patrick Jenkin – Environment Secretary – finally visited Liverpool in June having been in contact with the council for some time. Upon witnessing the standard of housing that Militant were seeking to rectify, he said Liverpool had: 'Deplorable conditions which have to be tackled as a matter of urgency.' It was a politically unwise comment, despite its truth. It meant that the government had to give something to Liverpool – to Militant – and Thatcher didn't want to.

Arthur Scargill and the miners were taking up most of her energies, so Jenkin was told to pacify the socialists. After weeks of talks with council leaders a deal was hammered out. Militant would get money from 10 Downing Street: £130 million. If this was a war, then they were winning. At least that's how they spun it. Hatton hailed it as a 'victory for our party'. The right-wing press reacted angrily. "Today in Liverpool, municipal militancy is vindicated," stated the Times. "It is the Tory government which has given away the most," argued the Daily Mail. They attacked Jenkin: "He has set a precedent. He has allowed defying the law, or the threat of it, to pay off," moaned the Daily Star.

It looked like the Liverpool rebellion was going to be successful. At the Labour Party conference in Blackpool later that summer, Militant leaders bathed in adulation. They had gone from unwanted outcasts to strategic winners.

But it would be short lived. Tory MP Teddy Taylor warned a prominent Militant representative before a TV appearance in Scotland: 'You do realise that we had to tell Patrick [Jenkin] to give you the money? At this stage we want Scargill. He's our priority. But we'll come for you later.' The short-lived joys of 1984 - the Garden Festival, the European Cup and the money for Militant – rotted in 1985 into something bitterly inedible.

Daniel Fieldsend

IMAGINE

Unemployment blanketed Liverpool in misery in 1985. David Alton, MP for Mossley Hill, had been preparing his speech for Parliament all week. He stood up in the spring, fumbled through his notes and declared: "The picture is depressing. About 88,000 people are registered as unemployed and only 2,025 jobs are advertised as available... Imagine life in an area where a major employer, such as United Biscuits, suddenly decides to pull the rug from under the feet of its 2,000 employees. What prospects do those people have of finding another job? If it goes on much longer, the area will become the Siberia of western Europe."

Like in Russia, there was appetite for revolution. Liverpool's landscape demonstrated what could be achieved and then left to wither if uncared for. Had Merseybeat ever existed? El Dorado was more likely. But still, prevailing in the hearts of locals, there was a sense of enjoyment to be had.

They were optimistic that things were about to change, especially following the nuggets of joy collected in 1984. But the Tories had other ideas. Patrick Jenkin was given a slap on the wrist for his frank comments about the city's condition and was told to say nothing more on the matter. The council would not be getting the £130m for new houses as agreed – the government denied having ever made such a promise.

Kenneth Baker, Minister for Housing, shrugged the speculation off, telling the press that Militant had been 'living in cloud cuckoo land' and the offer had never been submitted. With another budget set too low, Militant continued to battle with Whitehall. The city's reputation was becoming dangerously rogue.

The political engagement that typified Liverpool at the time, displayed by strikes, marches and general discourse, was not limited to just adults however. Youngsters had been listening at the dinner table and they whipped themselves into action. April saw the first ever organised school strike, aimed at protesting the government's YTS scheme which was viewed at the time as a way of exploiting young people into providing cheap labour.

Arriving at St George's Hall, tens of thousands of schoolchildren overwhelmed volunteers and the police, and ran the entirety of the route down Dale Street towards the Pier Head before dispersing all over town. What had been a word of mouth proposal had grown into a massive event with many schools closing for the day.

In Cagliari that month an 11-year-old schoolboy was performing in a play. Andrea Casula's character had him wearing a fake moustache and thick glasses as a disguise. His mother developed the photo of him wearing it a few days later, and she placed it on his desk in his bedroom next to a framed picture of him and his father, Giovanni, watching the sun set low and orange on holiday the year before.

His desk was where he did his homework. It was made of unfashionable light wood, with toy cars on and an unfinished *Calciatori* sticker album (he had two players to go). He'd been to see Juventus play when they came to Cagliari, but when his father told him he'd be going to the final to see them at Heysel that month... he became the envy of all his classmates. His joy was indefinable – he loved *calcio* and played and watched it every day. On 29th May he tied a black and white handkerchief around his neck and excitedly set off to Brussels with his father.

As mayhem reigned all around, a young doctor from Tuscany, Roberto Lorentini saw the lifeless body of the boy, Andrea, on the floor. As people scrambled to flee, Lorentini stopped and risked his own life. Kneeling at the boy's side, he attempted to resuscitate him. Lorentini could have escaped, but his nature forced him to help. Within a few minutes, he too had been trampled to death by fleeing supporters.

It is a tragic story. Roberto, 31, posthumously received a silver medal for civic duty. His father, Otello, found Roberto lying at the bottom of a pile of bodies next to a small boy and his father. He'd campaign for the rest of his life to prove that UEFA were culpable in the deaths of those people.

The accounts of the victims of Heysel are hardly, if ever, recounted. The fear innocent people felt as the fence came down before they fled for safety is seldom retold. Heysel, in Italy and in England, for supporters of teams not involved that night, instead became an opportunity to score points. It was weaponised. 'It's a haunting thing,' says Kevin Sampson, 'because nobody should ever go to a football match and not come back.'

A disaster of such magnitude had been coming. In 1984, twelve Liverpool fans were injured when a wall fell down in a Milk Cup semi-final at Walsall; Graeme Souness carried a child to safety. The facilities were poor and a culture of violence had married a deteriorating society. 'Violence always goes up when poverty rises and it was a particularly violent time,' Tony Evans plainly states.

A few weeks before Heysel, at a game between Birmingham City and Leeds United, 45 policemen were injured and 125 fans arrested in scenes likened by Popplewell – the investigating judge - to being more like the Battle of Agincourt than a football match. Another boy, Ian Hambridge (15-years of age) had retreated to a wall for shelter. It fell on him and killed him. It was his first game.

That same day, 56 people died at Valley Parade as a small fire started by a dropped cigarette quickly engulfed an entire, highly-flammable stand, which had locked turnstiles and no extinguishers. Legislation for protecting fans was not in place. The mood around football was at an all-time low.

Despite the times, Liverpool fans still had a good reputation. They'd been in European competition for 21 years prior to 1985, encountering remarkably few incidents of repute in that time. The match against Juventus in May was to be their fifth European final in eight year.

Accounts of the day vary. It began well, apparently, and was sunny with a good atmosphere, with the Grand Place in Brussels acting as a fine point of congregation for all fans. They met up, got photographs together and swapped memorabilia. The black and white of Juventus mingled comfortably in with the red of Liverpool for most of the afternoon. Gerry Blayney, a devoted supporter, wrote: 'The day started brilliantly. Everything seemed so special. There was loads of friendly banter with the Italians and the atmosphere was almost perfect.'

Other accounts say different - stating that there'd been a nasty undercurrent from the off, evident in Ostend the night before. News came out then that Joe Fagan was set to retire after the match, and that Kenny Dalglish was to take his job. It was most untypical for Liverpool to approach business in such a manner - to announce something so big before such a game - but a lot of that occasion was to be atypical.

Throughout the 1980s fans from other clubs in England had been travelling to European Cup finals to soak up the occasion (there'd been a great number of Scousers in Rotterdam in 1982 watching Aston Villa beat Bayern Munich, before returning to Liverpool with new trainers). With Brussels being a simple ferry journey from Dover, hundreds of non-Liverpool supporters made the trip over. Was that a factor in the disaster? To suggest so would be astonishing. When the footage of the charge that led to the deaths of 39 supporters came out afterwards, it was led undeniably by Liverpool supporters.

There were two sides in Belgium that day. Both were mostly made up of good people, while both had others seeking the thrill of – having been steeped in – a culture of violence. In the 1970s *Ultra* groups in Italy had been purveyors of local heritage. They had a code of honour and a way of acting that projected their communities positively. But in the years immediately before Heysel that code had disintegrated into misbehaviour, attracting young men who were absorbed in the more aggressive aspects of the movement, given publicity by the media.

They'd have a role to play in Brussels, too.

As morning became afternoon and the sun continued to beat down, 'banter' was replaced by edginess. Fans-come-writers Brian Reade and Tony Evans both describe the sweeping mentality among fans that this day wasn't going to be like Rome; that Scousers were ready for potential violence and organised ambushes. 'It wasn't about getting revenge,' says Evans, 'it was about not being caught out again.'

There had been minor scuffles at points throughout the day and a bit of a mood, but nothing as sinister as Rome the year before. Gerry Blayney recognised that things soured overwhelmingly later in the day, outside the ground, as the sight of the stadium was met with the presence of heavy-handed policing. Keith Cooper of UEFA had been attending a ceremony in the centre of Brussels with all of football's bigwigs. He'd visited Heysel in the afternoon and returned with a piece of rubble. 'This is from the stadium,' he told them. They already knew.

UEFA were well aware of how dilapidated Heysel was, but they let the game proceed regardless. Arsenal had complained to them about the stadium in 1981. It had a reputation already. Back in 1984 Liverpool's CEO, Peter Robinson, knew that there would be trouble in Rome but held faith in football's governing body and refused to ask for a change of stadium. 'It is not in Liverpool's style,' he'd said. But the following year as soon as he saw that the final was set to be played at Heysel he immediately requested an alternative location.

He was rejected. Riot police set the tone for the occasion with random beatings outside the ground, while the perimeter of the stadium was kicked in by fans wanting quick entry. Huge holes in the exterior allowed anybody to walk through. Tickets went unchecked. Inside the ground, rubble was thrown at Alan Hansen and Alan Kennedy as they walked past Juventus' end.

Did Juve supporters already resent Liverpudlians before the game? The socialist wing of the European Parliament in their 'Against Racism and Fascism in Europe' report, published in October 1986, said so: *"On the Italian side it was discovered that young fascist militants had also travelled to Belgium with the intention of having a confrontation with the Liverpool "Reds". They had been told that Liverpool was run by a communist-dominated administration,"* in reference to Militant. It looked in hindsight to be another wild pointed finger.

Heysel's 'neutral' section, Block Z, was filled with Juventus supporters. Some of them threw missiles into Liverpool's end and the gesture was returned; there were charges back and forth between the two sets of supporters as well - standard behaviour for the time. A competent police force would have dealt with it easily. But one week earlier the Pope had visited Brussels. It had been a massive security operation and the very best of Belgium's riot force had served overtime. They were allowed to take the final off, leaving a squadron of misfits in charge of the European Cup final.

Events would be contextualised by a 2005 BBC documentary which determined that, firstly, Liverpool fans had been attacked in Block Z. They then tore down the chicken-wire fence separating them from the assailants. Reds charged the area. Police offered no resistance. Juventus fans fled to safety. They tried to climb a wall to escape. The wall crumbled. It fell on top of the people below at 7:31pm. Contrary to popular belief, according to the BBC, the falling wall did not kill fans. Rather, it released pressure and allowed many to escape. The victims died from suffocation, having been trampled on by others trying to flee.

Liverpool did that: a collection of the club's fans caused that terror and confusion. In one brief moment, the local stereotype shifted from one of laughter to slaughter.

Heysel stadium didn't have a police command section, but word spread quickly of the incident as Juventus' fleeing fans jumped into other sections of the ground. There was an announcement in Italian and then, suddenly, a group of Juve fans came marching towards the Liverpool end, seeking revenge. One of them had a pistol. As far as the majority of Liverpool's support was concerned, oblivious to events, it was because of this mad behaviour by the Italians that kick-off had been delayed. Liverpool fans shouted abuse at them: they were the ones acting like the bad guys it seemed to most in attendance.

Juventus were the ones who had destroyed the stadium. They had fought with police. They'd brought a massive 'Red Animals' banner. They were the ones on the running track looking for confrontation, and now they had a pistol?

George Sephton was inside the command centre observing events. For a third time at a European Cup final he was threatened with a firearm. 'After the disaster, the UEFA delegate came to see me and my opposite number from Turin and said to us that we must tell the fans to keep off the pitch, otherwise the game would be abandoned. I said *"that's crazy, if one team score all of the fans will go on the pitch to try and end the game."* I refused, so he returned with a policeman who pointed a gun at me and told me to do as I was told. Phil Neal came in having heard all of this and laid into the both of them.'

With dead bodies lying around the stadium and panic reigning supreme, UEFA decided to play the match. Juventus won 1-0. Despite knowing people had died, the majority of Juventus' squad celebrated crazily. Their fans were bemused – some stood there transfixed despite having ripped clothes and bloody faces. There had been no mention on the loudspeaker of anybody dying; things couldn't have been that bad?

Coming out of the ground thousands of *Juventini* were cheering in delight. But when they found out that their own fans had died following a charge by Liverpool supporters, their mood changed instantly. The police and army were finally prepared. Horses kept the Italians away from Reds, who were herded onto buses and sent away.

Inside the stadium (now a crime scene), Liverpool's teenage reserve keeper Chris Pile from Huyton went for a walk with Craig Johnston. They saw imprints on the pitch from hooves and saw debris everywhere. They took a wrong turn and, according to Pile: "Ended up in a gym where some of the bodies were being laid out."[xv]

With Brussels in chaos, Roy Evans sat in a local hospital. Mark Lawrenson had gotten injured in the 3rd minute of the game and was operated upon. When he awoke, there was an armed guard at the foot of his bed. Hospital staff asked Evans to remove his club colours in fear of people being antagonised, but he refused. He didn't know the full extent of what had happened, but in his view the actions of a small few did not represent the whole; Evans and the staff had done nothing wrong.

Liverpool fans would be generalised as 'murderers' instantly. 14 people were found guilty of manslaughter. Of the 25,000 Reds in attendance, 0.06% caused people to die. [45]

Kevin Sampson recalls the reaction: 'It only emerged for us a few hours after the game about there being deaths and how many. We were staying in Ostend and everybody knew we were Liverpool fans. We felt as low as possible and couldn't wait to get home. When we got back to the city there was a palpable post-apocalyptic mood with people asking what went on. Everybody was trying to process it and comprehend how such a joyful day ended with scenes of such horror.'

*

Joe Fagan cried on the runway when the plane landed. His great career in football had ended under a cloud. "He found it incomprehensible. He lived with it all it his life," his grandson would say. "He had served in the Royal Navy during the war; he understood what was a game and what was not. He never really talked about it at home, he simply carried it with him."[46]

For weeks after the disaster Heysel dominated news segments. Every day there was a different photograph on TV with a circled 'wanted' face. 'Initially there was massive denial,' remembers Tony Evans of the immediately days. 'One of the reasons was because we were so used to our name being blackened and the wagons circling that the default response was to say "bollocks to that". Another reason was because that's not how we generally acted.'

Margaret Thatcher was involved from the off. Peter Robinson knew what her decision was going to be. A year earlier, before Rome, he'd stated "If things go wrong, we could find Liverpool winning the European Cup yet banned from playing in it again next season. It's as serious as that." There was a desire to end match violence.

In *Two Tribes*, Evans wrote that the morning after Heysel, Thatcher summoned a collection of football's most renowned journalists for a meeting. She assembled them to hear their perspectives on what had caused the disaster, but

---

[45] Of the 25,000 Reds in attendance, 0.06% caused people to die. Of the 771,000,000 Liverpool fans worldwide (according to Forbes) then 0.0000018158% can be labelled as 'murderers', although to do so would be over-simplistic and narrow-minded. The majority of the 771m were born after 1985. 'Murderers' is chanted by rivals to elevate their sense of self, caring not for the people who passed away.

[46] 'Found in a loft: Fagan's secret boot room diaries | The Independent'

refused to listen when she found that their opinions contrasted her predetermined views.

She believed that the trouble at football matches was because of flaws in the makeup of the individuals involved. The assembled journalists tried to force upon her the view that social economic neglect in working-class areas, from which football fans were drawn, played a significant part in the unruliness of matches. There were two schools of thought at play. The perspectives were divided on political grounds. Neil Kinnock was with the journalists when he said:

"The problem of football crowd violence is deep-rooted and it has many causes, of which one of the most important is long-term unemployment, especially among the young. We cannot hope to tackle this problem so long as we have a government which gives no priority whatsoever to tackling unemployment."

Labour's was considered to be the open-minded stance. The Economist – centrist – wrote: 'We have to ask ourselves not what is wrong with football, but with Britain as a whole.' But Thatcher saw it as the responsibility of the individual to act accordingly. She would publicly state her bemusement that two sets of fans could not stand alongside each other without the desire to fight. She was naïve to the conditions of the time. And where had this frenzied Prime Minister been when Liverpool fans had been hospitalised *en masse* in Rome?

Her office had been waiting to enforce draconian measures for some time and roundly decided to ban all English sides from Europe – not just Liverpool FC, but every qualifiable team. She sent her measures to the Football Association to carry out, which they did.

Everton's camp rose in bemusement. They'd won the league and were at their greatest ever point. It wasn't their fault. A collection of their players would concede in later years (particularly the liberal thinking duo of Peter Reid and Neville Southall) that the ban came from a desire to stamp out a working-class pastime, and that it was another opportunity to blacken the name of a city already out on its own.

The absurdity was complete when, despite being banned from competing, FIFA's president Joao Havelange named Everton as the World Soccer team of the year a few weeks later.

Then began the season of reports. First came the Popplewell investigation into crowd safety, which had been commissioned prior to Heysel but was extended to incorporate the disaster. It found that the first disturbances occurred in the Juventus end of the ground, with fighting between supporters and the police. This, the report wrote, led to missile-throwing in Block Z. Prosecutions came from television footage of the charge, which had been the third in a few minutes and had caused the death of 39 people (no amount of prior context excuses the savage thinking of a third charge). 26 supporters stood trial, 14 were found guilty of involuntary manslaughter and were sentenced to three years in prison. £5m was awarded to the families of the victims in damages – token money: something the living do to smooth over the dead.

Then came the charges elsewhere. The police captain responsible for security that day was sentenced. The general secretary of the Belgian FA, Albert Roosens, was given six months for negligence. Two senior police officers were named for extraordinary negligence. UEFA barred Belgium from hosting another final for 10 years. UEFA had taken 85% of the profits from the occasion, did they not have a duty of care? It seemed that they did: Jacques Georges, the president, and Hans Bangerter, his Swiss colleague, were given conditional charges.

Otello Lorentini, father of Roberto, discovered that both Juventus and Liverpool had refused to play at Heysel because of its condition, but UEFA dismissed their complaints and forced the game to go ahead. The Belgian government sat and said nothing. Eventually an inquiry by Marina Coppieters (a leading EU judge) found them culpable for 'a catalogue of incompetence'. With all things considered, Nick Hornby reflected in 'Fever Pitch' that the disaster and the ensuing ban could easily have been caused by Arsenal or any side competing that evening.

But it was Liverpool. And any fan involved who took reassurance from other sentencing did so with false comfort.

Alongside the imprisonments, many members of the public suggested a return of compulsory national service for all men of age – '*that ought to sort them out*'. Smouldering from his failed takeover of Manchester United, Daily Mirror owner Robert Maxwell asked: "Why have the Liverpool fans turned nasty? The answer is the Militant Tendency, as an example in Liverpool that has taken over. They have shown elected councillors and MPs they don't care for society, or civilised behaviour. This is the kind of thing that encourages hooliganism." It was a bizarre link and an easily refutable statement.

Militant, for all their criticism, were the first group to ensure that Liverpool as a city did not shirk away from its role in events. Almost immediately the City Council reached out to their opposite number in Turin. It was decided that a group of delegates would travel over on a peace-giving mission. 'We will be exchanging views with the Turin authorities about how we should jointly tackle the social conditions which lead to much of the violence happening in society,' said Derek Hatton. As a manufacturing area, Turin too was struggling with economic decline.

Representatives from Everton and Liverpool FC travelled to northern Italy with church leaders Worlock and Sheppard, as well as Hatton and Mulhearn. The Echo pleaded: "Let us for once forget politics and act in a manner worthy of this moment."

Had Liverpool City Council failed to reach out to the grieving people of Turin, they would have been tarred as heartless. It would seem that they couldn't win: 'It is insensitive and too early,' said local Tory leader Chris Hallows. The Daily Mail too wrote: "Liverpool Militants leading [the city's] peace mission over the Brussels disaster turned it into a political football yesterday as they flew to Italy." The press felt it was all distasteful and in the wrong spirit. Hatton had said before departing: 'We will be going to establish links with the socialist parties and trade unionists in Turin, collectively to fight the root causes of the hopelessness felt by many young people.' It was easy for the press to skew such a comment.

The delegation visited factories in Turin and met with the local socialist Mayor. Militant even sent Terry Harrison to Milan to speak at a meeting organised by the Italian Communist Party about 'the struggle for socialism in Europe'. Was Militant capitalising? They denied it. Hatton and other members of the council reported how friendly the families of victims were to them, and how seemingly appreciative they were of the visit.

It was then decided that there would be ceremonies in both cities to mark the disaster. But Turin would only hold one more mass in the next thirty years, with the disaster hushed by both Juventus and locals alike. Andrea Lorentini, Roberto's son, would campaign heavily for the club to recognise the victims. He'd go on to write how the bereaved were faced with "bewilderment, reticence, guilty silences and suspicion," by Juventus.

For the majority of Juve supporters, they won their first European Cup in 1996 against Ajax - 1985 would be just a statistic. Gianni Agnelli, the club's owner, had been flying to Heysel but turned his helicopter around when he heard of the violence. 'We have not won the European Cup,' he said later. 'Winning in those circumstances did not count.' Platini, having celebrated like he did, tarnished his reputation. Taking on a role at UEFA further villainised him to many Juventus fans. With dead bodies in the car park, the players had chanted '*glory, glory, Hallelujah*' together. Then afterwards, despite fully knowing how many people had died, Juve's defender Sergio Brio posed for photographers lifting the trophy high above his head. It was all too distasteful to bear.

Council leaders and delegates agreeing to meet up was one thing – they were paid for their professionalism - but for fans of the clubs to meet just a few months after the disaster was an entirely different matter. Negotiations were complex. The inner-circles of both groups had to be consulted. Links were tenuous but grew out of a connection between Kevin Sampson and a *Juventini* named Mauro.

He recalls where the friendship began: 'We were playing Roda in Amsterdam in a tournament in the early '80s and were waiting for a ferry at the port of Calais. This lad came over who looked a lot like a Scouser and said: "Excuse me my friend, is it possible to have a beer?" He introduced himself by his second name and said he was a Juventus fan. They'd been playing Celtic and he was hitching his way back to Turin. We got talking and swapped addresses. I got a letter from him which wrote '*It is my dream to stand on the Kop and sing the song of scarves*' meaning 'YNWA'. That was around 1981 and he used to come every winter. He loved Liverpool at Christmas, with all the girls singing in the pubs. Obviously the big thing we said was "*wouldn't it be great if we played you*" and it happened. And it was Heysel. It's amazing that our friendship survived that because he was under pressure from his mates to fuck us off. The opposite was true however. Roy Bentham was connected to the City Council somehow and Peter Hooton was a youth worker and they went to Town Hall and said that they'd like to do a friendship trip as a gesture. I was the conduit to the Juventus fans and we brought over a coach-load of 45 of them and took them around the city.'

Before they came, the visit had to be given the blessing of the main hardcore *Ultras* at Juve. The 45 fans who flew over were given free accommodation in the Holiday Inn on Paradise Street; they were taken to State and given free drinks; restaurants in town provided free meals – there was a sincere desire to repair the damage. At Town Hall, they were greeted by City Council representatives who took them on a tour of Anfield where they had their pictures taken on the Kop. A concert had been organised for them on the Royal Iris ferry which John Peel DJ'd, with songs from Groundpig and the Farm. When Peel played 'Solsbury Hill', an inebriated contingent of fans took to the stage in the middle of the Mersey: Liverpool, Everton and Juventus alike. 'Our friendship, rather than withering, actually flourished,' said Sampson.

While the people of Liverpool – both in power and on the ground floor – attempted to present themselves in the best possible light, the higher echelons of

British society continued to berate them. At a conference in Mexico City, Thatcher described Scousers as being from "a city possessed with a particularly violent nature."

It had become a hushed policy to isolate Liverpool, reinforced by the written media, in order to deter other councils from taking an equally militant stance. As well as using Heysel, the press began to refer to Liverpool as 'smack city' despite heroin being an overwhelmingly British phenomena, from Edinburgh down to London (*'choose life'*).

Data collected by the Home Office found that heroin usage was in decline on Merseyside and on the rise elsewhere in the country from 1985, particularly in Greater Manchester and London. The report also showed that drug usage in the Ford Estate in Birkenhead had been brought on by 'despondent unemployment' in the first instance. It was easy to label Merseyside as the main consumer region, especially after a Pakistani ship carrying £1m worth of heroin was very publicly seized in Ellesmere Port.

Tony Mulhearn wrote about the attempts to stand the city out on its own: "The government confidently expected that this isolation would evoke a more responsible attitude by the Labour movement. A chastened Liverpool would carry out the same kind of compromises as other councils had done."

In the end Thatcher needn't have worried. Militant orchestrated their own downfall. With money running out, the council made the fateful decision to issue fake redundancy notices to its entire workforce. 31,000 letters were sent out by members driving door-to-door and by local private taxi companies too. It was insensitive and bizarre. The point Militant were attempting to make was that unless more money was made available to Liverpool from the government, then jobs would really be on the line. Accompanying the redundancies was a note stressing not to worry, that they had no intention of actually letting anybody go.

But with a redundancy letter in their hands, what were people to think? Panic ensued. The trade unions instantly removed their support. The reaction blew out of Militant's control. It had been the most incredible miscalculation. They imploded. On the morning of September 16[th,] the decision was to be taken on approving the redundancy notices, but a local member had locked up the Town Hall and barred anybody from entering. There was a security force outside and other local members denied Militant the opportunity to democratise.

In October the NUT brought legal action against Militant for the notices; but the killer blow came at the annual Labour Party conference in Bournemouth. Neil

Kinnock finally came down hard on Tendency with the nation watching. In his speech, he said:

> "I'll tell you what happens with impossible promises. You start with far-fetched resolutions. They are then pickled into a rigid dogma, a code, and you go through the years sticking to that, out-dated, mis-placed, irrelevant to the real needs, and you end in the grotesque chaos of a Labour council – a Labour council - hiring taxis to scuttle around a city handing out redundancy notices to its own workers."

It was met with rapturous applause. Hatton shouted '*liar!*' - Heffer stormed out. Kinnock had used 'scuttle' as a metaphor for a sinister form of vermin, unwanted in a home. October saw thousands of people march against Militant, using the mobilised tactics inspired by them, against them. They gathered at the Pier Head and chanted for Labour to 'kick them out'. There was even an anti-Militant record released.

The purging of councillors then began. The district auditor banned many of the most familiar faces from public office for five years. Housing chair Tony Byrne was out, so too was Derek Hatton. The Liberals capitalised on their community politics of the time and exerted a major influence on the council... anything but the Tories. And next? It took 15 years to pay off the loans Militant took out from Switzerland and Japan. Tony Mulhearn became a taxi driver; Terry Fields worked evenings in a pub. Derek Hatton embraced capitalism.

He'd always been the face of the movement ("It was like a pop group - you needed someone upfront," said Terry Fields), so Hatton turned to Max Clifford to restore his image, who arranged for him to be snapped coming out of nightclubs with upper-class women. The tabloids enjoyed him: '*Di's Cousin Dates Degsy!*' wrote the Sun. He set up a PR firm, did television presenting, attended horse shows, starred in a watch advert, flashed his DEG5Y number plate on the back of his Jaguar; played King Rat in a Christmas panto, recounted battles with Thatcher and Kinnock in lucrative after-dinner talks, and left Liverpool with the highest council tax in the country.

1985 had been the most distressing of years. A divided council; a broken football club. 38 people trampled to death, the 39th died three months later. 32 Italians, 2 French, 4 Belgian, 1 Northern Irish. It wasn't until the year 2000 that Liverpool officially commemorated the anniversary of Heysel. Eventually a memorial plaque was hung outside Anfield. The website made a permanent place for Juventus' badge a few years later.

But the dead were part of a forgotten disaster, in both countries. Indeed, *L'Equipe* editor Jean-Philippe Leclaire wrote in his book on the disaster that: "Juventus have been as keen to forget Heysel as the club they beat that night." For Liverpool supporters who were there that evening, sorrow remained a genuine and permanent part of their lives. It went unspoken for many of them because of the pain of events.

For fans of other clubs, the 39 were collectivised into a stick to beat Liverpool and Juventus with. When the Reds played Fiorentina in 2009, a collection of their *Ultras* tried to twin a friendship with Kopites, unfurling a banner the length of *Curva Fiesole* which read: 'Welcome Reds – your story is for us a legend'. 'I looked at it and knew they weren't talking about five European Cups,' says Joel Rookwood, a university lecturer from Childwall. Thankfully Liverpudlians were just about culturally aware enough not to be used as pawns for Juventus' rivals.

In England, none could name them, nor indeed appreciate their nationalities, nor understand the circumstances of how they actually died, but many of Liverpool's rivals demanded Justice for Heysel. Not for the dead, who received some degree of it, but for themselves and their clubs, which was as distasteful and depraved as anything else.

And in the walled city of Cagliari, hopefully unaware, Andrea Casula's mother Anna would go in and dust the desk in her little boy's room. She, without a husband and a child, somehow attempted to go on.

Riposare in Pace:

Rocco Acerra, (29). Bruno Balli, (50). Alfons Bos, (35). Giancarlo Bruschera, (21). Andrea Casula, (11). Giovanni Casula, (44). Nino Cerullo, (24). Willy Chielens, (41). Giuseppina Conti, (17). Dirk Daeninckx, (38). Dionisio Fabbro, (51). Jacques François, (45). Eugenio Gagliano, (35). Francesco Galli, (24). Giancarlo Gonnelli, (20). Alberto Guarini, (21). Giovacchino Landini, (50). Roberto Lorentini, (31). Barbara Lusci, (58). Franco Martelli, (22). Loris Messore, (28). Gianni Mastroiaco, (20). Sergio Bastino Mazzino, (38). Luciano Rocco Papaluca, (38). Luigi Pidone, (31). Benito Pistolato, (50). Patrick Radcliffe, (38) Domenico Ragazzi, (44). Antonio Ragnanese, (49). Claude Robert, (27). Mario Ronchi, (43). Domenico Russo, (28). Tarcisio Salvi, (49). Gianfranco Sarto, (47). Amedeo Giuseppe Spolaore, (55). Mario Spanu, (41). Tarcisio Venturin, (23) Jean Michel Walla, (32). Claudio Zavaroni, (28)

Daniel Fieldsend

ALL TOGETHER NOW

It is 1986. At the seaside resort of Mar del Plata, four hours away from the city, the biggest teams in Buenos Aires are about to meet up for a tournament. Local fans will travel down together and portray the best of the city's football scene. Underneath the sunshine the determined young *bravas* will do anything to gain entry into the wide, open stadium, so they can stand together with supporters from other neighbourhoods. They'll climb up onto the roof of the ground; they will scale through high windows; they will forge tickets.

Outside the ground families congregate and eat *empanadas* and have barbecues and drink beer while their children play. They've come to watch San Lorenzo from the Boedo neighbourhood; Racing Club and Independiente from Avellaneda, whose stadiums are a mere block apart. They have come for River Plate and Boca Juniors, the dockland clubs, and for Arsenal de Sarandi, Quilmes, Lanus, Banfield, Tigre, Ferro and Gimnasia too, who make up the other teams.

It is a venue for civic pride and although it is four hours away, Mar del Plata offers itself as a scene of great localism, self-pride and identity. On this day the Reds of River Plate take over the city, winning *Torneos de Verano*. They prove that they are best team in the world: they have won the Libertadores and have beaten Steaua București in the Intercontinental Cup. Their fans show everybody that they are the best and most determined, risking life and limb to get into Mar del Plata, with the whole country watching.

Except in 1986 the best team in the world was Liverpool FC, and it was their fans who risked their lives on a much greater magnitude, climbing to the top of an 100,000-seater stadium because it was already overfilled by about 30,000 people (the upper rafters of Wembley – usually spacious – swelled with numbers as turnstile workers took sly tenners). It was Scousers, not Argentinians, who made the leap of faith to a window at Wembley, having shimmied up a 30-foot metal fence. And the Intercontinental Cup winners would have been Everton: the Blues were twice as good as the dour București side and could have taken River Plate, too. An English side had won 7 of the past 9 European Cups and Everton were Cup Winners Cup champions: they'd have been the bookies favourites for everything.

If *Torneos de Verano* was an opportunity to display civic identity for the people of Buenos Aires, then the FA Cup final of 1986 was a far greater magnification of this sentiment. Merseyside had the two best teams in the world and a populace surging with more civic pride than anywhere in the world, too.

On 10th May 1986 at 2:45pm the culmination of forty years of difference boiled up into one spectacular roar. As the last few bars of *God Save the Queen* settled down, the chant of 'Merseyside, Merseyside, Merseyside... Merseyside, Merseyside, Merseysi-ide... Merseyside, Merseyside, Merseyside. MERSEYSIDE, MERSEYSIDE!' belted out. It was louder than the climax of *Bohemian Rhapsody* two months later when Queen played Wembley, and was followed by the reinforced question of: 'Are you watching Manchester?'

Blues and Reds were supposed to be divided because of Heysel but they went to London with a city-first mindset. John Motson said as much: 'The whole world will have its eyes on Wembley today, to see how the fans act.' It had been a news topic on the morning of the final. BBC reported on the Hindawi affair, on the Wapping dispute, on the violent murders in Alexandra (South Africa), and on how Merseysiders had been behaving in London that weekend ("perfectly well," they said).

It had never been the 'friendly derby' like the press believed. There had been tensions in the past – in 1985 at Goodison a tiny group of fans pointed and chanted 'killers, killers!' at a group of Reds - but it had never been toxic like most other British derbies. Given the socio-political nature of the times, both sets of fans headed down to London fully aware that their city's reputation was on the line, a city they shared a passion for.

As was the case in '84, Scousers travelled down together. Father Brian Crane, the Everton chaplain, was filmed by cameras getting picked up at St Mary's church wearing a blue and white scarf over the top of his clergy shirt. 'We're all mates and neighbours, we can't fall out,' explained a fan with a large red rosette. David Sheppard spoke from the middle ground: 'It's been marvellous that both clubs have done so wonderfully well and it feels as though the city has picked up again [since Heysel]. The pride is very much ramped up with both clubs being in the final.'

If the occasion was a scientific experiment it'd show quite definitive results: 'pride' increased clearly when tangible 'neglect' was encountered. Nobody could measure it, only anthropologists could speculate. But the truth of the times was that Scousers in London had a heightened awareness of who they were and what it all meant, purely through the friction they had encountered with others.

Scouse journalist Linda Grant described the era: 'You felt as if the rest of the country wanted Liverpool drowned just off the coast of Ireland with all its whingeing population. Liverpool was Britain's Detroit, a city that had died through its own irrelevance to the modern economy.'[xvi]

Gary Shaw was aware of that sentiment. 'As far as you could tell the city was hated to a certain extent, both politically and socially. You understood that when you went to see Liverpool play away: everyone hated you; for being Scouse, for being working-class and having an opinion, and for thinking for yourself and for being a football fan... the sport was hated then.'

In 1986 the idea of being Scouse was in the gutter. Pubs in London wouldn't accept £20 notes because they believed them to be forgeries; shop owners followed Liverpudlians through the aisles; unemployment jokes became the norm. And it wasn't all imagined. 'People would flinch when you talked to them,' says Tony Evans.

Before the final, the BBC showed two rants from their go-to character Alf Garnett. Again, he spoke for the nation (why else would he be on national television?) when he said:

"They're so poor up in Liverpool with all their unemployed; how is it if they're so poor they can afford to be here? It's welfare isn't it, that we're paying? Both grounds are packed to the rafters and none of them are working up there so where is the bleedin' money coming from? The whole town is on the dole. It's costing the nation bloody millions. Where's the motivation? Can't get into Europe because of this bloody lot... coming down here... they don't pay rates up in Liverpool with that council. Hooligans, aren't they? Got us all banned out of Europe. It's not a European Cup is it? And all because of a load of drunken Scouse gits we're banned. They couldn't hold their duty-free liquor. Brand them for life..."

He then began shouting at the top of his voice and gesticulating:

"Brand them across the foreheads! They're muggers, rapists, unemployed and unemployable! We can see them! Whack them! Castrate them!"

Taking a sip of whiskey from the bottle, his act mellowed and he sighed his conclusion:

"We don't want a bloody Scouse cup final, do we?"

Back in the studio Des Lynam laughed: 'We always like to give you a level-headed point of view.' Jokes about castrating an entire city of people was seemingly normalised enough to be shown on the BBC as part of their FA Cup final build-up entertainment. There had been no such gags towards people from the mining town of Sunderland, the socialists from Manchester or the steelworkers from Wolverhampton when their teams played in finals during the '80s. Such areas had also been bastardised by Thatcherism - their populations had fallen and their manufacturing sectors had been killed - yet only Liverpool, it seemed, was joke-worthy.

Nine days earlier a comedy had debuted on TV about a family from Liverpool who stole things and cheated the system but saw it all as one-dimensional enjoyment. It was written by Carla Lane from West Derby and peaked at 21 million viewers, allowing a stereotype to flourish that Liverpool-people were criminal careerists. 'Obviously Bread didn't help,' Brendan Wyatt says. 'The media turned over a course of a decade, from 1977 until after Heysel.' Other cities were poor, but they were less amplified in the national psyche than Liverpudlians. 'We'd rub it in, we'd shout as loud as we could about how great we were doing, but the city was on its arse and we didn't have anything else to shout about.'

The Boswell/Lane image became an unfair stereotype which'd linger over Liverpool for thirty years. Steve McMahon knew the reality of the times. He'd been Kenny Dalglish's first signing in 1986 and, as a former Everton captain, had the weight of the city on his shoulders – a city he knew well.

'Growing up in Halewood was tough, but I didn't know anything else; that was just the way things were. I knew I had to go to school and knuckle down. My dad was a scaffolder who was unemployed and my mum was a dinner lady so we were the opposite of wealthy. It was difficult for me, I had to scramble to get to training. But when you have desire then it triumphs and that's all I ever wanted.'

McMahon came from a family of Blues. He'd been a ball boy at Goodison and became the player all of the Liverpool team hated most when he was captain of Everton's reserves. Aggressive, confrontational, determined, brave and a good player too. Howard Gayle couldn't stand him. He made his Everton debut in 1980 and was the fans' player of the year in his first season. A die-hard supporter himself – they loved him instantly. But the club sold him to Aston Villa and told the press that he'd wanted to leave: 'They cashed in on me because I was a commodity,' he said. 'They needed to sell me for financial purposes. Instead it came out that I wanted to leave and the whole thing was on my shoulders. That wasn't the case; I was portrayed as a Judas.'

At Aston Villa he maintained his standards and looked to be the nearest thing to Graeme Souness in England. Dalglish wanted to replace the bite that had been missing in midfield. 'If I hadn't been successful at Liverpool there might have been two sets of supporters hating me! It could have gone pear-shaped and I could have fallen by the wayside, because pressure is a big thing when you join Liverpool Football Club. You might be talented but you've got to handle pressure too. It's everything that comes with it. For me it was just like a hand to a glove, straight away I took to it.'

He endeared himself to the Kop instantly, scoring the winning goal against Everton in only his third appearance for the club. 'It just confirmed for the Evertonians what they perceived me to be. The Blues who I met were angry, because they saw one of their own leave and then later do well at Liverpool,' he said.

Playing against Everton in the FA Cup final could have given him some personal redemption. Not that he needed it. But despite the tie being set up for him, McMahon was injured. It appeared for Everton that selling him was the right thing to do, because their team, with the money recuperated, had become the envy of the nation.

Gary Lineker arrived from Leicester City at the start of the season and had scored 30 league goals, attracting interest from Terry Venables' Barcelona. With Mark Hughes already in Catalonia (hanging a Wales flag from his apartment balcony), Venables wanted to tap into the Heysel ban which would entice Platt, Waddle, Hoddle and Rush to the continent. Everton also had Graeme Sharp who'd score 19 goals, and Peter Reid who had been named the 1985 PFA Player of the Year. Neville Southall was the best goalkeeper in Europe and Kevin Ratcliffe was in the form of him life. They were formidable. But Liverpool were the champions.

Everton lost the title on 30th April when an Oxford United side containing John Aldridge and Ray Houghton beat them 1-0. Beforehand, they'd only lost two out of their last 29 matches. Liverpool were going into the final having been unbeaten in their past 17 games, with nine wins on the bounce and only one goal conceded in ten games. Merseyside's clubs were a class apart; 'The capital of football,' said John Motson during the build-up. Liverpool alone had won 30 prizes in the past 20 seasons. Andy Grey reluctantly conceded that they'd been the most successful team in the world in that period.

High above Wembley helicopters whirled, horns blurred, coaches sardined together and crowds gathered. Every ward inside the Royal hospital and Fazakerley hospital had wireless radios tuned in. Alder Hey was bedecked in red and blue bunting: nurses and doctors wore team rosettes. Excitement was at fever pitch. Sir John Moores took his seat with the other dignitaries. 90-years of age, he was a major shareholder in both clubs and had financed the possibility of the fixture years before.

The week leading up to the game had been a long one. Nobody could talk about anything else. '*Are you going*?' and '*how are you getting there*?' led the basis of every conversation. On the bank-holiday Monday Liverpool's team went to Haydock races to unwind. Sammy Lee had a horse running called Mr Quick. 'It certainly wasn't named after me,' he joked. 'If I hadn't been so heavy, I think I'd probably have been a jockey.' Peter Reid had gone to Haydock too – the teams were close friends. 'We can't let them win the double,' Reid told reporters.

Billy Butler (blue) of Radio Merseyside and Johnny Kennedy (red) of Radio City engaged in a week of back-and-forth mickey taking. On the Thursday Anfield hosted the final of the Unemployment League Cup – 98 teams whittled down to two. Mark Lawrenson was filmed playing a match against Gary Lineker at the Southport Snooker Hall. 'What's your biggest break?' Lineker was asked. 'A tackle from me,' Lawrenson quickly joked.

In Liverpool the Albert Dock, continuing its restoration, had its huge columns painted red for the incoming Granada studios. There was a sense of pure local optimism. Tickets began going on sale for a concert at the docks for later in the summer: Chaka Khan, UB40, Spandau Ballet, Run DMC and Frankie Goes to Hollywood would all be coming to town. But first, somebody had to win the final.

Scallies held on to the Everton coach as it drove down Wembley Way. The Blues were mobbed when they got off. There was a huge Italy flag waving in the Liverpool end. 'English football is desperate for this game to be a cracker,' said John Motson. A banner in the Everton end poked fun at somewhere down the Lancs: '*City of Manchester – Trophy Free Zone*'... 'Abide with Me' was drowned out emotionally and impressively by 'YNWA' by the Red half of Merseyside. Both sets of fans then claimed harmoniously: '*We're the pride of Merseyside*!' The whistle blew. It was time. The first ever Merseyside FA Cup final began.

*

Daniel Fieldsend

Back in the 1950s there were supporters who'd alternate between Goodison Park and Anfield depending on who was playing at home. There'd be Reds who went to watch Everton and Blues who'd go to watch Liverpool, but it wasn't entirely fluid. They weren't conflicted in their support – they knew which team was theirs.

Dave Bilsborrow, 80, has dedicated a life towards supporting Liverpool. He recognises a shift in the relationship between the clubs: 'I used to go to Everton games if Liverpool were away. We'd go in the Wilmslow and I'd be with my mate Tommy. A lot of fellers used to do it; Evertonians would go to Liverpool with their brothers. We all got on. Then it just changed. When I hear them called Blueshite now I don't take part in that. I used to drink in the Legion and if somebody said Redshite I'd just go away. I can't be doing with that.'

Immediately after the 86 final however the closeness was such that Steve McMahon said in an interview: 'It's just a pity one team had to get beat and there's heartbreak for some in the city. It was a fantastic occasion for Merseyside.' He was sat next to Graeme Sharp waiting for their joint flight back to Liverpool.

Kopites came out of Wembley delighted at having won the double. Evertonians were absolutely gutted. There was no animosity, no desire to fight, just an unspoken understanding. Reds needed to celebrate without Evertonians bringing them down and Blues needed to drown their sorrows without Reds in their faces. The two sets of fans went their separate ways.

Like with the Basque derby, fans knew that their actions had consequences for the local image, so they acted on their best behaviour. Scotland Yard said afterwards 'They can come back anytime' and Ian Ross of the Daily Post wrote: "A combined lap of honour in front of a sea of blue and red was confirmation, should it ever have been needed, that whatever divisions may exist in Liverpool the proud people of a much-maligned city are united by their common love of sport." Waiting for their older brothers and dads to come home, youngsters on Saxony Road in Kensington had a street party and shared two cakes.

The next day the players presented the trophy. Fans of both clubs came out to watch. 'Back in the day we were two rivals who were trying to win trophies,' says the player from Sparrow Hall, 'but you'd still see Everton and Liverpool fans at each other's side.'

They'd travelled down to Wembley together and had returned home together. Even though Everton fans had been denied the opportunity to watch their side play in Europe, and despite the fact they'd been pipped to the double themselves,

Locāl

they stayed and clapped Liverpool's players off the pitch. The following evening Tony Wilson sat down to anchor Granada Reports. He led with the sentiment of the occasion - a reference to a tough, long, post-Heysel season: 'Football,' he said, 'is standing back on its feet once more.'

Daniel Fieldsend

PASS IT ON

The European ban was a massive disappointment but was not initially a source of antagonism. "That's the only way you lot can stop us," Blues had joked. Both sets of supporters were just gutted that they couldn't pit their teams on the continent, but they both believed that before too long they'd be back competing. That wasn't to be the case and both Liverpool and Everton went through major changes after the ban. Arguably, their golden eras had ended years before it was lifted.

After the FA Cup final Gary Lineker was sold to Barcelona. He'd state later that he didn't really want to go, but £2.8m was good money and Everton wanted the cash. It was spent on relatively unknown figures, such as Stoke City winger Neil Adams and Wigan Athletic midfielder Kevin Langley who both arrived for a combined £270,000. Dave Watson – who used to thumb lifts to Liverpool away games – was signed from Norwich for £1m. Ian Snodin came in the winter for £800k. It worked in the short-term and Everton won the league in 1987, but things were already in decline. The board gave Howard Kendall a half-baked offer so he left for Athletic Bilbao, recommended to them by Liverpool's wily CEO Peter Robinson.

Everton stuttered, which was tantamount to taking a backward step in a fast-moving football world. Liverpool had done something similar after winning the double in '86, so they spent big on Beardsley, Barnes, Aldridge and Houghton to ensure it didn't happen again (it was football's loss that John Barnes was unable to play in Europe). Everton's investments didn't work out. McCall, Cottee, Hinchliffe and Newell didn't have the same effect as Liverpool's purchases. In 1992/1993 Everton signed nobody.

With the advent of the Premier League, clubs had more money than before. Football became big business and TV deals created stars of players. Everton were

Local

right there at the start with Philip Carter advocating for its formation and spending big once again. But the club misspent. Graham Stuart, Earl Barrett, Daniel Amokachi, Craig Short, Claus Thomsen, John Oster, Thomas Myhre, Olivier Dacourt, Ibrahima Bakayoko and Alex Nyarko were signed for high fees throughout the '90s but failed to deliver. The glue of success that bound Everton had gone ... the desire and ambition had faded. With a solid structure, the real talents enticed to the club would have stayed, but the likes of Gary Speed, Andrey Kanchelskis, Peter Beardsley and Martin Keown quickly moved on and had better careers elsewhere.

As Manchester United and Arsenal, who were very much on par with Everton a decade before, exploited new commercial opportunities, the Blues remained insular and barely upgraded their facilities and merchandising operations. Their executives appeared to be drawn from Lilliput. The club flirted dangerously with relegation at several points in the '90s and Mike Walker, who had cut his cloth at Colchester United before being given the Everton job, tallied a meagre 17%-win record.

1995's FA Cup victory was sandwiched between two nearby final-day escapes at Wimbledon and Coventry City. Fans invaded the pitch in 1998 after staying up on goal difference, but that joy quickly turned to anger at the chairmanship of Peter Johnson. Joe Royle left the squad in disarray; captain Dave Watson took over; Andy Gray was offered the job, but he got a better offer from Sky.

Howard Kendall became manager for a third time, but he was battling personal issues. Thriftiness was employed by the club as a legitimate measure. BBC Watchdog found that Everton had placed stickers of new sponsors One2One over the logo of their previous sponsors Danka. In this climate of weariness, Duncan Ferguson – the only person showing a willingness to fight for the shirt – became a legend. Captain Gary Speed was sold and was forced to sign a confidentiality agreement to not spill the beans on what was happening at the club.

John Moores died in 1993. Lord Grantchester left the board in 2000. When David Moyes arrived in 2002 the club re-mortgaged everything it had to remain active. There was constant talk of administration which contributed to a mood of dejection and annoyance. *'Everything would have been different were it not for the Heysel ban,'* became the rhetoric for fans, understandably. And it might have.

As the years progressed and Everton's fortunes worsened, Heysel became a reference point for their downfall. Had they won the European Cup in 1986, they may have grown into a larger club with an international fanbase and therefore would not have fallen into the Premier League wilderness. Or, on the other hand, the victory (had they actually won in '86) could have become a relic that stood for nothing at all. After all, did Aston Villa's and Nottingham Forest's European Cups prevent them from being relegated? At the end of an extremely hypothetical day, Everton still had the same unambitious, behind-the-times board, investing in under-par players.

But Forest and Villa fans had their day in the sunshine and Everton were denied theirs, and that left a sour taste for many. After their near relegations, a period of reflection took place. Instead of looking inwardly and recognising the major failings of the board, many pointed across Stanley Park and determined that the Heysel ban had ultimately, more than anything, ruined their club. As well as the poor, sorry and forgotten dead fans in Brussels, a small contingent of younger Blues grew up regarding themselves as the other victims of 1985.

'I think Everton's problem was they were given a diet of success and then starved of it,' says Joel Rookwood, 'and they didn't know how to deal with that. It was a good job that we weren't actually winning titles ourselves at the time.'

Throughout it all, though, Everton could win at Anfield. Between 1994 and 1999 Joe Royle's 'Dogs of War' went nine games unbeaten against Liverpool, with many Goodison Park victories thrown in the mix for good measure. But as the financial differences between the two clubs grew and derby successes dried up, so increased the animosity.

A flawed theory grew from Liverpool fans that they were innocents of any (if there was) genuine tension. Gary Ablett had scored on his debut as a teenager for Liverpool in the mid-80s. He was a regular for Kenny Dalglish but got less game time under Graeme Souness. By 1992 he was available for a transfer and received two offers: one from Tottenham and one from Everton. For as much as he loved the club, he loved the city too and wanted to stay local. He had a young family – son Fraser was only 1 – and the wage was higher at Everton, so he signed for them. Within a week Liverpool fans had graffitied the word 'Judas' on the wall of his home and had egged his windows. The hostility didn't last, but was it ever necessary?

Everton's great captain Peter Reid – an ardent supporter of the club and a beacon of Scouse identity, whose career was heavily affected by the Heysel ban – maintained a balanced view of what had curved the arc: "There were no attempts to find an alternative punishment [after Heysel], despite Liverpool's decision to withdraw from European competition," he wrote. "Margaret Thatcher wanted us all to suffer because that suited her dogma and the class warfare she was raging."[47] Reid points to the decision made after the disaster, when FA chairman Bert Millichip stood on the steps of Downing Street and announced that they'd adhere to the government's decision to ban all clubs, as a critical and largely forgotten moment.

What followed was a petty type of rivalry built on 'he said/she said' incidents, enabled in later years by social media friction, with a multitude of digs based around the idea of locality (and having ownership over it). Central to all antagonism was Heysel. Shouts of 'murderers', 'wall pushers' and '39 Italians' displayed partisanism without compassion.

On the periphery of Evertonian consciousness had been Manchester United's mockery of the disaster and their chants of 'Justice for the 39'. Joel Rookwood takes issue with the language used there, specifically the word 'Justice' as it referred to Hillsborough and the campaign led by Liverpool (and Everton) fans following what he describes as: '30 years of mistreatment, hurt, pain and anger, and of collective action to oppose it. And they know that. It is sly terminology.'

In return, a handful of Liverpool fans stoked the flames with jibes about Steaua Bucharest winning the European Cup in 1986. For many Evertonians, what actually riled them above all else was the condescending attitude of Reds who pretended not to care about them, downplaying the rivalry, whilst at the same time taking banners about Everton to European away matches.

For the authentic, activist, Liverpool fans – who enjoy Evertonians and wish them 'Happy 21st' birthdays and wave Tesco bags at Goodison – it is a myth that Reds don't care. 'It's your derby,' says Chris Hudson of the Spion Kop 1906 group. 'The first two fixtures I look for are Everton away and then Everton at home.' His twin brother Andrew Hudson agrees: 'It's red over blue. Fowler over Ferguson. If you're playing football on the pitch as kid and you're pretending to score past somebody, it's against Everton. I was jealous of Man United because they won everything but Everton is your derby.'

Andrew Hudson feels the Manchester United rivalry was built-up by Sky Sports and takes issue with the idea of it being a 'derby'. Joel Rookwood agrees: 'I think part of us pretending not to care about Everton is that there is a conscious thought process which goes into how we want our relationship with our rivals to be viewed, by them and by others. I think sometimes we act like Everton don't

---

[47] 'Heysel hit Everton harder than we thought says Peter Reid' – David Prentice – the Liverpool Echo.

matter, but I don't want Manchester United to think that we are their biggest rivals. They are not ours.'

Underpinning everything – the point scoring, tally keeping, being both obsessed with and offended by everything, collectively – was tribalism, in various manifestations. Rookwood states that: 'We won't sit here looking down on people for being tribalistic, because when Origi scores a last-minute goal all we want to do then is sing about them,' but there is a line to stay behind, and portraying tribalism in a non-violent and creative way is the only sound approach, he feels.

Steve McMahon played for both clubs. He sees what the rivalry is like now and remembers what it was like back in the day. 'There's a definite divide between the two sets of fans,' he says. 'All my family are Evertonians and I see how bitter it is now. It's like a religion for the people, like being either Catholic or Protestant – there is no in-between.'

But are things really that bad? 'Not really,' McMahon admits. 'You still see families who support each club so it's not beyond repair, there is just a few ardent fans on either side. In general, it's a rivalry, albeit a big one. I don't think it's as hostile as elsewhere.' Of that point he is correct. In Glasgow supporters go to the toilet in pairs on derby day whilst one fan watches the other's back.

In Liverpool it is uniquely different. There had to be a relationship between the clubs because both were linked tightly to the city, and the city to them, and they all shared (share) the same physical space.

Simon Hughes provides the perfect leveller: 'It might sound dramatic, but if you were out and there was a fight starting in another city and you heard a Scouse voice, you wouldn't wait to find out if he supported Liverpool or Everton before you jumped in to help him out: you'd help him out. I think that idea sort of erodes this perception of nastiness.'

Hughes' stance is a calming one: 'I don't see the relationship as being that bad to be honest. We co-exist; some of my best mates are Evertonians who I'd do anything for. It has become a bit pettier in recent years particularly with the rise of social media, but that hasn't helped things for anybody. We have loads in common. Everton do things a bit different, they want to be incorruptible and ultimately, they want to win. Liverpool on the other hand seems more united currently. We're accused of being deluded at times, but that delusion can help.'

Joel Rookwood has a theory: 'When we forget what matters and focus solely on the tribalism of footy, we're divided. But whenever we're faced with circumstances which require a response, we are united.'

Locāl

Nobody has more in common with local Reds than local Blues – two legions who dress the same, vote the same way and retain the same morals. When times were tough, the fans were there for each other. When Thatcher invaded the city, all Scousers came together to beat her back. When the dockers needed support, blue and red t-shirts became a feature. When Liverpool banned the Sun newspaper, Everton followed suit. When the city struggled to eat, the Blue Union and SOS came together to organise foodbanks. When Rhys Jones died, Liverpool stepped up for Everton, and when 96 Liverpool supporters died at Hillsborough, Everton stood with their neighbours. Every single step of the way.

Daniel Fieldsend

FEARLESS

'You say the hill's too steep to climb'

Merseyside was finally on the up. In the City Council elections of May 1987, the 33 wards voted out every single potential Conservative councillor in a cannon shot of the anti-Tory sentiment which would go on to typify Liverpool. Sir Trevor Jones' Liberals were beginning to grow in influence despite Labour's ruling, now that the Militants were all but gone.

But Liverpool was still Liverpool. The Beastie Boys had used the city as a springboard for popularity that month, staging a faux riot at the Royal Court – leading to the arrest of band member Adam Horovitz. It caused international news. "The audience chanted, *'We tamed the Beasties'* as the group left the stage," wrote The New York Times. It was all just a publicity showpiece for the band's tour, but it worked.

That summer the Maritime Museum opened on the prettier-by-the-day Albert Dock as Liverpool realised it was able to celebrate itself commercially. The following summer Prince Charles (without fangs) came to officially re-open the docks on a floating platform as champagne fizzed into the proud dark water. 1988 also saw the launch of *This Morning*, which simultaneously turned Richard and Judy into national icons and birthed the daytime TV market.

In September 1988, the most famous man in the world at the time, Michael Jackson, came to Aintree Racecourse for a one-off concert, conspicuously arriving with three black limousines and a police escort which travelled through Aigburth and Otterspool. 125,000 people attended the concert – the largest crowd for a solo artist in UK history, and his music could be heard all over north Liverpool, carried by the summer wind.

Good music, however, had a more homegrown flavour as just one month later the La's released *'There She Goes'*: a soundtrack of the times. As exciting as

Jackson may have been, coupled with the regeneration work taking place, nothing was as breathtaking as the Liverpool team of 1987/88.

Kenny Dalglish had built a formidable squad. Liverpool teams of old had always been robust, clever, talented and blessed with a knack for winning. This side was typified by flair: back heels, quick flicks, one-twos, outside-boot passes and dummies.

It wasn't until September 12th that home fans were able to see this assemblance of talented footballers. A sewer beneath the Kop had collapsed and needed repairing, having not been touched since it was built in 1860. John Aldridge had already broken scoring records by then. Liverpool would go on to amass 90 points over the course of the 'Samba' season, scoring 87 goals and lifting the league trophy with four games left to play.

Hansen, Nicol, Barnes, Mølby, Whelan, McMahon, Aldridge and Beardsley were amongst the most talented footballers on the continent in their positions and would almost certainly have beaten PSV in the European Cup final (in the same way Everton would have beaten Steaua) with ease.

Tom Finney – the best player Bill Shankly ever saw – was from a level-headed generation, but after Liverpool defeated Nottingham Forest 5-0 in May (it could have been 11 or 12), he gushed:

> "[The performance] was hard to describe. It was one of the finest exhibitions of football I have ever seen in my life. The speed the game was played at was tremendous. It was an exhibition that will never be bettered I don't think. There are so many good players in the side who work for each other and that makes all the difference. You see them up one minute then defending together the next. I think they are (the best of all time), you couldn't see it bettered anywhere, and I've seen Brazilians play. I'd put them above the Busby Babes and other teams."

1988/89 started with much of the same optimism. John Barnes breezed past defenders so fluidly it was almost impossible to stop him. The rhetoric in the press that he didn't turn up when he played for England only endeared him further to the Liverpool supporters.

In August, Ian Rush returned from Juventus. Nobody saw it coming. Fans knew that he hadn't exactly settled in Turin, but it wasn't until Radio City announced his return on August 18th that Scousers were aware. There was no press speculation, no jabbering from taxi drivers. Liverpool called a random press conference and out stepped Rush to everybody's shock. John Aldridge was unphased by it all, though, keeping the Welshman out of the team for most of the season.

Liverpool struggled in the league initially and were 7th after 9 games, with Millwall 2nd behind Norwich City. By December Liverpool had crept up to 4th having only lost once in their previous ten matches (an inspired teenage Paul Ince of West Ham had knocked the Reds out of the Littlewoods Cup), but then with 17 games gone Liverpool were quickly back down to 6th. It was becoming a rollercoaster campaign. Despite having 4 games in hand on Arsenal in February, Liverpool languished in 8th and Stan James put them at 9/1 for the title.

They'd failed to get going, but as was so often the case throughout the previous decades, something clicked for the Reds and they went on a tremendous run of form, not losing in the next 24 league and cup matches.

By mid-April Liverpool were bearing the fruits of their form and found themselves level with Arsenal: 32 played; 63 points each. Next up was the FA Cup semi-final against Nottingham Forest. It was the day that football stopped.

*

Back in 1981, scores of Tottenham supporters climbed out of the Leppings Lane terrace at Hillsborough and sat behind the goal because they were being crushed. 38 fans suffered injuries that day with numerous broken arms, as well as broken legs and stitches. After the crush the stadium was deemed unusable for semi-finals and was not selected between 1982 and 1987, but in 1988 Liverpool were made to play there.

The 1988 semi-final was dangerous. Sheffield Wednesday didn't have a safety certificate. After the game a panicked Kopite wrote to the FA:

"The whole area was packed solid to the point where it was impossible to move and where I, and others around me, felt considerable concern for personal safety. As a result of the crush an umbrella I was holding in my hand was snapped in half against the crush barrier in front of me... My concern over safety was such – at times it was impossible to breathe – that at half-time I managed to extricate myself from the terrace, having taken the view that my personal safety was more important than watching the second half."

The FA didn't respond. Not only did they neglect to review the safety of supporters, they chose the same venue again the following year for Liverpool versus Nottingham Forest.

Local

In between fixtures, there had been the appointment of a new face. Match commander Brian Mole had worked with Sheffield Wednesday for years and knew the stadium inside out. He knew football inside out too. Following a prank in his division when a new constable was kidnapped by several officers and held at gunpoint in a fake robbery, Mole was forced to move on. The incident had nothing to do with him. 19 days before the semi-final David Duckenfield was appointed as match commander, his first big job.

Few people were thinking about danger on the morning of the game, especially not the Liverpool supporters who made the trip to Sheffield. It was the most beautiful of beginnings: a tapestry of blue sky over a warm Saturday morning. There was a man on the corner of the Leppings Lane end selling sunglasses. Nothing could lessen the mood of the occasion, not even the roadworks on the M62, nor the policemen stopping cars to search for alcohol who caused a delay. Scousers had backed the miners years before and South Yorkshire Police remembered that fact (Scousers had reminded them of it in '88).

But the Reds arriving at Hillsborough were not late. In fact, given that the FA-produced ticket advised supporters to arrive at 2:45pm, they were early. But at 2:20pm there was a scene of mayhem outside the ground. The issue was the design of the stadium itself. The Leppings Lane end could only be entered midway through a terraced street. There were 7 turnstiles for 10,100 fans to get through. Nobody seemed to be moving anywhere. It was a bottleneck design and the absence of stewards giving instructions, or police officers filtering fans into the ground in stages, caused a mass congregation of people.

The main police presence came from mounted horses in the middle of the crowd who took up space and pushed people backwards through their own natural design. One of the horses got spooked, causing scores of people in its proximity to panic. The mood changed in an instant. Nobody seemed to be in charge. Normal procedure would have been to delay kick-off and reassure fans that they'd get into the ground eventually, where they could be directed into the appropriate spaces. But the match control office stayed quiet. Duckenfield stood watching the screens as police on the ground waited for instructions. '*For fucks sake open the gates, open the fucking gates!*' one officer shouted over the radio. Policemen did not swear on the wireless – clearly things were desperate.

Duckenfield panicked and gave the order. Gate C was opened by the police. But there was nobody waiting on the other side to direct the incoming fans – no police, no stewards. Just a huge tunnel and a sign that read: 'STANDING'. The central pen was already full. The West Stand around the corner was barely signposted or visible. People went straight down the opening. Had the match commander shown just a small degree of organisation and prior-thought, then disaster could have been avoided.

Peter Carney was amongst the fans who entered the directly facing tunnel. 'Let me tell you that there was no fucking pushing from the back. I shuffled down that tunnel and then hurtled by accident into it. What people don't know is that there was as a slope in the tunnel, so when you got to the edge you lost your footing and people caused a momentum.' Instantly there were people facing backwards; people on the floor; people climbing for their lives.

'My dad was there and he was above the Leppings Lane end,' says John Aldridge. 'He saw everything and said it was like a sea going out and leaving dead bodies behind it.' For those at the front it was like a tightening vice of pressure. Fences to the front and to the side, there was nowhere to go. Hundreds blacked out. The result was chaos and people instinctively started fighting for their lives. Peter Carney: 'I know fellers who had to crawl over others to get out of the pens. I know fellers who were on the floor and had to push bodies off them to get up themselves. That's you fighting to survive, and you were put in that situation by the people who made the arrangements.' There were people already dead stood on their feet. Others were distant, their features turning blue.

'If you have survived then well done you,' says Carney. 'And if you have survived and then helped somebody else then well done you, and well done you again. That's a completely different narrative than what was put out there afterwards.'

Phil Thompson was reserve coach at the time. He came out of the changing rooms and saw the police pushing Liverpool supporters back into the terraces, stating so in his autobiography. 'That's dead right,' says Carney, 'they had to fight to get past the coppers. The rescue started in the pens.' Fans began pulling others up out of the central pens by their arms – some already broken.

At 3:06pm the game was stopped. With supporters on the pitch having climbed to safety, and with others getting out through a tiny gate in the fence which had been opened, the referee ended the match. Nottingham Forest fans thought it was crowd trouble. '*You Scouse bastards,*' they chanted and '*Sign on, sign on*'. The police formed a cordon in front of them to stop fans from fighting, as per their instructions. In retrospect it showed a line of 150 coppers stood doing nothing to help while people in the Leppings Lane end were dying.

Local

42 ambulances lined up outside the ground but the police reported crowd trouble, so only 2 got onto the pitch. Fans became the heroes of the day, ripping down advertising hoardings to use as stretchers, pulling each other to safety and giving the kiss of life to victims. David Duckenfield stood watching from his control room. When FA secretary Graham Kelly stepped in to see what was happening, Duckenfield lied to him. He said that the fans had broken down Gate C and stormed in ticketless. Kelly reported this to the media. John Motson reported it to the nation. Nobody thought to question anybody else.

There were policemen and policewomen who were incredible in that moment, who acted instinctively and whose good natures ensured that lives were saved. They were on the ground floor doing the very best they could. Then there were those higher up who were part of an organisation that had a 'rotten leadership culture', inflicted with a desire to protect themselves at all costs, having shown at Orgreave in 1984 the little remorse they had for people – for their own people.

Outside the ground fans were confused, angry, sad, scared, numb: there was not one defining emotion. Bodies lay side by side outside the stadium walls – the police having formed a wall around them to prevent fans from seeing. Almost instantly the need to preserve themselves kicked in for those in the echelons of power. With the metal inside twisted like a warzone and with human debris on the terrace - shoes, spectacles, scarves - and with the bodies not yet cold inside a dark gymnasium, the *lies* were spread.

It fell from the mouths of coppers and it was pronounced on BBC News immediately: Liverpool supporters, seen drunk and without tickets, had stormed down Gate C to gain entry into the ground. But Gate C was intact. And none of them had seen it for themselves. Did nobody consider any collusion?

For SYP the cockroach-like instinct for self-preservation went from speculating to media sources to creating an actual case against fans. Senior officers told a shell-shocked force not to write anything in their pocket books (a bobby's bible) despite there being nearly 100 people dead. Then, against those poor innocent people who lay next to each other in the gym, a case was formed. The police checked their names against the criminal database and tested them for blood alcohol levels. Little boys with paper-rounds who'd gotten to the ground early and stood at the front so they could see the players they adored up close were checked for alcohol.

In his autobiography Phil Thompson referred to the lies. He was told by a policeman that Reds had broken down the gate: 'It sounded like people were getting their stories together,' he wrote. And they were. At the SYP social club that night, the Niagara, word spread of drunkenness and savagery from Liverpool fans. Insistent coppers were determined they'd be on the right side of any potential smear campaign.

Worried families who'd heard nothing from their loved-ones gathered at Lime Street station and waited for trains coming back from Sheffield. One by one a load of worn-down young fans arrived, were embraced and left with their relieved parents. Then there'd be only 3 trains left. Then 2. Then 1. Then there'd be parents left behind in an empty station with no son or daughter fearing the worst and not knowing where to turn.

So they drove to Sheffield with news reports on the radio telling them that almost 50 people had died. Then 60; 70; 80... And they were taken to a boy's club and told to wait in anguish together with other lost and anxious families, before being led to a room with a board on the wall. On it was a huge collection of polaroid pictures, with faces of bruised dead people on, and they were told to pick out their child or partner. The pictures were not in order so they had to look at every face. Then their loved one was wheeled out to them for confirmation, but if they broke down and tried to hug the body, they were shouted at: "This is now the property of the coroner," the police said. Families, numb, were asked to give a statement about their loved ones. Every question was about drink.

It was unfathomable to understand the pain they felt. They were on their knees in pain – the entire city was keeled over – which for a colluding press and establishment was the perfect time to kick them.

'Blame the victim,' says Peter Carney. 'Blame the victim, blame the victim. It goes on all of the time. Those who have power, the control, the means, they're always putting the victims down. It's a fight and a struggle. The whole thing about Hillsborough was to blame the victim.'

Uncaring toward the sensitivities of the situation, that families were shocked and in mourning, four senior South Yorkshire Police officers and their local MP, the Conservative Irvine Patnick, clammed up and closed ranks, sourcing to White's News Agency in Sheffield a series of smears which would pervert justice and flat-out ruin lives.

Families woke up having to digest their new realities – that they'd never see their loved ones walk in the room again, or hear their voices or their laughs and see their mannerisms, or watch them grow and succeed and have futures. Then on top of that deep unnatural pain, they had to suffer the press headlines on show in every corner shop in the country:

'DEAD FANS ROBBED BY DRUNK FANS' The Daily Star.
'They were drunk and violent and their actions were vile...' The Daily Mail.
'Police saw sick spectacle of pilfering from the dying,' The Daily Express.
'YOBS IN SEX JIBES OVER GIRLS' CORPSE' The Sheffield Star.
'Thousands of latecomers tried to force their way into the ground...' The Yorkshire Post.
'Fans In Drunken Attacks On Police' The Sheffield Star.
'Ticketless thugs staged crush to gain entry... attacked an ambulanceman, threatened firemen and punched and urinated on policemen as they gave the kiss of life to stricken victims.' The Sheffield Star

Peter McKay wrote in the London Evening Standard: '[The] catastrophe was caused first and foremost by violent enthusiasm for soccer and in this case the tribal passions of Liverpool supporters [who] literally killed themselves and others to be at the game.'

McKay's version of events was backed up the head of UEFA, Jacques Georges (the same fellow who was in charge of Heysel and was later given conditional charges, who almost definitely saw Hillsborough as an opportunity to credit himself). Georges pointed a fat finger wildly and sent the rhetoric continent-wide: "One had the impression that [Liverpool fans] were beasts waiting to charge into the arena." It was strange that he held such a view, given that he was not actually there.

Worse still for families, the journalistic desire to sensationalise was present closer to home. John Williams of the Liverpool Daily Post wrote: "The gatecrashers wreaked their fatal havoc ... Their uncontrolled fanaticism and mass hysteria... literally squeezed the life out of men, women and children ... yobbism at its most base ... Scouse killed Scouse for no better reason than 22 men were kicking a ball."

It must have felt for Brian Reade that he was swimming against the tide. He was a Huyton lad, still somewhat new to the profession, who, unlike the rest, had actually been at the game. For the same paper as Williams, he wrote with passion and conviction about what had happened.

> *"There were ticket problems last year and they were foreseeable this time. The fans complained and Liverpool FC complained to the FA and to the police. Nothing changed. The decision stood. For "safety reasons."*

It depends on your definition of safety. Mine does not include cramming one end of a ground while leaving enough space to play five-a-side on the opposite terracing.

On Saturday afternoon as I looked down at the heart-breaking sight of bodies piled up on the pitch below me, to my left there were clear gaps in the huge bank which had been set aside for the Nottingham Forest fans.

The families of the dead will not agree with the police idea of safety, especially as many policemen were assigned elsewhere. Ensuring safety.

As the Liverpool fans drove off the M1 they were greeted by 20 to 30 police who pulled them off the road and searched their cars, vans and coaches for drink. For safety reasons. On the main road into the city all pubs were shut. For safety reasons.

Outside the ground this year police say they saw large queues forming, so they opened the gate. For safety reasons.

Inside the ground when people turned blue as the life was crushed out of them, they pleaded with the police to let them out. But they were kept in their cages. For safety reasons.

When people needed medical help as they lay on the pitch drifting near to death, the response of the police was to form a line round the terraces and across the pitch, and to bring on the Alsatians. For safety reasons.

The Alsatians got into the ground but the ambulances didn't. Dozens more police were drafted in but the doctors and nurses weren't.

There was no shortage of boys in blue in the stadium but there was a critical shortage of oxygen machines.

But then this was only a football match. You wouldn't expect the authorities to have any contingency plans for dealing with people being crushed to death in a 50,000 crowd.

No. Just keep the animals in check in their cages. That's all you've got to worry about. That way there'll be no trouble and everyone will be safe. And if there is trouble, well, they'll probably deserve it. They're only football fans. They're only hooligans."

Reade was affected by what had happened then and like most people there would be affected for life. His article was perhaps the only version of truth available, and while it was an honest account, it was washed back by a massive tide of vilification, falsities, misconceptions and misplaced anger from elsewhere. On Wednesday came the biggest wave of all.

'THE TRUTH' wrote the Sun. It was the last headline Kelvin MacKenzie decided upon - he originally wanted to go with 'YOU SCUM'. As Britain's biggest selling newspaper, their word was taken as gospel. Harry Arnold had written about the allegations in a nuanced manner, but as he was leaving the office on Tuesday evening MacKenzie was busy sensationalising his article into a front-page spread, built on stereotypes.

The Sun stated that Scousers had robbed the dead, urinated on police officers and beat them up while they attempted to resuscitate other supporters. They painted Liverpudlians as being animalistic, savage, untamed and less than human. And the public believed them.

They believed them because they already had an idea of what Scouse people were supposedly like.

Dehumanisation happens over many years and is never an accident. When Ramsay MacDonald as acting Prime Minister said: 'Liverpool is rotten to the core and we better recognise it,' then people in corridors of power listened. When the press wrote about communist agitators on the docks and idle workers; of constant simmering tensions of one form or another... when they wrote about 'the harshness of waterfront life and bitterly combative Irish exile content,' which made the city seem lonely, and when they highlighted the 'festival of litter' and bare-faced drunkenness, 'a desire to live for the day' and spoke *about* but never *to* the people, it did something. It objectified them, and objects could be discarded.

This was a city known more recently for rioting, Militantism and Heysel. It was the place where you 'couldn't make water float upstream'. The people were regarded as animals, hence why the Daily Mirror got away with writing in 1982: "They should build a fence around Liverpool and charge admission. For sadly it has become a showcase of everything that has gone wrong in Britain's major cities," The Liverpool Zoo in 1982, The Liverpool Syndrome in 1981... Then on top of that, not only were the victims of Hillsborough mostly Liverpool people, they were also football fans, which according to the Sunday Times was: "A slum sport watched by slum people in slum stadiums."

Dehumanisation as an act allows other people to believe that the victims of an incident (or series of incidents) are less than human. It keeps a group at bay and enables them to be walked upon. There is a lack of dignity displayed to them, a complete lack of compassion, allowing certain powers-that-be to get away with literal murder, often profiting at the same time. Slave owners deployed it, Nazis deployed it, POWs suffered it, Muslims continue to suffer it – African Americans do too.

The fact that dehumanised people are likened to animals convinces the wider public that they don't feel in the same way that they do; they don't love or care or aspire like them. They should drink out of a different tap... sit at the back... sterilise and quash. When catastrophic things happen to a group of dehumanised people it is probably their fault; they act like animals anyway. When a group of dehumanised people die at a football match, it is somehow fathomable that the surviving members of the group would take out their penises and urinate on caregivers, because that's something an animal would do. Normal people would feel nauseous, but animals wouldn't. Lies were easily spread because of the preconceptions already well rooted in the minds of the majority group.

From Churchill sending gunboats up the Mersey to Alf Garnett making gags about castrating Liverpool people, pieces of information joined together like a whirlwind for suburban Brits to create a very vivid image of Scousers – 'a Sasquatch on our streets'. From the quiet of his study looking out onto Camden, Alan Bennett mused: "It would be Liverpool, that sentimental, self-dramatizing place. Liverpudlians have figured in too many plays and have a cockiness that comes from being told too often that they and their city are special." It would be Liverpool, he reckoned... Hillsborough had to happen to Liverpool.[48]

The Sun had an increasingly deteriorating readership on Merseyside anyway. It was Thatcherite in its essence and poked at Scousers weekly. But as soon as that article hit shelves the paper turned into a bastard overnight, burned on the streets of Kirkby and left untouched by delivery drivers all over the city. Not that the Sun cared. Rather, it continued to push a story that was selling well. 'I WAS ROBBED BY KOP YOBS' came Friday, and then the next day again 'THEY DRANK US DRY' – an interview with a Sheffield publican.

They were determined to find dirt on the people who had died. And *why*? Was it not tragic enough that people had died in the first place? Family members were harassed outside their homes and on their way to school. The Sun found out where they worked and camped outside. They were hounded. The Sun also attempted to pay neighbours tempting sums of money so they could hide in their house all day and take photographs of the grieving family members. With funeral

---

[48] Merseypride: Essays in Liverpool Exceptionalism. (2006), John Belchem.

Local

arrangements still yet to be made, the families were subjected to inhumane treatment.

*

Numb. The day after the disaster people got up (they hadn't slept) without any real idea what to do. There was no indication or spoken call to pilgrimage, yet spontaneously from early in the morning many supporters began congregating outside Anfield. Some people went to church and mourned, wept and prayed, while in the evening the requiem mass at Paddy's Wigwam overflowed with parishioners. But at Anfield throughout the day people continued to gather. More and more, unspoken they arrived at the Shankly gates with flowers and parcels. So many arrived that Peter Robinson decided to open the gates at noon. The club roughly organised the pilgrims into lines and offered unofficial counselling.

George Sephton was there. (His son had been in Sheffield on Saturday and had rung late on from a phone box in the hills of Yorkshire to tell his parents he was safe). 'My wife and daughter came with me to Anfield and we went up to the TV gantry. There was a sea of flowers which surpassed the half-way line. I was in shock that day.' For the next few weeks the Candy Lounge in the Main Stand would be open each day for counselling.

All that mourners wanted to do it seemed was be near the club. They laid flowers and paused, attempting to reflect upon what had happened. It was a reaction drawn from the 'Celtic' traditions of the city, as Grace Davie wrote: 'In coming to terms with their grief, Liverpool people found innovative and unusual ways to express themselves. Ways that drew from the depths of the city's history and culture.'

The Sunday pilgrimage to Anfield was a natural response for so many. They queued for hours in complete silence. By 5pm the Kop was awash with flowers. Scarves were tied around barriers – many in dedication to the fans who'd stood behind them. Over the course of the coming week, the flowers would reach out towards the centre of the pitch in a carpet of lilies and hydrangeas. One million people passed through Anfield – twice the city's population.

An overwhelming majority of the people who passed through Anfield were not personally bereaved. They were shaken by events and were either locals from the city or supporters from elsewhere, but were not all members of family. In their public grieving they displayed to the nation a form of community solidarity following death that had not been seen before. It reinforced Liverpool's sense of togetherness, something that was not accepted plainly. Edward Pearce of the Times continued with the same tiresome rhetoric:

> *"In the wake of the disaster the shrine in the Anfield goalmouth, the cursing of the police, all the theatricals, come sweetly to a city which is already the world capital of self-pity. There are soapy politicians to make a pet of Liverpool, and Liverpool itself is always standing by to make a pet of itself. 'Why us? Why are we treated like animals?' To which the plain answer is that a good and sufficient minority of you behave like animals."*

What Pearce failed to appreciate – he being an Oxbridge fellow from Shropshire – was the wraparound of familiarity which typified Liverpool people and Liverpool life. The city was built on a base of mutual support which, for others, was difficult to understand. As an outsider he was unappreciative of the need people had to come together *en masse*, describing it all as tawdry sentimentality.

For those affected by the disaster, it was enormously reassuring to experience. 'I love that word, community' said Frank Carlyle, mulling over its use: 'Liverpool city is a big community.' Tom Fairclough experienced a similar level of support when his mother died in 2011. 'Liverpool is a very emotional city and we celebrate our successes in a way some people say is over-celebrating, and we mourn in a way people say is over-mourning. There is a community thing about Liverpool that can set it apart.'

In the weeks after Hillsborough, the continuous visits to Anfield allowed people the opportunity to display quite publicly how they were feeling. It was new to Britain and confused many stiff-upper-lip types. 'Middle-class people throughout the country saw on Merseyside a model for the handling of grief to which they aspired, yet lacked the communal identity to achieve,' explained Tony Walter.[49] Classmates wrote messages for their friends who'd died that were shown on national news programmes. The constant flow of people felt more genuine than any official ceremony would have been.

At this time Kenny Dalglish was shown by cameras almost every day alongside one of the two leaders of the city's faiths: Catholic Archbishop Derek Worlock and the Anglican Bishop David Sheppard. All sects had been affected by the disaster, including those of both Red and Blue persuasion. It would become so common over the years to see church leaders on Merseyside together, but in 1989

---

[49] The Mourning after Hillsborough - Tony Walter, 1991.

it was still a very recent thing. A single generation earlier the two churches had not spoken, let alone stood together. Football had overtaken religion as a venue for identity and antagonism and the churches seemingly went along with the shift.

In its services commemorating the disaster, the Metropolitan Cathedral presented a huge red banner with a Liverbird sewn on by one of its sisters. Football related gifts were left rather than Christian tokens by the hundreds of people who gathered at the cathedral for services. When people were unable to get in due it being full, they laid their gifts down outside beneath a makeshift altar covered by a Liverpool banner. With Anfield described as a cathedral and the mourners referred to as 'pilgrims' by the press, the boundary between churchdom and footballdom blurred into one.

Both faiths offered counselling to the families and victims affected. Other relief was offered unexpectedly by the footballers and their wives. In the Candy Lounge, a rota was drawn up for players to go to funerals. Roy Evans wrote: "Young lads, usually focused on playing football, suddenly focused on helping people who had been struck by tragedy. Nobody backed off. To a man, they coped incredibly well." They attended half-a-dozen funerals each and watched their supporters grieve.

Ronnie Moran went to that of Paul Hewitson, a lad from Crosby who was a friend of his son Paul. Roy Evans went to that of his mate from Kirkby. Terry McDermott came home and went to 9 funerals with Phil Thompson. John Aldridge went to 12. It was true that everybody was affected by what had happened. Did Aldridge feel a mistrust of the establishment after it all? 'Oh yeah, 100%.'

*

Despite supporters attempting to get the truth across, the 'Lie' – floated by Duckenfield, Kelly, Patnick and other coppers – was already entrenched in the minds of the nation. Kevin Sampson remembers the time: 'I was working in London. It felt like we all had to go to Anfield, there was something quite comforting about laying flowers. I was unaware that there was an alternative narrative going on until I got into work on the Tuesday and the first thing I got was a couple of lads I was friendly with saying "Mad your fans though aren't they?" and I said *what do you mean?* They said, "You know, booting the gates in and jumping the turnstiles." I said *that's not what happened* but they were saying "Come on, no smoke without fire." That was right from the start.'

Scousers were not being listened to. The only bit of control they had was over what they consumed. People rang up Billy Butler day after day repeating the same message of boycotting the Sun, and while radio shows typically have a thirst for new content, Butler was more than happy to let them repeat the message. Corner shops sellotaped the same message to their windows on ripped out pieces of card: 'We don't sell The S*n'. It was a fight-back, an attempt to set the record straight.

Chris Horrie's book on the newspaper estimated that the boycott would go on to cost News International £15m per month for the next thirty years. The vivid image of women burning it in Kirkby was, according to him, the first time newspapers had been publicly burned on Britain's streets since the 1930s, when Jews in East London burnt copies of the Daily Mail in response to their front-page endorsement of Oswald Mosley and his pro-Nazi Blackshirts.

Sales in Merseyside dropped from 524,000 to a sorry figure just floating above one thousand in a decade. Sun editor William Newman replied in typical Sun fashion: 'If the price of a free press is a boycott of our newspaper, then it is a price we will have to pay.' The only apology was forced upon Kelvin MacKenzie by Rupert Murdoch (out of compassion or a concern at losing money?) although he later went on to say: 'I was not sorry then and I'm not sorry now.'

When the Hillsborough Justice Campaign began in 1998, the still-grassroots boycott became mobilised and was seen on stickers, banners and badges; visible in house windows and on the side of Hackney cabs. Simply, it became entrenched in local identity, deep within the fundamental principles of a Scouse constitution.

'People are conditioned in a way in which they don't really know the truth. They are guided by the media,' says Howard Gayle. 'The *'Don't Buy the S*n'* campaign has been massive because that paper should not be in this city and it will never come back. Those people who used to buy it were also governed by it; they thought if it was in the Sun it was true. A lot of people are like that, they don't source true information.'

'I don't buy the Sun,' says Steve McMahon. 'It's a Liverpool thing because of the stigma attached after what they printed. We discovered recently the whole circus afterwards was to cover the police's arses because they made mistakes and then blamed Liverpool supporters. It was a double whammy, people perished and then they lied and turned them into scapegoats.'

Did the players see the lies that were being printed? 'Of course, of course,' says McMahon. 'It was so easy for them to blame the fans because they didn't have a voice, but history tells us that the people of Liverpool have a very strong voice. Hillsborough was initially localised. If I was on a train in London and I saw a feller reading the Sun I'd pull him to task over it and say '*what are you doing reading that?*' but he probably wouldn't be fussed. Maybe that's just me, but I wouldn't be seen holding it.'

John Aldridge knew from the off that the newspapers were lying, because his dad told him plainly what had happened: 'He saw how the police were and he told me afterwards, "Nobody picked any pockets, nobody peed anywhere, nobody did anything wrong." My dad and I knew straight away what they were trying to do and I tried to help in whatever way I could, to get out there what the actual truth was. I had to say it for my own principles.'

The legacy of the article was not only to delay justice (akin to denying it) but it also reminded the public what a Liverpool person was apparently like. It affected Rickie Lambert early on in his career. 'I kind of knew the perception people had of Scousers from the way the Sun made us out to be. I knew people called us robbers and things like that, but when I moved away I could see it more. The outlook people had of us from outside of Liverpool was not nice. I've had arguments with fellow professionals in my team who've said something untrue and I've had to stand up for the city or for the Hillsborough victims. I was 10 when the disaster happened, so that was most ingrained in me. I grew up knowing how unjust it was and then I became aware of what was being said about us. I remember how Thatcher dealt with it and I felt separated from the government. It was like 'us' against 'everyone' and although there was still love for Scousers, there was a lot of hatred as well.'

For many, it was how Thatcher failed to deal with the disaster that was so shocking. A massive loss of life in her own country with so many children dead on a sunny afternoon, she refused to investigate the police force, or condemn them after the Taylor report came out. She failed to criticise any party involved and when the opportunity arose to campaign for justice for those who lost their lives, she did nothing.

It is rare to find any commentary from her surrounding the disaster, although an interaction she had with Margaret Aspinall, mother of James (18), inside Liverpool Cathedral in 1989 is telling:

Thatcher: "There were 750 police officers on duty on the day of the disaster."
Aspinall: "Please, tell me what they were doing, then?"
Thatcher: "Their job, my dear, their job."
Aspinall: "Well, how come 95 people [sic] died if they were doing their job?"
Thatcher: "I think I had better step away because you are so angry"

Daniel Fieldsend

It was at this moment that Margaret Aspinall realised the enormity of the battle the families had on their hands, against a government who were quite willing to walk away. It still remains unclear the extent of Margaret Thatcher's opinions on Hillsborough, but it was revealed thirty years later that she was cautious to back the criticisms of the police in the Taylor report: "The broad thrust is devastating criticism of the police. Is that for us to welcome?" she asked.

What is known is that upon visiting Hillsborough she was told by SYP that Liverpool fans were to blame, and by Douglas Hurd that Liverpool fans were historic trouble causers, and by Kenneth Oxford that ticketless fans were notorious for misbehaviour. Her mouth, the 'rottweiler' press secretary Bernard Ingham relayed the opinion that was fed to them both in April 1989, as Thatcher was walked through the deserted post-apocalyptic stadium by David Duckenfield. In a letter to Liverpool fan Graham Skinner, he wrote:

'Thank you for your letter of June 13th. I am sorry you were disgusted with the uncomfortable truth about the real cause of the Hillsborough disaster. It is my unhappy experience to find that most reasonable people outside of Merseyside recognise the truth of what I say.

All I get from Merseyside is abuse. I wonder why. You are at least right in believing that you will have to put up with my discomforting views. I cherish the hope that as time goes on you will come to recognise the truth of what I say.

After all, who if not the tanked up yobs who turned up late determined to get into the ground caused the disaster? To blame the police, even though they may have made mistakes, is contemptible.

Yours sincerely,

Sir Bernard Ingham.'

All of the letters, the articles, the lies and misconceptions from an establishment seemingly well-versed in deflecting blame show now the absolute weight of the task that families faced. But they took on the bastards.

'We stand up for our rights in Liverpool and that never subsides,' says David Fairclough. 'If you see a wrong being done you have to say something and I feel as though that's a Liverpool trait. It's in our make-up.'

'There was a long time when we thought *this isn't going anywhere*,' adds Kevin Sampson. 'It was only our immediate people in the city who knew what happened and it formed a siege mentality because nobody believed us. But we knew we were right. And we were going to fight.'

And fight they did.

Local

A timeline

19th April 1989. Wednesday. A packed crowd of 73,000 fans roared for A.C. Milan in the second leg of the semi-final against Real Madrid. Rijkaard, Gullit, van Basten, Baresi and Maldini – this was the best team in the world, led by Arrigo Sacchi, the best coach in the world. Milan's supporters were desperate for a win. The score was tied at 1-1 from the first leg. It had been a scrappy game to begin with, but Milan were just starting to get a hold of the match when the referee Alexis Ponnet from Belgium blew his whistle 6 minutes in.

He picked up the ball and the players stood still. The coaching staff on both benches stood up, as too did every supporter in the stadium. A tannoy announcement in Italian muffled something about *'Inglese'* and *'Sheffield'*. The whole stadium politely clapped. Despite being drenched right though, the Italians stood to show their respect. Then it became audible – not a growing noise but one that emerged straight away, collectively - the *Ultras* in Curva Sud were singing. *'Walk on, walk on, with hope, in your heart, and you'll never walk alone, you'll never walk alone...'* Ponnet put down the ball, gave it to Ancelotti and play resumed. Milan would go on to win 5-0. They'd win the cup the following month. (Forza Milan and Forza *Fossa*).

Although Liverpudlians were made to feel alone at times, especially by the media, they received a lot of support from a lot of good people following Hillsborough. Pope John Paul II, who had visited the city in 1982, sent his condolences. As too did George HW Bush and Queen Elizabeth. Gianni Agnelli, following Juventus' UEFA Cup triumph, said that his thoughts were with Liverpool. From Goodison Park, Everton linked two hundred scarves together – red and blue – which reached through Stanley Park and into Anfield's grounds. In Nottingham that same Sunday a minute's silence was being observed. Every ground up and down the country had some form of Liverpool memorabilia tied to its gates. Bradford City and Lincoln City had not met each other since the Bradford Fire Disaster in 1985, but they organised a friendly together and gave the money to the Hillsborough families.

Then came an appeal fund at the end of April 1989. The government gave £500,000. Liverpool FC donated £100,000. The city councils in Nottingham, Sheffield and Liverpool all donated £25,000. Schools and small businesses donated too. Within days the appeal had gone past £1m and would eventually reach £12m. *You'll never walk alone.* It was in this spirit that Glasgow Celtic organised a friendly match through John Smith and Kenny Dalglish. The player-manager was 38 and was going to funerals each day, whilst managing the biggest football club in the world. John Aldridge was publicly considering retirement from the game. 'The thought of training never entered my head. I remember trying to go jogging but I couldn't run. There was a time when I wondered if I would ever muster the strength to play,' Aldridge said.

Liverpool's terrace anthem went from being an historic battle cry at the start of the month to being a promise, a hymn and a fitting message of reassurance by the end of it. When Celtic supporters belted out 'YNWA' in their thick Glaswegian accents on the 30th April, it meant more than they probably realised. Celtic had reached out an arm to lift Liverpool back up. The Reds won the friendly 4-0, Aldridge scored 2 but didn't celebrate. John Smith told the press that the occasion had cemented the relationship not only between two clubs, 'but two cities'. Celtic supporters had their arms around Scousers inside the Jungle. When Reds presented a 'Thank you Celtic' banner, they were equally made up. '*Liverpool, Liverpool, Liverpool!*' chanted the Scots, once more in their distinctive accents. The Celtic supporters donated money into the thousands of charity buckets available throughout the ground during the game. Some £400,000 was raised inside Parkhead that afternoon – Glasgow council donated a further £25,000.

Of course, Liverpool's first competitive game after Hillsborough had to be against Everton. The Blues read out their sympathy on a tannoy as '*Merseyside, Merseyside, Mersey-si-ide!*' was belted by both sets of fans. After the minutes silence there was a spine-tingling rendition of YNWA from all supporters, perhaps for the last ever time. A flag went around the outside of the ground, a French tricolour of red, white and blue which read: 'LFC FANS – THANK – EFC FANS'. Another banner read: 'THE KOP THANKS YOU ALL, WE NEVER WALKED ALONE'. There was one more chorus of togetherness: '*Merseyside, Merseyside, Merseyside...*'

In May 1989 the Hillsborough Family Support Group (HFSG) was founded by families travelling to and from court for the Taylor Report inquiry. They met at the Vernon Sangster and elected a committee – a group that would go on to fight together for the memory of their loved ones.

On the 20th May the eventual FA Cup final was played. The fact that it went ahead felt insincere for many. They didn't know whether to celebrate or not when Liverpool beat Everton – who unfortunately for them were little more than a support act in something bigger, so wrote Brian Reade. The FA took fences down for the final - those metal barriers of death - yet some idiots still ran onto the pitch at the final whistle. Could people really be so thoughtless? After the game Roy Evans took the cup to a family in Kirkby who'd lost a loved one. Local kids saw him approaching the house and asked if they could play with it. He told them they could have it for fifteen minutes, that he trusted them. He entered the house to speak with the family and sure enough, fifteen minutes later, the kids knocked on the door with the cup.

Arsenal won the league at Anfield on the 26th May with the last kick of the game. Liverpudlians stayed behind to clap them, but life had been firmly placed into perspective. This, a last-gasp loss, was only football.

A moment of vindication came on the 1st August. Nobody expected anything from Lord Taylor. He was by all appearances another member of the establishment, and what had they ever done? Then he came on television with his findings: "It is a matter of regret ... that the South Yorkshire police were not prepared to concede that they were in any respect at fault. The police case was to blame the fans for being late and drunk ... It would have been more seemly and encouraging if responsibility had been faced." He pointed the finger not at fans, but at the police, which for so many people involved felt like a relief. At least now the media campaign against Liverpool fans could stop...

After the report came out, Douglas Hurd knew that the chief constable in charge would have to resign, or worse, because in his words "the enormity of the disaster, and the extent to which the inquiry blames the police, demand this." But Thatcher sent him a memo. "What do we mean by 'welcoming the broad thrust of the report'? The broad thrust is devastating criticism of the police. Is that for us to welcome?" Hurd was stuck. He couldn't call for Peter Wright's resignation. If he did then SYP would have to accept all responsibility. So they continued to lie and cover.

Then on the 30th August came the first legal blow: The Crown Prosecution Service decided that there was 'insufficient evidence' to carry out criminal proceedings against any person or group involved. South Yorkshire Police and Sheffield Wednesday Football Club were let off the hook.

As families readied themselves to fight again, Bert McGee (chairman of Sheff Wed) put the blame back on the fans: "They came to Hillsborough without tickets in the knowledge that if they created enough mayhem the police would open the gates." The media used their freedom of press to reinforce the view, as the full Taylor Report came out. "Taylor is reluctant to accept that 95 Liverpool fans were killed by the thuggishness and ignorance of other Liverpool fans crushing into the ground behind them," wrote the Sunday Telegraph on the 4th Feb 1990. A week later the Observer said the same: "They milled around the gates and stampeded down the tunnel because they couldn't bear the thought of missing the kick-off." (11/02/1990).

In an era before mobile technology and internet, the rest of the nation only got their information from print media, and whatever the newspapers wrote was taken as gospel.

In October 1990 SYP admitted they were negligent and that they failed in their duty of care to keep the people attending the game safe. But then just one month later at an inquest in Sheffield, they renewed their claims that drunk fans turning up late without tickets were to blame for the disaster. This was the first inquest.

Dr Stefan Popper limited the inquest, which began in Sheffield on the 19th October, by asserting that there was a cut off of 3:15pm, and that all victims who died had irreversible brain damage by then. In stating this, Popper covered the police, ambulances, fire service and local hospitals from being fully investigated. The 3:15pm verdict also grouped all victims together and failed to acknowledge each individual case. It was rumoured that Popper, a local coroner, was influenced by senior police members within SYP and was said to have been celebrating with them after the inquests. Family members in court had to sit and listen as the blood alcohol level of their loved ones were read out (again, even the children's). The levels were then printed in local Yorkshire newspapers the following day.

The 18th March 1991 inquest saw the assemblance of a local jury, all drawn from the Sheffield area. They had read local coverage of the disaster, such as the Sheffield Star's account: *"Many supporters were still propping up the bars at 2.30pm. They raced to the stadium arriving at the Leppings Lane end at the height of the crush. Some of them were the worse for drink, others without tickets were hoping to sneak in. Hubble bubble toil and trouble... drunkenness and ticketlessness were now added to the equation."*

It was unsurprising when, on the 28th March, the jury came to the conclusion of 'accidental death'. That 95 people [sic] had died and that it was somehow just an accident. The court doors closed and the families were left outside distraught.

In May 1991, a delegation of Borussia Moenchengladbach supporters flew over to Merseyside for a friendship visit. They donated a cheque for £7,000 to Hillsborough families – a much appreciated gesture.[50] Then, in October, with

---

[50] A link would be maintained from then on. Gladbach fans would come over once a year, go to the bars on Mathew Street and tell the locals how great they were. Liverpool fans would then travel to

police disciplinary action being taken against him, David Duckenfield retired on medical grounds. He said he had depression and post-traumatic stress disorder. He probably did. But his retirement prevented disciplinary action from being taken against him and enabled him to claim a full pension (still being paid up to the time of this publication).

13th January 1992. Because of Duckenfield's retirement, the only other disciplinary action being taken, against Bernard Murray, the police control commander at Hillsborough, was dropped as it was 'unfair' to continue to discipline him. Unfair on whom? The families suffer another knock.

Later that year Bernard Ingham, frightened of falling into obscurity in a post-Thatcher world, made another claim about Liverpool fans in relation to the findings of the Taylor Report. Knowsley MP George Howarth tabled a motion for Labour in Commons: "That this House deplores the comments made by Bernard Ingham in the Daily Express of 5th March 1992 concerning the Taylor Report into the Hillsborough disaster." Thatcher's 'rottweiler' began to resemble an unwanted mongrel.

After the poor baby boy James Bulger was horrifically murdered in February 1993, the national press again dismissed the city's sense of communal mourning, likening it to the Hillsborough disaster. Ian Jacks (the Independent) wrote: "Scousers acted out of a script as if they expected it now, mugged by one disaster after another until a particular kind of martyrdom has become part of the municipal character." And then Jonathan Margolis (the Sunday Times): "Does anyone dare wonder how many of the Anfield faithful solemnly observing a minute's silence at last week's home match were, to put it crudely, getting off on the 'city in mourning' theme?"

On 3rd March 1993 Tony Bland's life support was withdrawn having shown no signs of improvement, after a court order allowed for him to die with dignity. He was 18 at the time of the disaster but 22 when he became the 96th victim. 'Always loved', the Weetabix Kid, Rest in Peace.

A judicial review tabled by six families into the initial inquest verdict was rejected on the 5th November 1993. The apparent favouring of coroners toward judges continued, with Lord Justice McCowan ruling that the 3:15pm was accurate: "I see no fault in the coroner on this matter. He made a full inquiry... In my judgement it would not be right to quash the verdicts and order a new inquest

---

the Old Town of Gladbach, go to Fanhaus – an old army barracks turned into a beer garden – and tell the German's in return how great they were.

on the strength of these allegations made against the investigating police officers," McCowan decided.

Perhaps bitter that he'd gotten Nottingham Forest relegated the year before, former football manager Brian Clough bid for relevancy in his 1994 memoirs. "I will always remain convinced that those Liverpool fans who died were killed by Liverpool people." He maintained: "They were drunk. They killed their own." Liverpool City Council suggested a boycott of his book, only for Clough to respond: "Half of them can't read anyway". Garston MP Eddie Loyden kicked off in Commons against the remarks, tabling:

> "That this House condemns the actions of Brian Clough in his allegations that Liverpool supporters were responsible for the Hillsborough disaster; notes that such an insensitive statement will do nothing to assist the bereaved families in dealing with this terrible tragedy and loss; concludes that this is a cynical attempt to boost the sale of his autobiography; and calls on him to withdraw his statement, and to apologise to the people of Liverpool and to the bereaved families in particular."

No apology was forthcoming. When Clive Anderson asked Clough on his chat show if he regretted his remarks, he said: "No I don't regret it at all. It wanted saying. I was there. They brought the tragedy on themselves. The ghost writer actually watered that part of the book down because I would have got into more trouble if it all got in." 24/10/1994

Roger Cook had created a niche with his TV show 'The Cook Report' travelling the world and investigating injustices. Following refusal after refusal, Anne Williams turned to TV companies. An edition of The Cook Report concerning her case went on television in early June 1994. They determined on the show that Kevin Williams, her son, deserved an inquest.

Eddie Loyden, a former Navy man, stood up in Commons again, tabling: "That this House calls on the Attorney General to study The Cook Report on the Hillsborough Disaster that provided new evidence that in spite of previous rulings, victims were still alive long after the recorded time of death, underlining the case made by the bereaved families that serious questions remain unanswered."

The following month Eddie Loyden stood up in Commons once more with a follow-up on the progress of the case: "This House congratulates Liverpool City Council in calling an extraordinary meeting to debate a motion supporting the Hillsborough Disaster Working Party's demands for a fresh and scrupulously independent inquiry to investigate evidence and related matters disclosed in February 1992, and referred to in the Cook Report television programme on 2nd June concerning the circumstances surrounding the death of the victims and particularly the death of Kevin Williams, and calls on the Attorney General to order a fresh inquiry as soon as possible." 40 Labour MP's signed the motion, including Jeremy Corbyn and Dennis Skinner.

Eight months later Anne Williams' MP Sir Malcolm Thornton presented her information in Commons in front of Sir Nicholas Lyall, Attorney General. Lyall agreed to look into the report. Within its findings was the story of Tony Edwards, the only paramedic to make it onto the pitch at 3:35pm because police claimed fans were fighting. His testimony bore out the evidence of off-duty policeman Derek Bruder and special police constable Debra Martin, who both said that Kevin had shown signs of life up to 4pm - Bruder said he found a pulse when giving resuscitation at 3.37pm, while Martin said Kevin opened his eyes and said "Mum" just before he died at 4pm. Both Bruder and Martin said their statements were changed after visits from the West Midlands police to suggest there were no signs of life.

Williams was eventually told that a new inquest "would not be in the interests of justice". Optimism had been drained yet again.

In June 1996 the mongrel continued to bark. Glenda Jackson stood up in Commons and tried to put a muzzle on him, tabling: "That this House deplores the insensitive and ill-informed remarks, regarding the Hillsborough disaster, made by Sir Bernard Ingham, during BBC Question Time on Thursday 6th June; condemns his illogical disregard for the findings of the official inquiry into that disaster, by his apportioning blame for the tragedy to football supporters, dubbing them 'yobbos', and calls upon Baroness Thatcher's former press secretary to apologise, not only to the families of the 96 innocent victims killed on that terrible day, but also to the cities of Liverpool and Sheffield for the grievous pain and distress his intemperate comments have undoubtedly caused." 64 MPs signed the motion, but not one single Tory acknowledged it; the party in office that day had fallen silent on all matters regarding Hillsborough.

Another side of the story - that of the families - was presented to the nation on 5th December 1996 when Jimmy McGovern's Hillsborough docudrama was released. Two mothers had approached McGovern and asked him to tell their story. He was so angry at the injustice they'd suffered that he drafted in journalist Katy Jones to ensure the picture was not biased. Christopher Eccleston's performance of Trevor Hicks was so powerful that it ignited a public reaction and led to calls for a new inquiry. It was the first time that the view of a police cover-up had been presented to the British people.

Hope returned in 1997. In the March, Andrew Devine – who was said to have had similar conditions to Tony Bland – came out of his coma and was apparently able to communicate using a touch-sensitive pad. In May came the Hillsborough Justice Concert organised by HFSG at Anfield. 34,000 people attended and enjoyed some of the best musicians in the country. Early on, local band Space had the crowd lapping up their aptly titled *'Me and you versus the world'*. John Peel acted as compère, introducing the likes of Dodgy, Lightning Seeds and Stereophonics. As dusk fell *'Life of Riley'* had the crowd bouncing. Paul Heaton's silky voice sang *'Rotterdam'* with the Beautiful South, before his own poignant version of *'Lean on Me'*. The biggest act was supposed to be the Manic Street Preachers. Lead guitarist Nicky Wire stepped on stage in a Bill Shankly *'The socialism I believe in'* jumper, but the band refrained from singing their new track *'South Yorkshire Mass Murderer'*. The concert ended with Trevor Hicks – chairman of HFSG – announcing: 'From today the legal battle will start again'. The entire audience (including 'Baggie' Frank Skinner) cheered and swayed to You'll Never Walk Alone.[51]

The following day Liverpool fans travelled to Hillsborough for the last league game of the season versus Sheffield Wednesday. SYP confiscated flowers and banners from fans which were a tribute to the dead (somehow deeming a rose to be a weapon). Supporters were furious and began organising a boycott of Hillsborough. The following season, Sheffield Wednesday allowed the fixture to be sponsored by the Sun, a thoughtless piece of business. Only 14% of the allocated tickets were taken by Reds for the Hillsborough fixture on the day of the eventual boycott.

As promised, the new Labour government ordered a scrutiny of all evidence in June 1997. Lord Justice Stuart-Smith was placed in charge of proceedings. Early on outside the Albert Docks, he joked: "Are there more families to come? It's not like Liverpool fans to turn up at the last minute." Not only were families already waiting upstairs for *him,* Smith, representing the establishment, was joking about the disaster's main misconception. He was forced to apologise.

Despite finding that South Yorkshire police changed 164 officers' accounts of the disaster before sending them to Justice Taylor back in 1990, and that David

---

[51] Why don't fans sway anymore? Nothing looked better than a swaying Kop.

Duckenfield had 'lied disgracefully' when he blamed Liverpool fans for opening the gate, Stuart-Smith rejected any grounds for prosecution and maintained the original inquest verdict. Jack Straw nodded. He didn't believe there was sufficient evidence for a new inquiry. Tony Blair asked *'What is the point?'* and the door closed once again with the families left outside by their government.

Following the death of Lady Diana, the nation was plunged into a scene of collective mourning. Euan Ferguson of the Observer looked upon the flower-laying and hugging and winced. He created a term for it: "It was John Lennon's narcissistic emoting which began the Liverpudlianization of Britain and turned us into a country that fills its gutters with tears for girls we've never met." Once more, the national press dismissed sorrowfulness as being a distasteful Liverpool attribute.

After Hillsborough there were 700 plus people in hospital injured, as well as thousands upon thousands of survivors with unseen injuries and mental traumas. In light of this, the Hillsborough Justice Campaign was founded in February 1998 after a number of families decided to incorporate 'survivors and supporters of Justice for all'. They took up premises on Lower Breck Road and stepped up campaigns to raise public awareness for the disaster. Peter Carney says: 'A lad called Tony Barnbrook had won a case in 1998 through McGee solicitors, who were experts in PTSD, which was a big push in making the Justice Campaign happen.'

In August 1998, the HFSG put the money raised from the previous year's concert towards the private prosecutions of David Duckenfield and Bernard Murray. After a six-week trial, the jury found Murray not guilty of manslaughter and, despite eight days of deliberation, were unable to reach a verdict on Duckenfield. He walked free again.

Phil Scraton was sat in the House of Lords reading room at the time sifting through police statements. He found something shocking. There were three pieces of paper for every statement: a handwritten original, a typed version with amendments on, and then a final clean submitted version with obvious alterations made. All mention of fans being drunk or misbehaving were left in, whilst any criticisms of senior police officers or mentions of leadership being poor on the day were removed. David Conn gave an example many years later of a senior SYP note: "Last two pages require amending; these are his own feelings. He also states that PCs were sat down crying when the fans were carrying the dead and injured. This shows they were organised and we were not. Have [the PC] rewrite the last two pages excluding points mentioned."

Daniel Fieldsend

Junior Justice Minister, Maria Eagle – MP for Liverpool Garston – stood up in Commons and launched an attack on Norman Bettison in late 1998. "The institutional behaviour of South Yorkshire police was appalling," she said. "I stand by the comments I made in the House of Commons at the time. This was a black propaganda unit, engaged in a conspiracy to cover up." It later emerged that two police CCTV videos went missing from the locked control room on the night of the disaster, one of which had footage of the gate opening. It read like a wild Kremlin spy story, but was rooted in truth and set in *Great* Britain.

Jack Straw quipped in 1999: 'You know what Scousers are like, they're always up to something.' It was another example of the perception of Liverpool people within certain corridors. City Council leader Mike Storey condemned him: 'It's a constant drip, drip of stereotypical views,' he said. Stan Boardman returned to say: 'Once again it's someone in power having a go at Liverpool. It's something you'd expect from a Tory, not a Labour minister.'

A survey later that year found that 59% of Sheffield locals felt Liverpool fans were to blame for the disaster, despite the findings of the Taylor Report. This, ten years after Hillsborough... By now at least three people who had survived were known to have committed suicide. There was another nameless survivor in psychiatric care, not to mention the many addictions to drugs and alcohol and broken families on Merseyside and beyond. Anfield hosted a 10-year service. Ray Lewis, the referee from 1989, blew his whistle at 3:06pm to start a minute's silence. Thousands of fans stood on the Kop and listened as Trevor Hicks pleaded for new action to be taken against those responsible for the disaster.

But the families would be defeated again. There was a hopelessness, a feeling of getting nowhere. Murray was acquitted in a private prosecution at Leeds Crown Court and Duckenfield was cleared by the judge, Justice Hooper. The Sunday Mirror led a two-page headline on the amended statements but it came to nothing.

FHM magazine in 2002 thought it was acceptable to joke about the disaster. They likened the crushed fans to shoppers in a sale and called the victims lying on the pitch 'lazy'. Liverpool FC issued a statement: "The club is absolutely sickened to think anyone could try to find humour in such an appalling tragedy. The captions reported to us are nothing short of a disgrace and it's beyond belief that anyone considered them worthy of publication."

But the ignorance would continue. Boris Johnson in 2004 was Vice Chairman of the Conservative party as well as editor of the Spectator. He gave the nod allowing an incredibly incorrect article to be published, which said: "The deaths of more than 50 Liverpool football supporters at Hillsborough in 1989 was undeniably a greater tragedy than the single death, however horrible, of Mr Bigley; but that is no excuse for Liverpool's failure to acknowledge, even to this day, the part played in the disaster by drunken fans at the back of the crowd who mindlessly tried to fight their way into the ground that Saturday afternoon." Party leader Michael Howard ordered Johnson to visit Liverpool and apologise. The Guardian wrote: "If only Bron [Waugh] (former editor) could have seen it. For years, he told the readers of the Spectator that Liverpool represented everything hateful about modern England, with its idle, drunken 'workers' and its 14-year-old girls who could be had for a Mars bar."

Manchester United fans visiting Anfield in January 2005 held up pictures saying 'Vote Boris' and 'Self-pity City' as the 'Republik of Mancunia' – a supposedly socialist heartland – looked to capitalise on Johnson's Hillsborough remarks. Liverpool fans pointed back and shouted: '*Tory, Tory, Man United*!'

But the sentiment refused to go away. Alex Ferguson responded to the conduct of his prized striker: 'Rooney's from Liverpool and everyone from that city has a chip on their shoulder, so if an injustice is done to him on the pitch, of course he is going to react.' From a domestic standing, it was as Kevin Sampson says: 'If we *are* carrying a chip on our shoulders then we have every justification for being that way.'

Knowing full well that her little boy was alive at 4pm on the 15th April 1989, and that his last ever word was '*Mum*', Anne Williams went to the European Court of Human Rights in August 2006, seeking to overturn the 3:15pm cut off.

Three years later, in March 2009, Williams was told by the European Court that her submission was out of time, and that it should have been provided back in 1997. She composed herself to say: 'I'm used to the setbacks now. Interestingly, they've not refused me because I'm not right, it's because of timing.'

And then came the big day: the 20-year anniversary. In recent years the memorial services had averaged 8,000 people, however some 28,500 people turned up on 15th April 2009. All four stands had to be opened for the unexpected numbers. Jamie Carragher and Steven Gerrard awarded the families the Freedom of Liverpool. 96 candles were lit. Kenny Dalglish read a passage and Rafa Benitez let 96 balloons go free into the sky. But the biggest moment came when Andy Burnham stepped up to deliver a speech.

Few people knew who he was. An Evertonian from the Old Roan and Sports Minister for the government, Burnham appeared to be just another trim-suited member of the establishment. He was not. 'The Prime Minister has pledged that 96 football supporters will never be forgotten,' Burnham began – a token line heard before. "*We want Justice!*" a heckler shouted back. 28,000 people stood and pointed at Burnham – the loudest chants of '*Justice, for the 96*' were directed his way. After a minute he nodded. 'Okay', Burnham mouthed ... It was raw and angry and emotional, boiled up after 20 years of frustration, but, finally, it seemed that the message had gotten through to somebody.

*

Burnham and Maria Eagle went straight to Parliament and demanded full disclosure of all Hillsborough documents. In July 2009 the Home Office agreed. An online petition in 2011 demanding the documents be released reached 139,00 signatures. Kenny Dalglish, in his second stint as manager, said: 'This isn't a political issue – it's a humanitarian one, so at least common sense has prevailed.' The Hillsborough Independent Panel was founded in January 2010 and received the blessing of the government to scrutinise all new information. Steve Rotheram described it as a victory for democracy 'but it is yet to be seen whether it will be a victory for the families?'

The panel was chaired by James Jones, the Bishop of Liverpool and contained Raju Bhatt (lawyer), Christine Gifford (information expert), Katy Jones (journalist), Bill Kirkup (medical officer), Paul Leighton (constable), Phil Scraton (professor), Peter Sissons (broadcaster) and Sarah Tyacke (national archives). As they sifted through 400,000 new documents, a series of disappointments occurred.

In June 2010 Culture Secretary Jeremy Hunt was made to apologise after he described Hillsborough as a 'hooligan' event. Labour MP Derek Twigg asked Home Secretary Theresa May: 'How can the [relatives] have trust in the government that they will see through the proper release of the Hillsborough files given that's the view held in high parts of the government?'. Then in October 2011 Sir Oliver Popplewell blurted out that the families of the Hillsborough victims should look at the "quiet dignity and great courage relatives in the West Yorkshire city had shown in the years following the tragedy." Popplewell had chaired the inquiry into the Bradford Fire and continued to say: "The citizens of Bradford behaved with dignity and courage. They did not harbour conspiracy theories. They did not seek endless further inquiries. They buried their dead, comforted the bereaved and succoured the injured. They organised a sensible compensation scheme and moved on. Is there, perhaps, a lesson there for the

Hillsborough campaigners?" Steve Rotheram was there once more, rebuking him in Parliament for his misunderstanding of events.

In 2011, 22 years after giving his ticket to a friend who died in the disaster, Stephen Whittle took his own life. He left £61,000 in his will to the Hillsborough families. If only he knew that it was never his fault.

In August that year Peter Hooton had been planning an anti-Sun newspaper concert. He was joined on stage at the Olympia by Pete Wylie and Mick Jones of the Clash. They formed a single band and played each other's songs. Jones – taken back to his younger days by the sense of protest - proposed afterwards that they took the band on tour. Hooton consulted the Hillsborough families who agreed and the Justice Tonight tour began. In Manchester, the Stone Roses reunited for the concert, while the likes of Hard-Fi, Primal Scream, Manics, Cast, Shane McGowan and Billy Bragg also made appearances elsewhere. At the concert in Lyon, Eric Cantona came on stage and pledged his support for the campaign.

On the anniversary of the disaster that year, Alan Davies, a "comedian", said on his podcast: 'Liverpool and the 15th, that gets on my tits that shit. What are you talking about? *"We won't play on the day"* Why can't they? My mum died on 22nd August. I don't stay in all day on 22nd August.' Davies received thousands of comments on Twitter. He offered to donate £1,000 to the HFSG but they declined. He then posted on Twitter: "Going out later. I've decided to get a disguise." The Tweet was accompanied by an image of an Enfield stereotype Scouser tracksuit.

In response to the upcoming Hillsborough verdicts, Manchester United's board and Alex Ferguson condemned their fans use of the chant *'Always the victims, it's never your fault'* when singing about Liverpool. They said: "The club deplore it. The manager has made the club's position very clear on this matter; it's now up to the fans to respect that." Despite the pleas, United supporters still sang it after a 4-0 victory against Wigan.[52]

But on the 12th September 2012, none of that mattered. The Independent Panel had reviewed all of the documents and published its report. It concluded that 164 statements had been altered. It exposed the police's campaign to blame supporters. Crucially, it highlighted that 41 of the 96 could (and should) have been saved, had the emergency services reaction been good enough. It stated that

---

[52] Tom Fairclough says: 'A lot of clubs are happy to pledge support to the Hillsborough campaign on one hand, but then sing 'Always the Victim' on the other, which I don't care what anyone says, it is a dig at Hillsborough.'

fans who were merely unconscious were put on their backs and covered, rather than placed in the recovery position. Theresa May ordered a new criminal inquiry straight away.

Peter Carney says: 'You had 55 dead and 41 who could have been saved, which is down to the lack of response and resources. I was unconscious on the terrace and it was Liverpool supporters who saved me. I knew it was down to whoever was managing the event, the coppers and that shithole of a ground, but how do you get that across? And besides, I was left for dead on the terrace.' The panel was about to finally reveal the truth.

Reverend James Jones' report (titled 'The Patronising Disposition of Unaccountable Power') laid out the main reason as to why it was so easy for the police and media to appropriate blame at the feet of the supporters: "Although by no means all of the bereaved families are from the city of Liverpool, I was told that press coverage of Hillsborough, combined with negative stereotypes of Liverpool and Liverpudlians, acted itself as a barrier to truth and justice, in that it affected people's willingness to engage with the families' campaign."

The Daily Mirror then found that £1.5m had been paid out to members of the SYP force – around £330,000 each – for trauma, but found that families of the deceased had only received roughly £3,500 each. The injustice was blinding.

Outside the High Court in December 2012, the verdict of 96 accidental deaths was quashed. There was a massive weight of relief for the families as a new inquest was finally ordered. Lord Justice Igor Judge found that the initial inquiries were not 'properly conducted' cueing gasps of shock in Commons – but the people of Liverpool were not shocked; they had known all along. The house of cards began to wobble.

On 18th April 2013 in Birkdale the ferociously determined Anne Williams died of cancer. She had gone to the memorial service three days earlier and told cameras 'I really wanted to go, not to say goodbye though, because I'll be going to him soon.' Williams was posthumously given a BBC Sports Personality of the Year award. She'd fought tirelessly for her boy and was the real 'Iron Lady'.

A new inquest began in Warrington on 31st March 2014. It would go on to be the longest ever inquest in British history. Families travelled up and down the M62 every day for two years.

Several politicians in Parliament knew the wind had changed. John Hemming, MP for Birmingham Yardley, tabled in September: "That this House notes the organised cover-up of the truth about Hillsborough; commiserates with the

Hillsborough families; thanks the many campaigners for not giving up; further notes that there is evidence of other cover-ups of wrongdoing that has not been brought to light; recognises that the judicial estate of the constitution is vulnerable to cover-ups; and calls for consideration as to how allegations of other cover-ups can be better considered to get to the truth in less than 20 years."

Before their match against Newcastle United that week, Everton FC presented a tribute to the Hillsborough families. A little girl in an Everton kit with '9' on the back of her shirt walked out of the tunnel holding hands with a little boy in a Liverpool kit with '6' on his back. They stood in the centre circle as the Hollies' 'He ain't heavy, he's my brother' played over the tannoy. The song had been re-recorded by the Justice Collective and released in December 2012, featuring Paul McCartney, Robbie Williams, Rebecca Ferguson, Holly Johnson, Gerry Marsden, Paul Heaton, Glenn Tilbrook, John Power, Melanie Chisholm, Paloma Faith, Beverley Knight, Eliza Doolittle, Dave McCabe, Peter Hooton, John McLure, Shane McGowan, as well as Bobby Elliot and Tony Hicks of the Hollies, and former footballers such as Peter Reid, Alan Hansen and Kenny Dalglish. It became the Christmas number 1 and raised money for both HFSG and HJC.

In February 2015 Everton unveiled a plaque in honour of the 96 in the Park End, with the image of the little boy and girl carved in. Everton fan Stephen Kelly, whose brother Michael died in the tragedy, said: 'I have always been grateful of the support from the blue side of the city. I hope that when Evertonians look at this they will feel proud of the way we've supported our neighbours.'

Then there was the 26th of April 2016 – a day which for anybody associated with Liverpool the city and Liverpool the club, produced a moment when time stopped. Everybody in later years would remember where they were when they found out. The world's media lined up outside Warrington's courts, pointing their cameras at the door as families walked in to hear the jury's verdicts.

It proved to be heart-in-mouth. The greatest fear was the jury finding that fans had contributed to the unlawful killing of 96 other supporters. There would be no coming back from that. It'd be a permanent stain. One by one the questions were read out:

1. **Basic facts**: "Do you agree with the following statement: "Ninety-six people died as a result of the disaster at the Hillsborough stadium on 15 April 1989 due to crushing in the central pens of the Leppings Lane terrace, following the admission of a large number of supporters to the stadium through exit gates?

'Yes' ...

And then 2. (**Police planning**): "*Was there any error or omission in police preparation? ... Yes...* As the judge, Sir John Goldring, asked for her answers, the juror rattled them out like gunfire: 'Yes,' 'Yes', 'Yes'. For the Hillsborough families, the survivors, the friends left lonely, those suffering with mental health and then every Liverpool fan who'd defended the Hillsborough victims against the mouths of ignorance for the past 27 years, the potential for exoneration boiled down to the next two questions.

6. Unlawful killing: "Are you satisfied, so that you are sure, that those who died in the disaster were unlawfully killed? And that the breach of Mr Duckenfield's duty of care caused the deaths?"

'Yes'

Get in! Families in court punched the air, others bent forward suppressing screams. But they were only halfway there. If the next question fell in the wrong direction, then the people at Hillsborough and the wider city would be forever tarnished, found to have killed their own fans.

> **7. Behaviour of fans:** "Was there any behaviour on the part of the football supporters which caused or contributed to the dangerous situation at the Leppings Lane turnstiles?"

'No'

Screams. Delighted jubilant screams. No European Cup victory ever felt like this. Across the road in room 401 of Birchwood Industrial Park, the assembled survivors and other campaigners fell to their knees having watched a live stream of events. Others jumped up and ran a little bit, most were instantly crying, drawing huge, huge breaths. This was the moment of total exoneration. All of the dirt thrown at them for 27 years fell in an instant. The '*why don't they just get over it?*' and '*no smoke without fire*' rhetoric was gone. The same establishment that had lied for a generation had now just admitted the truth. The Truth. "*Have that MacKenzie*". Fans behaviour played no part in the disaster. Outside the court, the cameramen smiled as the families came out punching the air. There was still anger laced within it all – for 27 years they'd been lied to for - but the hugging;

the laughing. Liverpool fans were not culpable and now the whole world knew the truth.

That truth was put out there by the entire global media force. It was on the front page of the New York Times - "Britain faults police in 1989 soccer crush" - and was inside *La Stampa*, *Le Monde*, *Die Welt* and *Bild*. In Britain the word 'Justice' featured on the front pages of the Daily Mirror, Daily Star, the I and New Day. The Guardian's first 7 pages were dedicated to the victims, telling of how their deaths were now firmly pinned on the police. David Conn was given five pages to retell the story of the tragedy and the history of the inquests. It had been Conn's article in 2009 questioning the police statements that helped the campaign turn a corner. Brian Reade was given a front-page platform to explain how the families felt. The Liverpool Echo had 37 pages of coverage, more than any piece of news in the city's history. They spelt the word 'Families' with a capital F throughout: those now with vindication. "What the authorities failed to recognise is that they were not dealing with ordinary people and that Liverpool is not an ordinary city," the paper said.

But the Sun didn't put anything on their front page... Nor did the Times (both owned by News International). There was a civil war within the offices of both about the striking lack of compassion. The Sun had relegated the story to pages 8 and 9 and wrote another fruitless apology on page 10, because they had to but didn't want to.

David Cameron's apology on behalf of the government was instant and sincere:

"With the evidence presented today it makes clear that the families have suffered a double injustice. On behalf of the government, I am profoundly sorry that this double injustice was has been left uncorrected for so long. The false version of events ... not enough people in this country understand what the people of Merseyside have been through. The appalling death toll was compounded with an intent to blame the victims. A narrative about hooliganism on that day was created which led many people in the country to believe it was a grey area. Today's report is black and white: Liverpool fans were not the cause of the disaster. I'm sure all sides will join with me in paying tribute to the incredible strength and dignity of the Hillsborough families and the community that has backed them in their lost quest for justice."

Andy Burnham stood up in Parliament the next day and demanded accountability. He thanked the jury for seeing through the lies and blamed a police force for putting protection of itself above protecting others. He then cited a complicit print media and a flawed judicial system for their roles. The collusion between the media and the police had caused most harm. 'In court the families were told to show no emotion while their loved ones were smeared by lawyers,' Burnham reminded Commons. He saluted Theresa May for her stance in righting the wrongs of the establishment. But more than any other member of the house, he himself deserved the most praise. He'd been as good as his word.

The exoneration in 2016 was a huge release for so many hundreds of thousands of people who had tentacles in Hillsborough. They were never whingeing, or wallowing in self-pity like the media made out. The Johnsons, Pearces, Jacks' and Margolis' of the Fleet Street hate gang couldn't have been more wrong. In fact, far from wallowing, every time a Scouser was heard talking about Hillsborough putting their version across, they were fighting back. Every time they refused to read a certain newspaper or opted to boycott a certain brand, they were fighting back. And they won.

Howard Gayle turned down an MBE that summer. He cited historic British slavery as one reason, and Hillsborough as the other. In 2019 he reaffirmed his stance: 'You'll find that the vast majority of players who accept gongs don't come from Liverpool. When you're brought up here as a socialist then you have a certain way of thinking and a certain dynamic,' a Scouser affected by Hillsborough wouldn't cosy up to the establishment. 'No other city would have achieved what those Hillsborough families did, they kept on going and they did not give up. I think other cities or clubs who found themselves in that position would remain in it; the fact it was Liverpool meant resilience against an epic story of lies and now the government has got to own up to those lies.'

During Everton's immediate home game against Bournemouth, the club paid tribute to the victory. Members of the HFSG were invited onto the pitch as all four corners of Goodison Park stood in applause. The Hollies played once again and there was a banner which read: 'JUSTICE AT LAST, BROTHERS IN ARMS'. It inspired collective goosebumps. Bill Kenwright, the Everton owner, put it best when he took the mic:

"They picked on the wrong city – and they picked on the wrong mums."

Local

HEART AS A BIG AS LIVERPOOL

There became a tendency for people, albeit unaware, to collectivise the victims of the Hillsborough disaster into one number – into 'the 96'. They were individuals, each with their own wants, habits, loves, humour and aspirations. The following brief descriptions are taken from the BBC, the Liverpool FC website and the Liverpool Echo, from the inquests. Notice how all of the people who died were on the cusp of starting something new; every single victim had plans for the future. Notice how many were recently married or engaged, wanting to start a family – or how many more were just schoolchildren beginning their lives. Now consider their families, left without them. The 96 are individuals; they are more than a number.

John Alfred Anderson, 62: married his wife on Valentine's Day in 1946. They toured the country on his motorbike. He loved taking her and the kids to New Brighton to play. Had gone to the game with his son.
Colin Mark Ashcroft, 19: had attended special schools but strived in life. He got a job as a gardener on £35-per-week and saved up for a season ticket. It was his first away game.
James Gary Aspinall, 18: eldest of five children. Shared a room with his two younger brothers. Born with a kind nature, he caddied for elderly gentlemen at a golf club. They rang the house on Sunday 16th April '89 asking if he could work that day. The line fell silent at the news.
Kester Ball, 16: when he was 11 he wrote about his desire for the future for a school project. "I want to get married and have two children. When I am 17, I would like to take a driving test. For my 18th I would like to have a big party. When the year 2000 has arrived, my family are going to meet up to celebrate." A bright lad whose dream was taken.
Gerard Baron, 67: a postman who had served his country in Burma and India in WW2. Had been pinned down by a tiger in the jungle during his service. Married

Winifred and had 7 children. A doting grandfather.

Simon Bell, 17: a clever lad who went to Merchant Taylors. Was a cricket fanatic. Told his mother he'd be back later after the game as he was going to pop into the cricket club. She told him to come straight home.

Barry Sidney Bennett, 26: a properly caring family man. When his brother moved to London for work, he had no money; Barry furnished his flat for him. He worked on the tugs, wanting the adventure of working at sea.

David John Benson, 22: a twin brother and a cracking footballer. Loved budgies and had an aviary. Had a two-year-old daughter. She grew up and married, and her uncle (twin Paul) gave her away. Her first dance was to Luther Vandross' 'Dance With My Father Again'.

David William Birtle, 22: cultured and handsome. Had lived in Birmingham and Oman as a child but moved to Liverpool when he was old enough as he loved the people. His mum was in Oman on 15th April and put BBC World Service on at 3:10pm UK time as she had a strange feeling.

Tony Bland, 22: A Yorkshire lad who loved games of pool and snooker down his local, but was a diehard Red too. Got a paper round as a kid so he could go to Anfield. Got a job as a young man to see his team play home and away. Was made up when they came to Sheffield.

Paul David Brady, 21: worked hard and thrived as an engineer. Had his own van and apprentice. Had been abroad with his mates and was saving up to travel Australia.

Andrew Mark Brookes, 26: loved all things Liverpool and soaked up the city when it was shown on TV. A patient, honest and dignified man. Was raised to respect the police and turn to them when needed.

Carl Brown, 18: born with a zest for life. An extrovert with intelligence and so much potential. A champion chess player, a skateboarder, BMX biker and a computer whizz. Was about to go to university.

David Steven Brown, 25: it was love at first sight when met his future wife. He was passionate about her and desperate to start a family. Said for years he wanted a daughter called Samantha. When he found out his wife was pregnant, he felt fulfilled. He never got to meet Samantha.

Henry Burke, 47: always had people in fits of laughter, a natural comedian. A true Scouser. Kids loved him. A family man who adored his children, wife and siblings. Doted on his younger brother who had Down's Syndrome. Promised he'd take care of him once his parents died.

Peter Andrew Burkett, 24: a Birkenhead lad with a huge family. Had a 'smile that'd warm a persons' soul'. Was close with his father, like best friends. 'You were my legacy to this world,' he wrote.

Paul Carlile, 19: was born 4lbs and fought to survive. When his granddad died he moved in with his nan so she didn't have to be alone. Of a Friday he'd go to his mum's and bring her favourite sweets. Had a big heart. Neighbours requested the street he lived at be renamed Carlile Way. The council agreed.

Raymond Chapman, 50: a loving husband and father. He'd worked hard all his life to build a future for his family. Was looking forward to retiring and spending time with his wife. Drove to Sheffield with 4 friends; only 2 came back.

Gary Christopher Church, 19: had been a choir boy and had been in the Scouts. A happy lad. Became a joiner and worked *hard*. 8am shifts through to 10pm. Was happy to be in work given the times. LFC was his release.

Joseph Clark, 29: a shy lad from a huge family who loved get-togethers. Met his wife-to-be aged 18 who he adored. They had a son and daughter. He was playing with them when his mates pulled up to drive him the match. '*See you later*' he said, giving them all a kiss.

Paul Clark, 18: his room was decorated in Liverpool curtains, bedspread, rug, lamp... he got his love of the Reds from his father. Full of life, he'd just bought a car so he could stop cycling to his apprenticeship.

Gary Collins, 22: a Red from a family of Blues. A much-loved son, brother, nephew, cousin and grandson. His mum waved him off that morning: 'Good luck son, I hope they win.'

Stephen Paul Copoc, 20: a gentleman who had a love of nature. Trained in Botany and Horticulture and became a gardener in Mossley Hill. Knew what he wanted from life. Was engaged to his sweetheart and was saving to buy his parents a house.

Tracey Cox, 23, and Richard Jones, 25 (boyfriend and girlfriend): Tracey was the youngest of five children. Richard was the eldest of three. Tracey moved to Sweden as a little girl and was known for her intelligence. Richard was a protective older brother to his siblings and wrote poetry as a boy. They met at a youth hostel in the Lake District and kept in touch. Both later went to Sheffield University. They shared a flat and were in love; a bright couple. Tracey was proof reading her dissertation the morning of the match when tickets became available. She received her degree posthumously.

James Delaney, 19: loved animals. As a boy he gave his mum pet worms. Found an injured hedgehog aged 6. Mended its broken leg with lollipop sticks. Cared for pigeons and ferrets and loved his little brother who asked to go to the game with him. James said *no,* but he'd take him to the final.

Christopher Devonshire, 18: a darling of a child with white-blonde curls who was doted upon by his whole family. Grew into a wise young man with an interest in social issues. Showed an interest in sports journalist. Was appalled at the conditions fans were subjected to.

Christopher Edwards, 29: had the voice of an angel and was in choirs from a young age. Religion was very important to him and he was heavily involved in his local church. Was close to his sister and made sure he was with her at all the toughest moments in her life.

Vincent Fitzsimmons, 34: a brave man. Almost drowned in the canal as a boy but was saved. Relocated to Seattle as a child with his family and overcame bullies. Was carving a fine life out for himself going to night school midweek and seeing his son of a weekend.

Thomas 'Steve' Fox, 21: was so caring, he took a first aid course when they were rare. Was also a qualified lifeguard. Got his mother to sign an organ donor card for him as he wanted people to live if he was ever unfortunate.

Jon-Paul Gilhooley, 10: just a baby. Loving and affectionate to his family. Saved money and bought bottles of perfume at a jumble sale for his mum, two aunties and three cousins. A big football fan who never got to see his cousin Steven captain Liverpool. Never got to grow up and fall in love and have his own children.

Barry Glover, 27: ran a greengrocer business in Ramsbottom with his dad. Was recently married. Would drive his van to villages and serve many isolated people. When he passed away, the streets were lined and the church was full, such was his worth and regard in the community.

Ian Thomas Glover, 20: a young lad with impeccable taste in clothes and music: Deacon Blue, Supertramp, the Waterboys, Hall and Oates... He also adored his mother. Her 50th birthday was two days after he passed but flowers still arrived from him – he'd ordered them before the match.

Derrick Godwin, 24: a quiet young man who was kind by nature. A geography whizz who knew all of the capitals of countries. He didn't drink or smoke and was helpful to his parents – a nice person with his whole life ahead of him.

Roy Hamilton, 33: worked for British Rail and used passes to go abroad with his wife and children. Had just got a new home and car for his family and had received a promotion to senior technician. Was a rock for his children. Had recently booked a hall for his wife's 40th and daughters 18th birthday parties.

Philip Hammond, 14: an avid all-round sportsperson who played football, basketball, cricket and golf. The weeks of April '89 were sunny and he played golf every evening. He had a tournament on Sunday 16th April which he prepped for the night before. Was excited to be going to his first away game.

Local

Eric Hankin, 33: a staff nurse with a big personality. Loved helping people. Did a 24-hour football tournament for charity and ran sponsored marathons. Was a caring tower for his son and daughter. When she wanted to go an under-14s nightclub, he reluctantly agreed. Afterwards when picking her up he said the car wouldn't start and got the other kids to give it a push – to her embarrassment. Left so many memories for his family.
Gary Harrison, 27: the youngest of seven children. A talented footballer and a huge Liverpool fan. Was on Everton's books and insisted on taking his red kit to training. Grew to be a proud family man. Was happily married. His son went on to sign professionally for Liverpool. Had gone to Hillsborough with his brother (and best friend) Stephen.
Stephen Harrison, 31: fell in love with his soulmate aged 14 and they married aged 18; had four children together. Loved to cook and kept notes of all his recipes. Was extremely house-proud and immaculately dressed. Had went to Hillsborough with his brother (and best friend) Gary.
Peter Andrew Harrison, 15: always the tallest in school – he grew to be 6 ft 4 at 15. A funny boy who was always laughing. The family recently moved to a new house and Peter finally had his own room away from his two younger brothers who he loved very much. He'd get up at 4am before school and help deliver milk. Was about to move to Jersey where he'd have had a good life.
David Hawley, 39: was on holiday as a young man when he saw his future wife. Sold his camera so he could stay an extra week and ask her out. They married and had 3 children. He had been planning to take them all travelling. Was the life and soul of parties.
James Hennessy, 29: a music lover who enjoyed the *Eric's* scene. A die-hard Red who'd been to the Paris and Rome finals. He'd started a plastering business and was in a new relationship. Adored his daughter and worked hard to provide for her.
Paul Hewitson, 26: came from a large group of friends. Had saved for a car so he could take his mum for her weekly shop. A motivated and hard-working young man who'd just established his own roofing business.
Carl Hewitt, 17, and Nicholas Hewitt, 16 (brothers): played football together at the back of the house in all weather. They loved holidays together with the rest of the family. They'd go ice-skating together with their cousins. They both had season tickets and had travelled to Sheffield together.
Sarah Hicks, 19, and Victoria Hicks, 15 (sisters): Sarah was gifted and turned down Oxford and London Imperial to study in Liverpool. Was torn between pharmacology, medicine and architecture. Victoria was as bright and as

determined. Wanted to be a sports reporter and typed wonderfully biased reports after Liverpool games. Hid them under her bed so nobody could read them. Both had talent and compassion.

Gordon Rodney Horn, 20: was fostered by a loving family who visited him often in his care home as a boy. He'd stand in the port hole window waving at them. Was shy at first but his came out of his shell when he lived with his new family. Was musical and enjoyed playing the flute. Aged 17 he moved to a halfway house but was planning on moving back in with his family in 1989.

Arthur Horrocks, 41: a much-loved man. Had been a Cavern kid who'd go to shows during school lunch. Went every Liverpool home and away game until his children were born. Never witnessed violence at matches, not even at Heysel. Was an insurance agent, 'the man from the Pru' who was immensely popular.

Thomas Howard Snr, 39, and Thomas Howard Jnr, 14 (father and son): Thomas Senior had been in the Merchant Navy and travelled to the far east. At 6 ft 3 he was known as the 'gentle giant'. Met his wife-to-be while on leave. They had 3 kids. His eldest Thomas Junior wanted to be just like his father. Wanted to grow up and be tall, too. Was taking karate lessons and proudly showed off his moves. Was excited about going to the match with his dad. Waved his mother off at the end of the path.

Eric George Hughes, 42: 'Eric the Red' was devoted to Liverpool FC. Missed a trial with Tranmere Rovers because he went to Anfield for a match. Educated his children on the teams of the '60s. Took them all over the country watching LFC. Always managed to get them tickets. Didn't manage to for Hillsborough.

Alan Johnston, 29: loved live music and had recently watched the Rolling Stones and Elvis Castello play. A Kop season ticket holder. Most of all he was a giving person who worked for the NHS and donated blood regularly.

Christine Jones, 27: a good person with a wonderful nature. Worked as a radiographer at Lancaster Infirmary. Met her husband whist working there. Loved music and was into contemporary bands. Became a vegetarian after hearing the Smiths' 'Meat is Murder'. Owned a rescue dog.

Gary Jones, 18: Fazakerley-born. Fashion conscious, always in Wade Smith. Was at Hugh Baird looking to pursue a career in electronics. Loved music and was saving for a guitar. Big fan of the La's and Deacon Blue, had a ticket to see them live but never got to. They dedicated a song to him.

Nicholas Joynes, 27: a popular young man with many friends. His future wife was at his 21st party at the Kirkby Civic Suite. They were seeing each other for years. She was an air hostess and together they travelled the world. L.A., Hong Kong, Dubai, New York, Spain, Greece... they were looking forward to the future.

Local

Anthony Kelly, 29: was born prematurely, weighed 2lbs. Christened straight away, but he came home and grew strong. Became a fine drawer and joined the army. Was brave all of his life.
Michael David Kelly, 38: loved to read and could get through Tolstoy in one sitting. Enjoyed John Lennon and Bob Dylan songs. Had followed the Reds since the old Second Division. Then, in the navy, he saw the world and all its wonder.
Carl Lewis, 18: worked hard, harder than most, to provide for his partner and daughter. Got paid of a Friday night and always took his girl out. His dad paid for his lads to go the match. He went to Sheffield with his brothers and his mate Paul Carlile (19).
David William Mather, 19: his parents tried for 7 years to conceive him. He loved playing video games and snooker. Loved reading Stephen King; loved bananas and custard from his nan. Loved to drive – was his family chauffer. Loved the Reds.
Brian Matthews, 38: a good man. Met his future wife at the Halfway House in Walton. They married in 1977. He raised thousands for charities, including Round Table, Help the Aged and RNLI. Walked from Liverpool to Manchester for Children in Need dressed as a clown.
Francis Joseph McAllister, 27: was named after saints. Was generous to everybody. Gave up his '74 FA Cup final ticket to his cousin who was emigrating to Australia. Joined the fire brigade and helped a great number of people.
John McBrien, 18: a richly talented and humble youngster. Had just received an unconditional place at Liverpool University studying social economic history. A good actor who had the world at his feet.
Marian Hazel McCabe, 21: her brother got her into football. She became ardent. Travelled up from London and spent all her money on Liverpool. Worked overtime to save for Liverpool games. Had been planning on travelling Italy for World Cup 1990.
Joseph McCarthy, 21: won sports awards from the age of 7. Became school football captain, then prefect, then chairman of the debating society. Popular with everybody. Had the potential to go far in life.
Peter McDonnell, 21: was the baby of the family. Always loved taking things apart and seeing the mechanisms. Aspired to start his own business. Was forced to follow work down to London. Was shocked at the levels of homelessness there and gave his coats to people in need.
Alan McGlone, 28: as a boy he was a table tennis champ sponsored by Fred Perry. Met his wife-to-be when they were 12. Married at 22. A falcon would visit the house, he fed it and rescued a nest of birds. Was looking forward to a party

after the match. A sunny Saturday.

Keith McGrath, 17: his dad and 6 uncles got him supporting Liverpool. Went to his first away game aged 13. At 16 he planned to set up a painting and decorating business once he finished his apprenticeship. Had a wonderful future ahead of him.

Paul Murray, 14: would always carry his elderly neighbours shopping for her. Was a member of the church choir. Played in the school football and basketball teams. Was a pleasure and always helpful.

Lee Nicol, 14: the youngest of 3. Loved school, didn't understand why people did not. Had a pen pal in Barcelona. Wanted his hair cut like Bon Jovi. Got a paper round to contribute toward his season ticket. Innocent things. An innocent thing. Was an organ donor too. Just 14.

Stephen Francis O'Neill, 17: considerate and kind. Attended church every Sunday. Spoke about the future with his father – starting 'O'Neill and Son' business. Was studying in college. Went to Hillsborough with his father, cousin, friend and his uncle Dave Hawley. God bless them.

Jonathon Owens, 18: bright and cheerful. So many friends. Lived all over the place in his young life. Cardiff, Southport, St Helens, Chester. Things just begun to settle down. Became mates with his colleague Peter Burkett. They went to Sheffield together.

William Roy Pemberton, 23: witty, that dry Scouse wit. Very clever lad. Was fluent in Latin. His passion was with computers. At 14 he wrote and sold his first software programme. It funded his entry to university. What a future he had.

Carl William Rimmer, 21: an animal lover who'd come home with stray dogs. His dad was a taxi driver working nights. Carl looked after his mum, renting her films before he went out. Was saving up his 21st money to propose to his girlfriend. Had bought his mum a satellite dish which arrived late April.

David Rimmer, 38: it was love at first sight for him and his wife. Had two children. He doted on them, reading bedtime stories. Had their first holiday abroad the summer before. Sat listening to the crickets at night. Felt content. Life was good.

Graham John Roberts, 24: committed to everything he did in life. A protective big brother. A season-ticket holder for years. Had his wedding booked for the following summer. Worked for British Gas. Had a t-shirt from them which read: 'I'm a *wonderfuel* person'.

Steven Joseph Robinson, 17: confident, charismatic and a character. Aspired to join the police. Was a leader and would have done well. Worked in a newsagents and of a Saturday morning put a Jackie magazine under his sister's pillow. Music lover. *Together in Electric Dreams*.

Henry Charles Rogers, 17: an all-rounder. Played football, golf, tennis, basketball and could swim. He even skateboarded. In school he'd read the Financial Times and was working towards an economics degree. Had all the potential in the world.

Andrew Sefton, 23: developed a social conscience as he got older, marching against unemployment. Had high morals and principles. Had to follow work down south. His mates there wanted to go to Israel or Portugal with him in the summer. He didn't get to go.

Inger Shah, 38: a loving, devoted mother. Warm-hearted and intelligent. Believed in human rights and justice. Was born in Denmark in a small fishing town. First came to London in the late '60s as an au pair. Lived in India for a spell. Supported Liverpool forever. Started going games after Heysel as she felt this was when the club needed her support most.

Paula Smith, 26: went to her first Liverpool game with her brother aged 6. Grew to spend her money on LFC paraphernalia. A true fanatic. Shy by nature, she knew everything about the team. Kenny Dalglish was her hero. Kenny Dalglish attended her funeral. It shouldn't have happened.

Adam Edward Spearritt, 14: he loved life. He loved football. Read Roy of the Rovers, played Subbuteo, collected Panini stickers. Was such fun. Went to Anfield often but Hillsborough was his first away game.

Philip Steele, 15: like his father, supported Liverpool. Read books on the Reds all of the time, of heroes past and present. Was an alter boy. Never said a bad word about anybody in his life. Had arrived at Sheffield early with his family.

David Thomas, 23: used his 21st birthday money as a deposit on a house. Had started up his own painting and decorating business. Would have given the shirt off his back to whoever needed it more. Had a sincere will to help others.

Patrick Thompson, 35: a hard-working family man. Once did a 26-hour shift for British Rail. Had five children all aged under six. Was devoted to them, as well as his wife, mum, dad, brothers and sisters. And to the Reds. Had been at Heysel but knew of no violence. Was supposed to be working nights on Saturday 15th but got his shift changed.

Peter Thompson, 30: had been a role model all of his life. Enlisted in the T.A. before working for British Aerospace. Worked in Canada, USA, Norway and The Netherlands. Met his wife in Eindhoven. Was expecting the birth of his daughter.

Stuart Thompson, 17: one of six children. Had so many friends and always wore a smile. Enjoyed animals and the zoo. Sent off for snakes. Didn't tell his mum. She opened the box and had a fright. Swapped them for a ferret. Didn't tell his mum.

Had just started his driving lessons.
Peter Tootle, 21: was shy by nature. Didn't like his picture taken. Didn't drink – the pub got Lucozade in for him. But cared so much about his family. When his granddad died, he went to his nans every night and made her dinner for her. Had met a girl. Was about to go on holiday with her. First time abroad.
Christopher Traynor, 26, and Martin Traynor, 16 (brothers): Christopher was a talented craftsman who made furniture for his family. Worked on destroyers at Cammell Laird. Later worked for the council. Had been renovating his family home with his wife. Helped his elderly neighbours with shopping. Christopher saved the life of Norman Langley at Hillsborough. Martin was a prefect at school who looked after younger pupils. Played for Parkside FC with Jason McAteer. A future in boxing was anticipated. Was on a YTS as a joiner. Stopped his neighbour's house being robbed. Both were caring people.
Kevin Tyrrell, 15: a polite young man. Spent all his time playing football. Was going through a trial at Tranmere Rovers at the time. Never got into any trouble. Had not long received a season ticket. Hillsborough was his first away game.
Colin Wafer, 19: as a lad he liked maths and art. Liked snooker, the Waltzer's, Battenberg cake, playing football, Deacon Blue, his job and Liverpool FC. He enjoyed his life. Hillsborough was his first away game.
Ian David Whelan, 19: was finding his feet in life. Loved his girlfriend. Loved U2. Loved the Reds. Before Sheffield that Saturday he called by his girlfriend's house and left two red roses on her doorstep.
Martin Kenneth Wild, 29: the eldest son. Lived with his grandmother in Derbyshire and loved her very much. Worked in a fabric factory but went to every match at Anfield. Was passionate about speedway too.
Kevin Williams, 15: had an endearing sense of humour. Had pictures of Barnes, Rush and Dalglish on his wall. Did his granddads shopping for him, who's leg had been amputated. Left an entire community distraught.
Graham Wright, 17: a good lad. A practising Catholic. Tried to raise awareness for 3rd world countries. Enjoyed walks with his girlfriend. Was about to become a blackbelt in karate. Was awarded his belt posthumously.

Rest in peace, the victims of Hillsborough. You'll Never Walk Alone.

Local

WALKAWAY

'That's what they say'

Michael Heseltine was a man of resolutions who'd ask his supplicants to bring him their problems on an A4 piece of paper. When other politicians seemed to turn their backs, he still remained involved in Liverpool's development, long after 1981. On one occasion in the mid-80s, he corralled a bus-full of CEOs from London's big businesses for a tour of 'dark Liverpool', driving them around the areas of modernist failure. They saw the unfinished housing estates of Cantril Farm and Netherley, and the abandoned high-rise houses that had replaced Everton's Georgian terraces. It was Heseltine's way of kicking things into action.

The ink was still wet on his 'City Challenge Programme' (an initiative designed to regenerate deprived urban areas) when he heard about the opinion polls. Labour were 18% ahead of Thatcher's Conservative party. Her cabinet whispered plots against her. A change was in the air. He'd always had an uneasy working relationship with the Prime Minister – his self-appointment as 'Minister for Merseyside' (albeit with a nod of approval) in 1981 had been seen as a counter attack of her political hostility towards Liverpool – and now the time was right, he felt, to knock her off her perch.

In November 1989 he resigned from her cabinet and spoke against her to the press, quickly tabling a leadership bid. But Thatcher wasn't soft. After the first ballot she agreed to resign, on one condition. She'd go, provided none of her remaining cabinet voted for Heseltine. In his own words he'd later reflect: 'He who wields the knife never wears the crown'. They swore John Major into office in the second ballot and the hefty political lion was left to lick his wounds. Nevertheless, despite not having won the seat of power, he'd done Liverpool another favour. Michael Heseltine had ended Thatcher's 1979-1990 era of old boys misery.

Daniel Fieldsend

The 1990s was a much quirkier decade than those before it. Adults played video games shamelessly and watched on as the left-field became mainstream. Common-speaking artists like Tracey Emin and Damien Hirst became millionaires. Scruffy was made acceptable by Blur and Oasis and to be working-class was to be trendy, explained by Pulp's 'Common People'. *Smoke some fags and play some pool, pretend you never went to school, but still you'll never get it right...*

Politicians started cosying up to football stars and pop stars, building up to a chorus of John Prescott being soaked by Chumbawamba at the Brit Awards in support of the sacked Liverpool dockers (more later). *You'll never fail like common people. You'll never watch your life slide out of view...*

In Liverpool, kids had more 'stuff' than ever before. Girls danced around in their jelly shoes and Bon Bleu outfits, while the boys ran about in their light-up trainers and buttoned up tracksuit kecks. They played outside with bottle tops and skipping ropes and got on with life unaware of their centrality to Britain's future. The country was moving away from the stained smoke walls of the gentlemen's clubs, as decisions were being made with an eye on the reaction of the people. By the end of the decade these kids would be potential voters, which mattered all of a sudden. They'd also be the target of massive industries in a consumerist society, too.

Football, as well, was just about realising its value in a paparazzi decade. Players soon became global superstars. The humble talented striker from an egg-and-chips background was able to reinvent himself as a celebrity of considerable status.

But in Liverpool at the start of the decade, football mattered less than it had ever done before. The shadow of Hillsborough was rightly present, with life put into perspective.

When the league title was won in 1990 it was taken for granted. Kenny Dalglish came off the bench for his last appearance as a player against Derby County and, having secured his status as the most legendary footballer to ever play for the club, was comically booed by the Kop. With Liverpool champions and top of the league by three points the following February, it shocked the world when he decided to resign. He was mentally exhausted after the disaster, and the strain caught up with him. The national press camped outside his home in Birkdale (Marina offered them tea and biscuits, but no comment). They wanted to know if he'd be coming back, but it wasn't to be. The Dalglish era was over and so too was Liverpool's age of dominance.

Local

One of the more unspoken achievements of Dalglish's tenure would eventually prove be his attention to youth development. Although he never bore the fruits of his investment, Dalglish did his utmost to ensure that the incredible young talents Steve McManaman and Robbie Fowler signed for Liverpool and not Everton, their boyhood club.

McManaman was a skinny kid from Kirkdale who could dribble past opponents as if they were mannequins, breezing forward effortlessly every time he received the ball. His dad Dave had been classmates with Tommy Smith and was the star footballer of the area; young Steve grew up hearing that he'd 'never be as good as his arl feller'. In an interview with Graham Hunter, he'd recall: "I'd be in the pub with my dad on a Saturday waiting for the pink Echo to arrive with all the local results in it. Working-class Liverpool was just amazing. I loved sitting and listening to the stories of my father and his mates. I felt like a man, like I was part of it."[53]

With both dad and lad being Blues, Everton tried for years to sign Steve. But in 1986 Davie Aspinall, the legendary Liverpool scout, picked up McManaman and his father and drove them to Anfield to meet the club's manager. There, in Dalglish's office, the young talent stood mesmerised by a pair of golden boots on the Scotsman's desk that he'd been given in Japan. 'You can have them,' Dalglish offered, tempting the lad to sign.

The current head of local recruitment at the academy, Ian Barrigan, has a framed picture of Aspinall, Fowler and McManaman on the wall of his office. He remembers the day McManaman signed, because it was his birthday and he was going out with Aspinall's daughter (who'd later become his wife). 'Jimmy had spotted McManaman in a 7-aside match at Anfield,' says Barrigan. 'He knew he was fantastic at 10 years of age. We'd gotten beat by Everton at home 2-1 that day but went on to win the double in the end, and that was the day McManaman signed. Because it was my 21st birthday, Jimmy got me to ring Dalglish to tell him.'

Robbie Fowler (still known as Robert Ryder then) was shining for Liverpool Schoolboys in the late '80s. He'd been invited to LFC's centre of excellence but hadn't yet signed. One icy Tuesday evening as he was stood waiting for his bus back to Toxteth with his dad, a white Mercedes pulled up. *'Need a lift?'* asked Dalglish. He took them all the way home. When they got to Toxteth, young Robbie took an eternity to get out of the car, hoping his friends would see Kenny Dalglish

---

[53] *El socio del Todos.* McManaman interview with Graham Hunter, 2016.

waving goodbye. 'But you know what,' he wrote, 'not one of my mates walked by, and not one of the neighbours stuck their heads out their windows, even though they were all nosey buggers!' Fowler decided to sign for Liverpool despite being a Blue and became a defining symbol of the 1990s.

Roy Evans remembers when he first came across Fowler at youth level. His lad Stephen was playing in goal for West Lancs Schoolboys against Liverpool Schoolboys. Robbie was playing up front for Liverpool: "And although I'd obviously heard of him, I'd never seen him in action. I'm not sure how many he scored but he gave Stephen a pretty torrid afternoon." He made scoring look easy. At the academy, Fowler and McManaman became friends despite there being three years between them. At a tournament in the Netherlands they got to play together, and although there were various famous teams with famous academies at the tourney, they were the two best players there.

Graeme Souness gave Fowler his debut in a League Cup tie against Fulham in 1993. He scored one at Craven Cottage, and then in the return leg at Anfield scored five. It was astonishing - Kopites were delirious. Here was a natural born finisher, a teenager, a rogue, a street kid and a Scouser. He was instantly endearing.

The Liverpool staff on the bench had been hopeful that he'd make an impact but they had no idea that he'd be *so* impressive – not since Ian Rush ten years earlier had a player scored five times in the same game. Ronnie Moran knew that he had a job on his hands keeping the talent grounded. After the match, he stepped into the dressing room and quipped: 'I don't know what you're looking so smug about. You should have scored seven!'

That night Fowler went back to his mum's house and had special fried rice from the chippy and a can of Irn Bru. The next time he went, his picture was on the paper that his chips were wrapped up in. He scored against Oldham in his next game, then bagged a hattrick against Southampton in the Premiership. Against Aston Villa live on Sky he scored again, then bagged two against Spurs. By April he'd scored more goals than he'd played games and was talked about all over the country.

The press announced him to be the greatest goal scorer since Jimmy Greaves. He was still just seventeen. Before long Nelson Mandela would be asking for his autograph.

Fowler was dubbed 'the Toxteth Terror' by an obsessed written media. "I always think deep down it was a little dig in some way, suggesting I was this scally who had crawled out of the gutter... if there's one thing that does my head in, it's all the stuff banging on about Toxteth being this shithole, the inference being that it was miraculous I managed to claw my way out of there... I remember it being a safe enough place to grow up, and I don't remember having much trouble as a kid," Fowler wrote in his autobiography.

After his goal-scoring exploits he became an overnight star. But he had no publicist or understanding or control over the situation. One minute he was cleaning the baths at Melwood, going home to his mum's terrace where his nan and granddad also lived, 'The next I was all over the papers and across the telly.'

Sky Sports decided to do a feature on his Toxteth life. 'Because I've grown up here, I can see nothing wrong with it,' he said of his neighbourhood as he walked alongside a reporter... 'Here's one of my arl houses here.' Outside the house was a local Scally. Fowler pointed him out: 'See that kid there, he was being dead cheeky to me one day so I chased him and I volleyed the ball at him and he ducked and it went *rar* through the window. The window shattered. The ball ended up in the washing machine so I just jumped over our fence and hid in the bin shed.'

As the feature progressed, Fowler was followed by more and more children. A woman saluted him – 'Hiya Robbie' – 'Alright June?' – she was his old lollipop lady. The mismatched entourage eventually reached an empty football court. There, Sky tried to ask Robbie whether he'd play for England or Ireland? But the lad would rather play football. The interviewer then spoke to his dad, Robert Fowler Senior, who pointed at his son in the background. Junior was visible dribbling the ball on his head like a seal past all of the children, in an impromptu game of knockouts. 'Look at him now, he looks like a schoolboy there – them kids are not far beneath him,' said Senior. Caught between being a youth and one of the biggest names in football, the interview offered a portrait of the innocence of an emerging international star.

Despite Fowler's arrival and the excitement he was bringing, the city was firmly in the national eye as a spectre of misery in 1993. In January it was recognised by the EU to be one of the poorest urban zones in Europe. Then in February the poor innocent two-year-old Jamie Bulger was kidnapped from Bootle Strand and horrifically murdered by two ten-year-old boys.

Such was the fish bowl attention afforded to Liverpool from 1985 to 1995 – by outsiders looking in - Fleet Street likened Liverpool's communal reaction to the murder, once again, to Hillsborough. Jonathan Margolis for the Sunday Times wrote an article titled 'Self-pity City' – a tag that would prove difficult to scrub away:

"Liverpool has a dark and ugly side to its character which has belied the cheeky Scouse image it loves to promote. Most liberal of people can turn out to hate or at least be irritated by Liverpudlians, however much you like the city. Liverpool culture seems to combine defeatism and hollow-cheeked depression with a cloying mawkishness. Liverpool is stuck in a groove, refusing to listen to criticism, clinging to past charms and triumphs, desperate not to be seen provincial but managing to appear just that by cutting itself off from the world. When the world is against you, how gratifying it must feel to know that you really do walk alone."

It was a shocking article, an horrific piece of casual slander. Totally without compassion, did Margolis expect Liverpudlians to beg for forgiveness and popularity whilst mourning the most inhumane tragedy, which had happened upon their own streets? In the weeks and months to follow the press laid the blame of Bulger's murder at the feet of an entire city. In return, locals reacted angrily against their intrusive presence. Fleet Street continued to tarnish them.

There had been thousands of flowers and teddy bears stacked on the grass verge at the back of the Strand. They'd been bought by people who had little financial means but who wanted to show genuine, sincere sympathy. The press referred to the post-Hillsborough 'Liverpudlianization' again, with Charlotte Raven for the Guardian adding to Margolis's piece: "A classic piece of self-delusion. Scouse propensity to linger over every misfortune until another comes to replace it makes them uniquely suited to the demands of the Bulger mourning marathon."

Football, tragedy and mourning were inseparable in the eyes of the written media. Tony Walter explained the issue, writing that the working-classness of such displays seemed to offend 'the cultural sensibilities of mainstream English reserve'. Distancing themselves meant the issues lay at Liverpool's feet, not Britain's.

Within the flowers and even the protests was a sense of community that bemused a public who only saw the crime itself. Ralph Bulger, the father of innocent James, tried to explain afterwards how Bootle was/is: 'A great place full of warm people'.[54]

Margolis's sentiments were not lost on Brendan Wyatt: 'I think that's why we get this Self-pity City tag, because we come together after something has

---

[54] Quote sourced from 'As If' by Blake Morrison, 2012.

happened, like Jamie Bulger and even when Madeline McCann went missing. Ken Bigley too and Hillsborough, and Anthony Walker as well. We come together and support our own. People see it as though we're wallowing, but we're not.'

Jonathan Margolis had been a writer for the Financial Times and TIME magazine but, back in 1978, was unsuccessful in a job application for the Liverpool Daily Post. In 2003 he conceded that his 'Self-pity City' article had been written in anger and that the reaction to it was surprising. He'd received more pats on the back than condemnation for it. In an apology, he wrote: "Over the weeks after my article appeared, I became horribly aware that across Britain there is a very real, casual racism - and I don't use the term loosely - for Scousers. It starts about halfway along the M62 to Manchester and gets worse from then on." None of it was fair.[xvii]

The same lack of affection given to Fowler's Toxteth in the 1980s was afforded to Bootle in the 1990s. Jamie Carragher grew up in and remains entrenched to the town, and the press coverage afforded to the place did not accurately depict the Bootle he knew.

Carragher describes his hometown as a venue for fierce communal spirit. 'I feel blessed to have been born there,' he said, explaining time and again how the values he upholds and the principles he personifies, firstly as a player and later as a torchbearer for the city, are the principles of Marsh Lane: a community where the most destructive weapon he ever saw was a sharp tongue in the Chaucer pub. In his autobiography he goes into detail:

"Marsh Lane is the type of area that has contributed to Liverpool's reputation. It's a mad mix of cynical and kind-hearted, funny yet tough personalities... For generations the people here have been bred to be survivors. Bootle was bombed to virtual destruction during the Second World War. Later, poverty set in because the dockyards, once the main source of employment, were abandoned.... You've got two choices in a situation like that: sink or swim. Ninety per cent of people here keep their head above water... You need to be shrewd as well as resilient where I'm from."

In the mid-90s when he was just about on the fringes of first team football, local kids would stand at the end of his Knowsley Road path and look through the window of his house, waiting for Carragher to give them a nod and a wave. 'I'd be watching Sky Sports and eating my tea,' he recalls. 'I was probably just having my fish of a Friday with a few chips and peas that I got every week like a good Catholic lad for my mum. I don't think I've changed too much.'

As he matured, Carragher became the perfect reference point in conduct for all local players: appearing everywhere, presenting awards, never acting ostentatiously and always crediting his family, community and city for his achievements. By the end of his career almost everybody had a positive encounter with him at some point. He became an exemplary face for his town.

'I see myself as lucky to be from Bootle,' he says. 'Predominantly most of my soccer schools are here. Some people say *"I got out"* about themselves, but that doesn't apply to me. I love where I come from. I still like to be around the people I grew up with and I drink in the same pubs. I just see myself as fortunate because I was able to do what most kids grow up wanting to do and play for Liverpool or Everton, which few local lads have actually gone on to do.'

Those local Liverpool and Everton lads who emerged to play for the club in the 1990s were tough kids. Michael Ball, Tony Grant, Steven Gerrard, David Thompson, Alan Stubbs, Francis Jeffers - their upbringings were visible in the way they played. When Fabio Capello tried to lure Jamie Carragher out of retirement for England, he paid flattery to those mental attributes as 'strong intangibles'.

Liverpool, as a city region, had hard characters, but they were resilient and certainly not all criminals like the press made out. Historical crime data on the government website today shows that from 1990 to 2001, the total amount of crime in Britain was consistently higher elsewhere than it was in Merseyside.

Police force	Theft offences	Vehicle offences	Criminal damage	Fraud or Forgery
Avon and Somerset	29,257	39,801	17,216	6822
Cheshire	13,342	14,606	8,518	1679
Devon and Cornwall	26,163	22,488	12,940	3704
Greater Manchester	63,201	103,874	57,909	11,034
Merseyside	*32,425*	*37,705*	*21,814*	*4150*
Metropolitan	205,705	209,383	144,210	36,000
South Wales	26,591	46,879	28,329	3027
South Yorkshire	23,363	31,814	16,216	2014

Thames Valley	41,800	46,266	20,618	5183
West Midlands	50,015	84,321	39,555	6291
West Yorkshire	48,530	73,632	36,496	5574

The stats show that Liverpool was much similar to everywhere else in the country in regards to crime, apart from London, Wolverhampton, Leeds, Oxford, Birmingham and Manchester, whose levels of criminal activity were much higher and left Liverpool far behind (perhaps some inward reflection was – and still is – required by travelling supporters?).

So why did Liverpool retain a criminal perception? Tony Evans often refers to history: that the Irishness of Liverpool meant any whiff of wrongdoing appeared more sinister to the British public; that happenings inside Scotland Road seemed more dramatic than the actions of gangs from Birmingham, like the Peaky Blinders, and Salford, like the Scuttlers.

In the 1990s the traditional charm of Liverpool was moulded into a different form of television fascination for the public. The decade started with 'Waterfront Beat' and ended with 'Liverpool 1': police dramas set in the city with Scousers playing bad guys. Mike Storey, council leader, stated: 'What concerns me is that it harms our city's image and puts off potential investors who might get a distorted image of Liverpool.'

And it wasn't a case of delusion. In 1991 an estate developer in Grantham (Thatcher's birthplace) renamed a street from 'Liverpool Close' to 'Ipswich Gardens' because sales were poor compared to other streets. In Bournemouth that same year, locals acted out against the number of Scousers who'd moved down to work in the town as labourers, with the Independent reporting:

> "A take-away owner having trouble with local youths likened their behaviour to that of 'a bunch of Liverpudlians'. Scousers had taken over the medial tasks of the town and encountered 'white racism'. The local Bournemouth FA created a ruling that each team could have no more than five Scousers. Bournemouth West Tory MP John Butterfill described Liverpudlians as "drop-outs pursuing a parasitical lifestyle."

Simon Hughes remembers growing up and it being a matter of life that Liverpool people were viewed in a certain way: 'Criticisms were given as naturally as breathing and sex for people. Now, I've reached the point on a personal level where I feel there is no point arguing with them because their views are so entrenched across society. Why do we need the seal of approval from somebody who is not from the city? I think Liverpool is far more culturally rich than the vast majority of other places anyway.'

TV shows in the 1980s and 1990s rebranded the Scouse accent as something else. It had always been the sharp-end of Liverpool's speared identity. Then Harry Enfield satirised it, put it in a tracksuit and made it appear angry and stupid.

Enfield distorted and simplified Scousers and in doing so enforced a bias against the accent. The Independent – so often willing to question accepted British norms - ran a piece on it. This time they wrote: "That thick Scouse accent has turned into a social affliction and a real disadvantage at work in other parts of Britain, and some Merseysiders are not joking when they refer to the scourge they call 'Scouseism'."

Sheila Coleman told the paper of an incident at the House of Commons: "We were stopped for a routine security check," she said. "They immediately recognised my Liverpool accent and one of them said, 'Look out, lock up the silver, the Scousers are in the House'. It was offensive in the extreme and to my mind revealed a deep-rooted prejudice."

A fair comment was made by a presenter from Crosby who'd been made to have elocution lessons as a child to lose the best part of her accent and identity. Anne Robinson said: "When I hear a Scouse accent I brighten up because I know the speaker is going to be brighter and probably a lot more entertaining, in a witty way, than the rest."[55]

But by 1995, a very firm image of Liverpool and its people had been presented to the public. The city had fallen in national regard. Just thirty years earlier the accent had been copied and adored, but in the mid-90s the Liverpudlian character was questioned - in shops, on television and in newspapers. If the city had indeed fallen, then it only had one option.

Jamie Carragher referred to the Marsh Lane mentality – of resilience and grit. That way of thinking swept over every borough of Liverpool. It was sink or swim. So they kept their heads above water, drawing upon what Winston Churchill had coined as "the spirit of an unconquered people". They'd survived his attack beforehand in 1911. They'd survived the Germans afterwards, as well as poverty, dehumanisation, disasters and public vilification, all through their own grit and community. It was to be more of the same.

---

[55] 'Racism, sexism, now scouseism' | The Independent, 1997.

Local

This was still a city of musical and artistic flair. It had refused to accept criticism and retained belief in the beauty of its buildings beneath the soot. Eventually, with a bit of a clean and a lot of investment, the rest of the country would come to hear about – before discovering for themselves - Liverpool's genuine exceptionalism.

*

In 2019 TripAdvisor named it as the third best destination in the United Kingdom, behind London and Edinburgh. Liverpool, that port town out on its own, was placed ahead of Bath, York, Jersey and the usual upper-class getaways. Liverpool: ahead of every other unmentioned city in the UK. In 2018 the Guardian named it as one of the top 40 destinations in the world, between the palm trees of the Seychelles and the temples of Laos.

The city's buoy came from an obvious place: from outside. Help came from the continent, from Brussels and the European Union.

The EU had initially played a part in Liverpool's demise, rendering its docks and its geography irrelevant. In the mid-80s however the Union started handing money to the Council for rejuvenation projects. They set up an office in Brussels for the city in 1994 and awarded it 'Objective One' status – such was its state of destitution.

One of the big difficulties from that point was securing British funding to match the investments made by the EU. They gave Speke airport £23m; they gave £5m for Bootle town centre; £900,000 for a North Huyton community project; £16m to improve transport links in South Liverpool; £20m for a Merseytram scheme (no UK funding to match the initiative scuppered this); £3m towards restoring St George's Hall, and then £50m towards restructuring the King's Dock.

The city started to peacock itself for outsiders. Liverpool Football Club joined in, flirting with internationalisation in the late 1990s as advances in communication made the world seem smaller than before. Foreign fans, tourists, players and coaches began to enter Britain and Liverpool more regularly. It had always been a venue for settlers from around the world whose communities became historic and deep-rooted, moulding the city into a unique hotbed of cultures. In the 1990s, though, fandom, specifically authentic local and traditional fandom, was threatened by tourists for the first time.

Studies were conducted on the influx and active targeting of Scandinavian supporters in the '90s by academics across the continent. Clubs would become brands, deliberately exporting themselves for consumers. Manchester United became known for being the best at it, and while Liverpool were not on their level commercially, they were still good at selling themselves.[56]

English football had been televised in Scandinavia since the 1960s and the Liverpool 'Norwegian Supporters Club' was formed in 1980. By the late 1990s there were some 90,000 members of various Liverpool clubs in Scandinavia. De-localisation of support within Anfield went from being a welcome accident to a very real pursuit, and a grey wasteland of ticket scrambling was born. It felt like social exclusion for those who had always supported the club. For them, an agenda became obvious: there was now another economy to compete with and a new form of marginalisation.

The Scandinavians who started coming over more regularly were ardent fans, respectful and fundamentally good people, who cared for Anfield's surrounding area. They had more successful alternatives elsewhere to follow but instead chose Liverpool, and, because of that, were welcomed on the whole. But from the stadium being a place of escape for locals during uncertain times, there was now competition just to get inside. '*Any spares?*' became a standard question asked before every match and would be forevermore.

As football grew to be more commercialised, it left symbols everywhere. Carlsberg paid for a bronze statue of Shankly to be placed outside the Kop. They scribed the words 'Bill Shankly was probably the greatest manager in the world' together for its unveiling in a tawdry display of commercialism – something Shankly, the teetotal socialist, would have hated. Why hadn't the club paid for it to begin with? Many fans felt they should have been guilt-tripped into doing so.

In January 1994 Roy Evans fulfilled John Smith's prophecy from twenty years earlier and became Liverpool manager. He was to stand as a guardian of the old Boot Room ways – the Liverpool way – in this globalised age. The Souness era would boil down to the narrative that he changed too much too soon. He'd also be remembered for his interview with the Sun newspaper.

Under Souness, Liverpool finally re-joined European competition following the Heysel ban. Legislation meant that he needed six English players to be in his squad, but Liverpool had a 'foreign' team: Grobbelaar was Zimbabwean, Molby was Danish; Rush and Saunders were Welsh; Nicol was Scottish, while Whelan, Houghton and Staunton were Irish.

---

[56] Andersson & Radman, 1999: 68... Goksøyr & Hognestad, 1999... Lee, 1999: 89... R Nash, 2000.

Local

Souness only had a few English lads, namely Wright, Burrows, Tanner, Barnes and Ablett. Because of this, he blooded raw prospects Steve McManaman and Mike Marsh, and even gave a game to a kid signed from Prescot Cables called Barry Jones.

It didn't take off and following a draw with Portsmouth in the FA Cup Souness was hospitalised with a serious heart condition. The Sun came to see him and did a full spread of him in hospital alongside his partner (headlined '*Loverpool*'). It was only three-years after the Hillsborough disaster and supporters were furious. Such was the strength of civic feeling towards the newspaper in the city, the manager tarnished 15 years of legacy with a ten-minute conversation. On top of this, Phil Thompson had been sacked from the Boot Room – which was then knocked down and forgotten.

It all felt uneasy. The players were not good enough and Ronnie Moran would fume that they no longer cared like those before them. Roy Evans in 1994 stepped into a difficult situation.

In his first home game as new manager he appealed for unity, writing in the programme notes: "I'm a local lad. I stood on the Kop as a youngster and understand the expectations of all our supporters. I was a 15-year-old lad when I was presented in front of Bill Shankly. '*You are joining the greatest club in the world,*' he told me in his office. I believed him then, and I believe it now. I come from a similar background to a lot of our supporters and we have a common bond." Evans still had Ronnie Moran there and he hired Sammy Lee to work under him, preserving something traditional and now seemingly precious.

Everything was changing. Because of legislation following the Taylor Report, the famous standing, swaying and spontaneous Spion Kop was set to be demolished. It had stood since 1906, but in May 1994 bulldozers knocked it down.

Every home match leading up to the 30th April was a 'Flag Day', in which Kopites brought in their old banners, brollies and wavers to create a visual spectacle. They knew that in a few short months football's greatest monument would be gone: more important to fan culture than the old Wembley (a once-a-season venue) or anywhere else.

The atmosphere was electric against Everton, enhanced by an old wartime air raid siren smuggled in, and against Chelsea and Sheffield United too. On the 16th April against Newcastle the Geordies realised the significance of the occasion and joined in with 'You'll Never Walk Alone' as the Kop swayed back and forth.

Daniel Fieldsend

Liverpool's last home game of the season against Norwich City went on general sale just a few days before the match. Tickets were £8. The queues were old fashioned, snaking all the way down Skerries Road at 6am on the Tuesday morning like they had done in the pre-Heysel days.

Leaflets had been produced and handed out at Newcastle and at West Ham away, explaining how exactly 'Flag Day 5' against Norwich – The Kop's Last Stand – was going to be organised. It instructed fellow Kopites to arrive at Breck Road at 1:45pm. They were reminded to sing YNWA slowly, and make as much noise as possible throughout the game by joining in with every song without reservation (not that they needed telling twice).

The club had not regarded any of the other flag days, but the leaflets suggested that 'FD5' would be different. "Rumour has it the club are planning some appropriate celebrations. About bloody time too. If they do provide some kind of party we should join in where appropriate. Ignore the '60s pop stars, professional Scousers, entertainers and hangers on. We don't need them. They only turn up at cup finals and take tickets from *YOU*," the leaflet read. "Don't let the club hijack our day. It is our Kop and we should show the world just how proud we all are to be Kopites."

As it happened, the club brought out former players before kick-off, adding to the sentimentality of the day. Confetti flew and brollies spun. George Sephton played 'She Loves You' like the old days. A banner outside the ground read: 'SPION KOP 1906-1994 RIP – REDS IN POWER'. Mike Nevin's dad took a camera to capture the day. Outside Anfield he filmed Dr Fun (Lenny Campbell) and his puppet Charlie, dressed all in red entertaining fans who entered the Kop. A bloke walked past the camera with a huge Liverpool-Genoa poster worn as a hat. There were more Italian flags inside the ground, for Roma and Juventus who were symbols of the club's recent finals.

Joey Jones' tapestry was proudly on show, as every section of the Kop boasted colour. The thousands of fans packed together roared throughout in unison - none of it cheapened by the sight of a camera phone. Brian Hall took the mic and introduced Liverpool's former players one by one. Albert Stubbins first, then Billy Liddell (who ran onto the pitch despite being 72 years of age). Tommy Smith next – '*Ohh Tommy Tommy*' – before Ian Callaghan, David Fairclough, David Johnson, Stevie Heighway, Craig Johnston and Phil Thompson were introduced.

The two biggest roars of the day were for Kenny Dalglish – not seen for ages – and for Nessie Shankly, Joe Fagan and Nessie Paisley – not seen for longer – who came out in a trio. '*Amazing Grace*' filled the air, creating an emotional moment.

Local

Nobody had wanted this day to come, but come it had. Grown men cried sporadically throughout. They were mourning a part of themselves, their own identity and mortality. For them, it was the end of fandom as they knew it.

Norwich won the game. Liverpool's players were poor but their fans were rich in humour; "*You're supposed to let us win*," they chanted to the Canaries. Nobody wanted to leave afterwards; the police had to intervene and shepherd them out. At Flagpole Corner the masses stood, looked back one last time, welled up and walked out forever. The Kop and its Kopites had been special, not bettered anywhere else, and now it was over.

John Garner would go into folklore as the last person to score in the old Kop end, dressed as a Spion Kop war veteran in army gear, with a fez on like Poor Scouse Tommy. He jumped the barrier at the end of the game and ran towards goal, encouraged all the way before he put a shot in the top corner.

*

The Independent knew that Scousers didn't usually wear fezzes. In 1995 they wrote: "Despite its image as a run-down and depressed city, its people are prepared to pay high prices to dress well. Staff at Wade Smith, whose annual turnover is a staggering £5m-plus, never cease to be amazed by 16-year-olds spending more than £150 on a pair of Versace jeans."

Liverpool in the '90s still had its own unique fashion and music taste. Wade Smith's had moved to Mathew Street with female shoppers part of the clientele now too. All of the new, trendy young footballers went there. They'd browse the records at the back of the shop and look at the new Helly Hansen and Meccano jackets at the front.

Jamie Carragher remembers being an emerging talent spending his money there: 'You'd be bouncing in to town all those years ago and getting what was on offer there. I always say that [rhetoric] of Liverpool being fashionable and people try and take the piss out us from that Harry Enfield sketch, but you'd do well to find any better dressed fellers or women than us, especially of a Saturday night in town.

'I certainly didn't want to be a fashion icon like you see certain players wearing flamboyant outrageous gear now. I'd want to look smart and I think that's the best way of summing it up. You don't want to go over the top, which goes back to not wanting to draw too much attention to yourself or think you're bigger and better than anyone or whatever it may be.' Carragher presented himself in such a manner because he knew in Liverpool upstarts are quickly brought back down to earth.

It was in this mode of thought that the Farm band were styled. They dressed like working-class, match going locals, 'which had always been the point of the band,' says Kevin Sampson, their manager. 'They had to look the part so the audience could identify with them on every level. Wherever you were from you could go and see them.'

Liverpool was blessed with many bands in the 1990s who made relatable music, not about love and hand holding like in the 1960s, but about optimism for jobs and even casual drug use. And they all looked like typical Scousers: Cast, the La's, the Farm, the Lightning Seeds and Space walked onstage in bucket hats and branded jumpers, not suits and bobbed haircuts. Most endearing for fans was how they refused to shy away from typically divisive issues for media savvy bands, such as football and politics. Lee Mavers was a Blue and John Power was a Red and everybody was fine with that.

No longer a dominant Atlantic seaport, the city learnt to redefine itself in other ways. Bands were just one manifestation of Liverpool's musical evolution. Africa Oye festival began in 1992 and grew year upon year. Young adults went to Voodoo, the Quad, the Conti and the 051 for a dance. Electronic music was encompassing all types of people. At the forefront of it all was Cream. 'That grew as a super-club which was unprecedented,' says Sampson. 'Local lads started that and watched it travel the world.'

The club was more of a lifestyle than anything else and was founded by James Barton, Andy Carroll and Darren Hughes. They named it because 'the cream always rises to the top', which proved to be true. By 1995 Cream had events in Ibiza, Buenos Aires and Moscow. If the Beatles were at the forefront of music in their day, so too, in its own right, was Cream.

The events attracted young, single and free people from all over the country, keen to be seen at one of the trendiest venues in Europe, wearing stylish clothes and having a good time. Naturally, it attracted Liverpool's young squad of footballers.

They'd been dubbed the 'Spice Boys' by the Daily Mail because of their good looks, modelling contracts and youthful zest for life. The tag stuck, but not in endearment. They were synonymous with the '90s New Lad era, fostered by an interview that appeared in Loaded magazine, who'd taken Fowler and McManaman to a bar in the afternoon and left the mic running while the interviewer disappeared to the toilet. Their off the cuff conversation, together as two young Scouse lads, was used sneakily and made to appear as though they'd had a night out with Loaded and confessed to a life of hedonism. They had not.

There had been an explosion in earnings and an erosion of privacy which the players felt a consequence of. But that was nothing new: from George Best to Frank Worthington, footballers had always enjoyed the benefits of fame. The Independent cut through the fascination to the truth of the media obsession: "Liverpudlian youth has had a poor image outside the city. Brian Clough's infamous jibe about Scousers stealing hubcaps was just one manifestation of a common belief that the city's young men were more interested in taking cars and drugs than earning a living," (1997).

Fowler and McManaman were misrepresented for being seen in the city centre, but in truth they spent most of the time in their mothers' houses in Walton and Toxteth respectively.

The 1996 FA Cup final would become notorious for the cream Armani suits and mobile phones on the pitch (Roy Evans and Ronnie Moran refused to wear them), but little would be said about the press intrusion leading up to the game. For three days the tabloids wrote about Fowler's parents' break-up. He was still living at home with his mum and had only ever been on holiday to Wales, but here he was, exposed to a new world in which people like Robbie Williams hung around with the team and rejoiced in their fame. Manchester United, like Liverpool, had a young squad, with players like Scholes, Giggs and Beckham starting in 1996, but they were able to prepare for the game without intrusion (the 'Becks' obsession came later).

Liverpool lost to Manchester United and the result summed up the decade. United had become Liverpool's envy. 'They played the kind of football that we in our heart-of-hearts longed for Liverpool to play, which we had been doing in the decade before,' says Sampson. 'We spent the 1990s watching them chip way and get closer to what we thought was an unassailable 18 titles. It is a difficult decade to celebrate.'

A few months later, domestic football was replaced by the international game. Anfield had hosted the European Championships qualifier between Ireland and Holland in 1995 as the Dutch and Irish used the city as a venue to drink together all day, spontaneously organising an impromptu match between fans in Stanley Park. The Dutch won that particular match, as well as the official one a few hours later, and qualified for the tournament in England.

Daniel Fieldsend

A few months after the FA Cup final, in the summer of 1996, Holland played in the quarter finals of the tournament against France at Anfield and locals (those who could afford to go - ticket prices were extortionate) got to see new stars like Zidane, Kluivert, Thuram, Seedorf and Deschamps in the flesh at a time when big European names were not coming to Anfield. They saw Maldini for Italy, as well as two impressive players for the underdogs Czech Republic: Pavel Nedved and a suave young Patrik Berger.

Roy Evans had tried for years to sign Lilian Thuram and Marcel Desailly, as well as Jari Litmanen for the Reds, but the club refused to pay out big fees for them and, as a recovering place, Liverpool lacked panache and attraction as a club, with England in general having little desirability as a league.

The English national team had failed to qualify for the World Cup in 1994, adding a degree of expectancy to the 1996 Championships. St George's flags were bought again all over the nation and the Lightning Seeds' nostalgic song 'It's Coming Home' provided an anthem for the summer. In most of Liverpool, though, there was a lot of bemusement: why did Venables not play Fowler, and why was McManaman wasted out wide? Such conversations were typically followed by an ending of *'who's arsed anyway?'* England was becoming an unpopular London team in the minds of many.

From this point on, the decade, which had started slowly, built up to a crescendo. In 96/97 Reds boycotted Sheffield Wednesday and then lost to Paris Saint-Germain (a club that was younger in existence than captain John Barnes) – whose supporters presented a banner saying 'Welcome to the Legendary Fans' to the travelling Kop. It was also the season of emerging talents: David Thompson, Jamie Carragher and Michael Owen.

Sport on Merseyside helped to improve Liverpool's image, especially after a suspected IRA bomb was rumoured to have been planted at the Grand National. Some 500,000 people were evacuated from the course and were fed and housed by the residents of Aintree Lane, Warbreck Moor, Walton Vale and Ormskirk Road.

But the most defining image of communal support, from a sociological perspective, came against Norwegian side Brann in March in the Cup Winners Cup.

After scoring his 113th goal for the club (still aged only 21), the third goal of the evening, Robbie Fowler lifted up his club jersey to the fans. Underneath was a red t-shirt: a familiar image with a message of Scouse community: 'Support 500

Locāl

Liverpool doCKers - Sacked Since September 1995'. Fowler risked his commercial potential but secured his image as a working-class champion. It became the most defining portrait of the 1990s.

Daniel Fieldsend

STAND BY YOUR MAN

'Nearly everybody that lived near us went to sea or worked on the docks,' said Fred Windsor of the olden days. 'People in our street whose fathers went to sea, well they always had a parrot hanging outside the door.'[57] Liverpool's most important street wasn't Bold Street or Church Street, but the sea itself. Chris Lawler explained his desire to be near the coast, wherever he may be. 'I moved to Norway coaching for a bit but still had to live near water,' he said. 'It must be a Liverpool thing. I played for Bangor in Wales and moved to Anglesey because it was by the water. I joined Stockport County at the end of my career because it was the closest ground to the Mersey.'

Water was (and is) central to Liverpudlian identity. LFC's first badge was that of seafaring legends: it was a Liverbird flanked by Neptune (the Roman god of freshwater) and Triton (god of the sea) with 'Liverpool Football Club' written underneath. The stands at Anfield were full of seamen: cooks, shipmates and deck officers. And they were full of dockers, too, which at one time was a rite of passage.

But it wasn't an easy job. There was no guarantee of work, hence why – as discussed – dockers became creative with their time and resources. The introduction of the National Dock Labour Scheme in the 1950s effectively got rid of casual employment after dockers fought for their rights, receiving proper contracts and proper employment.

But the advent of containerisation rendered most of them obsolete – there were too many dockers and not enough jobs. Machines did most of the work now so traditional workers were not needed. Relations between the Mersey Docks & Harbour Company (MDHC) and its dockers became strained. MDHC wanted to

---

[57] In conversation with the Museum of Liverpool Life.

get rid of great numbers of dockers (they could afford to, but didn't want to, pay for them all), so they created legislation meaning they could call dockers out at any time of the day – or night – and make them work. MDHC didn't ask, they made it compulsory. Families of dockers had their lives restricted. They'd get home and pull their phone wires out and say it had slipped, or they'd tell their kids to lie and say they were out – anything to regain control over their lives.

Standards of living deteriorated and incomes nosedived. The working-classes saw themselves threatened once more by capitalism. Old school dockers retired as soon as they could. 'I'm glad to be leaving,' they'd say, and 'it's getting to be like the old days'. They were right. Retiring dockers saw their jobs replaced by sub-contracted workers who belonged to new (worse) working conditions. Typically, they belonged to Torside Limited, a third-party employer. The old school dockers' view of them was a belittling one – they were young lads, hungry for work, who'd accept any contract, but were untrained, untested, unsafe, and not proper dockers.

Accidents became a daily sight. Between 1983 to 1989, docker numbers nationally fell from 14,631 to 9,400, and in a much smaller window (from 1989-1992) there was an 80% increase in dockers leaving the industry. The ship was literally sinking.

MDHC didn't care: tonnage increased threefold from 1983. Casualisation began to sneakily return; at Seaforth, lads revolted against plans to reintroduce gate selections, like it had been back in the days. Overworked, underpaid, with no job security... revolutions had been started for less.

Across the world dockers became disillusioned. They were waiting for a spark to light the flames of change. Of course, given the city's nature, it happened first in Liverpool.

On 25th September 1995 80 younger dockers were dismissed by Torside over an overtime row. MDHC sacked all involved. The Torside workers refused to accept this and, the following morning, drew a picket line outside the gates of the Liverpool Docks. 328 men refused to cross it. Some of their fathers refused, too. The old school dockers stood up for the young lads; 500 of them were sacked.

These were no rag-and-bone workers. They'd go on to be painted as dinosaurs, but months earlier Lloyds List (a company that had been assessing standards since 1734) had called the Liverpool dockers: "The most productive workforce in Europe." They were the best in the business.

Daniel Fieldsend

Despite knowing that it was going to happen sooner or later, the Transport and General Workers Union declared the strike unofficial because no ballot had been taken. They'd give money to the dockers hardship fund, but, otherwise T&G did nothing to help. Many of the sacked dockers saw this as a betrayal. Unionism without the support of a union? They were out on their own.

For 28 months they stood out there together, that group of men, unless some died, which they did, or got injured by a passing vehicle, which most did, in the wind and the hail together, standing for their class and pride, and on one of the lads' birthdays they'd all have a cake together and a pint afterwards. Every cake had either a blue or red football kit made out of icing on it depending on the leanings of the feller, and they'd come back again the next day and strand strong again, with their yellow stickers and CK t-shirts, in a display of brotherhood, love and unity. 'The best in Europe'. They'd form a line and block the cargo for as long as they could – ten mins, an hour – and they'd have their kids with them on some days and their wives with them on others, and they'd all take the piss out of each other in turns, but they'd unite whenever a member of the Scab Port was spotted coming and going. *"Fucking scabs"*. In the end they were fighting for each other and for a bigger purpose: they were fighting for the very idea of trade unionism.

Kev Robbo summed it up when told reporters: 'My father, his father, my two uncles, they fought for better conditions on the docks. Some men gave their lives. We can't go and throw those hard-won rights away and sell out the future generations.'

Days were long and weeks felt never-ending, especially when nothing was happening. Whispers of support supposedly coming in from this place and that were taken as nuggets of gold, pure gold, to be collected and turned into victory. Somehow.

In December 1995, three burly Scouse fellers flew over to New York and headed to the very mouth of the Hudson River – to New York Harbour: one of the biggest docks on the Atlantic – where they stood outside its gates and drew a picket line. It took real *cohones*. But their brothers in New York were ready and they agreed. The mini-strike caused stoppages in New York and American Atlantic Containers agreed to a one-month boycott of Mersey Docks, citing the sympathy action taken by East Coast dockers. That contract, to MDHC, was worth £4m.

The dispute coincided with the emergence of the internet which the dockers used to their advantage. The national media were not giving them any attention, not even BBC Merseyside, so they looked out to sea for support.

Local

So fiercely respected were the Liverpool dockers that 30 ports across the world came to a standstill at various times. In Germany, Norway and Japan workers refused to unload Liverpool ships. In Antwerp, Zeebrugge and Gothenburg it was much the same story. And in South Africa all ports were closed down "in solidarity with the Liverpool dockers who stood by us during apartheid".

Robert Irminger of the Port of Oakland, California, was asked to name his workers who supported the picket. 'A lot of the information I don't have,' he said, 'but of course, if I did know their identities, I would not divulge them. Ordinary workers see the sense of solidarity.' Cargo ship Neptune Jade was bound for Canada, but longshoremen refused to cross a picket line, so it went to Japan, where it was the same story. It settled in Taiwan, some 1,300 miles away from its original destination. 'The corporate world does not have a clue about solidarity,' said Irminger. 'They think there has to be someone at the top giving orders.' If only the T&G union had decided to bridge the global support given to the dockers...

Mersey Docks and Harbour Company soiled themselves. Profits fell for the first time in 10 years in 1995 to 31.7 million, a trend that would continue throughout the dispute. 23% less ships were using Liverpool's docks than before. Yet for as much as those dock workers around the world were supporting Liverpool, they were also looking after themselves. Their union rights could one day be under threat, too, they understood. It was wise to remind employers where the real authority lay. It was power to the people, *right on*.

While MDHC took a financial battering, the dockers and their families on the picket line were no better off. In fact, they were poorer. Because of the circumstances of their plight they couldn't claim dole. They couldn't work, either, because that would scupper the movement. So they were forced to use foodbanks. Life depended on donations from outside. One day, an 84-year-old widow came down with a cheque for her late husband's earnings. He'd been a miner and had told her to save it for an emergency. This, she felt, was one.

Dan Carden – current MP for Walton – stood with his father Mike on the picket line. He was 8-years of age. 'The Trade Union building which you can still see in town as the Unite building was the Transport General Workers building then, which became a second home for me. It's where I went to get my Christmas presents and I'd skive off school of a Friday to sit in meetings. Then I'd go over the road to the Lord Warden pub and hang out with old dockers, where of course football and horse racing would be talked about.'

It was there that the famous Calvin Klein t-shirts were sent. Fellers in ale houses across the city would be sat in a red, royal blue, navy or sky blue doCKers t-shirt most days for 28 months. It became both a commercial success (money raised went into the hardship fund) and a visible token of support for the dockers. Slowly, the t-shirts began to be seen more and more across Liverpool.

Dockers were sat in the Lord Warden on the night of 20th March 1997 watching the Liverpool match on telly. There was a muted cheer when Fowler scored the third goal of the night, then an instantly frenzied one when they saw his celebration. *'He's got our t-shirt on!'* they shouted at each other.

The significance of the moment was huge. There'd been a lull in support for the dockers nationally. Momentum had begun to waver. For most of the dispute, media sources and celebrities wouldn't touch the dockers with a barge pole.

Mersey Partnership had run a campaign in 1995 before things kicked off, attempting to get businesses to invest in the city. "Ian Rush and Robbie Fowler are the only strikers on Merseyside," they boasted, riding the popularity and reputation of football in the city. But here was Fowler, two years on, backing the sacked dockers.

He'd gotten his t-shirt through Steve McManaman: 'One of his uncles was having a tough time,' Fowler said, 'and Macca brought us two t-shirts to put under the kit to show our support. We planned to [unveil] it after the game but I scored and lifted it, and the amount of publicity it got for them was great. We believed in what they were trying to do. I got fined the equivalent of £900 at the time but it got the point across.'[58]

The fine was tuppence for Fowler (he'd received the first 'teenage millionaire' contract under Souness), but the gesture was astronomical. The dockers got together for their weekly meeting afterwards and discussed what Fowler had done. They were unanimous that it was awful how UEFA had chosen to fine him. One of the fellers, who'd been using foodbanks for months, shouted up from the back "Let's have a whip-round for him, we'll pay it!" He was half-serious.

'It was one of the biggest moments of the strike,' says Dan Carden. 'I've still got a picture of that in my office in London which the Casa Pub gave to me. The image went around the world and made a real difference, bringing global attention to the dockers' dispute. It was so important and was one of *the* major sporting political moments that I think there has ever been.'

---

[58] In conversation with Liverpool FC TV.

Locāl

Carden's dad had been sacked. His mum was struggling working part-time for the NHS. Families involved quietly questioned it all, watching as their sense of purpose evaporated more and more each day. 'So to have something like that happen as a kid filled you with pride,' Carden says. 'I think that's what Liverpool the city is all about and what our politics is all about.' Unity is strength, as the old saying goes.

Echo and the Bunnymen frontman Ian McCulloch said of Fowler's act: 'I can't really see Beckham having done it. Doing those things that you're not supposed to do, that the authorities look down on, whether that was in school, or to the police or with the government. All those things add up to him being the most fitting footballer for our team, more than any other player we've ever had.'[59]

Although it was McManaman who had bought the shirts, and although it was his idea, and although they'd both planned to display the shirts after the match to the crowd, it was Fowler who created a legacy. Perhaps had they done as planned then UEFA would not have noticed and the act would have been less fulfilling. Either way, Fowler added to his image of roguishness and symbiotically linked himself further to the fans, appearing as though he was prepared to risk endorsement, his own image and a fine, just to connect himself with a pressing current political issue. Would it ever happen again? Had it ever happened before?

After the match, Norwegian full-back Stig Inge Bjørnebye collared Fowler in the dressing room and asked what the t-shirt was for? Bjørnebye was a cultured young lad, always thinking about current issues. The local players got into a discussion with the him and the other foreign players about it, which piqued Bjørnebye's interest. A few days later he went down and stood on the picket line with the sacked dockers. Not at the front, but shoulder to shoulder with them without any real ceremony.

It opened a floodgate. The London Palladium hosted a 42-man benefit concert in aid of the dockers cause, in which Rob Newman, Lee Hurst, Jo Brand, Eddie Izzard, Steve Coogan and others did routines. It was a sell-out. 'Their dispute is at the heart of what's happening politically,' Newman told the press, 'but it hasn't gotten any media coverage. This should start a discussion on the casualisation of labour.'

The picket line wasn't solely a Liverpool FC dispute, even if Fowler's image became synonymous with it. Duncan Ferguson - the son of a gas rigger from the

---

[59] Also in conversation with Liverpool FC TV.

Fife coast - made a five-figure donation to the fund, while Alex Ferguson – steeped in the values of the Clyde shipyards - offered signed merchandise to be raffled off for money. Billy Bragg did a song and Greenpeace got involved. It was very much now front and centre of national awareness.

But the biggest support had always been a local one: it had been the dockers wives. In January 1996 the 'Women of the Waterfront' (WoW) sent a delegation down to Downing Street to campaign. They'd backed their husbands from the off. Small choirs of them would stand outside the homes of scabs and sing to the women inside: *'Stand by your man, and show the world you love him'*.[60] Their very presence as females was unique in trade union history. They brought food and attended pickets like the miner's wives had done, but also formed a recognisable group, spoke at rallies and campaigned for funds.

Jane Kennedy – a lecturer in social policy at the University of Liverpool at the time – told the Independent in 1997: "An unusual aspect of this dispute is the role played by culture," she said. "The collective history of the docks - an organised, solid, militant history - may no longer be based in a geographical community, but it is still very powerful. Without the unquestioning support of the community, I doubt the dispute could have continued this long." She continued. "For decades, Liverpool has effectively been a city under siege. It has suffered years of severe poverty and unemployment, coupled with ridicule from the rest of Britain. Their past has given them a sense of solidarity, attaching a strong 'under adversity' label to the city."

Churning in the background of the dispute was the false promise of a new Labour government. Tony Blair was young, charismatic and tapped in to the optimism of the 1990s with his chumming-up to pop stars and footballers. Labour came into power in May 1997, winning 409 seats and knocking the Tories down to 177. But any optimism the dockers had was quickly dispelled. 'New Labour' was not Labour in the traditional sense and was no ally to this body of struggling workers.

---

[60] It's difficult when writing a football book not to focus heavily on masculine achievements, but the history of Liverpool – especially moments of truly great strength – has belonged to Scouse women. From the Blitz workers to Bessie Braddock, to the Hillsborough mums and dockers wives: they've been the city's backbone. Liverpool women are stronger than the rest; better than most and more stoic than their hot-headed, daft partners.

Local

Despite the party owning a 14% share in the Mersey Docks, they largely ignored the dispute. Tony Blair felt that the dockers were responsible for their own misfortune through their unwillingness to alter their views and "long-standing abuse of monopoly power". The New Labour government failed to reverse anti-trade union legislation enacted by the Tories under Thatcher. They were only Labour in name, it seemed. Wolves in sheep's clothing. 'Whose side are you on Tony Blair?' placards outside the docks asked each day.

Eventually Merseyside Police had enough. They began turning the screw. They increased their presence each day towards the end of 1997 and took action against picketers. 13 dockers were arrested in late August alone. Anybody nicked was then prohibited by bail conditions from standing anywhere closer than 25 foot of the picket line. The end was on the horizon.

On the 26th January 1998 the sacked dockers accepted a settlement. It secured continuity of their pensions but didn't reinstate their jobs. Many were against the settlement but the majority voted for it. It was all over.

After the strike had finished, the Liverpool dockers got in touch with their comrades around the world, sending letters of thanks which, according to the Oakland committee upon receiving it, incarnated the great trade unionist James Larkin: "Who is it speaks of defeat? I tell you a cause like ours is greater than defeat can know. It is the power of powers." They had awoken an international response through their dedication and loyalty to each other. 'If we absorb this message,' stated the Oakland workers, 'then it will be a victory for the Liverpool dockers.'

Afterwards, socially conscious pop stars were looking for something genuine to grasp. They deserted New Labour faster than former Tories flocked to it. Jarvis Cocker, Ian Broudie, Cerys Matthews and Ian Brown wrote a condemnation in NME at the government for turning its back on its social reform promises. In this fashion, Oasis, Primal Scream, Chemical Brothers, Paul Weller, Billy Bragg, Cast, Dodgy and Ocean Colour Scene released an album called 'Rock the Dock' aimed at lining the hardship fund for the dockers who failed to qualify for redundancy packages. 'It's a disgrace their cause has been largely ignored for so long. People need to support them,' said Noel Gallagher.

Support came in another strange way a few months later. Chumbawamba drummer Danbert Nobacon ran over to John Prescott at the Brit awards and poured a bucket of icy water over his head. The band's song Tubthumping could easily have been dedicated to the sacked dockers, especially the repeated line: '*I get knocked down, but I get up again, you're never gonna keep me down.*' At the

Brits they changed the lyrics to: *'New Labour sold out the dockers, just like they'll sell out the rest of us.'* Nobacon's action was a publicity stunt above all else, but one that a few dockers sitting dry at home may have secretly smiled about.

As the dust settled, the dockers began to look to the future. They wanted to invest their leftover money into something noble, something with a social heartbeat. The Casablanca bar on Hope Street was reborn. 'The Casa', as it would be known, was named after the socialists who fought in the Spanish Civil War. It became a community centre and a bar. It'd go on to offer free advice on housing and employment issues, on benefits and asylum and family law. The one constant in life is the potential for hardship. The Casa, dockers hoped, would be a remedy to ease people's concerns. Between 2000 and 2015, some £10 million worth of free advice would be given to people in need. *Unity is Strength.*

The strike was the longest ever industrial dispute in British history. It transcended politics in the end, welcoming football and the arts too. Above all else, the dispute would be remembered successfully in that it provided a new-age example of unionism, collectivism and solidarity during a decade of brands, bands, daft pop, consumerism and false consciousness. Liverpool had again shown a resolve that transcended its small population and displayed the values of working-class unity at a time when nobody was really sure whether such a thing still existed.

*

When New Labour took over the country in a fanfare of popularity, Liverpool again went against the grain. Mike Storey of the Liberal Democrats was elected as leader of the City Council and promised to restore the city's reputation. 'Liverpool voting has always gone against the rest of the country,' says Simon Hughes. 'It tends to be that those in power don't deliver on their promises and we're the first ones to say *"actually, what the fuck are you doing?"'*

In 1998 a defining figure of Liverpool FC's success was set to depart. Ronnie Moran had been at the club for 49 years. He'd sat on the bench for 1,365 games, missing only one match in that time. Under his employment the club had won 10 league titles and 4 European Cups – making him arguably the most successful coach in world football. From being the boy recommended to the club by his postman, to becoming captain, trainer, assistant and manager for a short while, he knew Liverpool inside out. When it all ended Kenny Dalglish said: 'I don't think it's a coincidence that in the most successful spell in the club's history, Ronnie Moran was there.'

Steven Gerrard said later: 'The reason our club has a fantastic history is because of people like him,' while Alex Ferguson added: 'I wish I'd had a pound for every argument I've had with Ronnie, but after the game he was always the first to offer you a drink. There is no question Ronnie Moran is one of Liverpool's all-time greats.'

For better or for worse, Liverpool FC was dipping its toes in the future. The club planned to fill the first team void with a thinker from the North of France. Gerard Houllier had taught in the city, working as an assistant French teacher at Alsop Comprehensive in 1969. He'd lived off Faulkner Street, drank in the Royal Oak and wrote a thesis paper on social conditions in Liverpool. He'd stood on the Kop and watched the Reds beat Dundalk 10-0. He loved Liverpool and always longed to return.

Houllier worked his way up in football from coaching little Noeux-les-Mines – Raymond Kopa's first club – who he took from the 5th to the 2nd division, before being appointed as the thinker behind the blueprint for France's 1998 World Cup victory. Celtic wanted him to be manager in '98 but he joined Liverpool instead. When it came to thrashing out titles with the club, it was decided that he'd become 'joint-manager' with Roy Evans: the first such pairing in British football.

Now Liverpool was half-international, half-traditional. There'd be conflicts. The French speakers would sit together and the English and Scandinavians together too. Jamie Carragher and Rigobert Song from Cameroon became training ground rivals. Titi Camara and Djimi Traore struggled to adapt. Throughout it all, Robbie Fowler remained Liverpool's best player.

He was a former Evertonian and somebody with self-confidence; he always scored past them and the Blues hated him for it. They whispered vindictive rumours throughout the week that he did drugs in town. If some saw him, they'd shout the accusation across the street. Fowler was unapologetic for his quality and continued to perform. On one occasion his mother came home to find the word '*smackhead*' graffitied on her house, a visual attack on her son.

He'd grown up hating drugs – consumption had taken the lives of two of his cousins. He told the Guardian in 2005: "If people only knew the reason why I hated drugs so much, maybe they'd have been a little slower to throw this mud at me. Drugs are nothing but evil."

It got to the point where his financial advisor went to Liverpool and told them that the abuse was hurting his mum and dad too much. Liverpool issued a statement in 1998 telling people that, on top of Sport England's regular checks, they did their own drug tests at Melwood and Robbie Fowler was clean. He'd been forced to do drugs tests non-stop since becoming a professional a few years earlier. Nevertheless, despite the factual statements, he continued to receive stick and his family were feeling the brunt of it. By 1999 he'd had enough.

In previous derbies he'd been the primary target of vitriol. Despite Everton almost going down the season before, Liverpool hadn't won a derby in five years. On the 3rd April '99 Everton were once again languishing around the relegation places. They'd won only 2 league games since early December. *'Blue shite going down, they're going down, they're going down, they're going,'* taunted Kopites inside the Albert. Duncan Ferguson had been sold, Peter Johnson had bailed, Philip Carter had taken over. Evertonians were angry with it all. Anfield was a cauldron.

Both sides had a number of strong characters. Everton had Michael Ball, David Unsworth and Dave Watson. Liverpool had Steve Staunton, Dominic Matteo and Paul Ince. Tackles flew in from the off. Early in the game the Frenchman Olivier Dacourt scored a screamer on the volley. The Blues were delirious. When Paul Ince was brought down by Marco Materazzi six minutes later, Robbie Fowler stepped up to convert the penalty. 1-1. In celebrating the goal, Fowler instantly fell to his knees and mimicked snorting the line, as if it were cocaine. McManaman – his best mate – pulled him up to his feet, but Fowler did the celebration again and danced a jubilant jig. It'd become an infamous image.

The match would go on to finish 3-2 to Liverpool: another for Fowler, one for Berger and then a goal from 18-year-old Franny Jeffers later on. Everton would have won the game were it not for two goal-line clearances from young right-back Steven Gerrard. But in the end, it was to be remembered for Fowler's actions.

He was fined £60,000 and given a 6-game ban for his celebration. It caused faux outrage within a mostly a middle-class Fleet Street press. But Fowler didn't regret it – he felt a statement had to be made: 'It was a way of telling them that if they carried on with all that abuse, then I was going to stuff it up them even more,' he wrote. 'It was an attempt to make them stop. And it was supposed to be funny.'

The strangest part of the affair came afterwards when Gerard Houllier claimed that Fowler was only copying a Cameroonian celebration he'd picked up from Rigobert Song in training. Behind closed doors Houllier had already marked Fowlers card. Despite the striker being a firm favourite with the supporters,

Houllier wanted to phase him out. A few years later he did do, preferring to partner Emile Heskey with Michael Owen instead.

The French manager was building a fine squad. Players of the calibre of Dietmar Hamman, Stephan Henchoz and Sami Hyypia arrived in 2000 to compliment the attacking talents of Steven Gerrard, Michael Owen and Robbie Fowler. Steve McManaman was not to be a part of the continental revolution. He'd already decided to leave the club a few years before and departed on a free transfer.

McManaman had spoken honestly to the Independent in 1997: "I do admire foreign football and the idea of a different culture. I was aware of Italian football from my early days at Liverpool with Ian Rush and Graeme Souness playing there. I've spoken to Gazza and Chris Waddle, while Paul Ince speaks highly of it. But I'm a Liverpool lad and I love the club. As long as Liverpool want me, I'll stay."

Liverpool did want him. They were reported to have offered the same terms as Real Madrid. He'd already turned down a casual approach from Juventus and a very serious bid from Barcelona (£12m). There were other factors at play for McManaman. He was yet to pit himself in the Champions League - did a player of his talent not warrant the opportunity? It had demonstrated Liverpool's demise when Roy Evans rather poetically said 'Liverpool without Europe is like a banquet without wine.'

McManaman's mother was ill, too, seriously ill. Such a situation made life seem all the shorter and a football career seem shorter still. He was in his mid-20s already, no longer a whiz kid. The offer presented itself at a pivotal time and McManaman left on a free transfer. For Liverpool fans, it hurt.

But he'd always been a 'continental' type of player. He was never shouty, like other Scouse footballers. He was a prince, a pearl, with an effortless breezing style. For McManaman the decision to move would be justified by the end of his first season.

Initially at Real Madrid he was taken aback. The facilities were better at Melwood, Butruegeno wanted to know all of Liverpool's secrets and John Toshack had the squad doing training sessions that had been created by Joe Fagan in the 1970s. By the end of his first season however, he was a European Cup winner. He'd win it again two years later playing alongside Roberto Carlos, Zinedine Zidane, Luis Figo and Raul. He'd be called 'a partner to everybody on the pitch' – the most important player – by an observing Johan Cruyff. His dad Dave had lost his wife and his son had moved from home, but after that season, everything was vindicated.

When McManaman won La Liga in 2003 he was joined in Madrid by his old mate Robbie Fowler for the celebrations. The Toxteth striker was given a Real Madrid tracksuit to wear and joined the tour bus with the rest of the Galacticos. At *Cibeles* fountain he was asked to get off the bus and join the team, but he refrained and lay low nearby, only to be spotted by a group of British tourists who – while confused – chanted his name.

1998/1999 was recognisable for Fowler's celebration and for McManaman's decision to leave, but it would become most notorious for the emergence of a young right-back from Huyton with a mispronounced surname: a tough tackling, passionate, skinny but impressive kid with a shaved head called Gerrard. If the '90s was to be defined by a changing of the guards, from the traditional age-old ways of the Boot Room to a new, slow, somewhat awkward continental era, then the mid-2000s would be defined by Liverpool's catapulting into Europe head first. For both the city and the football club, Steven Gerrard was to be more than anybody else the face of the success to come.

Local

MERSEY PARADISE

During the Second World War, schoolchildren in Huyton were not evacuated. They stayed inside the town and watched each day as it was taken over by strangers. It became home to three camps: an internment camp, a prisoner of war camp, and a base for American servicemen. In May 1940 the town became home to potential threats to national security, too, who were put up in new empty houses, secured by high fences and barbed wire. After the war when everybody had left, that group of houses became the Bluebell Estate. It was here during the 1980s, in a cul-de-sac street called Ironside, that Steven Gerrard grew up.

Modest and working-class, the concrete road in front of number 10 was Wembley for Gerrard. He'd play outside each day and pretend to be John Barnes. The lads his age weren't good enough, so he played with his older brother and his mates. They were 9 and 10. He was 6. They all wanted young Stevie on their team. On one occasion he was shoulder-barged into a fence and had his face cut open by a nail. He knocked on his granddad Tony's house, received butterfly stitches, and went back out to play again. Huyton was hard and Gerrard was a product of his hometown.

If it was sunny, they'd play on the field at the back of Ironside. One time when the ball got stuck inside the perimeter of nettles, young Gerrard tried to scoop it out with his leg. His foot went through a rusty garden fork and got wedged. His neighbour Neil came running and called an ambulance. Stevie Heighway drove to Alder Hey when he heard the news and stressed for surgeons not to amputate his toe – this lad was going to be special.

He'd been recommended to Dave Shannon at Liverpool by his coach at Whiston Juniors, Ben McIntyre. 'You could see straight away he was immensely talented,' said Shannon to the Liverpool Echo. 'He had a fantastic desire to play and compete. He wanted to be the best at everything. He was just born to be what he is.'

When Whiston won an U12 tournament in the Netherlands, Sammy Lee presented the young captain with the cup. Two Scousers who were the best in the city for their respective age groups, who'd work together at Liverpool years later.

The club fast-tracked him up the ages. At Vernon Sangster he was mates with Michael Owen and Jason Koumas. Hughie McAuley, their coach, remembers the three of them gravitating toward each other: 'Good players automatically seek each other out,' he acknowledged.[xviii]

But then tragedy struck. Granddad Tony came around on the 16th April '89 to tell the Gerrard's that their nephew and cousin, young Jon-Paul had died at Hillsborough. Gerrard had gone to bed the night before and prayed. They'd played outside Ironside together for years. There was just one year between them. After the tragedy, the Vernon Sangster was shut for weeks. When it reopened it was a different, much more sombre place.

Over the years Owen and Gerrard were treated like prized assets at Liverpool. Stevie Heighway took them to Wembley in 1992 to watch the Reds. They were allowed to have a look at other clubs by Heighway, too, confident that Liverpool would secure their loyalty. Gerrard played a game for West Ham, had a look at Everton's facilities and met Alex Ferguson at Manchester United. Fergie was desperate to sign the lad, but Gerrard would never go to Manchester. Back when he was a boy his dad had clocked him out of the window wearing his mates blue Man United shirt, pretending to be Bryan Robson. He was bollocked and told he'd bring shame on the family if he was seen wearing it. 'Dad wasn't having any son of his dragging the Gerrard name through the Huyton gutter,' reflected Gerrard.

Playing as captain, his Cardinal Heenan team went unbeaten for 3 years. He signed his professional contract and posed for pictures at the school – shaved head, wearing a navy-blue Lacoste jumper. Even before he was on the periphery of the first team everybody in Huyton knew who he was. Gareth Roberts remembers: 'I'd get my haircut in the barbers on Twig Lane and their used to be a drawing of Gerrard in a Liverpool kit above the mirror, and that was before he'd even played a game for the first team. He'd have been about 17.'

The happiest time of Gerrard's career was pumping balls up at Melwood as an apprentice. There were no worries, other than the smell of Joe Corrigan's morning shite wafting in from next door. He'd enjoy messing about with his mates in the reserves, but later acknowledged he never wanted to be caught acting a 'tit' in front of older Scouse lads like Fowler and McManaman.

His mate Michael Owen was world famous by the time Gerrard began training with the first team. In his first week at Melwood he made an impression, hitting Paul Ince hard with a tackle. 'What do you think you're doing?!' Ince barked. 'Shut the fuck up!' the teenager from Huyton snarled back. Gareth Roberts has a fond view of the encounter: 'Ince turned up at Liverpool and called himself 'The Governor' – a Cockney who'd played for Man United – I love that the Scouse lad smashed into him and said *"welcome to Liverpool."'*

Jamie Carragher, another local lad with a fiery streak, remembers it well: 'Stevie was 18 and Ince was Liverpool's captain; had captained England and had played in Italy. There is a type of conviction that you get with the best Liverpool-born players. Wayne Rooney has similar qualities. There was a belief and grit in Stevie's play combined with technique... Nothing was going to get in his way. He wasn't going to let anybody beat him without a fight.'[xix]

Gerrard was a right-back initially. Fans would stand and roar in celebration in the Centenary and Main Stand whenever he flew into a crunching tackle. There was something so masculine, aggressive, determined and 'Scouse' about the way he played, it turned them into barbarians. He channelled that Huyton upbringing into brave performances, replicant to how fans believed they would play if they had the opportunity to do so.

Gerrard went beyond that standard in matches against Everton and Man United. He said of the Trafford club: 'In Huyton I, and every other kid from a Red family, had been taught to loathe Manchester United. It was drilled into our brains, hardening our hearts and conditioning our souls as Liverpool fans.' That regard led him to write in his autobiography: 'During ninety minutes of football, I want United to die.'

In 2000 on the approach to Old Trafford, the window near Gerrard was attacked, causing it to splinter. He almost received a brick to the head. It had been built up by the press as a battle between Roy Keane and himself, which inspired the Scouser to put in a strong performance. The occasion would be marked by violence on and off the pitch. Liverpool won 1-0, their first victory at Old Trafford in ten years (a symbol in itself of the shift between the two clubs). It all felt like the '80s again.

The rivalry with Manchester United always had a different complexion for Liverpool fans than the one with Everton. The Blues occupied the same physical space as Reds and there was a limit on the degree of venom that could be afforded to them. Because they lived together in the same city, the derby would be rescued by significant moments of civic important (Hillsborough, Rhys Jones' murder...) but Manchester United fans were nameless and faceless. They were the imagined enemy – Mancs from up the road. Only human decency prevented encounters from sliding into anarchy.

On occasions decency was forgotten. Fights in 'dog shit alley' were regular throughout the '70s and '80s, no more so than in 1985 when the frustrations of life under Thatcherism – a slow building rage born out of a lack of opportunity for both groups of supporters – boiled over into a display of hooligan behaviour at Goodison Park in an FA Cup tie between Liverpool and United.

Inside and outside the ground fans fought with each other. Brian Glanville penned an account: "Coaches and trains of United's supporters were stoned. Mechanics would run out of garages to scream abuse at the coaches as they went by... Journalists see little or nothing from the press box, nothing of what goes on in the surrounding streets and alleys, at railway stations..."

'People were just attacking each other wherever they could,' Tony Evans remembers. 'All of the pubs on Walton Lane had the windows smashed.' He reflects, though, that the fixture happened in an era of general anger. 'Every night you'd turn on the news and there'd be fighting on the picket lines, Northern Ireland was burning and British life was being consumed in violence, so why would it be any different in one of the poorest cities in the country that was being starved of resources?'

The following year, Man United's team coach was attacked with tear gas outside the Main Stand. The unfortunate victims were school age Liverpool supporters who'd been stood waiting for autographs from arriving players. They were taken into the United dressing room and looked after by United's squad – Bryan Robson in particular acting with care.

Tension had been whipped up by a number of factors. By Old Swan's Ron Atkinson who was happy to play the pumpkin-headed pantomime villain; by the history of that ship canal too, apparently, although it was never a problem before. By the column inches Man United received from a biased media. By the Beatles being superior to the Hollies and, on that note, by Merseyside's clubs being far better than Manchester's.

Like Liverpool, Manchester was a city of historic Irish immigration and was a hotbed for socialist discourse. Ian Brown of the Stone Roses once said that they were two ends of the same city "and if we'd get it together, London would never have [get] a look in." In that vein, there had been a lot of good incidents between the two tribes. Stephen Monaghan and Brendan Wyatt both have stories of being looked after, and looking after, Manchester United's inner circle in Europe when their paths have crossed. In 1986 Tony Wilson organised a benefit concert 'With Love from Manchester' in support of the sacked Liverpool Council members to raise money for their families and for legal fees. The Smiths, the Fall and New Order played – Derek Hatton spoke with Morrisey beforehand to seal the deal.

Although it was a factor, the rivalry was not directly between the two cities (recent sandwiches put out for Manchester United fans in Everton's (Red) Brick pub on County Road testify to that). Tension was mostly inspired by historic competition. 'I've worked in Manchester and they'd love to have what we have,' says Andrew Hudson, while his brother Chris points out: 'The only other set of fans that come close to us are United, who have a similar mindset and culture. There is no other team who travel up and down with their mates like we do other than United. Even the music and the way you act at the match, they're similar.'

Matt Busby had conceded way back in 1957: 'Liverpool have some of the finest followers in the land. Only a man who has worn the red shirt of Liverpool, when the home team are attacking the Kop goal, knows and appreciates the value of those supporters.' He was Man United manager at the time.

Dave Bilsborrow remembers the late-50s as an age before total animosity: 'There wasn't a great rivalry with Man United. I went to matches and we drank in the pub together. You'd go in groups of ten or twelve and so did they. There would never have been chants about Munich. When it happened I was so upset. Duncan Edwards was brilliant and it was unfortunate he died. Chants like that came in in the '80's.'

By the early 2000s such chants were commonplace. As too were ditties about Hillsborough and crushing gestures from supporters in the Stretford End. Graffiti about the disasters accompanied the walk to both grounds on the day of the game. Other songs centred around unemployment.[61]

---

[61] Risk of long-term unemployment in Liverpool in 2012 was 12%. It was 17% in Manchester. 'In current poverty' in Liverpool was 4%. It was 7% in Manchester (Source: Experian). 1 in 130 people in Manchester are homeless (2018). They are sad statistics detailing a sad state of affairs nationally under Conservative rule. They should not be sung about or celebrated, especially not from the high balcony of a weak glass house.

It showed the degeneration of society that people on either side chose to score points from deaths. It was a greater demonstration of the degenerate nature of the individual when they sought to justify their chants on the basis of a *'he said it first'* rationale. Thatcher had treated football supporters like schoolchildren, and schoolchildren they were not. Some kind of macho affirmation was associated with the singing of the chants in the '90s - that they were authentic fans for doing so.

That perception changed in later years, but in 2001 hostility was at fever pitch. Manchester United were chipping away at Liverpool's record number of league titles. They were a glamorous, global club. Liverpool were still provincial, limited by the locally owned Moores family. The Reds were a standard below new emerging forces like Lazio and Valencia. But in 2001 they did the double over United – the first time in 22 years. At Anfield, Robbie Fowler and Steven Gerrard scored in a 2-0 win - they being two central characters in a homegrown story. Fowler strutted past the United fans during his celebration and shook his fist at them triumphantly.

Liverpool's unexpected growth continued under Gerard Houllier. By the end of the season Liverpool had won three trophies – the FA Cup, League Cup and UEFA Cup, with their triumph in Europe exceeding financial expectations.

In 2001 Liverpool made revenues of £130m, compared with Manchester United's gains of £217m... Real Madrid made £192m and Bayern Munich made £173m in the same year. The Reds were a cut below.

In terms of spending money on quality players, Newcastle had spent £15m in 1996 on Alan Shearer and Real Betis had bought Denilson for £21m in 1998... and later still Lazio broke the bank for Hernan Crespo (£36m), as Internazionale signed Christian Vieri in 2000 for £32m. But Liverpool's most expensive purchase over a five-year period was Emile Heskey for £11m. They would not spend over £30m on a player until a decade later. They were falling behind the times.

In 2000/01 Nick Barmby was Liverpool's most expensive purchase having been signed for £6m from Everton. According to Bill Kenwright, Barmby had said the 'worst 6 words in the English language' to him that summer: "*I want to go to Liverpool.*" Houllier was asked by the press if it'd cause any issues? 'Why? Is he changing his religion, or politics, or what?' he responded. Barmby became a hate-figure for Evertonians, especially after he claimed to have always been a Liverpool fan.

Local

As the first player to leave Everton for Liverpool since 1959 he received dog's abuse. *'Nicky Nicky Nicky, die die die!'* many in the Gwladys Street chanted. He'd been Everton's player of the year in 1999 before turning down the most lucrative contract in the clubs' history to force a move to Liverpool.

For the Reds, he'd become a lynchpin of their 2001 side, alongside the 35-year-old free transfer Gary McAllister. Both started away in Rome in the last 16 of the UEFA Cup in the February, against an old enemy. Once more, Stadio Olimpico was a colosseum of fire.

The 'CUCS' *Ultras* in Rome showed that previous violence afforded to Liverpudlians in 1984 was no coincidence, with incidents outside the ground and on D'Aosta bridge, as well as around the city. It proved that Roma supporters retained a deep hatred for Liverpool FC. Six Reds were hospitalised and 22 were stabbed in the arse in a further display of Roman shithousery.

The Italian club had one of its greatest ever sides: Cafu, Samuel, Batistuta and Totti would go on to win Serie A under Fabio Capello's stewardship that summer. But they couldn't beat Liverpool. *'We always win in Rome, we always win in Rome!'* jubilant Kopites gloated on the way home.

*

They lived long enough to see Liverpool step back onto a respectable perch before passing away. After the treble was secured, Joe Fagan, his old colleague Tom Saunders, and all-time hero Billy Liddell all passed away in the same July week. Although they were older men, it was a shock for the club.

Joe Fagan was still spotted about, sitting on the promenade in Crosby with his wife Lil most mornings. Gerard Houllier called Saunders his 'Liverpool father' and they chatted at Melwood every day. Saunders had been in Dortmund two months earlier watching Liverpool win the UEFA Cup.

Fagan was laid to rest at Anfield crematorium over the road from his house (facing the ground and Stanley Park). In life he was tied to the club and in death he'd forever face the stadium. With Evans and Moran no longer working at the club, all ties to the Boot Room were now gone. A realisation dawned on supporters that there was now no going back.

Supporters had flown to Germany from the newly titled 'John Lennon Airport' – rebranded as a coat-tail to the £938m pumped into the city by the European Union throughout that year. As the club and city expanded and evolved in an attempt to manifest into something more - more continental, sophisticated and more welcoming - Scousers reacted in a different way.

Daniel Fieldsend

It may have been tongue in cheek, but the 'Keep Flags Scouse' movement which began during that tournament showed the value given to (and the desire to maintain) localism in a new global age. A watershed was happening; something was under threat. Historically, banners had been creative and celebrated cult heroes for Liverpool (though not all of them were innovative, despite the rosiness of time), but as nouveau supporters from elsewhere made their own banners in the 1990s to take to matches, traditional fan culture – the most visible face of it - was perceived to be at risk.

KFS was a joke, except it wasn't... many a true word is said in jest. There had been incidents of banners being taken down, damaged or (as legend goes) cocooned around their owners if they caused embarrassment to Liverpool's inner circle of supporters. St George's flags were at risk throughout that UEFA Cup run and the subsequent Champions League era to follow. St George was a symbol of nationalism for right-wing supporters. It was also, more accurately, an easy and unoriginal flag – a club title in each corner of the cross (MCFC, CPFC, TRFC, LUFC...) – and, given that Liverpool supporters regarded themselves as unique, cultured and different to the rest, they refused to be associated with it.

The Guardian caught wind of the campaign and did a piece on it, referencing the humorous 'Keep Baby Names Scouse' follow-up, only for online comments to describe it as elitist, self-righteous and parochial. "Out-of-town fans have threatened violence against anyone who touches their flag," the article reported. What was originally a funny joke inspired by the 'People's Front of Judea' – *'fuck off*' – 'Judean People's Front' nature of Liverpool's supporter (in that fans could hardly agree on anything) had stirred a debate, albeit a welcome one. By 2002 the Echo was asking: "Should the Kop be for locals only?"

KFS was an attempt to reclaim the culture of LFC, which new fans were attracted to, which traditionally was always just an expression of Liverpool-city culture anyway. The campaign would never have happened had authentic long-term supporters not felt marginalised by the changing nature of both football and fandom in England.

In response, as an unspoken way of educating rather than excluding fans, away games – especially in Europe – were coloured by an increasing number of Kirkby, Kirkdale, Halewood, Bootle, Huyton et cetera banners (red background, white text) claiming cultural ownership over the spectacle and the experience. It would remain the case throughout the years, with banners that have been given the seal of approval being draped over the top of ones that are considered embarrassing.

Local

A trend had been started that was impossible to reverse. Brendan Wyatt explains how it developed: 'Around 2001 we had a bit of a change when we won all of them cups, but it was much more prevalent after Istanbul. As the team progressed, you'd see more and more tourist fans flying in from everywhere. When we played Cardiff at Wembley in 2012, I hung my Kirkdale banner over the front and this woman asked *"Where's that?"*'

The response from local Liverpool fans was natural and explainable. They were disenfranchised. Their resistance made for a powerful image. 'Look at those photos from Rome in 2001,' says Chris Hudson, 'when we're all at the front with the Kirkdale banner hanging down and not one lad has any '*Casual*' clobber one. They're all genuine Scouse lads with a number 2 [haircut] all over and a pair of Stan Smith's on.'

Other clubs in England went abroad and were defined by images of St George flags and Burberry caps. Liverpool had adopted another new trend. The lustrum of the Lacoste tracksuit had begun. It had been worn since the 1980s following Scouse pilgrimages to the continent: a French tennis brand with a refined reputation. By the early 2000s it was pure Liverpool Scal. Tracksuits cost in excess of £130 each – expensive for the period – and came in a variety of colours. 'I had the all-red one; I must have been bouncing around looking like a post box!' jokes Chris Hudson... 'It was boss though.'

There was also the club tracksuit period: a Nike 'Valencia' or adidas 'Milan' (or Argentina) rig-out proving to be particularly well favoured in Liverpool. But above all else, the most defining staple of attire for Scousers (which remains) was the AirMax 1995 training shoe.

More commonly known as a pair of 110s (due to their cost)[62], the shoes became iconic. Andy Hudson tells a story about being in L.A on holiday visiting exclusive trainer shops: 'I was reading books about collectors and what they liked. Every single one of them said that the most sought-after trainee is a neon 110. I was thinking "Come to Liverpool, everyone has a pair."'

Wade Smith remained central to the new look, and indeed all other looks to come until its closure. Adidas chose to promote their latest football boot outside the shops' Mathew Street store, with Michael Ball and Steven Gerrard receiving a

---

[62] Chris Hudson: 'Mad the way they're still known as 110s just because they were once £110. They're like £170 now. If someone calls them AirMax 95 you're like "*what are they?*"'

black and red Predator boot from a security guard. They, both clad in a tracksuit and cap, looked quintessentially like normal local lads. Which was important.

There remained a prevailing mentality of *'who are they?'* in the city which deterred upstarts from getting too big for their boots. Jamie Carragher stated the importance of looking 'normal' for himself and Steven Gerrard throughout their careers. 'You don't want to draw too much attention to yourself or think you're bigger and better than anyone,' he said.

Peter Carney believes that the presence of that mentality keeps people in check, while Simon Hughes thinks that it is an important part of the Scouse character. 'Nobody gets ahead of themselves here otherwise they'll get put down for talking shite. There can't be big heads in the city.' Foreign purchases like Sami Hyypia and Dirk Kuyt, who appeared humble, gained the respect of local supporters faster than flamboyant footballers, such as El Hadji Diouf. Ronnie Moran had kept things in check for years, calling any player with a degree of vanity a 'big headed bastard'. His was a Scouse message: be outstanding but never appear to be bigger and better than anybody else.

That conflict of what was in and acceptable, versus what was out – Wool, unacceptable, Tory – weighed heavy throughout the ensuing years as Liverpool was faced with more 'outsiders' than before; and not just in terms of visitors. Increases in communication through advancements in the internet, as well as the onslaught of reality television shows, mixed society together more than at any time in history. People had a greater exposure to 'others', and, as a consequence, came to define what was normal and homogenous behaviour. In other words, they decided, against opposing forces, what was acceptably 'Scouse' for a new age.

Local

GOOD ENOUGH

At the start of 2003 Liverpool was overtaken by propaganda stickers. There were posters in the receptions of offices and schools; inside hospitals, hotels and the backs of taxis. The message was everywhere. Liverpool was going to win. In five short years it was going to become the European Capital of Culture.

After the city's victory was announced, Tessa Jowell headed up to Liverpool. There had been scenes of jubilation. At Lime Street she was met by grinning schoolchildren holding up homemade placards, accompanied by a military band playing old-time tunes. She was taken to the Empire Theatre where she read out a message of congratulations from the Prime Minister. Council Leader Mike Storey followed up. He said: 'This is as good as Liverpool winning the Champions League, as Everton winning the double and the Beatles getting back together on the same day.'

Although every ward on Merseyside had a Labour MP (other than Southport), the City Council was still a Liberal organisation. Since 1998 Mike Storey and then Warren Bradley had spearheaded the city centre's revival. Chavasse Park was transformed, Liverpool One was approved, the waterfront was named a World Heritage site and now the European Capital of Culture victory had been secured.

When the announcement was made, the Liberals set off fireworks at the back of the Town Hall. Newcastle and Cardiff were shocked at having lost. They were further aghast that it was Liverpool that had won. Tessa Jowell had the council's back: 'Their vision, passion and enthusiasm - coupled with a really spectacular year-long programme - impressed the judges, who chose them from a very strong field.'

The Liverpool bid had celebrated the city's face: its museums and Georgian buildings, as well as its people. Scousers were considered to be a unique selling point. John Belchen determined that Mersey Partnership's idea to market civic identity was "forward-looking self-promotion, not self-pitying nostalgia."

They managed to tap into the historic ripples of difference. Representatives from the port cities of Marseille, Istanbul, Bremen, Gdansk and Naples brainstormed with Liverpool and decided to identify themselves as 'Cities on the Edge' in time for the final award. Their intention was to: "Strengthen the narrative of their peripheral commonalities," celebrating how they: "Exist out of the dominant notions of time, space and nation." In other words, they looked to market themselves organically as independent spaces with their own particular identities. "The plan includes," the Financial Times explained, "rebel lectures in cities with rebellion running through their veins." It proved to be the right approach.

The first ever European Capital of Culture city had been Athens back in 1985. The very idea of Liverpool ever receiving such an award back then was unfathomable. It had been the brainchild of the European Commission, who described it as 'a golden opportunity to show off Europe's cultural richness'. The event, they said: 'Is so attractive that Europe's cities vie with each other fiercely for the honour of bearing the title.' Melina Mercouri wanted to bring the European community closer with it. From Athens in '85 it went to Florence, Amsterdam, West Berlin and then Paris – places of already-outstanding beauty. Did they require further celebration? Did they need more money?

When Glasgow was presented as the European Capital of Culture in 1990 it signalled a new beginning for the award, now seen as a marker for regeneration rather than a status symbol. Glasgow went from being notorious for decay and relative poverty, to somewhere with obvious culture and international potential. Restoration then occurred in Antwerp in 1993, Rotterdam in 2001 and Lille in 2004.

Now Liverpool was going to be the European Capital of Culture. Locals didn't know exactly what that meant, but they liked it. The city was about to get a makeover. It was going to get more money. It was going to be understood at last, appreciated too. A line was going to be drawn under every conceivable negative that had ever happened, right?

Speke airport went from being an outhouse to the fastest growing airport in Europe. Tourists began to flock in daily just to sample Liverpool's vibe - that tangible atmosphere which set it apart. The mud was being polished off the diamonds. Following Jowell's announcement, the Liverpool Culture Company was founded, promising to host events, grow infrastructure, attract investors, create jobs and generate spending. It was all very exciting. A new era was dawning.

*

Sami Hyypia hadn't been in the best of form throughout 2003. Gerard Houllier thought a change was needed. He asked Steven Gerrard to see him in his office after training. Sat alongside Phil Thompson, he told Gerrard that he wanted him to be the new club captain. Everything had been smoothed over with Hyypia – he understood – and this was the decision. Houllier told the press: 'When he was young, all he needed was time to mature. Now he is 23 and he is ready.' Gerrard was shocked. For the next few years he'd pull over his car periodically on the drive home from Melwood, amazed by it all. His dream had always been to play for the club, but this meant something else entirely.

Once again, despite the optimism, Liverpool people had to move mountains in order to shift deep-rooted public opinion of them. Ken Bigley, an engineer from Walton was kidnapped in Iraq in September 2004. His family clung for hope of his release for 22 days. Billy Connolly joked about his potential beheading: 'Aren't you the same as me, don't you wish they would just get on with it...?'

Bigley was killed in October. He was a week away from retiring. He was a month away from meeting his grandchild. That same month, Boris Johnson edited a Spectator article which said: "The extreme reaction to Mr Bigley's murder is fed by the fact that he was a Liverpudlian... they cannot accept that they might have made any contribution to their misfortunes, but seek rather to blame someone else for it, thereby deepening their sense of shared tribal grievance against the rest of society."

It was a nod to the Hillsborough Justice campaigns being led in the city. Later that year Norman Bettison said Liverpool city centre at times resembled "Beirut on a bad day". Then, the following evening, Sir David Henshaw, Chief Executive of the council whose job it was to bring in investment, said at a dinner: 'Liverpool can still be the most mind-bogglingly awful and whingeing place, where the glass is always half empty.' He was addressing a room full of tourism delegates.[xx]

Back in late October 2002, Liverpool (Premiership leaders) had been humbled by Valencia in the Champions League. The Argentinian midfielder Pablo Aimar was slick, creative and infamously impressive. When their coach Rafa Benitez was hired as new Liverpool manager in 2004 Liverpudlians salivated. 'I want the supporters to be proud of the team, of the manager, of the players and of the club,' he said.

Would they now play football like Valencia? In spells, it would be breathtaking. At other times it was effective. But Michael Owen would not be a part of any of it, even if Roberto Ayala and Pablo Aimar were expected to be purchased at some point. Thailand's Prime Minister Thaksin Shinawatra was also supposed to buy the club that summer, putting the club on a higher financial plane.

Owen had run his contract down and departed to Real Madrid for £8m plus Antonio Nunez. He'd been named as Europe's best footballer just two years earlier and was still only 24-years of age. The fee was measly.[63]

In actuality, rather than raiding Valencia, Benitez brought in Luis Garcia, Josemi and Xabi Alonso from Spain. Djibril Cisse had been pre-purchased by Houllier and arrived for £14m. The squad was, as John Williams described, 'An uneasy mix of local heroes, young Spaniards and soon-to-be outcasts.' Little was expected from Liverpool. A revolving door of outs (Murphy, Heskey, Diao, Diouf and Cheyrou) were replaced by marginally better ins. Benitez met with Gerrard and Carragher to discuss his plans.

His captain had been touted as the next Duncan Edwards years earlier, but Benitez felt he ran too much to be truly effective. Carragher had iron will, which Benitez appreciated, but was not valued nationally. Sol Campbell, Ledley King, Rio Ferdinand and John Terry (Southern-born lads) all started for England over him. Sami Hyypia made the cut. He was Finland's captain and had European pedigree. Xabi Alonso was just as cool on the ball, possessing incredible talent which was understated by his boyish floppy hair. Benitez had four high-standard players, enough for him to build upon.

Results were mixed to begin with. Liverpool's hopes of qualification from the group stages of the Champions League hinged on a win against Olympiakos in December. Ten days earlier Rafa's rag-and-bones side overcame English champions Arsenal – a great squad of Ljungberg, Cole, Henry and Vieira – at Anfield in a presentation of things to come. Neil Mellor had been the hero that night and he'd be the hero again.

Liverpool had to beat the Greek side 1-0 or by two clear goals if they conceded to go through. Sure enough, just before half-time, they went behind. Rivaldo – who was supposed to meet with Liverpool executives in 2003 – dribbled past

---

[63] Fans were dismayed. Real Madrid had paid £39m for the 2002 Ballon d'Or winner Ronaldo from Inter. Was Owen not worth a similar value? It emerged later that he ran his contract down in pursuit of the Champions League. Had he stayed at Liverpool...

three players before earning himself a free-kick at the edge of the box. He got up, placed the ball down and scored, giving Liverpool a mountain to climb.

Benitez brought on Sinama-Pongolle at the interval. The young French striker had been signed in 2001 aged 16. It had been a coup for Liverpool to have gotten him at the time. At the FIFA U17 World Cup that he'd been named 'Best Player' beating Diego of Brazil, Andres Iniesta and Fernando Torres of Spain, as well as Carlos Tevez, Pablo Zabaleta and Javier Mascherano of Argentina to the award. Every club wanted him. But his career wouldn't take off as expected and, like Mellor's, would be remembered for this night.

Pongolle pulled one back in the 46th minute. *"Come on!"* screamed the Kop. Olympiakos sat deep and tried to soak up pressure. Gerrard hit the post with a nonchalant flick, but time was running out. Gerrard then scored a volley from 25-yards and Anfield erupted, but the referee ruled it out for an earlier infringement. In the 78th minute Neil Mellor was brought on to make a difference. Carragher was clattered inside the box in the 81st, but the referee ignored it. Pongolle picked up the loose ball and floated it toward the back post. Nunez headed it straight at the keeper who parried to the floor. In slid Neil Mellor on the half-volley, blasting it into the back of the net. *"Fucking come on!!"* the Kop roared as people tumbled over rows of seats.

Gerrard was everywhere, breaking up play and moving the ball forward. But time was running out. Fans kept glancing at their watches. Not long left. On the 86th minute Xabi Alonso battled to keep the ball in play. He pushed it out to the left where Jamie Carragher received it. He swivelled back onto his right foot and whipped a cross into the box. Neil Mellor was there, and he cushioned it down into space. *"Come on, just one more goal..."* Gerrard danced around the flight of the ball and adjusted it to his right foot. '22-yards lay between myself and glory,' he said. It whistled in. The Kop erupted. People fell further. Limbs were everywhere. It was deafening. As had been the case in 1977 against Saint Etienne, Liverpool had scored in the dying moments of the match and were going through to the next round.

But it was more than just qualification. The context of the win would be significant. The timing of the goals and the emotions attached to them – as is so often the case – inspired belief and proved to be a catalyst for the campaign. Had Liverpool won 4-0 easily it would have been a different story. Now the city was full of self-belief and the team reflected that optimism. Anything was possible. Back in '77 Saint Etienne were beaten by a good side who were expected to triumph in Europe. But this was a different story, and Liverpool was a different, much battered but potentially better place. Scousers were imbued with a new belief in life.

Still, little was expected outside of Liverpool. In the next round they drew Bayer Leverkusen. Klaus Augenthaler, their manager, told *Bild* he was happy with the draw. The consensus in Germany was that Liverpool were the weakest team left in the competition. Leverkusen had already beaten Roma and Real Madrid in the group stages and fancied themselves to go through. Liverpool won 6-2 on aggregate.

Then on the 18th March the draw for the next round was made in Switzerland. Everybody's heart sank when it was announced. 20 years since Heysel, Liverpool were set to play Juventus. Rick Parry, Chief Executive from Ellesmere Port, gave the club's view: 'There is quite a deep friendship between the clubs and I think between the two sets of fans,' he said. But that wasn't true.

When Liverpool tried to force a friendship before the game with a mosaic saying *'Amicizia'* (friendship), presenting a banner to the 2,600 Juve fans in the Anfield Road that said 'In Memory and Friendship', the *Juventini* turned their backs and raised their middle fingers. Earlier when the City Council had handed them welcome packs at Speke airport (JLA) they either refused or dropped them on the floor. Juventus were not here to make friends.

Why? All behaviour can be explained. For 20 years the name Liverpool had manifested into a symbol for them. Fiorentina, Napoli, Lazio – all of their major rivals who visited Delle Alpi chanted *'Liverpool, Liverpool!'* at them. Heysel had been celebrated disgustingly in an *Ultras* war without boundaries. A red shirt was used to antagonise Juve's supporters – a reference to the supporters who had caused involuntary manslaughter. Now they were finally on Merseyside.

Liverpool won the game 2-1. Sami Hyypia scored a controlled volley ten minutes in, before Luis Garcia lobbed Buffon from thirty yards in the 25th. Cannavaro equalised, but that wasn't the story which carried across the continent. The whistling, the fingers and the gestures – that was more newsworthy. It led the press to believe there would be a vendetta in Turin for the second leg.

Local daily newspaper *La Stampa*, accused of being pro-Torino by Juventus fans, wrote: "At the festival of friendship, ignorance wins." While the national paper *La Gazetta dello Sport* had on its soft-pink pages: "It was an embrace that died against a wall of indifference, which was unfortunately coloured black and white." Newspapers were less impressed by the sporting feats of a 19-year-goalkeeper called Scott Carson who, for the most part, kept out Nedved, Del Piero,

Trezeguet and Ibrahimovic, but instead focussed on the social connotations between fans.

Kevin Sampson and his mates had been in touch with Mauro since the draw was announced. They hoped for some kind of reconciliation. 'When we arrived he took us to some bars around Turin. I asked "are we going to be okay?" and he said *yeah* because we were with him. You could feel that people were only shaking our hands through gritted teeth. That sense of responsibility and guilt is there and it'll take a long, long time to get out of the system. It's for the people most closely affected to decide when the time is to move on, it's not for us to say.'

There had been an attack on the Tuesday night in Turin, but most of Liverpool's hardcore support were wise enough to stay in small groups and avoid the city centre, keeping a low profile. Police, thankfully enough, kept a high profile. People of influence in Turin made statements calling for peace. Andrea Lorentini, whose father had died at Heysel, wrote in *La Stampa*: "I have felt the terrible consequences of violence. I know what it means. So this evening leave hatred and everything else behind." While captain Alessandro Del Piero said: "The tribute at Anfield gave the Liverpool fans the opportunity to say sorry and we have to remember that these fans were not the ones that were at Heysel."

The statements were made through necessity, because they knew what the reception was going to be. Juventus supporters were teargassed outside the stadium for trying to get to Liverpool's buses. Helicopters circled overhead. Inside the ground the Juventus fans threw seats and bottles into the Liverpool end. The stewards and police stood back and watched. One of the less barbaric banners read "Easy to Speak, Difficult to Pardon. Murderers" while a more sinister one read "15.4.89 - Sheffield. God Exists", as if Heysel was neutralised by Hillsborough for them. Coming out of the stadium after a 0-0 draw with the sight of a police car on fire, it was plain to see that forgiveness was a long way off. Nobody was seriously injured, though, and Juventus had made their point. Liverpool FC progressed to the next round.

Liverpool, that plucky team from an emerging city, had beaten another favourite for the competition. Barry Glendenning, who had been covering the game for the Guardian, sulked: "Liverpool are through to the semi-final. No disrespect to the Harry Kewell, Igor Biscan and Djimi Traore-carrying Scouse outfit, but if that doesn't devalue the whole competition, I don't know what does."

In another fine display of class appreciation, the impression was given that Britain's press wanted Liverpool to lose to Chelsea in the semi-final. Where was their sense of romance? Scousers were in dreamland. Houses in Speke, Walton,

Page Moss, Bootle and the other nuclei of the city began dressing up. Red scarves were placed on window ledges to begin with as a faint display of encouragement, before an Echo spread went up in the windows of a scattering of homes. 'Come on Lads' was the message. Such displays were reserved for cup finals in the past, not semis, but people were giddy. Liverpool had been starved of major European success for a generation. The Chelsea game was the talk of the town.

Rickie Lambert lights up when he thinks back to the buzz of that period. He was a teenager, just about to make his way in the game: 'That's exactly why I got carried away! Some of the best nights I've had in my life was going to watch Liverpool in the Champions League that season.'

Olympiakos was unexpected. Leverkusen was routine. Juventus was a relief. But this was Chelsea. This was pure nerves. Liverpool were 31 points behind the league champions. They'd just wrapped up the title. They'd already beaten the Reds three times that season and were 11/10 favourites to progress into the final. Nobody outside the city fancied Liverpool.

6.6 million people watched the first leg in Spain. *Marca* had coined Liverpool 'the 21st team' of La Liga. But this was a game of greater social magnitude than what international viewers understood it to be. It was Liverpool versus London; the provincial city against the capital. 400,000 people against 8.2 million. It was Djimi Traore from Laval who'd cost £650k against Didier Drogba from Marseille who'd cost £27m. Steve Finnan from non-league Welling United against Claude Makelele the '*Galactico*'.

It was tradition and values against new money and new success. Chelsea were the team of George Osbourne and Jeremy Clarkson – Liverpool was the red-hot town of leftists. Back in February, Chelsea fans had sung *'There's only one Boris Johnson'* after their Carling Cup victory over Liverpool – the reference obvious. They had waved £20 notes in the air and sang about slums. They had screwed up their faces beneath their Burberry caps and screamed *'You're not famous anymore!'*

It was the start of a faux rivalry. Chelsea's values opposed Liverpool's, but that was nothing new. Reds were used to the Big Smoke. "London Stinks of Rat Piss" noted a banner draped over the high walls of Trafalgar Square.

Inside Stamford Bridge, Reds sang 'La Bamba' for what seemed like an hour. The Rafa-lution was in full-flow and became a studied portrait of globalisation. Not one Spaniard had ever played for Liverpool in 112 years, nor managed the club, yet Spanish flags began to appear on the Kop as songs emerged, tailored for

Local

the nation. Everton adapted to it all in typical fashion, creating a song about Liverpool (albeit humorous) for their upcoming summer signing: '*There's nobody better than Mikel Arteta he's the best of the Spanish we know*'. Merseyside had been infected with a Castilian fascination.

The first game was a tense 0-0 draw. Mourinho began the mind-games immediately afterwards: '99.9% of Liverpool fans think they are through to the final,' he said. Phil Thompson responded on Sky Sports: 'Mourinho's wrong. 100% of Liverpool fans think they're through!'

A few days before the second leg a story appeared in the Liverpool Echo saying that Chelsea had hired a venue on Castle Street for their post-game celebrations, expecting to win. Jamie Carragher used the news as motivation. As if the teams were not fired up enough, a back-and-forth exchange of mind games added weight to the occasion.

The greatest nights in Liverpool's history had often been midweek European games when Anfield was still light and the day had been sunny – it meant they'd gotten far in the competition; this was such an occasion. It seemed as if there were more people on Breck Road than inside Anfield's ale houses, with singing near Flagpole Corner reaching full-pelt decibels. Two hours before kick-off, the turnstiles began to click. A burly Scouser in the middle of the Albert had waited for the last few lines of 'Fields of Anfield Road' to end before shouting a command across the pub: '*Let's get in that fucking ground!*' ... there was a roar of approval as scores of Reds poured out, like a Germanic tribe before war. It was 6:30pm. None of it was normal.

'I have never experienced an atmosphere like it,' Steven Gerrard said. The team came out to do their stretches 45 minutes before kick-off. Typically at such times Anfield was empty. 'I couldn't believe my eyes or ears. Anfield was three-quarters full. The stadium was bouncing,' he recalled in his autobiography. Gerrard stood and stared at the Kop. He was mesmerised. The banner of most distinction in block 202 simply read: 'Make Us Dream'.

3 minutes in Luis Garcia scored. The confusion surrounding whether the ball crossed the line or not made the goal sweeter for delirious Reds. Immediately after it, Chelsea were inspired. They were everywhere; Gerrard stated that it felt like 13 players versus 11. 'We survived because of one man,' he wrote: 'Jamie Carragher.' The Bootle-born defender had been a rock in both ties. *En* route to the semi-finals, Chelsea had scored five times against Barcelona and six times against Bayern Munich, but Liverpool's number 23 denied them.

Daniel Fieldsend

Anfield bounced. Literally; the stands could be felt moving up and down. 'Fields of Anfield Road' – still a new and exciting chant - was deafening. Michael Owen and Steve McManaman, in the Main Stand, were on their feet taking it all in - would they have been playing in other circumstances? There was a surreal moment after Eidur Gudjohnsen's miss when people were just making noise, singing anything in pockets of 30 or 40, not hearing what else was going on around them. It was pure human jubilation.

The effect it had was mesmerising. Every single report after the game cited that hurricane of power. The 12th man, the Liverpool crowd, had surpassed its giant reputation. Roman Abramovich was seen laughing in the directors' box throughout You'll Never Walk Alone – but he couldn't help it. Jose Mourinho walked off the pitch and nodded towards the Paddock, clapping at them, crediting them for the victory.

Media reports focussed on something unseen before in a new hyper-communication age. "The best team may or may not have won, but the best supporters definitely did," wrote Clive Tyldesley for the Daily Telegraph. "Just ask them. Like Jose Mourinho himself, Liverpool fans are good and they know it."

Oliver Holt for the Daily Mirror described what it was like for a journalist to witness such a passionate anthem: "The most rousing rendition some of us have ever heard, it felt humbling to feel such passion. One of the great sights in world football right there in front of you. People stared at each other in awe."

"It was not just a wall of bulging, stretching, moving red shirts upon which Chelsea had to mount a long, fruitless and toothless assault here. It was a wall of noise too." John Dillon of the Daily Express wrote. "It's the kind of support that no amount of Abramovich's billions can buy," stated Ian Doyle of the Daily Post.

Henry Winter of the Telegraph penned how it was: "Just incredible…a wave of unbelievable noise rolled into Chelsea's players, knocking them back, scrambling their senses and lifting Liverpool…the pillars and rafters of this famous stadium were shaking as the songs, screams and chants cascaded down from all sides. It was impossible, at first, for the Chelsea players to communicate with each other."

In Italy, *Corriere dello Sport* pondered the beast that would be awaiting AC Milan should they overcome PSV: "The people, not only the team - because the magic of this stadium made the team - coached by the genius Rafa Benitez, made Liverpool unbeatable."

Perhaps the most wonderful image was painted by Chelsea captain John Terry in his autobiography: "No way will we lose this game tonight, I thought. But the Liverpool fans were amazing. I have never heard anything like it before and I don't think I ever will again. When I heard the final whistle, I broke down. I was crying. I sat there in the dressing room that night with a towel over my head, just crying."

*

George Sephton congratulated fans as they exited the stadium, telling them he'd never heard anything like it. As they walked down Utting Avenue people who couldn't get into the ground (a growing theme for years to come) came out of their houses and clapped. They applauded the fans as if it had been them that had won the game. Arguably, they had done.

Rafa Benitez called into a Formby pub on his way home. It was still chocker. Across the bar, separated by scores of wild fans, were two former Liverpool players. Drunk locals got in Benitez's ear. Among the poetic messages of thanks, they had a demand. 'You need to sign him back for us!' – 'he's better than Morientes' – 'he's God!' they pointed. Robbie Fowler was stood having a drink in the corner with Steve McManaman. It planted a seed in Benitez's mind.

One of the last flags to leave the Kop that night summed the whole occasion up. It was aimed at Chelsea and every other team in the land. Its message was simple: 'Your Dreams Are Our Reality'.

Daniel Fieldsend

THE WONDER OF YOU

Gerald Grosvenor was one of the wealthiest men on earth. 6 titles followed his name; he'd been president of 13 charities and his 4 children were Lords and Ladies who'd grow up to become godparents to royal babies. His honours and medals were boundless and his estates were worth millions. Grosvenor was at the top end of the class system see-saw, personifying the very ideas of Britishness – of knee bending entitlement - that seemed alien to so many Liverpudlians. One would not find him drinking in the Penny Farthing...

But he, more than most, deserved a pint from local drinkers. His company was commissioned by Liverpool City Council to develop the 'Paradise Project' in the early 2000s, taking the wasteland between Hanover Street and Strand Street and turning it into Liverpool One. Grosvenor said: 'I've known this city for many years, and for many of those years it has drifted. It has been very much regarded as the poor second cousin to all our other great industrial cities throughout the United Kingdom. But now it has a project which is a flagship. It has something that it can be deeply proud of.'

Building work was well underway by 2005. It swept away Chavasse Park, Canning Fire Station, Quiggins and the oldest wet dock in the world and replaced them with glass complexes for consumerism. Liverpool city centre was being transformed by the day, as the biggest project of its kind in Europe.

The comparison with Liverpool Football Club was obvious. In midsummer 2005 their supporters were on a pilgrimage to the furthermost corner of Europe. A modern stadium awaited them, out in the middle of nowhere, an almost dystopian vision on a freezing cold night that had been so warm just a few hours earlier. They were there to watch their club win and ultimately transform, butterflying into a new era of shallow consumerism. Or not, depending on perception.

Local

Every Liverpool fan who had baked on the Asian side of the city throughout that day had laughed to themselves at certain points, remembering between lulls of song and drink that they were in Istanbul for the Champions League final. *'What are we doing here?!'* This wasn't the domain of Liverpool Football Club anymore: much poorer than other clubs in England, let alone Europe. The word 'fate' had been as much of a cliché before the game as the word 'miracle' would be afterwards.

Following the Juventus victory, the Echo started twirling tea leaves. In an article in mid-April they pointed out the coincidences between other years when Liverpool had won the European Cup and 2005. In 1977 there had been a Star Wars film. The Pope had died in '78 and Wales had won the Grand Slam. In 1981 there had been a new Doctor Who, Prince Charles had married a new partner, and Ken had exchanged vows with Deirdre in Coronation Street. Sure enough all incidents reoccurred before Istanbul. The ever-superstitious Carlo Ancelotti must have shit himself when he saw Fred Elliot and Jack Duckworth dusting off their old suits for the second Barlow wedding.

Such omens worked their way into daily chit chat at bus stops, at work and over evening meals throughout Merseyside. Nothing else seemed to matter in 2005. Almost every car had miniature red and white chequered flags flying in their rear windows. Larger flags flew outside houses now, and red t-shirts were made tailored for the event with the badges of every conquered team on. 'In Istanbul, we'll win it five times' was the message. All along the wide streets of the city – Queens Drive, Edge Lane, Rocky Lane, Muirhead Avenue, Grover Street and so on – houses were unashamedly and without reservation decorated in red. Projecting team colours on the front of a home was both a wonderful statement of identity and a fanatic Scouse tradition.

Cup finals in the past had created a buzz of excitement and an obvious tangible atmosphere. But this was more, somehow omnipresent. Liverpool was blanketed by the occasion and for 6 months at least was defined by it. So close to obscurity, the idea of being relative again had everybody salivating. Every night out in town was topped off by a rendition of Johnny Cash's 'Ring of Fire', the anthem of the campaign. It had been introduced by Philly Carragher and the Bootle Reds earlier in the season and, matched by the twirling of a scarf in the air, created a tremendous vision at Anfield.

At midday on the 25th May, Tony Blair stood up after PMQ's and wished Liverpool "the very best of luck" for that night. His opponent, Michael Howard, said he took "particular pleasure" in seconding his rival's statement. The lar-dedar political elite, who'd so often in recent years ignored the city (Blair was cold-shouldered during the Dockers Dispute and during the campaign for Hillsborough inquests), were riding a feelgood national bandwagon.

Over in Istanbul, local ideals clashed against the cultural symbols of a nation and beyond. Not only were Carragher and Gerrard - Bootle and Huyton lads with hard knock expressions - coming up against the sleek compatriots of Alessandro Nesta and Andrea Pirlo, but there were conflicting flags and chants on display too. Among the banners on the restaurant face of Taksim Square was a gigantic St George. It stated across its face 'WEYMOUTH REDS' - breaking all of the KFS rules. Next to it, smaller and written on a bedsheet was the text: 'Pete Price is a Cunt'. Only half of the fans there understood it. Its satire meant both nothing and everything at the same time, depending on the reader.

BBC 5 Live positioned their young reporter Matt Williams in the square. At 6:15am he told listeners: 'There are already hundreds of fans here and clearly a lot of them haven't gone to bed. The bars are just opening now and Liverpool's day in the Turkish sun is just beginning.' At 8:40am, still too early, he simply stated: 'Taksim Square is now packed out.'

21 years away from football's zenith had created a buzz of anticipation for supporters. It also brought in fans who'd not particularly shown a great interest in going to Liverpool matches beforehand. Between Rome in 1977 and Heysel in 1985, the accents heard around the ground had changed; less Scouse, more 'other'. Between 1985 and 2005 not only had the accents changed, but the languages of Liverpool supporters had too.

Less Scousers, less tickets available for them, more foreign supporters now. For many of Liverpool's more hardcore support, Istanbul would mark the beginning of a battle to retain the club's soul.

Taksim Square was a large flat piece of concrete with a road dissecting its middle and a decorative statue on the other side. For two days it was enclosed by red banners and occupied by red shirts. Young Turks turned up in the morning expecting Liverpool fans to be organised, ready for a territorial battle, but were confused to find that Reds just wanted to drink and sing. Media companies too had a sketchy understanding of the occasion, attempting to draw links with Heysel 20 years earlier (this was Liverpool's first final since, against Italians once more).

The Guardian spoke with a Milan fan, Enrico Deaglio, who recalled the months after Heysel. "Twenty years ago, here in Italy we considered the people of

Liverpool to be the scum of the earth. We knew it was a decaying city and one in which nearly every kind of social problem existed..." Deaglio paused. "We wouldn't think of it quite like that anymore, I suppose." A lot had changed.

In trying to compare Istanbul to Heysel the press failed to acknowledge the climate and conditions of both times. Istanbul was a feelgood occasion during a period of civic regeneration for Liverpool. Heysel was, well... 1985.

Efes were drank and flags were waved. Paul Tomkins described his journey to the stadium which involved an old local man getting on his coach to sample the experience. According to Tomkins, the man – who didn't speak English – sat smiling looking out of the window, waving to the crowds of other locals outside as if he were 'the luckiest man alive'. Indeed, throughout the 2-hour journey, scores of Turks could be seen along the road and on the balconies of their apartment blocks clapping the visiting Red army on.[64]

At the Ataturk Stadium, Pete Wylie sang a collection of Scouse favourites for the early bird fans. During his version of 'The Wonder of You' hundreds poured on stage alongside him to the sheer panic of Turkish organisers – '*I guess I'll never know, the reason why...*' – "everybody get off! It is going to break!". John Power, who was set to follow on stage, was spotted half-drunk, jumping from roof to roof of parked coaches in a red bucket hat. Topping off this most Scouse of spectacles, Kevin Nolan walked past with his mates, tinny in hand.

Outside the ground fans intermingled with a global media force. French, Dutch, Italian, Spanish and American TV crews wanted to capture the occasion. A reporter from the Japan Times said: "With the exception of Steven Gerrard on a good day, not a single Liverpool player would get into the Milan side." He was probably right.[65]

That sentiment seemed to be the consensus – that Liverpool had overachieved already and would get beat. Every single Kopite inside the ground thought otherwise. Their banners were proof of that belief. Not exactly as poetic as the Joey Jones tapestry a generation before, the modern favourite 'Welcome To Hell My Arse!' had arrived at the Ataturk for all to see. It shared the defiance of its 1977 cousin: 'IF YOU THINK THIS IS HELL TRY THE GRAFTON ON A FRIDAY NIGHT'.

---

[64] Red Revival: Rafa Benitez's Liverpool Revolution. Paul Tomkins, 2006.
[65] Dida, Cafu, Nesta, Stam, Maldini, Gattuso, Pirlo, Seedorf, Kaka, Shevchenko, Crespo.

Back home thousands of more traditional supporters tuned into their wireless radios and sat down to listen to the game. On Radio City they heard John Aldridge and Steve Hothersall describe, with impressive composure all things considered, the most incredible match.

JA: I think this is the biggest game in Liverpool's history. A lot has happened between 1977 and now. We need to win here tonight. I just want to wish the lads the best of luck.
SH: John, before Chelsea you made a plea which sent the chills down my spine. What would you say tonight?
JA: Make sure when you're back in that dressing room after the game you've given everything. Blood, sweat, tears... and know you can't have given anything more...

SH: Immediately a free-kick to defend from the right-hand side. Andrea Pirlo will strike it. Two in the wall for Liverpool. Oh, it's a goal for Milan. It's been hit on the volley by Maldini at the age of 36...

SH: Milan score again! Crespo gets a second goal for the Italians. Was that a major injustice for Liverpool? Down the other end Luis Garcia was appealing for a hand ball and a penalty and Milan broke and scored.
JA: We need a minor miracle...

SH: Kaka turns his man. He plays a ball into the penalty area and it's chipped to the right-hand side of Jerzy Dudek. He's scored past the goalkeeper by the Milan fans in the south side of this stadium and they go into the break three goals up.

Barry Glendenning wrote for the Guardian at half-time: "If this Liverpool team was a dog, you'd shoot them." The Reds were 188-1 to win. The players went in with their heads down. Carragher felt too ashamed to look up at the red banners and the faces of the Liverpudlians who'd overtaken the stadium. He thought back to the piss-taking he'd received in the Chaucer after the loss to Manchester United back in 1999 and feared the amplification this occasion would summon. 'I almost began to regret reaching the final,' he wrote.

During half-time, Carragher and the players heard the fans singing You'll Never Walk Alone, louder and louder as they exited the tunnel. 'It wasn't the usual version though. There was a slow, sad sound to it, almost as if it was being sung as a hymn. The fans were praying on our behalf.'

Locāl

Filippo Galli played for and won European Cups with Milan. He wanted them to win. He'd retained a love for Liverpool since 1984, though. 'If you cut my arms open you will see Liverpool is in my veins,' he said. The Reds retained a mythological place in Italy. There was a history between the club and the country. Many of the Italian supporters in Istanbul, including Galli himself, had paid money just to hear the famous Liverpool fans singing their hymn, in the same way people paid to see the Haka performed, or went to the Olympics. The song had (has) huge cultural and sporting significance.

Milan's fans fell silent and listened to the 38,000 Liverpudlians at half time. Chills went up the collective spines of millions of people watching throughout the world. In pubs in Sydney at 5am Reds joined in. In Oslo, Seattle, Cape Town and Hong Kong, too, they sang along. Soldiers in Iraq squeezed around small television sets agonising for a comeback. In the village of Bambali in Senegal, a 13-year old Sadio Mane watched with his best friend, who'd ran off into the dark night overtaken by emotion before half-time. 'When he came back at the end, he could not believe it. Even to this day he cannot believe it,' said Mane.

The thoughts among the players was to reward supporters with a goal.

SH: *This is Xabi Alonso in the centre circle. Alonso plays it out to Riise on the left-hand side. Riise crosses but it hits Cafu. It comes back to him. He puts it back into the box and OH HE'S GOT IT. They may be three goals down Liverpool but Steven Gerrard has urged the Liverpool fans to get to their feet. It's 3-1 Milan.*

JA: *It was a great goal.*

SH: *Here's Alonso, to Hamman...*

JA: *Hit it.*

SH: *Hamman to Smicer – SMICER HITS IT! OHHHH!*

JA: *OHHHHHHHHH!*

SH: *HE'S GOT A SUPERB SECOND FOR LIVERPOOL. THE REDS ARE BACK IN THE EUROPEAN CUP FINAL. IT IS QUITE OUTSTANDING. LIVERPOOL ARE BACK IN WITH A SHOUT.*

JA: *COME ON!*

SH: *Here's a ball from Carragher. It's Gerrard!*

JA: *THAT'S A PENALTY!*

SH: *INSIDE THE BOX IT'S A PENALTY FOR LIVERPOOL! THEY'VE GOT A CHANCE TO LEVEL THE GAME UP AT 3-3!*

JA: *He's...he's*

SH: *He has given it hasn't he John? He's not waving it away?*

JA: *It's a penalty. It's a penalty.*
SH: *The referee is waving away the AC Milan players.*
JA: *They're trying to say that he should be sent off. He was last man.*
SH: *Xabi Alonso. He's an expert at the dead ball situation. 40,000 Liverpool fans inside here hold their breath. Hundreds of thousands hold their breath on Merseyside. Xabi Alonso for 3-3 ... IT'S SAVED! HE FOLLOWS IT IN – NNNNNN* (Hothersall's voice breaks) *– IT'S WONDERFUL. IT'S MARVELLOUS.*
JA: *OOOOAAAUUUALLLL! AAAAAA!*

Milan threatened time and again to score. Every time they got into the Liverpool box Carragher stopped them. It affected his body. He was limping, cramping up, stretching and blocking shots. No matter whether he was on Buckley Hill or the Ataturk, it seemed to be in his nature to win at all costs. "I'd come a long way from the snotty nosed kid who wanted to come off the pitch early because it was raining. As I deflected away another goal bound Milan shot, I knew dad must have been prouder than he'd ever been," he wrote.

SH: *It's extra time in the final. Liverpool were dead and buried at half time. They have produced a miraculous comeback. It is a spirit that is only found on Merseyside. Liverpool have a great shout of taking home the European Cup. Heads held in their hands on the Milan bench.*

The spiritual Italians believed it to be the grace of God, that Liverpool were going to win. Perhaps it *had* been predetermined. When Gudjohnsen missed in the 95th minute against Chelsea, when Cannavaro hit the upright against Juventus... now Dudek had saved Shevchenko's shot from point blank range. When the game went to penalties, at least 1,000 Reds turned their backs and couldn't watch. Some fans threw up on the terraces, so extreme were the butterflies they felt.

JA: *I think he's bottled it...*
SH: *Up steps Shevchenko. He scored the winner two years ago. He's up against Dudek. Will he hand Liverpool the European Cup?*
JA: *YAAAAAAAAAAAHHHHHHHHHH!*

SH: *AAAAAAAAAAAAAHHHH!* (Incomprehensible noises continue for some time) ...
SH: *TEARS AROUND THE LIVERPOOL FANS. IT IS THE ULTIMATE WAY TO WIN. Liverpool are crowned champions of Europe. All those dreams come to fruition! Merseyside and Liverpool are the kings of Europe! Back at the top of the European table!*

Local

In Liverpool the previously deserted streets erupted. Everybody spilled out onto the roads. Some people sprinted up and down, shouting deliriously. The euphoria was sensational. In town, buses were left deserted by their drivers. There were people dancing in the street. The fountains on Williamson Square became the scene of congregation as supporters ran through cheering, well into the early hours. *'We are the champions, champions of Europe!'*.

Stephen Monaghan had lost his father the year before. He'd been recognised in Halewood as 'Shankly' – the ultimate praise. Monaghan had visited Rome earlier in the year and by pure coincidence the Pope died while he was there. His corpse had been placed in a crypt in the Vatican, so Monaghan queued up to see him. 'I touched his body and said "*Look after my dad, and let Liverpool win the European Cup.*" When we won it, I looked up to the sky and said "That's for you dad."'

As Carragher and Gerrard ran around the track holding the trophy, jumping up and down singing 'Ring of Fire', the supporters chanted *'Are you watching Manchester?'* back at them. It seemed that their East Lancs rivals were.

Oasis were playing the Coronet that night but didn't come on stage until after the match had finished. They'd demanded that a giant screen be fitted for their fans to watch the game. When they eventually came on stage, the Gallaghers opted to come out to You'll Never Walk Alone rather than their usual 'Fucking in the Bushes' track, on a stage that was lit up red for them. Later that night Liam Gallagher dedicated 'Stop Crying Your Heart Out' to AC Milan's supporters.

The following morning when *La Repubblica* newspapers dropped on the cobbles of Milan, they had the headline: 'Milan suicide, Liverpool triumph'. The accompanying article stated: "One usually has to work hard for victories. Milan, instead, worked hard for a bitter defeat. Gerrard raised the cup; they did not steal it. It seemed they lost it, they won it. Honour to them."

The Guardian were more favourable toward the Reds: "The glory of Liverpool is reborn. They are not merely champions of Europe once more but the indefatigable creators of a victory that will be talked about so long as football exists."

Every newspaper worldwide carried the image of Liverpool's team celebrating with the cup – Josemi wearing a Spanish flag, Diao wearing a bandana, Baros wearing a red scarf. There was one imposter on the photograph alongside them: Lee Dames, a 19-year-old from Anfield who'd pinched a club tracksuit and ran on the pitch at the final whistle. 'Some of the players were nudging each other about me and thought it was funny,' he told the Echo. His arl feller Paul was in Sam's Bar in town watching: 'I spotted him and thought *'That's not my son, is it?'* I was flabbergasted.'

His face was clocked from Amsterdam to Buenos Aires – all over the world. Liverpool FC were back where they belonged. Their fans drew comments from the great and the good of football. Diego Maradona declared: 'Liverpool showed that miracles exist. They proved that football is the most beautiful sport of them all. After this game, my English team is going to be Liverpool. I came across some of their fans beforehand and they told me they were going to win, but that they would be made to suffer. Liverpool are the best team in the world for what they have done in this Champions League. They deserved the Cup.'

And Johan Cruyff stated: 'There's not one club in the world so united with the fans. I sat there watching the Liverpool fans singing You'll Never Walk Alone and they sent shivers down my spine. A mass of 40,000 people became one force behind their team. For that I admire Liverpool more than anything.'

Left behind in Turkey nursing hangovers in the sun, the fans in Istanbul had been disregarded by council planners when it came to that day's parade. If that was the price to pay for being there, it was worth paying. BBC estimated that close half a million people took to the streets of Liverpool to welcome the team home. At the Jolly Miller, Utting Avenue, Priory Road, Anfield, Everton Valley and Scotland Road, locals climbed up telegraph poles, wriggled to the top of streetlights, perched on road signs and stood on billboard ledges.

Crowds had been gathering at St George's Hall since midday. On a warm Thursday afternoon kids were kept off school by fathers who called in sick for work. In their full kits, children waved chequered flags on their parents' shoulders and blew horns to a monotone version of 'Ring of Fire'. By the time the bus arrived there were people everywhere – on top of the hall itself, on the roof of Lime Street Station and on every level of St John's car park. 'You'll Never Walk Alone' took on another version again.

Beside the huge columns of St George's Hall and with the circular splendour of the Picton Reading Room in the background – a collection of architecture so fine it belonged in Berlin or Paris – the masses stood together, beneath an actual golden sky. It looked like Rome in the days of Constantine's rule. *Populusque Liverpudlians.*

'I'd never seen such scenes,' said Jamie Carragher. 'You found yourself frantically moving your head from one side of the bus to the next to make sure you didn't miss any of the banners or homemade European Cups people were waving.' Carragher pointed toward the civic value the trophy win and the subsequent parade had. 'Even though Evertonians may disagree, it's the whole city that reaps the reward. Because of our efforts, the name of Liverpool was seen to represent something good, positive and noble.'

Liverpool City Council's department for ECOC08 had looked to market football in the city from day-one, regardless of the standard of the clubs. The two – LFC and the city - now complimented each other. On the front of the bus next to the European Cup and on St George's Hall was a massive yellow poster with '08' displayed on it. 'The two together symbolised the resurgence of a city that had been marginalised for so long,' says Joel Rookwood.

Because of the success of the football team, tourism in Liverpool boomed and the year of culture was given more exposure. And because of the economic transformation of the city, Liverpool FC was viewed as a more glamorous destination for cosmopolitan footballers in an age of greater player power.

Rookwood feels that stereotypes and dated perceptions slowly began to change from this point on: 'Having the Capital of Culture provided much needed development and it resurrected the city. Istanbul was a metaphor. At 3-0 down nobody gave us a prayer. In the mid-80s nobody gave us a prayer. Yet here we are.'

'Without Everton and Liverpool, I don't think this city would be what it is,' agrees Steve McMahon. 'You'd have Liverpool as a city but the two clubs have helped globalise the place. People in other parts of the world know more about the club than the city. It has been married to the success of the club.'

Rickie Lambert has his recollections of life at the time: 'Town was absolutely buzzing with the Capital of Culture bid and the football. Beforehand, the city had some lovely parts but was still a shithole in places and I think when the money came in the city just started to shoot up.' Lambert's view is more valuable given that he moved away from Kirkby at the time, relocating to Bristol as his career took off. He was able to appreciate the change all the more each time he came home: 'When I came back it was a completely different city. It was gorgeous. One of the best cities in the country. I couldn't believe it.'

Liverpool was always going to prevail at some point, Rookwood feels, 'in spite of everything.'

*

President Erdogan had a message for Rafa Benitez: "It was the best display of bravery and commitment I have ever witnessed." The Queen sent her congratulations to Liverpool. As did Tony Blair: "It was a magnificent achievement which will be remembered across the country."

Support for Blair was beginning to decline nationally and within Liverpool. At a conference at St George's Hall a few months after Istanbul, New Labour rounded up a collection of famous locals to reinforce the idea that they were the historic party for the city. Phil Thompson recalls in his autobiography sharing a stage with Craig Phillips of Big Brother fame and giving a talk for Blair, despite having been 'loyal to the Conservatives' for many years.

That form of thinking became dated very quickly in a city that looked towards its future. Steven Gerrard was the face of it all. He'd turned down Chelsea again that summer (*"how can I leave after a night like this?"*) much to the delight of supporters worldwide who believed that Rafael Benitez could build upon his misfit squad. 'Money Can't Buy You Love' was a Chelsea-inspired banner made by one Kopite. David Conn, Guardian journalist, had pointed out that Liverpool's success had been one of emotion and loyalty against heavily financed clubs, as football itself stood on the threshold of change.

LFC had to grow but stay true to its roots, like the city itself. Balancing international with local was of maximum importance. In choosing to stay at Liverpool, Steven Gerrard became the most famous face in the city. Alongside the youngster Wayne Rooney (who'd left his boyhood club for Manchester United a season earlier, thus highlighting Gerrard's devotion), he was the most famous local since the Beatles.

The London Evening Standard said as much. "He symbolises the club [and is] considered part and parcel of the city." In a two-page spread written by Vivek Chaudhary, the Standard claimed that Rick Parry had met with Gerrard's father Paul at the Birkdale Golf Club to convince him that 'his future lay at Anfield'. The article – from an enterprise always looking for a sensational story – dispelled the rumours of Gerrard being threatened to stay by unsavoury characters. Speaking to the Standard, a Bluebell resident, John Kendall said: "The Gerrards are well known and popular members of the Huyton community. If anybody threatened them then I would have liked to have met them. There are a lot of big, important families in Huyton and they would not have allowed any harm to come to the Gerrards."

Kendall's sentiment transcended the Bluebell. Gerrard had the backing of Red Liverpool in its entirety. But Huyton was in the headlines for an altogether different reason later that summer, following the racist murder of teenager Anthony Walker.

18-years of age, he'd just completed his A-levels and was walking his girlfriend home through Flower Park in St John's estate. It was 11pm on a Friday night when he was viciously attacked and killed by two males. The killers fled instantly. They were the brother (albeit estranged) and cousin of Manchester City footballer Joey Barton. Merseyside Police rounded the murderers up in Amsterdam and brought them back on an EasyJet flight to Speke where they then arrested them. As the pair languished in police cells that evening, some 4,000 people joined the Walker family on a candle-lit vigil through the park. It sparked a massive period of reflection. 96.6% of Knowsley was white, but did that make Liverpool racist?

The city had the oldest black community in Europe, but the city still clearly had its struggles with social integration. Joey Barton described the Walkers as close and loving, and explained that they stood out because they were the only black family within a four-mile radius.

It was a further tragic example of how much work was still to be done in the suburbs of the city, and how an undercurrent of racism, albeit a trickle compared to fifty years earlier, still existed. The city continued to heroize its white achievers but did anybody know about the feats of black pioneers, such as Clovis Roach, Daniel Ekarte, John Archer and Irene Afful?

Liverpool nevertheless retained within itself a desire to improve, collectively. If racism was present then it would be tackled. In ten years time the city would have a new star, a Scouser and a representative of the modern era whose talent would get all the recognition it deserved. And nobody would notice that he was black, just that he was Scouse.

Back in '05 at a summer camp Ian Barrigan spotted the 6-year-old playing for St Matthews school. He put him in his Country Park team and recalls now: 'When he played for me he would score ten goals a game. We had to play him at the back to stop him always scoring, but he'd still get the ball and take on everybody to get to the front of the pitch.'

Trent Alexander-Arnold dreamt of playing for Liverpool. That summer he sat on a wall by his house in West Derby and watched as the team paraded the Champions League trophy. 'You see your idols standing up there and you see a whole city so happy, and sitting in my mum's car driving around seeing everywhere red...' it planted a seed in his mind for the future.

Daniel Fieldsend

THERE SHE GOES

He got back into his car, grabbed the steering wheel and roared in delight. It felt like winning a trophy. 'We've just signed a player with a passion and a heart for this club that no amount of money can buy,' said Rafa Benitez. Fans on the Kop dusted off their old 'God' reference banners and went looking for their old shirts. Robbie Fowler was back.

When he signed for Leeds in 2001 he looked like a hostage. 'I have left Liverpool on good terms and I will never say anything against them,' he told reporters, citing a desire to get back into the England squad for the 2002 World Cup. It wasn't the full truth. Liverpool hadn't offered Fowler a new contract, Houllier wanted him out, yet he still refused to speak out against the club.

Going back to Liverpool in January 2006 was huge for him. He spoke about not realising how big Liverpool was as a youngster because he'd never known anything else. It was only when he left the club that he realised the magnitude of the Reds. 'I was away from the city for five years and getting a chance to go back home was everything.'

With society being on the threshold of great change, coupled with the world's attention being on Liverpool, people became nostalgic for the old times. Fowler's return was a concordant of that. Just ten years earlier he'd been top scorer in the Premier League with 28 goals. Back in 1996 there was no commercial internet unless you paid hourly for dial-up, and mobile phones were reserved for businessmen with suitcases. Fans in Liverpool were still only just getting used to an all-seated Kop.

Life, and especially life at Anfield, had changed beyond recognition by 2006. The atmosphere was awkward and the experience was dull. Something that had always been lively, creative, edgy and at times disorderly - which bubbled and hissed as anthropologists watched on – was now domesticated and unexciting. The once deadly Spion Kop had become a tame beast.

It was inevitable that the vast sums of money being pumped into the game would break the ties with local communities, as neoliberalism met globalisation. Everybody in Liverpool knew somebody who used to go to matches but had decided to pack it in. It was too expensive, they couldn't sit with their mates and they didn't like the direction football was heading in.

'Culturally there was nothing really going on,' says Joel Rookwood. 'We'd moan about a lack of atmosphere and we'd reference an ideal of a politicisation of fandom which was a response to locals getting squeezed. It wasn't as Scouse as it once was. We saw a trajectory which didn't look good.' Fans wanted to have a political way of being that could become part of a narrative of everyday fandom in the city. An organised group was required, but that seemed unlikely.

Peter Carney describes traditional, often local, hardcore fans as 'activist supporters' who he says 'see it as their right to influence happenings at the club.' But they were mostly working-class and either couldn't afford to go or couldn't access tickets. Supply clashed heavily with demand and Anfield's demographic shifted. 'After Istanbul we got this onslaught of new fans and things changed,' says Andrew Hudson. 'The atmosphere was dying and even though we were a good side, there was something missing.'

George Sephton had missed only one Anfield match in 40 years. 'I talked to the Scandinavians who were the same stock as us and were very respectful of LFC traditions,' he said, 'but a lot of the new guys who came from elsewhere hadn't got a full understanding of the etiquette of what being a Liverpool fan was.'

More than any type of fan or nationality, the biggest alteration to atmosphere came from design: specifically, compulsory seats. The actual physical requirement of sitting had a subconscious association with 'being quiet', like being at school, or church, or at home, or on transport. Standing up was for concerts and parties.

Brendan Wyatt used to sit in the Main Stand towards the away fans. 'If I started singing the people around would look at me,' he said. 'I've had the stewards looking at me for making a noise. There'd be Chelsea and United fans singing songs about Hillsborough, 3,000 of them, and if I stood up and gave it back, I'd be told to sit down or I'd be out.'

Around the time, Chris Bascome wrote an article about Liverpool's local fans that wasn't the most flattering of pieces. Dan Nicolson pulled him up on it with a reply that said: 'You shouldn't be calling out the local support, you should be putting pressure on LFC to ensure more locals can get inside the ground.'

A debate on the Rattle (RAOTL) ensued about the consequences of Istanbul and how it had: 'Brought a new fanbase that didn't respect the city and the culture of the club,' recalls Kevin Sampson. None of the traditional supporters took issue with Liverpool having an international fanbase as it was a result of their stature. They realised it was part of being a 'big club' ... 'But a lot of the new breed just didn't seem to get that Liverpool the club is enmeshed with Liverpool the city,' Sampson repeats, citing the qualifier against Bordeaux early in 2006 as an example, when people turned up at Anfield wearing "Scouser" (Enfield) wigs chanting *'Easy, easeh'* and *'Who are yer?'* – made famous by lower-league television show Soccer AM.

The issue was never out-of-town fans or foreign supporters (Liverpool fans prided themselves on having "Supporters All Over the World", even creating a scarf with various flags around a Liverbird in celebration of the fact), but more the way in which new supporters watered down Anfield's atmosphere and disrespected age-old traditions.

Fan values had been historic, built upon throughout the 1950s, and had been maintained by supporters like Bobby Wilcox who backed the manager and the players regardless of whether he rated them or not. If they wore red, they got his support. The new supporters needed educating in the ways of old.

The worst thing Sampson saw was a collection of visitors in the Stanley pub reading the Sun. Jegsy Dodd went over and set fire to the paper: 'And an incident flared up. The thing that smashed me was the amount of people in there standing up for the lads reading it.' The following morning, Sampson lay down a proposal in the Rattle calling for some collective resistance.

A group of devotees from all corners of the city met in Shenanigans pub on Tithebarn Street. They wanted to preserve something sacred and drew up a list of targets, chief of which was bringing together a core group of fans on the Kop. Rick Parry agreed with them, surprisingly, so they relocated their season tickets and block 306 became like the old 'middle of the Kop' where traditional supporters could congregate.

Parry said: 'Any initiative to improve the matchday atmosphere is warmly welcomed.' Part of the club's support for the cause was because they marketed the Anfield Atmosphere to tourists, which ironically had started the wheel turning. 'Moving 2000 like-minded people into one place basically created an away section in the home end,' says Joel Rookwood, 'with mostly lads who went everywhere and had an opportunity to be together. It gave us a sense of collectivity, we weren't diluted, we had a Scouse heartbeat and we were in one place.'

The Shenanigans group titled their campaign 'Reclaim the Kop'. For academics it displayed genuine cultural ownership from fans over their club. At the same time, many of Manchester United's inner circle broke away and created FC United, a new enterprise born with a spirit of disillusionment. RTK's founders were equally dismayed but they maintained different motives: their purpose was to recapture the match day experience at Anfield, not move it elsewhere.

A message was sent out to the new fans, addressed to those with 'replica shirts over their jumpers', who took photographs at the match, filmed You'll Never Walk Alone, didn't sing (or sang the wrong chants) and chose to slate the team when things were not going well:

> "Not so long ago we'd sing 'You got your education from the Kop'. Being a Liverpool supporter stood for something. Supporting this club brought responsibilities. You were different. You dressed different. You didn't follow the moronic chants that every other club came up with." The message went on: "Good fans no longer feel a part of the increasingly shallow Anfield experience and it won't be long before more and more start spewing it. We need a reasonable, sensible, enforceable charter that properly educates people as to what is required of them."

The people who coined the message remembered Anfield's halcyon days of the 1950s through to the 1980s, and saw a clear demise which didn't sit well. Singing was important, and songs had to be verified by authentic long-term dedicated fans who were part of the local community and who shouldered the reputation of not just the club, but the matchday atmosphere as well. They determined that substandard support harmed both their identity and the potential glory attainable by the team. Above all else, Anfield's atmosphere had to be constructed distinctively, with a nod to the city itself.

The eventual charter came on New Year's Day 2007, in line with the city's 800th birthday. It reinforced many of the traditions that fans were worried about losing. Just as the sacked dockers had done a decade earlier (without the obvious suffering they endured, clearly), RTK used the internet to get their message out to people from beyond the confines of their own immediate communities:

"First is that we are only custodians. The Kop is a spirit, an attitude, the heart and soul of Liverpool FC. No-one owns it, but together we are a legion; a force like no other.

"The Kop innovates. It has never followed. As Liverpudlians, we should never follow the rest of the country's trends and fancies. Whether that takes the form of lower-league grade chanting, overhead seal-clapping or the petty deriding of opposition supporters, the Kop deserves better.

"That means a song for every player. No booing. No heckling any Liverpool player while he's on the pitch. Respect the opposition when they've earned it. Applaud their goalie.

"As with songs, fashion and all aspects of terrace culture, we lead the way with flags and banners. These should always be a matter of pride to the club and relate to the club or the city. There are flags that are Liverpool – and flags that are just not on. No St. George's crosses. No localities from outside the L postcodes. No Confucius-style philosophical tracts. 'Keep Flags Scouse' is a tradition we uphold with pride.

"On 15th April 1989, 96 of us never came home. We will always honour the memory of those who died at Hillsborough. In our respect for them and their families, we will never purchase or read the Sun newspaper, and we deplore the reading of it by any Liverpool supporter.

"It is our custom and our privilege as Liverpudlians to welcome supporters from far and wide. We expect all Kopites of all ages, wherever they sit inside the ground, to show similar respect to the city of the team they support. You support the city too.

"We don't tolerate racism. Everyone knows LFC all around the globe. From Nairobi to Ngoya we have fans because we do things the Liverpool way. We have style, we have honour, we have principles. We are a global force with a local pulse. A club of the people.

"Our own icon, the symbol that makes the Kop a legend all over the world, is our anthem. Our hymn of triumph and occasional pain. Let's respect the anthem and do it proud, sing it slowly and with heartfelt emotion, right to the end.

The charter had a clear sentiment and was well received. There was a thirst for a campaign of such a kind, to educate and not isolate new supporters. An historic sense of how Liverpudlians regarded themselves came to the fore, which fused local identity and football together once again. Andy MacKenzie, a die-hard away fan maintains that: 'Supporting and backing the manager is number one for Liverpool Football Club. That's the role of the fans and we need to keep our core values. If you are a Liverpool supporter then there is a conduct and a way of acting. There was a lot of division around the Kop when new fans were trying to use generic little chants. We're not like the rest of England.'

RTK established itself as a group with clear aims and forged a working relationship with the club. 'Rick Parry gets a lot of stick, but he was always very fair with us,' recalls Kevin Sampson. 'We had a bucket collection for Michael Shields; the Bulgarian judiciary wanted €80,000 to return him to the UK. I remember Rick Parry saying to Ged Poynton – "we're not just allowing this – we're supporting it."' LFC allowed Michael Shields' dad to make a presentation to the Liverpool squad, who themselves donated money.

Liverpool then transported all of the buckets of money to the bank on the family's behalf. Rick Parry also trialled selling beer at the top of the Kop through plastic bottles, nudged along by RTK lad Alan Cook. Nobody rioted and before long lager was back on sale all over Anfield.

As well as forming links with the club, RTK also created a number of visible displays which set a benchmark for future fan groups. Before Porto in November '07 they organised a march from the Sandon in support of Rafa Benitez. Inside the pub, a sign was taped to the wall aimed at Liverpool's American owners: 'You are Custodians, but the club is ours. Rafa Stays'. Thousands marched down Breck Road, led by a framed photograph of a youthful looking Benitez. "Young and old, they chanted the name of their manager and listened to echoes coming back to them in the darkness," wrote the Daily Mirror.

An even bigger spectacle came earlier in the year before the third round FA Cup tie against Arsenal. BBC had hired Kelvin MacKenzie to be a presenter for the game, slapping every Liverpool fan in the face in the process - not just those watching at home, but those who had to share Anfield with him. RTK knew that BBC's cameras wouldn't focus on any mosaic that came *before* the game kicked off, so they organised one for *during* the match. It was an unavoidable and "phenomenal exhibition of solidarity" according to the Echo.

Even more shocking on the BBC's behalf was that, just a few weeks before the match, MacKenzie had been recorded at a fancy after-dinner event in the North East saying: 'All I did was tell the truth. There was a surge of Liverpool fans who had been drinking and that's what caused the disaster. I went on World at One the following day and apologised. I only did that because Rupert Murdoch told me to. I wasn't sorry then and I'm not sorry now.'

When 'Truth Day' arrived the Kop was decorated in white and red leaflets forming a 'Truth' mosaic. 12,000 people chanted '*Justice, for the 96*' continuously as soon as the '6 minutes for the 96' banner at the front of the Kop went down. One of the more poignant banners asked four questions: 'How did it feel when you couldn't find your mate? – did you feel guilt that you didn't share his fate? – how did you feel when you couldn't find your bud? – and later when MacKenzie dragged your name through the mud? NEVER FORGET, NEVER FORGIVE, JFT96'.

MacKenzie's frontpage spread and headline was still a point of anguish on Merseyside and beyond, and his lack of remorse cut deep. A few days after the game he was on BBC television again, this time on the Question Time panel. Once again refused to apologise, stating how: 'That story has been caught up in a battle between [the fans] and me that no matter what I said would resolve the issue.'

But 'Truth Day' had done its job. It kept Hillsborough and the demand for Justice within the public eye. 'It felt like one of those times when us everyday fans were capable of making a difference,' says Sampson. Reclaim the Kop had done good. It had reinforced the value of traditions and brought activist fans together. But when Liverpool's American ownership were proving to be too incompetent, a need for a more organised and political group emerged. The Spirit of Shankly was formed and RTK became a footnote in the grander scheme of things to come.

*

Workers at Town Hall began compiling statistics in 2007 investigating whether the European Capital of Culture had taken off. They found some very interesting things, especially regarding how Liverpool was being presented to the rest of the country. In the national press there had been a 25% increase in 'culture stories' about the city, compared to 2003. Events, in particular, had received a remarkable rise in positive coverage. Back in 2006 only 21% of press stories relating to the city were about arts and culture, but one year later in 2007 it was up to 83%. 2.7 million people were reading about Liverpool, they found, which was far in excess of the national average.

It was working. Visitors were coming and people were beginning to change their perceptions. But then, in August on a warm Wednesday evening, a stray bullet went into an innocent little boy and changed everything.

Rhys Jones was walking back from football training. He was crossing the car park of the Fir Tree pub when a bullet intended for a rival gang member hit him and killed him. People from the community rushed to help but were unable to save his life.

Croxteth Park was at one time the largest private housing estate in Europe. It had been built in the 1980s and, like everywhere else, quickly rooted itself into the identity of the residents. But it also developed a problem with youth gangs – with youngsters whose prospects were so limited that they determined other youths from a mere neighbourhood away, who were receiving the same economic uncertainty, failed educative system and governmental neglect as them, to be the enemy.

When Howard Gayle was a young lad he was in a gang in Norris Green and experienced several brushes with the law, simply because there was nothing else to do other than play football, get into mischief and have fights. With narrow prospects and with no opportunity for personal development, youngsters achieved a comforting degree of purpose in a gang.

In 2007, drugs and guns had been added into the equation and territory became significant. A number of terraced streets across Liverpool saw the letters 'FTM' graffitied onto walls by youngsters, which stood for 'Fuck the Matrix'[66] and was, more than anything else, a symbol of an irritated and directionless generation. They were young and angry, which was understandable, but a poor little boy who had just finished his SATs, who was getting ready to go up into big school, got caught in a needless crossfire and died as a consequence.

Rhys Jones' death became a national tragedy. Gordon Brown called it a heinous crime "that has shocked the whole of the country," adding: "The people responsible will be tracked down, arrested and punished." Merseyside Police unleashed their boiling frustrations on the case, deploying some 300 people to investigate. Nine weeks later the gunman was arrested.

Football had been a visible element of the mourning process throughout. Rhys Jones played as a midfielder for his local team and was an avid Evertonian (Little Boy Blue). His small coffin was of Everton FC design and at his funeral, everybody who attended wore either Liverpool or Everton colours. The Echo started a campaign called 'Liverpool Unites' and sold purple ribbons (the amalgamated colours of both clubs) to raise money for the Rhys Jones Memorial Trust.

---

[66] Matrix was an anti-drugs and anti-gun programme founded by Merseyside Police two years earlier, which saw yellow police vans patrolling the city breaking up gangs of youths.

An article in the paper suggested for Liverpool FC to play the 'Z Cars' theme tune – Everton's anthem - at Anfield in a tribute to Jones before their next game. The piece only intended to test the water, but the Echo was bombarded with letters from fans who supported the idea and before Liverpool's next match, a Champions League qualifier against Toulouse, the club willingly agreed.

Brian Hall had been involved with the family throughout. He introduced mum Melanie, dad Stephen and older brother Owen at pitch side, all in Everton shirts, and informed the crowd of the club's desire to mark respect and remembrance of Rhys: 'To demonstrate that all football fans are united with them in their sorrow.' After Z Cars was played, Anfield serenaded the families with a version of You'll Never Walk Alone.

Rhys's uncle Neil had told the Liverpool website before the game that it would be a fitting tribute, that: "Rhys will have a little mischievous grin on his face at the thought of being the cause of it." Liverpool's staff and players wore black armbands. Rafa Benitez embraced the family and later, despite being Inter Milan manager, donated a considerably large sum of money to the Rhys Jones Memorial Fund because he was touched by the cause. He said there were "people who would like to do so too but cannot afford to." It showed the kind of social conscious Liverpudlians expected of their sporting heroes.

Jamie Carragher was aghast at the murder of the schoolboy but also noted that: 'One of the best things about this city is that people pull together when it matters most and this is one of those times.'

Once again, the city mourned collectively. The Rhys Jones Memorial Fund went towards building sports pitches in Croxteth, inside Langley Close, near the Fir Tree pub. It'd give kids a place to go and play football, deterring them from gang warfare, strengthening the community.

There was enough happening in Liverpool; being said, being done, being built, being felt and being hoped for, that the city was not going to allow itself to be known only for incidents of criminality alone. Everybody was certain of that. The city refused to sink like it had in the past.

The European Capital of Culture, a title so perfect it could have been created by Paul Du Noyer with only Liverpool in mind, could now be seen on the horizon of the Mersey. The people of its banks buoyed in anticipation.

Local

WHICH SIDE ARE YOU ON?

Usually a decent barometer of what is a truly globally significant news story is whether or not it is in the New York Times. A civil uprising in Africa; a catastrophe in Asia. If it is noteworthy, it makes the daily broadsheet. On the 10th April 2008 the headline 'Ringo Loses Leafy Head' made the (no pun) cut. "A vandal chopped off the head of Ringo Starr from a life-size topiary of that former Beatle over the weekend in Liverpool, England, while leaving his band mates untouched."

Merseytravel were gutted. They'd hired Italian sculptor Franco Covilli to give South Parkway Station its own display of public art. The decoration of Ringo's head they got in return was as funny and as original as the topping off of the Duke of Wellington statue with a traffic cone in Glasgow. It was one for the citizens to enjoy and the councillors to tut at.

Why had it happened? Ringo Starr came to Liverpool in January to kickstart the Capital of Culture celebrations. A few weeks later he was asked by Jonathan Ross on his chat show what he missed most about the city? But Starr just laughed. Ross then asked him if there was anything at all he missed, to which he replied: 'Erm, no...' Starr then went on to admit that he was lying about a statement he'd made to a crowd of fans at the Cavern about 'wanting to move back' to the city, saying that he just wanted to 'please the Liverpudlian public'. The Echo received 1,500 angry letters from locals who felt patronised by him. Council Leader Warren Bradley acknowledged that Starr had visited Liverpool and done: 'A PR job for himself,' although he himself wasn't too fussed.

In speaking out against the city of his birth, Starr broke a sacred rule. He inflicted his own demise and was cast aside as an outsider, a traitor with a tarnished legacy. A fortnight after his comments, somebody went out at night with a pair of garden shears and took off his (leafy) head. A line had been drawn. This was modern Liverpool. What was in, was in, and what was out, was out.

American businessmen Tom Hicks and George Gillet skimmed past the headline in the New York Times. When they arrived in Liverpool, they had no idea of the extreme wrath a scorned Scouser was capable of pouring.

The club was a commercial sleeping giant and the city was on the up. They'd been attracted to the façade of the Albert Dock and the new builds; cranes were everywhere in an ever-changing skyline. There was a clear self-confidence about Liverpool that Hicks and Gillet liked.

A national museum had just been built next to the Liver buildings, modestly dedicated toward the city itself. Liverpool One – the largest retail scheme in the UK – had been fenced off for years, but suddenly opened up one day like a gateway into a new world. That was the tag the officials went with: 'The World in One City'. It was the capital of creativity, competition and culture.

Jaguar Land Rover in Halewood was hailed as the best car factory in the world and up the road was Europe's largest printing plant. Liverpool was now a centre for computer games design and had become a biotechnical hub with the largest centre for wealth management outside of London. It was now a centre for engineering, too.

The view people from outside had of Liverpool as a frosty place thawed with the increase of students coming to university. Many fell in love with the place and chose to stay and invest their ideas and futures. The city region expanded and so did its skillset.

Liverpool looked glassy, classy and new, but the direction of local wealth – real wealth – trickled away from residents. Where once upon a time local capitalists founded their own stores, like George Henry Lees, Owen Owen, Ethel Austin and Littlewoods, massive corporations swallowed them up and the money went to tax havens in the Caribbean. Lewis's Department Store had stood since the 1870s. It framed the festive season, hosting the first Christmas grotto in the world, and it retained a mythical status among locals who etched it into their folklore through songs. But in the late 2000s its doors closed and it ceased to trade.

Nevertheless, Liverpool had re-found itself. There was a creative industries sector and a rising employment rate inside the constantly opening hotels, bars and restaurants around town. It was worth £1.8 billion with a further £1.5 billion of developments due to be finished by the end of 2008. Forever living outside the framework of Britain, as the national economy slowed, Liverpool's sped up - a total reversal to the past 70 years.

The journalist who had called Liverpool 'Self-pity city' in the 1990s after the murder of James Bulger, who had tarred Scousers within their own nation, returned in 2008 to pass comment on the changes made. Margolis wrote:

> *"To be honest, all the stuff I'd read about urban regeneration and the fact that Liverpool has been crowned European Capital of Culture 2008 sounded like so much boring official-ese. But what I discovered here is utterly stunning. Trust me, they're building one of the modern wonders of the world beside that grey, choppy old Mersey. So much for 'Self-pity City', for 'shell suits', for "calm down, calm down" and jokes about Scousers nicking your hubcaps. What's happening here is real. And it's going to take the world by surprise.*
>
> *The rebuilding of Liverpool is costing more than £5billion partly from EU funds, but mostly private money. It's the biggest project of its kind anywhere, and there are plans to spend another £50b turning the whole of Merseyside into what I believe will be Britain's second city by the middle of the century. Every corner you turn, however far you walk, has some glorious old structure being restored, and to a stupendous standard.*
>
> *Across the city, as far as the eye can see, are cranes. Whole streets are being built. Astonishing new structures at strange, striking experimental angles accost you every corner you turn. That waterfront, the one with the Liverbirds building, is going to end up as beautiful as Sydney's if it's not careful. But buildings need people, business and a culture to match, and boy does the new Liverpool have all three. The place oozes confidence and prosperity.*
>
> *Across a range of crimes, from violence to burglary to bike theft, Merseyside is safer than Bedfordshire, Somerset, Devon and Cornwall and North Yorkshire. Violent crime is 32 percent lower than in bloody Hampshire, for goodness sake. And culture? I've never seen so much of the stuff in one relatively small city. It's almost ridiculous, bewildering."*

Liverpool had for the longest time been unvisitable, but for the grace of other football fans. Now the sound of foreign tongues joined the squawks of seagulls, giving town a unique ambience. The Albert Dock could have been mistaken for Genoa's Antico Port on a sunny day, especially with those pearl-white cruise ships at its banks.

David Fairclough remembered when tourists didn't want to visit at all: 'It was a place at the far end of the M62, and the other side was the sea. We were our own little place. Now we're this holiday resort-party town, it's kinda strange for us. I think Liverpool enjoyed being a republic. We are who we are and our true colours shine through. You're really proud to come from here.'

It was a republic that locals were keen to show off. Scousers found themselves going out of their way to offer directions to tourists each day, of whom by 2018 there would be 75 million-per-year of. Travelodge rated Liverpudlians to be 1st in a 'Kindest UK City' report.

'In the last decade you can credit a lot of change to the money that came in from the European Union and from the City of Culture victory,' reflects Peter Moore. 'I often think we were a city that was starved by London, and we did not get the investment that southern cities were getting. Manchester too got greater investment and there was maybe something the government did not like about Liverpool. Finally, this city is living up to its potential, having gotten the investment from abroad and from the EU.'

That period of reflection continued when Robbie Fowler – a baby of the 1980s and a symbol of the 1990s – said of the ECOC victory: 'If you went to Liverpool in the early 90's and suddenly you didn't go for 20 years you'd see a massive change. It looks unbelievable now, it's a fantastic place. Outside of London we've got the most listed buildings. The heritage and history and culture of the people makes it a fantastic place. I think there is a special Liverpool mentality.'[67]

Still, the balance between the daily aspirations of locals and the incorporation and welcoming of a new international world rested on a knife's edge. In Williamson Square, the LFC shop swelled with foreign tourists looking to buy memorabilia. Facing it, Scouse lads sold match-day programmes and non-official scarves and flags from their market stall, symbolising the polarity of new-Liverpool.

David Moores from Halsall had been LFC chairman since 1991. He was rich by British standards, but was not an oligarch and did not have state-backed finances like some of the new owners who'd changed football's landscape. 'The Abramovich era was upon us and I knew that I could never compete,' he later said. Liverpool had not won the league under Moores' tenure; doing so in this new climate was impossible.

---

[67] Niklas Holmgren podcast, September 2015.

It was time to sell. Bids came in from Taiwan, Thailand, Saudi Arabia and the UAE. All were rejected. Tom Hicks and George Gillet seemed genuine enough and purchased Liverpool Football Club in February 2007. Moores made an £88m profit.

There was a honeymoon period initially. Liverpool got to the Champions League final in Athens and purchased Fernando Torres afterwards for £27m. But the bid from Hicks and Gillet had been built on false promises – such as £215m for the development of a new stadium on Stanley Park. Cash was taken from the club's profits to pay for the American's assets.

Straight away Hicks emerged as the dominant partner. His comments, supposed to be endearing, would over time be his undoing: 'The first spade will be in the ground within 60 days,' he said, and: 'If Rafa said he wanted to buy Snoogy Doogy we would back him.' Rick Parry quickly realised he was the central subject of a Stealers Wheel hit. 'It became clear that they had very different philosophies on how the club should be run,' he coyly conceded.

In November, Benitez and the owners fell out over transfer targets for the January window. The Americans told Benitez to 'concentrate on training and coaching the players he already he had.' In a bizarre press conference, he repeated that line over and over. Things were clearly wrong. Liverpool's main core of fans were then tipped off by local journalists that Jurgen Klinsmann had been sounded out for the manager's job.

During an FA Cup tie against Havant and Waterlooville, in which Liverpool went behind twice, the Kopites who knew the extent of the wrongdoings at the club began chanting '*They don't care about Rafa, they don't care about fans, Liverpool Football Club, is in the wrong hands.*' They formed a vocal minority and their grievances were largely ignored. An emergency meeting was then called at the Sandon Pub – birthplace of LFC.

Three hundred die-hards turned up having found out about the meeting through word of mouth, message boards and texts. Plenty overheard others on the Kop talking about it and moseyed down unexpectantly. Jay McKenna was only 20 at the time. He was a union rep in work but had no real history of activism. One of his workmates told him about the meeting, so he went along and sat at the back. 'It was like at the match, you'd nod at people whose face you recognised but that was it.'

Paul Rice chaired it. He'd been involved with the Labour Party in the past, specifically with Liverpool Broadgreen and the City Council, and was asked to chair by Peter Hooton who considered him the best man for the job. Various groups attended, such as RTK, Urchins, different fanzines, coaches and mags. All had something to say. 'We hadn't been as political as we wanted to be,' says Joel Rookwood, 'but there but there was enough collective momentum to change that.'

Very quickly the meeting took on a trade union resemblance. McKenna sat at the back soaking it all up. History had shown that the people of the city were able to mobilise their collective anger into change, provided they had a voice. The first meeting determined just that. 'I don't think I really realised what was going on at the time,' says McKenna. 'Paul Rice heard me speak and asked me to get involved.'

'Sons' of Shankly quickly became 'Spirit'. The name itself had socialism at its core. John McDonnell, Labour politician who was born in the city, believes such a union could only have been founded in Liverpool: 'That's not me being arrogant about Liverpool but it's true. LFC has always had a huge supporter's base and it's always been the pride of the city. The supporters of Liverpool rightly believe they own the club. It doesn't matter who owns it financially, it is the supporters' club. That is the thing about Scousers, they don't just want to have their say: they want to be heard. They want to be part of the decision making, so such a movement could only come from here,' McDonnell said.

His friend and fellow activist Roy Bentham agrees that the first supporters union had to emerge in Liverpool. 'Politics has always been a part of football and to suggest otherwise would be a total fallacy. Especially here, since 1989.'

The spirit of the union had been around for a generation. Back in 1961 at an AGM, members of the Liverpool Supporters Association told the club how annoyed they were with its running. A local supporter, Mr Adler, called for a vote of no confidence in club chairman Tom Williams. This was the most radical moment of fan action in Liverpool's history to date. Williams would be re-elected but the act showed the power fans believed they had.

Spirit of Shankly's first protest came before, during and after the Aston Villa game in February with banners offering support for Benitez. Tom Hicks had been in attendance. Outside the Main Stand stewards formed a cordon to protect the American, but even they were singing against him. *'Tom and George tell lies, they tell lies.'*

There were other happenings at play which angered fans. The cost of football and the accessibility of tickets had reached a point whereby only a small percentage of the city's population was able to attend matches. A splinter club was formed in March named AFC Liverpool. Their intention was to offer affordable football to give youngsters some form of match-day experience.

They were a generation of fans who were on the outside of the club looking in. Football was little more than a television show for them; Brian Reade fittingly named them the 'Sandon Backroom Babies'. Tommy Smith bemoaned: 'Grossly inflated admission prices have made the sport elitist. The elderly and those on low incomes could once afford to watch top-division football. Not anymore.'

AFC Liverpool's sentiment was not a new or unique one, and it was not the reaction of one or two disgruntled individuals. It was born out of a long-standing, fair-striving Scouse philosophy. Like Spirit of Shankly, there was an unwillingness to accept ones' lot in life that typified them.

Communist sculptor Arthur Dooley had staged a protest in 1967 against the cost of exhibitions at the Bluecoat which were outpricing local artists. He hung artwork on the railings outside the building and encouraged a union of other artists to do the same, declaring to the masses: 'Art should be a part of everyday people's lives and it isn't. There is no real contact between the artist and the ordinary people.' Every word of his statement applied to football in 2008 (and beyond). AFC Liverpool became the Bluecoat railing of its day.

440 days after the takeover by Hicks and Gillet, the first spade was in the ground. Except it wasn't. SOS organised a protest in Stanley Park wearing high-vis vests and boots, pretending to be workmen digging. It was a bite at the '60 day' fib told by Tom Hicks. The union was receiving massive media attention at the time and Jay McKenna was becoming one of the faces of it all, speaking daily to the likes of BBC Merseyside and Granada, despite working full-time in the Job Centre at the same time. People started to ask him where they knew his face from? On one occasion when he was in a bar in town with a girlfriend, he appeared on Sky Sports and a man approached him and gave him £20 as a thanks for the union's work.

McKenna wasn't well received by everyone in the city, however: 'I remember a Facebook group was set up which made me laugh called: "I want to punch Jay McKenna in the head dead hard". I remember there was an Everton fanzine, too, which did a list of 100 irritating things. I was the highest placed Kopite - 9th – and they called me: James "Liverpool Football Club" McKenna. I beat Michael Shields and Dave Kirby. I came ahead of 'smackheads who ride little bikes'. Everton fans gave us shit and my mates who were blues would wind me up about it.'

During the whole period Liverpool were performing well in the league and in Europe. But uncertainty was a daily presence. Rumours circulated before the Real Madrid tie in March 2009 that Rafa Benitez had resigned. He hadn't and his team went on to win 4-0. Afterwards, Madrid legend Zinedine Zidane described Gerrard as the best player in world football. 'He might not get the attention of Messi and Ronaldo but, yes, I think he just might be,' Zidane said.

A genuine worry for Liverpool fans was the absence of other emerging local players. Gerrard had made his debut eleven years earlier and since then no other Scouser had tied down a long-term role in the team.

It brought about a debate on the importance of having local representation at Liverpool for the first time ever. Since Ian Callaghan's debut in the early 1960s, through to Smith, Lawler, Thompson, McDermott, Lee, Fairclough – Fowler et cetera, things had been taken for granted. Jimmy Case had his say: 'The fans need someone they can identify with, one of their own, and anyone who underestimates the importance of having a Scouser in the team is standing on shaky ground. I certainly don't think players from abroad can take it in.'

And Case continued: 'Even today, with so many foreigners in the game, it is important that Liverpool keep bringing through players who have the city and the club in their veins. I cannot think of another club where that bond exists to such an extent as it does at Liverpool. Give the fans everything, work your socks off and they will stick with you even when the going gets tough.'

In the stands and on the pitch, localism was under threat. Before a league game in '09 Ronnie Moran was told he couldn't come into Anfield without the correct accreditation. He'd played for, captained and coached the club all of his life but was told he couldn't come in freely. Sammy Lee – who was assistant manager – saw the encounter and sorted Ronnie out.

Lee went further and asked ground staff for a room at Anfield that he could recreate as a new boot room, in spirit at least. He gave Moran a job to do and tasked him with furnishing the room to recreate the old post-match think-tank he once knew. It had a fridge, beers, a table and chairs – nothing fancy. Lee would meet Moran before and after matches and they'd invite the opposition staff in for a chat. Bobby Charlton would come in and reminisce and Moran would take the mickey out of his knighthood. In training, Lee made sure all of the players knew who Moran was and what he'd done for the club, pointing out his image on the corridors of Melwood while the old man walked around the perimeter of the pitch outside. Football was changing but at least Lee, Moran, Gerrard and Carragher remained.

Carragher in particular began to personify everything Liverpool fans stood for. Franklin Foer wrote once about Javier Zanetti going to an underground *Ultras* meeting at the end of an Internazionale season to give out awards to the communist fans there. Foer wrote that if the club found out, they'd have asked questions of their captain. In early 2009 Jamie Carragher went to a Spirit of Shankly meeting and spoke honestly about the uncertainty surrounding the owners. If LFC had of found out... Jay McKenna remembers Carragher's presence: 'He spoke on stage openly, and another time came back from a family party with Sami Hyypia. A lad had to shoot off half-way through and Carragher lent him £20 for a taxi. There's a photo from the end of the night once the lad had come back of him trying to give Carragher the £20 back.'

Just like people from Huyton felt a stronger affinity with Gerrard because he was from there, McKenna and Bootle residents felt a greater attachment to Carragher. 'I remember playing footy in the park as a kid and he came and joined in because we were playing with his brother,' says McKenna. 'There's a Scouse thing between fans and players. You look at them and you think '*he's one of us.*' The kids in the street just want to be like them. You get a nice sense of pride by thinking 'by-ours' created one of Liverpool's best defenders and one of Europe's too. He's won the European Cup and is just a feller who used to play footy on the streets by ours.'

In the summer of 2009 Liverpool appointed Christian Purslow as managing director. He quickly labelled the SOS as 'Sons of Strikers' - a dig at the historic perception of Liverpudlians nationwide. They responded with a banner featuring the word 'Purslow' beneath a large cartoon penis. A few months later Tom Hicks Junior, a board member at Anfield and son of chief owner of the club, lost the plot. Stephen Horner, a fan, forwarded Junior an article from the Echo about Rafa Benitez's future. Junior replied almost immediately saying: 'Blow me, fuck face. Go to hell, I'm sick of you.' He was forced to resign.

Things were heating up. There was a mass meeting at the steps of St George's Hall on Independence Day (July 4th) 2010. Speeches in support of SOS were delivered by the likes of John Aldridge, Karen Gill, Steve Rotheram, Alison McGovern and Howard Gayle. John Bishop took to the stage and was met with a tongue-in-cheek chant of '*John Bishop is a Wool*'. He took it in good nature, replying: 'You know when we moved to Runcorn, I had to go... because I was 6. I said to the council "*I don't want to go, because one day I could be stood on the steps of St George's Hall and my message could be drowned out by some knobheads shouting John Bishop is a Wool.*" To be honest though, I'd rather be a

Wool than a Yank at the minute,' – anything but... He then credited the SOS, reiterating: 'We've got a voice now and we can make a change.'

Things got worse before they got better however. The owners sacked Rafa Benitez. Before he left his Wirral mansion for Inter Milan, he donated £96,000 from his severance to the Hillsborough families. Under Roy Hodgson Liverpool fell embarrassingly into the relegation places after a loss to Blackpool. It was the club's worst start to a season for 57 years. Dominic King wrote for the Echo that the club was: "On its knees, torn apart by an internal civil war... crippled by debt, possessing too many players who are not good enough." There was talk of potential administration and a nine-point penalty deduction.

Then Martin Broughton was appointed as Chairman. Billboards went up across Liverpool and Birkenhead funded by the SOS which simply said in bold: 'Debt. Lies. Cowboys. Not Welcome Here.'

Things started to accelerate. At the start of October there was a good chance Liverpool FC could have folded. SOS made a video that was widely shared online featuring famous Liverpool fans, such as Sue Johnston, Stephen Graham, Gerry Marsden, Paul Smith, Peter Hooton and Ricky "Mr Hicks my arse!" Tomlinson. *'Do one'* was the main message of the video.

Royal Bank of Scotland were owed a debt by Tom Hicks. They were prepared to place the club in administration rather than refinance. Hicks had to scramble for fresh credit. The 13th October was D-Day. SOS put on coaches from the Rocket for fans to travel down to London to gather outside the High Court of Justice. They waited there nervously to discover the judge's findings. It didn't take long. Justice Floyd determined that Hicks and Gillet were wrong to try and block any potential sale of the club and should therefore allow negotiations to continue. The club had two days to find new owners or it'd be in administration with 9 points deducted.

SOS activists travelled back with optimism. It'd taken so much to get to this point. Straight away an offer came in from New England Sport Ventures (Fenway Sports Group). They would pay off the debt and acquire ownership of the club. John Henry made a declaration to Liverpool fans as the final stages of his bid went through: 'We are committed first and foremost to winning. We have a history of winning, and we want Liverpool supporters to know that this approach is what we intend to bring to this great club.' Winning? Fans just wanted stability. The idea of silverware was ludicrous at such a time.

Local

Henry attended Liverpool's next game, the Merseyside derby at Goodison Park, and watched a Roy Hodgson team lose 2-0 to Everton, plunging them down to 19th in the league. Within a decade Liverpool would become Champions League final regulars and one of the most desirable teams in world football. Hicks and Gillet left Liverpool without a penny of profit after three years of financial abuse. In a small window of time, given the vastness of the club's history, the era demonstrated the repercussions that'd await any other owners who'd attempt to undermine Liverpool fans – who now had a strong voice.

*

Joe Anderson was elected as leader of the City Council in 2010 with a 'socialist agenda'. Labour ousted the Liberal Democrats from office, but in truth the city had maintained a map of red for some time. As Britain voted for David Cameron's austerity programme, Liverpool elected every form of Labour representation.

In the 1990s under Blair, Liverpool had one of the lowest voter turnouts in the country. People were exhausted from their battles with Thatcher and disillusionment ruled. But austerity was a blatant attack against the poor – against many wards in Liverpool – and the socialism that had always underlined the city resurfaced once again in a more blatant manner. Such a response was unsurprising. Throughout history Liverpool had been the home of radical responses.

Jeannie Mole had formed the 'Workers Brotherhood' – one of the first socialist societies in Britain – with her husband from their home on Bold Street in 1886. After the First World War, capitalist commentators acknowledged how the city held up the banner of the labour movement, which had beforehand been done in Glasgow. 'Red Clydeside' became 'Red Merseyside'. It marked Liverpool out as somewhere different. When the brazen fascist Oswald Mosley stood atop a van and drove down Queens Drive spouting hatred from a loudspeaker in the 1930s, he was showered by bricks from nearby rubble sites and put in Walton Hospital. Then in 1968, 300 women at the Ford plant in Halewood chose to strike in line with their co-workers in Dagenham.

It'd be naïve to suggest that throughout all that time Liverpool was anti-Tory, however. Footballers voted Conservative in favour of lower taxation and Protestants did before religious divides disappeared. Right up until the 1970s the Tories formed one of the two major parties in the city, running the council up until 1955. But in the 1960s 'class' replaced religion as the main purpose for voting and people became socialised toward the left.

Daniel Fieldsend

When both parties underperformed in their duties, voters in the city elected Liberals. There was a flexibility at the time – Labour were not cemented to civic identity. Tony Lane explained how things were in the late '70s: 'The Liberals have occupied a poetical space created by the sheer enormity of Liverpool's problems and by the failures of the Labour Party to tackle them.' At the time of Margaret Thatcher's election win in 1979, the Tories were 3rd in public affection. By the end of her tenure they'd been consigned to oblivion.

The Militant party emerged as the voice of the people against a visibly Blue-Oxbridge establishment and the more the city was attacked as 'the enemy within', the more anti-Conservative people became. The idea of voting Tory went against Scouse identity. By 2010 to be called a 'Tory' was the most powerful and venomous insult in the local vocabulary.

When Reuters broke the news in late 2011 that Thatcher had considered abandoning Liverpool into the Irish Sea in 1981 as some kind of physical pariah, it caused genuine shock and was taken up by the Independent, BBC, Guardian and Financial Times. The city found itself teetering on the edge of its nation, with its own set of ambitions and beliefs. But the revelation inspired no gasps in Liverpool.

John Aldridge's emergence as an LFC star coincided with the darkest days of Thatcherism. He knew what her agenda was and later retained a certain distrust of the establishment, which carried through to his career in the Basque Country with Real Sociedad. His comments, on the people there, relate in many ways to how Liverpool people came to regard themselves:

'They don't see themselves as Spanish; they should be their own country. It goes back to the days of [General] Franco who allowed Hitler to bomb a Basque village. He let them practice there which mutilated thousands of people (Guernica). When I found that out, I couldn't believe it... You can compare the regard people held for Basques to Thatcher's days; people lost their jobs.'

It was surprising that Labour hadn't won control over City Council sooner. Joe Anderson from Dingle had joined the Merchant Navy at 16 and become a union rep during his time with them. He'd sailed to Gydnia on the Polish coast and encountered an uprising. In South Africa he witnessed apartheid. After coming home, Anderson ran the Monroe pub on Duke Street before working as a social worker and then a councillor. Within five years he was City Council leader, taking Labour's total from 19 to 48 seats. He talked of socialism, naturally, and lamented a way of life that was disappearing by the day, when women scrubbed their front steps and kept pride in their community despite their poverty.

Anderson was tasked with maintaining a traditional socialist heartbeat while expanding the city internationally as a business hub. He had to do so under the austere programme forced upon him by Cameron's government: 'We have never faced such cuts as a city, even after the Second World War,' he said. Was Liverpool to be the new Bologna, one European magazine pondered? The Italian cobbled city had consistently elected a communist office since 1945.

Such comparisons were not needed; Liverpool had been left of centre for generations. Dan Carden, Walton MP, was raised on a diet of dockers discourse, union meetings and marches. He believes that Liverpool's embedment with socialism – which Peter Carney describes as a 'sweet-sounding echo chamber' – is fused by the influence of its ancient port. 'If you go back 100 years you had casual labour and you had trade unions which were organising, and because every family had links to the docks it politicised the working classes, probably more so in this city than in any other. We are a very proud here and it is quite unique that we still see the spirit of socialism and solidarity and speak with one voice, because that is how you change things.'

Those sentiments transcended class boundaries in the city for locals, even those catapulted from humble backgrounds into money. David Fairclough remembers the transition: 'I was brought up working-class: my dad worked six or seven days a week and my mum has always worked too. We come from a very social environment with Labour values. When you move into football it's weird. I remember hearing players talk about taxes when I was a youngster in '74. I wouldn't have even discussed it with them back then.'

Jamie Carragher provides proof to the belief that class is a mentality as much as anything else, and, despite coming into money, working-class norms remain deep-rooted: 'I wouldn't say I was somebody who went into the dressing room on election day and told everybody they had to vote Labour,' he said, 'although that's something I would do. My education of that stems from my upbringing and where I came from. My dad would talk about the miners' strike when I was a kid; I remember the Derek Hatton era as 7 or 8-year-old; Arthur Scargill and those type of people. Football is a working-class sport. You like to think that footballer's values and those of their families are to never forget where they come from.'

If there is a clear political leaning in a Scousers' makeup, where does that leave supporters from outside the city who retain contrasting beliefs? There are people who attend matches at Anfield from other parts of the country, who vote Tory and who buy the Sun. Is that an issue? Gareth Roberts believes that if you support the club, you are duty-bound to support the city too.

Jay McKenna agrees: 'The fanbase needs to have a conversation about what it is. Not all voices are equal in this debate, like it or not. Liverpool try to be all inclusive to everyone but at some point they need to find a balance and our fanbase needs to have that conversation too.'

He continues: 'If the fanbase is fragmented then we can't move forward. If you're a Tory and you see me saying this then you'll think '*He's a leftie militant, I'm not going to listen to him,*' but that doesn't make it untrue what I'm saying. The Sun thing I don't get. If you read it, you can't be a Liverpool fan. If we put that to the fanbase inside Anfield today, they'd agree. But in terms of people's political persuasions, well we need to talk about that. They might not agree with Bill Shankly's quotes about socialism, but that is who Liverpool are. He delivered certain things which the fans bought into, which made us the best in the world. You can't now change that because it was then and this is now. If you do, you're betraying your history.'

Those beliefs – of fairness and social equality – came into conflict with a commercially driven mega sporting institution at many times in the 2000s. At the top of Arkles Lane was a huge moneyed beast whose glass façade was looked upon but rarely accessed by its neighbouring community. Most disappointing for them was how it swallowed up the old terraces that helped to create their sense of place, leaving them to go derelict. Cllr Ian Byrne was part of that community: 'I live underneath Anfield and the club definitely played a role in the managed decline of the area. It created an environment whereby people were leaving in droves.'

The Guardian's David Conn, who had been a champion of the Hillsborough fight for justice for so many years, revealed the extent of Anfield's austerity programme in a shocking 2013 article. "People's farewells are bitter, filled with anger and heartbreak at the area's dreadful decline and at the club for deepening the blight by buying up houses since the mid-1990s then leaving them empty," he wrote. Conn explained that Liverpool began with Lothair Road, buying up empties and trying to tempt other residents to leave. They abandoned purchased homes for twenty years and engineered the decline of the area. The consequence of 'tinning up' those houses encouraged vandalism and fires. Residents feared they'd wake up to find the street ablaze. People moved out but the value of their homes had tumbled drastically. Conn pointed out that the club could have added temporary tenants to the houses, sustaining the community, but did not.

The grand Victorian houses on Anfield Road one season disappeared. Conn spoke with a resident who revealed he was offered £55,000 for his home on Alroy

Road, but refused outright having been forced to renovate it twice following vandalism. For one week of Stewart Downing's wage, things could have been done legitimately and with sincerity. Ian Ayre - from Litherland originally - told The Guardian that Liverpool aimed to expand the stadium but would not lower the cost of tickets (*"that's not realistic"*), another disappointment for local residents.

Then the Independent did a piece on the exclusivity of Anfield, speaking to a father who lived "2 miles from the ground" but had never been able to take his son to a game. Forever seen as an escape for local fans, the relationship between them and the club was stretching close to breaking point by the end of 2013.

Daniel Fieldsend

TRAMP THE DIRT DOWN

Then, on the 8th April 2013, Margaret Thatcher died. In West Belfast crowds gathered to drink outside the Sinn Fein office in Lower Falls Road. In Glasgow, champagne was uncorked. Derry and Bristol were decorated in graffiti, while in Brixton the local Ritzy cinema advertised a new film: 'Maggie Thatcher Dead'.

In Liverpool, a reaction had been pre-planned for years in advance. The Old Roan pub – which had stood for two hundred years but only ever sprang into life during Aintree Races – experienced the landmark night of its existence. From the moment the news broke at noon, people congregated there, entering, embracing and laughing. By 10pm the bar was dry, inspiring the youngsters (who hadn't lived through her tenure but provided a telling symbol of her legacy through their reaction) to head outside, set off fireworks and burn an effigy.

Across town drinkers in the Casa - a venue for sacked dockers – poured out onto Hope Street dancing, and regulars from the Yankee bar set off flares on the steps of Lime Street. The chant for Philippe Coutinho was amended to declare: *'Maggie's dead dead dead.'*

The jubilant few reminded confused passers-by that 'Thatcher', for them, was a noun, a symbol of an era of disregard, more than a living breathing human. She was the overseer of union demise, dockside trading neglect, media abuse and anti-Militantism. Liverpudlians grew poorer and felt despised by her government and remembered her for the negatives of her tenure. She had backed the police following the Riots of '81, considered managed decline, and, upon discovering 'damning evidence' of the police's role at Hillsborough, refused to condemn them.

Locals responded to her passing with relief. John Aldridge's mates went for a pint when they heard the news. He joined them. 'I hated her and everything she stood for. She despised our city because we stand up for ourselves. We won't be bullied and we won't let people tell us what to do.'

The Independent and the Telegraph fixed their gaze upon Liverpool's supporters for their next match against Reading. John Madejski, chairman of the club, displayed with his comments how polarised Thatcher's legacy was between the wealthy and the working-classes: 'We have got to appreciate that Margaret was a world leader who did so much for this country,' he said. He then proposed a minute's silence for her.

Madejski received a conga line and banners tailored for the event. 'You Didn't Care When You Lied. We Don't Care That You've Died' read one, 'You Picked on the Wrong City' read another. Both were references to her government's coverup of the failings surrounding the Hillsborough disaster.

A number of Socialist Worker fliers – handed out on Bold Street the day before the game – had reached the concourse. 'Rejoice, Rejoice!' they read – a mimicking of Thatcher's reaction to the sinking of the Belgrano ship in the Falklands War, in which 323 people died. "Gotcha" Kelvin MacKenzie picked as a Sun headline for the incident in 1982, a foreshadowing of the insensitivity to come.

Fittingly, the silence that John Madejski called for was granted. Not for Thatcher, that symbol of the booted establishment, but for the Hillsborough victims who were muddied by that very same boot. Before kick-off one fan who'd lost his son at the disaster climbed up to the rafters of the concourse and led chants against her.

Birkenhead-born actress and Labour politician Glenda Jackson stayed behind in Parliament the following day. She sat and listened as Conservative MPs eulogised the former Prime Minister, waiting for her opportunity to talk. 'I tremble to think what the death rate for pensioners would have been this week if that version of Thatcherism had been fully up and running this year,' she began. The blue-ties facing booed, but she continued: 'There was a heinous social, economic and spiritual damage wreaked upon this country by Thatcher. Every single shop doorway, every single night, became the bedroom, the living room, the bathroom for the homeless. People saw the price of everything and the value of nothing.'

Brendan Wyatt lived through it all: 'When I left school, she was turning the screw. There was no hope. I wrote letters everywhere but there were only eleven vacancies for apprenticeships for 2,500 kids.' Norman Tebbit told them to get on their bikes. 'So we did. We went across Europe on the Transalpinos.' Abroad had always retained great fascination for Liverpool people, more than any domestic greenery. Wyatt's clothing company – the name and the culture surrounding it – was a reaction to Thatcherism and an era where, despite the misfortune, some light could be gleamed, just by being a Liverpool fan.

Another positive from a negative, Howard Gayle reckons, is that her attempts to break the will and morale of working-class people had an opposing effect, uniting communities regardless of their colour. The people of Liverpool came together in a mutual loathing of Thatcher, and football became a canvass to display that sentiment.

When Liverpool FC completed its Main Stand redevelopment in 2017, fans were able to buy personalised bricks and plaques for the floor outside. Alongside the memorials and declarations from supporters across the world was a message paid for by a local: 'Maggie's In The Mud – 08.04.2013'.

And that was it. Done. 'I sang songs about Thatcher until she died and then I wouldn't anymore,' says Joel Rookwood. His stance was the most typical one. She was a period in time, of suffering and demise, but that was over with now. Liverpool was still on an upward trajectory and there was no point wasting time thinking about a serpent of the past, even if the scar tissue of her legacy had affected the way people thought and voted.

Local

LIVE THE DREAM

Like the old days, austerity was blinding the quality of life of enough of the city to dampen the spirits of everybody. Two thirds of the Council's budget was cut – some £444m. Joe Anderson told the Financial Times that his office received £174m in council tax but spent £172m on adult social care alone – 'It doesn't take a mathematician to see that this isn't sustainable,' he said. Per resident, Liverpudlians were £816 per month worse off than elsewhere. Homelessness rose, depression levels increased and families were plunged into poverty. Worse than that still, Infant Mortality Rate rose to 6.8% in Liverpool – twice what it was in London. Suicides became part of a statistic displaying the extreme measures people were taking to escape it all.

Mark Green from the University of Liverpool found that by the end of 2015 the UK had experienced the largest annual spike in mortality rates for nearly 50 years. The Independent opened a story one month saying: "The Conservatives have been accused of 'economic murder' for austerity policies which a new study suggests have caused 120,000 deaths." They followed it up one month later, writing: "In places like Liverpool, modern history tends to be told in the cadence of lamentation, as the story of one indignity after another. In these communities, Thatcher's name is an epithet, and austerity is the latest villain." David Cameron's 'nasty party' (a self-bestowed title) was overseeing a programme in which the rich got richer and the poor died.

In 2015 the Guardian made a movie on the 'Two Kensington's' – Liverpool's and London's. There were visible contrasts shown: in London, a Bentley was filmed zooming down a floral white-housed street; in Liverpool, a lad was filmed doing a wheelie on a bike down a bordered-up road. The intention of the movie was to show the polarities of Britain's economy and wider society in the run-up to the general election. John Harris, the documentarian, listed some statistics:

Liverpool's Kensington had 30% unemployment and a 48% rate of child poverty. London's Kensington had 2.9% unemployment and a 4% rate of child poverty. In Liverpool's Kensington, a house could be purchased for £1, a local initiative. In London, on Kensington Palace Gardens, a home was up for sale for £47.8m.

The movie pointed to the imbalance of life in an austere Britain. London was a 'Monaco', an offshore tax haven invested in by the rich. Liverpool on the other hand had its local SureStart centre for struggling mothers closed down. John Harris, after speaking with ladies who explained its essentiality for them, became emotional: 'Words like austerity can become very cliched until you see them in practice and see what they actually mean. Okay the government saves money in the most short-sighted, crass and ignorant way imaginable but places like this are threatened with closure.' There'd be a further £12b worth of cuts to come.

And what about football, that television show? Nobody could afford such an outlet. During David Cameron's tenure as Prime Minister, between 2010 and 2016, LFC finished 6th, 8th, 7th, 6th and then 8th again, with one decent season under Brendan Rodgers in between when they finished 2nd. The despondency of football mirrored life so well for so many.

Competitively void, a million miles away from the Chelsea's, Manchester United's and now Manchester City's of the league – and a trillion miles away from the Real Madrid's and Barcelona's - there was much uncertainty about what the benefits actually were to being a Liverpool fan, especially a local one? Wedged inside those Cameron years, though, was a valve. From his debut goal against Stoke City on a cold January night in 2011 to his oh-so-close tears after Crystal Palace in 2014, supporters were dead certain about their feelings towards Luis Suarez.

He was untouchable. He scored and chased and dribbled and won matches on his own. He seemed like he could have been the greatest Sunday league player of all time, often hunched and clumsy, but better than he realised and so deft, inventive and instinctive with his goals. Hattricks and theatrics defined him. He was a flawed phenomenon who'd grown up in poverty playing street *futbol* on his dusty Salto neighbourhood court, while his mother swept floors for money because his father had abandoned them.

He played like he was terrified that he'd suddenly be dragged back to the life he knew as a boy when he couldn't afford shoelaces, unless he fought for every win, as if he were resisting some unforeseen prophecy.

Locāl

For Uruguayans, his behaviour made sense. They loved him more than any other player in history. For Diego Maradona he was a misunderstood innocent who needed protection. For everybody else he was a portrait lunatic – the most hated man in football. But for Liverpudlians, with his urchin-like rebelliousness, he drew affection from somewhere deep within the local psyche.

Their love for him came from an historic Old Scotty shanty mentality, not from this new stoic cosmo-European city. He flirted with the wrong side of the law and the people liked that, building a cult around him that protected him from controversies. When he bit Ivanovic, a blind eye was turned; when he racially abused Patrice Evra the club embarrassingly backed him with t-shirts. Luis Suarez was on a trajectory toward being the best ever Liverpool player – all of the other greats said so – he'd even called his daughter Delfina, an anagram of Anfield.

But he'd wanted to leave before, choosing to train alone when Arsenal bid for him, and he wanted to leave again when Barcelona came in for him. Steven Gerrard – now 34 – negotiated with him to stay, but he was off a year later. For Gerrard, who himself never had the team built around him that his precarious talent deserved, it was more of the same. Suarez joined Javier Mascherano, Fernando Torres and Xabi Alonso in wanting to leave for better things. Liverpool Football Club had become a stepping stone, trapped in the middle of a pyramid of clubs, buying from below to sell to those above with no hope of ever truly competing.

At the same time, Jurgen Klopp had taken over at the financially fragile Borussia Dortmund. In 2005 they had been in $150m worth of debt and were days away from bankruptcy and relegation to the 5th tier of German football. In the years before his arrival they had finished 7th, 9th, 13th, 6th and 5th. He took over, spent hardly any money, made stars of youngsters like Robert Lewandowski and Shinji Kagawa, played a revolutionary type of football – aggressive yet technical and co-ordinated – mythologised the roaring home support and won trophies. His captain Sebastien Kehl said: 'He gave a new identity, not just for Borussia Dortmund, but for German football.' With his charisma, passion, blonde hair, glasses, cap, touchline sprints and massive hugs, Klopp had become the most recognisable coach in world football. Liverpudlians could only pine for such a manager.

*

It was naturally going to happen. The performances were mundane, everybody got used to sitting down, nobody knew the person next to them, everything was routine, tedious, unenjoyable. When teams came to Anfield and asked questions as to the location of its famous atmosphere, the Kop merely waved a hand in boredom, like an old lion swatting a fly. They'd dismiss such teams and chants as undeserving of a reply. The Main Stand and Anfield Road had neither the acumen nor confidence to reply at all and thus continued to stare straight ahead silently, with their bobble hats and flasks of tea.

'Even though we were a good side there was something missing,' says Andrew Hudson. 'For years you'd go the game and it was just boring... same songs being sung... little games were shite.' Fans had reached a glass ceiling and tried to break it in a way that demonstrated a process for others to follow. Many of the younger, like-minded, dedicated Reds who went all over the country to away games – who all knew of each other but flew under different banners – decided to come together, unite, and get their own coach. They stood together for the first time at Craven Cottage at the end of 2013 and then, at the start of the 2014 season, organised to bring out all of their banners for Notts County at home to make a display.

It was a follow on from the sentiments of Reclaim the Kop but was delivered by a younger demographic. 'We all spent a night in the pub painting flags and using bedsheets,' remembers Andrew Hudson. 'We must have had around 35 flags just for Notts County, and that was the first game for Spion Kop 1906.' His brother Chris continues: 'It went on from there into the development of social media accounts. In terms of visual strength, I don't think there's anyone better in the league than us at what we do.'

They did it because they backed the club and wanted the best for the team, making banners to fit various occasions – because the context of individual matches is usually unique, determined by off-field events – and worked as a group to give a face to the culture and identity of Liverpool supporters. They took banners to Old Trafford ('Scousers Rule And Don't You Forget It') and to Goodison Park ('18th Birthday – 1995 to 2013'), and they brought forward some of the more finely woven strands of authentic-support beliefs ('Anne Williams Iron Lady'). The club appreciated them and eventually opened a dialogue. But one of the most important things that Spion Kop 1906 did was team up with the Spirit of Shankly to campaign against the cost of football for all.

In December 2013 they took a banner to White Hart Lane - 'FAO Mr Ayre: Supporters Not Customers' - and backed the Football Supporters Federation's 'Twenty's Plenty' campaign to cap away tickets. Various banners propped up their stance, such as 'ɛNOUGH IS ɛNOUGH' and 'Football Without Fans Is Nothing' and they co-ordinated with visiting fans coming to Anfield to demonstrate the universality of the climate.

That mobilisation of football supporters led to a collective protest in London in August 2014, marching on the Premier League headquarters from central London. Simon Magner of Everton's Blue Union told the BBC: 'In an ideal world, all fans would be charged exactly the same as all other clubs in the same league.' But this wasn't an ideal world.

The movement had working-class socialism at heart. Premier League clubs were making record profits from TV deals but were not subsiding fans or rewarding them for their commitment. In 2015 against Arsenal, Spion Kop 1906 and Spirit of Shankly members protested against £64 tickets by staying in the turnstiles for the first ten minutes of the game. They put up a banner on the Kop the following month: '1990: £4 – 2000: £24 – 2010: £43 – 2010: ?'. It was all building up to something.

On the 6th February 2016, some 10,000 Liverpool fans walked out on the 77th minute of the game against Sunderland in protest at the clubs proposed £77 tickets. Black flags waved and the opposition applauded. 'People were cheering on the way out,' remembers Chris Hudson. There was something symbolic about them walking out of the ground early singing 'We love you Liverpool' at the same time. Andrew Hudson says: 'We'd been out since 9am, handing out leaflets trying to educate people on what was happening. The club have made huge strides since then. I think the penny has dropped for them and they get it a little bit now.'

The twins' tickets were actually going down in price, but they were protesting on behalf of everybody else. Inside the Solly where fans watched the last ten minutes, there were awkward cheers when Sunderland equalised – it proved that fans had value. 'Without them a club is nothing,' states Andrew Hudson: 'The fans who make the atmosphere are proof that Liverpool works because of what we do.'

The Premier League must have been watching because one month later they capped away tickets for all clubs at £30. "Is there a place for socialism in football?" pondered the BBC. In that ancient tug of war between boards wanting to make profit and fans fighting to retain their club, supporters had pulled back some ground.

But for many Reds, in January 2015 it felt as though the last part of the club's soul had gone. Steven Gerrard announced that he was leaving. He'd just scored two goals to rescue a point against Leicester City but he hadn't been given a decent contract and was set to leave for free – the news hit like a thunderbolt.

Daniel Fieldsend

He'd been a tough-tackling skinhead midfielder as a lad who battled with Keane and Vieira, before morphing into the best attacking midfielder in the game, adored by Kaka, Totti and Ancelotti. In recent years he'd evolved into an elegant, more refined player, controlling matches from deep. Earlier in the season he was sent off for a two-footed challenge on Juan Mata in an otherwise dull fixture. 'What he did was so Scouse because you don't accept anybody taking the piss,' says Gareth Roberts now. But his dismissal marked the end of the passionate era – for both clubs.

Gerrard was meant to be a one-club man. He'd rejected Internazionale, Real Madrid, Bayern Munich and Chelsea to give his best years to Liverpool FC. But as his career came to an inevitable conclusion, the club dallied and didn't give him a new deal until November. By then he'd agreed to move to Los Angeles.

Jamie Carragher Tweeted: "Sad day for Liverpool and English football. I think it's the right decision, all things considered." They'd been texting all week. Gerrard eventually told the Echo: 'If a contract had been put in front of me in pre-season, I would have signed it. I'd just retired from England to concentrate all my efforts on Liverpool.'

But it didn't arrive. Naturally when a player comes through the ranks, gives everything and then ages, fans begin to reflect upon their own mortality. Hernan Crespo from the suburbs of Buenos Aires penned a eulogy for Gerrard: 'It was a shot to the heart. When a champion like him leaves a club like Liverpool something goes away inside you. A piece of history is sadly leaving. I feel proud to have faced Steven, both in that final and when I was at Chelsea. I thought back to all the times we battled hard on the pitch but always as honourable men, filled with passion and love for football.'

The Spion Kop unfurled a banner for him in January 2015 before a League Cup semi-final against Chelsea. It said: 'The best there is, best there was, best there ever will be'. He loved it. The captain got in touch with the group and asked if they could come to Melwood to meet him. Chris Hudson was part of the contingent: 'We spent a good few hours there. I took my Istanbul ticket and he signed it. Everything he could do for us, he did. He went into the dressing room and came out with a load of Suarez gear; boots and what have you. We were gobsmacked, he was so genuinely nice.'

Spion Kop 1906 were just one face of the youth-inspired fan culture at the time, which would fuse together with other facets to form a bigger picture of Liverpool in later years. There was the 'Make Us Dream' banner that they took to Melwood for the title run in of 2014, a welcome form of trespassing that showed how much fans cared. That banner was there for the bus welcomes which spontaneously grew out of the King Harry pub on Blessington Road, which looked down over the docks and the Mersey beyond. The welcomes, intended to push the team over the line to secure league glory, bordered on the edge of the law and were designed to provide each team with a feeling of inspiration or intimidation.

Successfully lit flares sucked the daylight from around them – unsuccessful ones exploded and were cheered. Chequered flags waved, banners draped over houses, people climbed up walls and bottles flew through the air. Everybody followed the bus to the ground, shoulder to shoulder singing. If Blessington Road looked over the cranes, the Mersey, and then Ireland and the Atlantic beyond, then the watching world looking back could see the message clearly: *this* was Liverpool.

After the Man City victory in 2014 all of Liverpool's hardcore went straight to town for a Sunday Session with Boss Night: another facet of culture. There were that many people partying inside Sound Bar on Duke Street (Sound and Boss together), that the window went through and smashed on the floor. Lads emptied out onto the street and continued the party, only for the police to turn up with Alsatians, confused to find that there was no actual violence to worry about.

Boss Nights had grown out of the Boss Magazine founded by Dan Nicolson. Its concept was influenced by The End, but for a new era. It discussed pubs, songs and fashion and had an 'in / out' undercurrent like The End before it. Its '50 things not to wear in Liverpool' article became a timeless example of Scouse identification, disregarding items like: V-neck t-shirts, belts, wallets, vests and white socks, as well as a host of Manc/Wool brands like: Superdry, Hollister, McKenzie, Toms, Henley, Pretty Green and Moncler.

Every venue Boss Nights occupied filled up, fast. At OSQA's off Hardman Street it became the post-match routine. There'd be young and old groups of fans in there with live performances. When the nights moved to District – a warehouse in the Baltic Triangle – they became more organised with more banners, more performers and more flares. A lad with a shaved head off one of the coaches started playing old Liverpool chants and went down a storm. 30 or so match lads went to his gigs in town. Outside of that circle, at Boss Nights, he was known as 'that lad' initially and then 'Webster'.

Bus welcomes, Boss Nights, the Spion Kop 1906 banners; better football being played and a return of competitiveness: from 2013 things started coming together. It demonstrated what could be achieved if the team was up to the standards of the fans. Kevin Sampson glows when he thinks about the pageantry of it all: 'It's unparalleled, and its funny when you have big occasions elsewhere like with City and Chelsea and they leave flags on the seat. As a fanbase, in the best possible sense of the word, disobedience is in our DNA, and what everybody else is doing, well we have to do the opposite. I know I keep coming back to the idea of us being virally despised but I believe it comes down to good old-fashioned jealousy. The bit Melville wrote about with everyone enjoying themselves and living for the day is something we've taken into the stands.'

To be despised in England married up with being admired on the continent. Liverpool had links all over Europe, at Celtic, Inter Milan, Gladbach, Lazio, Ajax and Feyenoord (who'd join Liverpool's hardcore whenever possible). Things had only ever been mundane at Anfield because the performances of the team warranted it. And if Liverpool were envied nationally, it was because of a fan culture that had been drawn out by Bill Shankly in the 1960s. For things to kick on further, if the glory days really were to return, then another charismatic manager was needed.

Local

NEWBY STREET

They'd had him pinned as their number one target for five years - the perfect fit for the club - so FSG bided their time. They kept hold of Brendan Rodgers for the start of the season until Klopp was ready to end his sabbatical. Meetings took place secretly. The board *'Skyped'* his agent, Marc Kosicke, to inquire about the German's interest. In September, a meeting was arranged in New York between him and the owners. They sold their vision to Klopp and he liked what Liverpool stood for. It was a proper football city with a rich history. All of it appealed, the challenge, the struggle and the potential rewards. On the 8th October he became manager.

In his first meeting with club staff and players he told them how they were all responsible, together, for everything. It mirrored Shankly's doctrine of everybody working together and having a share of the rewards. Tom Werner took Klopp and his staff for a meal at the Hope Street Hotel and showed off the prettiness of his new rejuvenated home.

The following morning Liverpool fans worldwide tuned in for his first press conference. He was more famous than any player at the club at the time and he excited the supporters immediately. After apologising for his poor grasp of the language, Klopp proceeded to say in perfect English: 'Of course, at this moment we are not the best team in the world. What I saw from outside is absolutely *okay*. At this moment all the LFC family is a little bit nervous, a little bit pessimistic, a little bit in doubt.' He talked about expectation being like a backpack that can weigh a team down, and although it was nice to reflect on the achievements of 20 years ago, a new chapter needed to begin. Then came his defining statement: 'My message to Liverpool fans is that we have to change from doubters to believers, now.'

Jimmy Case liked him straight away: 'He's probably the closest you'd get to a Scouser in terms of attitude,' he said. The new manager's early tenure coincided with a number of subtle changes and appointments from Fenway Sports Group that'd bring the club back closer to the people of the city. From Florence Melly Primary School, walking distance of Anfield, FSG announced an initiative to offer tickets to local residents and local Primary School children. It was a small number, around 600 to begin with, and although it wasn't exactly a massive window sale opportunity like the old days, it was a start – a nod in the right direction.

At 20 Chapel Street, Liverpool's office block, positions were being filled by committed supporters. LFCTV, the face of the club to millions worldwide, began to celebrate authentic fan culture with their videos and documentaries, helped by the appointments of Phil Reade and Mark Platt ('every time our media team use the word 'Boss' I think it's significant, because it's a Scousism,' says Joel Rookwood).

At the academy, Alex Inglethorpe (hired initially by Brendan Rodgers) made it his agenda to ensure the best Scouse talents joined Liverpool and not their catchment-area rivals.[68] Jurgen Klopp supported the plan, saying to the press in his own carefree way: 'How many people live in Liverpool? 500,000? Iceland has 330,000 I think, so Liverpool should have enough people to create our own team... If I have two players, same quality, but one speaks proper English and the other one speaks Scouse, the Scouser is in, that's why we are Liverpool.'

Significantly, Tony Barrett – a man once likened to the Khmer Rouge by the previous American owners – was appointed as the head of supporter liaisons. He lived in the city, his mates were from the city, and he'd written as a journalist about ways in which the club could improve. They wanted to listen now, it seemed.

Suddenly LFC had a social conscience. Giving back to the community had always been the domain of Steven Gerrard and Jamie Carragher in the past. They'd donated so much money to local causes like Alder Hey and their foundations, but now everybody was chipping in. Mamadou Sakho was turning up at houses on Stanley Road to help with the painting, arriving with bags of sweets and drinks from Home and Bargain. Trent Alexander-Arnold, who'd made his debut in 2016, was involved, telling the Times: "Changing a life is best thing I

---

[68] I myself was brought in as a youth scout for a few seasons to help search for local talent.

can do in a week". Both players were representing Kev Morland's charity 'An Hour For Others', which asked people to give up their time and skills to strengthen the community.

Before long Jordan Henderson would be spending his Christmas morning with sick and underprivileged children at Hotel TIA, and Adam Lallana would be easing food insecurity with Red Neighbours. Andy Robertson, a Glaswegian signed for cheap from Hull City, who had been skint a few years earlier playing in the third tier of Scottish football, who more than anybody embodied this new, value-driven Liverpool, took a keen interest in helping with foodbanks as well. When a 7-year-old lad called Alfie Radford asked his dad Tom if he could spend his pocket money on food in Aldi to donate, Robertson found out about it and sent him a letter:

> "For you to give that up for people who are having a tough time and need some help to get by is absolutely amazing. Let me tell you now, that is brilliant from you and sets an example to the rest of us that showing a little care and thought for others is really important – it's also very Liverpool. Foodbanks are a cause very close to my own heart and what you've done will stay with me for a long time."

Robertson volunteered with Fans Supporting Foodbanks and drove around the city dropping off crates of food in a van donated by Peter Moore. Food poverty had grown since the introduction of Universal Credit, a benefits payment that took (takes) six weeks to arrive and forced people to miss their rent, pushing them into hunger and potential homelessness without support. Ian Byrne of the Spirit of Shankly and Dave Kelly of the Blue Union started collecting food in wheelie bins in September 2015 and since then the organisation had (sadly) grown.

Howard Gayle asks: 'How can it be, now, in the fifth richest country in the world, that we have people using foodbanks?' He sees it as a governmental failing. But Liverpool FC – New Liverpool – stepped up. Jay McKenna knows that the club would never come out and state its position politically - no sporting enterprise would ever alienate potential investors - but he sees the underlying meaning of their actions: 'What they're doing around foodbanks and the community is good because they acknowledge their role.' Ian Barrigan says that at their 2018 end of year party, the club collected food for the community: 'We have a duty and I like it. You see all the quotes from Shankly and Paisley... all our greats have been from working-class families and I don't want us to lose our background.'

A lot of the change seemed to come from Klopp's social and political philosophy. He knew that success would only happen if everybody was pulling in the same direction: the board, academy, management, fans and players – and the wider city of Liverpool too. He possessed an affable nature and spoke freely about matters of concern. To Raphael Honigstein he said:

"I'm on the left of course, more left than middle. I believe in the welfare state. I'm not privately insured. I would never vote for a party because they promised to lower the top tax rate. My political understanding is this: if I am doing well, I want others to do well too. Something I will never do in my life it is vote for the right."

The right-wing frightened him having been raised by a generation of Germans who remembered the war. In Liverpool, he found a city that was a solace from such political ideology. Historically whenever fascists tried to recruit members in Liverpool, they were beaten back. The English Defence League – a racist group – planned to march through the city in early June 2017. Seventy Lonsdale-clad men and women arrived at Lime Street, but despite being encircled by the police, got no further than the old Penny Farthing pub directly facing the station. Thousands of Scousers turned up to meet them, to send them back to whence they came. The visitors fell short of the standards of the locals and were heckled throughout. Chants displayed a feeling of difference, including the oft-repeated '*Scouse Not English*' and the impromptu, tongue-in-cheek '*Fuck off to England, the city's all ours*' – a comical yet telling exhibition of an evolved mindset.

Brendan Wyatt says: 'We put them on the train back. My dad fought the Nazis so I owed it to him to deny the fascists the chance to march in our city. They weren't far off them, those who came. I'm British, but people don't understand our lack of Englishness. It's a mentality from what we were subjected to.' For Scousers, the day had comedy value, especially when a loudspeaker played the Benny Hill theme tune as the EDL trudged sadly back to the train station.

That afternoon was in the middle of pre-season. Klopp was away, so he probably didn't see the event, but he was well aware of Brexit and had his views on Britain's decision to leave the European Union. He told Dan Roan of the BBC:

"History has taught us that if you are alone you are weaker than the unit. I have never experienced a war but the past has showed us that Europe is much safer if all of the powers are together. Yes, we have problems but let's solve them together." Klopp rhetorically asked Roan who benefits from countries like France and Italy becoming more right-wing? *"Stick together*

and calm down. I hope for common sense in the end because one [person] wants to benefit from the bad situation [here] and be Prime Minister from it. It is not right. For me, I live here (Britain) and it is a wonderful place in Europe and I hope it stays like this."

During the referendum Liverpool had voted to remain (more solace for Klopp), dividing the narrative that Brexit had been a northern uprising against the political class. The local stance prompted the New European magazine to lark: "Expect the red half of the city-state's population to immediately declare an independent people's republic. Followed by an application for EU membership, with Klopp as president of the independent republic of Liverpool. The 28th member state of the European Union."

Liverpool had been rejuvenated considerably by European funding over the previous two decades. A walking tour of the city's landmark attractions was spotted by tiny placards with a blue and gold EU flag, declaring *'This project was funded by the European Union'*. For many, the EU added to their socio-political identity.

Nicky Allt feels there is a link between football and the remain vote; that Liverpool is a continental city, made so by both its outward-facing geography and the exploits of LFC abroad, and therefore has inhabitants who favour Europe. 'If you consider Brexit, the majority of Liverpool and Celtic supporters would be against it and would be really proud to be European football clubs. A large part of Chelsea and Rangers supporters however would want to leave the European Union, so this is where the politics intertwines. There is also that belief that if you win the European Cup then you are a club with European pedigree and standing.'

Andy MacKenzie agrees with that and furthers the statement by saying that both Glasgow and Liverpool probably value the European Cup more than inland teams because of their geography: 'We're steeped in a culture of it historically that elsewhere has been deprived of,' - Glasgow voted 66% remain. If it was Europe that the people wanted, inevitably that's what they'd get. But LFC hadn't been good enough to win on the big stage for a long time. They were a relic of a club, like the two Milan sides and Ajax at the time – a memory of a bygone European age. Any optimism was reserved for the delusional, not just the casual 'believer'.

*

Mohamed Salah was not a big name when Liverpool signed him. He was a winger who'd underperformed at Chelsea but had done well since in Italy. At £36m he was cheap enough and young enough to make an impression, but there were doubts. Two former Liverpool players stated after his signing that he probably wouldn't start, while a reputable European journalist likened him to Juan Cuadrado (a flash in the pan winger) and said he lacked intelligence. Salah would go on to score more goals in a single season than any player in Premier League history and be named as the fans', players' and writers' footballer of the year.

He'd become the most famous Arabic man in the world and have his face plastered across Times Square. He'd unite a politically splintered Egypt. He'd fund hospitals, schools and ambulance units in Nagrig. He'd sponsor 450 families and donate £250,000 to the Egyptian state. In the March general election, 1.7 million people would vote for him to become Egyptian president, despite not being on the ballot. He'd be featured in GQ magazine, who'd write about his humble nature and disarming smile. CNN would write about his 0% body fat and explain that he used to play as Liverpool on FIFA as a boy, but and now as a man some 77% of its players had voted him to be the face of the next cover, which mattered all of a sudden. The Guardian would visit Cairo and report: "He beams out from billboards, selling everything from chocolate bars to soft drinks, mobile-phone tariffs and bank accounts." He'd be the face of New Liverpool.

The club had always had famous players in the past, from Billy Liddell to Kevin Keegan, through to Fernando Torres and Luis Suarez. But Salah was more famous and more socially, culturally and ethnically significant than any player in the club's history, more so than John Barnes in regards to his universal impact. What's more, Salah had not been a massive star beforehand. Only at Liverpool did he become an icon for Muslims all over the world. In Afghanistan and Iraq people crammed around televisions to watch Liverpool matches; in Lebanon, Tunisia and Morocco it was the same story. As Liverpool progressed in the Champions League with Mohamed Salah scoring goals, the club's star rose with his.

Locally, Liverpool was now fused together with the rest of the world and the growth of the club as a brand positively affected the mood of the city, because for proud locals they were one and the same. On Bold Street - with its array of restaurants from across the world, and its unique flavours, smells and accents - there were posters for Salah in shop windows and on flags above doors. Having a Muslim icon also bridged together people who previously stayed rigidly, or antagonistically, away from each other.

Mumin Khan, of West Derby Road's mosque Abdullah Quilliam (the oldest in Britain), told Simon Hughes for the Independent about how local non-Muslims had started popping in to have a look around the mosque, because they'd never seen inside of one before and were interested now, because of Salah. "He has painted a positive picture of Islam and it is helping communities with the same basic needs to understand and respect each other a lot better," Khan told Hughes.

On County Road – supposed Everton FC territory – the local Discount Store seemed to have a new Mo Salah banner over its door every fortnight, much to the delight of local Liverpool fans.

Researchers at Stanford University discovered there'd been an 18.9% decrease in hate crimes against Muslims in Merseyside since Salah had signed for Liverpool. The stat was no coincidence and displayed both how positive an impact he'd made, and how fickle and narrow-minded certain people had been beforehand. Authors of the report explained: "The public image of Salah as a hero of sorts, and the resulting normalisation of some Muslim practices, may have dampened the appetite for harassment and violence toward the city's Muslims."

Hate crime in Merseyside was already far less prevalent than elsewhere in the country, especially given that Brexit had created a surge in anti-Muslim sentiment elsewhere in Britain. Because of this tide of xenophobia, Channel 4 news, BBC, *Al Jazeera* and most other major media channels honed in on a Liverpool FC good news story in February 2018.

With Salah having already scored 30 goals, Kopites in Porto's Libertade Square on a rainy afternoon sang: *'If he's good enough for you, he's good enough for me, if he scores another few then I'll be Muslim too … / … if he's sitting in a mosque that's where I want to be.'*

A guest on Channel 4 News told viewers: "Unfairly the white working-class who are associated with football are often accused of being prejudiced … in one of the most important cultural parts of Britain, which is football, it is heart-warming that something like this is happening. The fact they have chosen to highlight his faith is quite respectful. Liverpool fans are a special breed and there is no coincidence that this has come out of Liverpool."

Salah acquired a number of chants throughout the course of the season to various songs, to 'Sit Down' by James, 'The Day We Caught the Train' by Ocean Colour Scene and to 'You Are My Sunshine'. It had so often been the case that whenever Liverpool were doing well, songs emerged easily, naturally and spontaneously. 2017/18 would go on to be the season of the Beautiful South's 'Rotterdam or Anywhere', Peter Gabriel's 'Solsbury Hill' and Righeira's 'L'estate Sta Finendo' – an obscure Italian disco hit from the '80s that Neapolitans had turned into *'Allez allez allez'*.

Back in August, Liverpool had to beat Hoffenheim to progress into the group stages of the Champions League. Their young coach Julian Nagelsmann said beforehand 'I'm not in awe of this club,' before admitting after losing that: 'Anfield turned us into headless chickens.' Away from home, Trent Alexander-Arnold scored a peach of a free-kick to secure the tie, despite still being just 18-years of age. Afterwards Steven Gerrard – employed back as a youth coach – spoke about Trent and recalled a moment when he'd visited the Academy looking for more tips on how to improve. Gerrard called him a "beauty" of a player. Jamie Carragher then shared a photograph of himself standing next to a young Trent as a mascot in 2009 – the baton passed from one local representative to another.

The group stage away matches provided the kind of charm that deterred a certain type of fan and drew the more determined. They were in Moscow, Maribor and Seville. The locations set a wheel in motion. It felt, being over there, as though this Liverpool side was capable of achieving something and that the fans were a valued part of anything to come. 'We have the resources to be successful now,' the recently appointed CEO Peter Moore said. 'Compare the squad we have now to the one we had two years ago. There is constant improvement. At the same time, you can feel it with Jurgen that we're onto something.'

The quarter-finals against Manchester City were hostile. They were storming the league, were favourites to win the European Cup, and, because of their constant presence, had become the new enemy of the Kop. 'We've always looked around for the team stopping us from winning trophies and made them the victim of our aggression,' said Joel Rookwood. Indeed, it had always been the case from Nottingham Forest through to Chelsea that rivals were determined by competition rather than culture.

Like other rivals, some City supporters began to draw on chants from the periphery of their consciousness and made shouts about 'bin dippers' and 'murderers'. It was new from them, but sadly inevitable. Liverpool fans were used to songs about economic deprivation and had been since the days of 'Bread' and 'Boys from the Blackstuff'. The irony was that Liverpool was now a wealthier and more handsome city than most others in the UK, including Manchester. 'It's pathetic really,' said David Fairclough of the chants: 'There's lot of contradictions in football.'

An army of rogue fans welcomed Manchester City's bus on Arkles Road on the night of the first leg with the kind of 'anti-authority spontaneity' that Kevin Sampson described earlier. Bottles were thrown and smashed against it, cracking the bottom left window. Was it a personal attack or tribalism? Was it obvious anti-social behaviour, or an attempt to intimidate the opposition and give LFC an advantage? Either way, Liverpool won 3-0. Guardiola was furious and the press were equally aghast. Liverpool FC received a fine from UEFA for the occasion. A bulk of those involved merely shrugged at the furore. They saw worse every October on Mischief Night.

Following the second leg, which Liverpool won 2-1 (5-1 on aggregate), Simon Hughes made a point in the Independent about the size of the remaining semi-finalists in the competition. There was Bayern Munich (whose civic population was 1.45 million), Real Madrid (3.16 million) and AS Roma (2.87 million) all vying for the trophy, compared with Liverpool who had a civic population of 491,500. Just being there in such an age was an achievement.

As Joel Rookwood said when remembering the days of Gladbach and Saint Etienne, there was a difficulty for non-capital city clubs to win big cups: 'Liverpool provides itself as the exception, we are the shining light as an opposition to that movement.'

Jamie Carragher was driving to his mum's house on Knowsley Road when the idea of Liverpool overachieving was put to him. He said instantly: 'I was thinking about this the other day. It's unbelievable. This city in the north west of England with 5 [sic] European Cups and still fighting. We've got the Beatles, LFC, fashion, music, the arts. I think it all comes from the people really; we don't accept second best and we're always fighting for something. We push the boundaries and never accept what we've got, and we always want to be better no matter what it is. I also think about that natural enthusiasm and energy that the people have got; everyone has that in them and there is a mentality of *"why should anyone be better than us? Nobody is better than us."* That belief and energy mixed together means we always seem to overdo what people expect us to do.'

When the draw was made for the semi-final in Nyon in April, it was inevitable that Liverpool would be drawn against Roma – they who believed themselves to be Liverpool's greatest overseas rivals.

In the first leg, with the police focussed on enclosing and monitoring thousands of Liverpool fans who'd arrived on Anfield Road to greet the teams, sixty Roman *Ultras* in balaclavas marched down Breck Road, the other side of the stadium, punching random Reds and whipping them with the metal ends of their belts. Sean Cox from Dunboyne was attacked for wearing a Liverpool scarf and put in a coma.

With his treatment taking place at Walton Neuro, Liverpool fans set up a fund to support his family during their difficult time in the city. The Spirit of Shankly's campaigning would in the end raise just shy of £60,000 for them. 'The Twelfth Man pub were the first people to offer support in terms of accommodation,' says Peter Carney, who then set about making a banner for Cox; it had 'You'll Never Walk Alone' in English, Gaelic and Italian stitched onto it, the message being one of unified peace.

Many fans were trepidatious about travelling over to Rome. It had been an unsavoury location for so long. The trip therefore appealed only to the exuberant, the brave and the devoted. It appealed to the type of fan who'd tailor a banner and take it to the centre of dynastic human competition, who'd stand outside the Colosseum with a token to 'them' from 'us' that read: 'Rome Wasn't Built In A Day... That Was Birkenhead'.

Such was the family atmosphere Klopp had nurtured at Melwood, Lucas Leiva helped arrange for the Reds to train at Lazio's facilities and sent a gift back for the cheeky canteen duo at Melwood: Carol Farrell and Caroline Guest (a Lazio shirt signed by the whole squad).

Afterwards, when Liverpool had defeated Roma 7-6 on aggregate to reach their first European Cup final in over a decade, Stephen Monaghan threw the Sean Cox banner down to the squad to hold up. It made for a famous image: young Liverpool fans at the front of the section singing *'allez allez allez'*, *'Gini Wijnaldum'* and *'Mo Salah, Mo Salah,'* together with their t-shirts, caps and shoulder bags - one mass force of 5,000 people pointing toward the team in absolute synergy. The scene was completed by Dejan Lovren and the players together holding up the Sean Cox banner in return, for all to see.

No longer was the club in the process of 'coming together', it felt as if they were close to a point of climax. Was this not it, what all fans aspired for? Simon Hughes met up in the Baltic Triangle for a coffee: 'This run to Kiev has brought a lot of people together,' he said. 'In Liverpool, people are feeling closer to the club. They're embracing fan culture more now. I think it's important to document what's happening at present.' But, as he continued to say, despite the progress 'they still have a way to go before they fully connect the local fanbase with the club.'

Locals, however, were willing to give temporary allowances, given the direction the club was heading in. The build-up to the final in Kiev was raw and exciting. All throughout May the city baked in one of its hottest recorded summers. Despite the warmth, determined mums kept their windows bolted shut because they were being used to hold up flags and banners for their sons, daughters and partners. For the first time in years everybody wanted a banner making, so they did it themselves, out on the garden with a red sheet and tub of white paint.

'I wondered if that had been lost in recent years,' said Tom Fairclough, 'but in May when you looked at the houses in the city there were flags everywhere. That reaffirmed to me how massive it is. I thought it had been watered down a little bit because 2005 was like nothing ever seen before, but May showed nothing had changed.'

Logistics made for enjoyable exchanges. *'How are you getting there?'* once again formed the basis of most conversations. Via Minsk, Riga, Sarajevo and Prague: the wanderlust spirit of the old days spiced everybody's plans. The difficulty of reaching Kiev was made easier by an inherent confidence and a degree of street-wisdom: people camped in haunted woods in Belarus and turned Odessa into Ibiza.

Once in Ukraine, the occasion was made easier by a Facebook group called 'Free Couch Kiev': an initiative started by locals who were unhappy at the extortionate prices hotels were charging, who themselves wanted to portray a kinder image of their city.

That underlying degree of human compassion defined the occasion. Kiev would, despite the potential difficulties, be brilliant: Shevchenko Park was sunny, the music was good, Webster played a fine mini-concert for Boss; the ale flowed and the locals intermingled with Scousers. Real Madrid's supporters were affable, cultured and, because they were used to such occasions, willing to contribute towards a light-hearted atmosphere

Even Rickie Lambert was there, back representing the club as a fan following his recent stint as a striker. His arc over a period of fifteen years in many ways mirrored the growth of Liverpool. Lambert had been let go by Steve McMahon at Blackpool as a teenager. He worked in a factory in Skelmersdale slicing cabbages and bottling beetroots, just to tide himself over until he got a new club. He trained with Macclesfield Town and waited for recognition and a contract. 'It was costing me £20 in taxis a day getting to training. I was lending money off my family because I had none. I was getting close to jibbing it,' he says. But he got his contract and worked his way up, scoring in all four divisions and then for England on his national debut. He'd played for Liverpool – who else in Shevchenko Square could say that? – and now stood in the sunshine with his mates wearing a red t-shirt with an Owen McVeigh badge pinned to it. His top reading: 'Liverpool - Possibly the Best City in the World'.

Things appeared to take a turn after the game when a group of Dinamo supporters stormed into the McDonald's on *Khreshchatyk* at 2am chanting something indiscernible, before they softened and quite randomly walked through the restaurant holding aloft A4 pieces of paper with Liverpool's badge on. They patted Reds on the back, shook their hands and then were gone as quickly as they came. Nobody understood why.

The occasion was not without its drawbacks, however. Flights were a letdown for thousands. People had to pay £2,000 for a room for one night, while others payed in excess of that for tickets. It had always been UEFA's intention to exploit fans at finals, despite them having paid all season to travel the continent endorsing their brand competition. There'd be no reward at the end. But the occasion – so out of the blue – inspired fans to pay regardless. Around 40,000 Reds travelled over to Ukraine, news reports stated.

'I was walking around bumping in to lads I know who I didn't even think were going,' says Hughes. 'It was a powerful image of Liverpool, and this is what people from outside the city don't get: success is important on the pitch but if people in the city see progress is being made and people are able to have fun along the way, then the support will continue.'

David Fairclough reflected afterwards in the quiet of Formby Village: 'It's unbelievable what Liverpool do – everybody saw Shevchenko Park. More than politics or music, football brings it back.' His friend, who worked as a presenter for Fox Sports, had visited before the final and told Fairclough: 'No fan group in the world would have gone through what Liverpool have done. There are teams in South America with fanatics like Boca Juniors and River Plate, but when Liverpool travel, nobody does it better.' That statement would appear even truer one year later.

The Reds lost the final, came fourth in the league and claimed no trophies in 2017/18. But it was a winning season. The videos, the foodbank support, the Boss Nights, the fans taking part in a fashionable movement, together as 'New Liverpool'. It all fed into a cycle of optimism that carried through into pre-season. There was no fresh start, just more of the same for 2018/19. After years of progress, Liverpool had been pushed back into relevance by the force of nature that was Jurgen Klopp.

Locāl

FORTUNE FAVOURS THE BOLD

The Unbearables: A season review and a change of tense

He was a teenage writer who'd never written anything of repute and had no inspiration, so in 1879 (a year after Everton were founded) Robert Louis Stevenson set off on a trip to France with nothing but a donkey for company. He was looking for adventure, for infamy on a Don Quixote voyage. What he found was something more natural and assuring. He found contentment. There are few things written in the 19th century that have any relevance to modern life, or fandom, but this does:

> "The great affair is to move; to feel the needs and hitches of our life more nearly; to come down off this featherbed of civilisation... Alas, as we get up in life and are more preoccupied by our affairs, even a holiday is a thing that must be worked for. To hold a pack upon a saddle against a gale out of the freezing north is no high industry, but it is one that serves to occupy and compose the mind. And when the present is so exacting, who can annoy himself about the future?"

Stevenson's description of life pausing whilst travelling with a purpose appears to be as applicable to today's world as it was then. If he were alive in 2018 wearing an Under Armour t-shirt and a pair of Vapormax, if he was in Kiev and had decided to follow Liverpool FC all over Europe, away from the featherbed of society and its confusing and stressful woes, he'd compose his mind for a moment, briefly, with a legion of fellows hugging and shouting together without the judgement of public glare, in a far-off land with a gale against his face – in Moscow or Maribor - and he'd realise that when the present is so exacting, who can annoy himself about the future?

There came a point when Liverpudlians realised that it was not about 2017/18 or 18/19 and the dividing lines between campaigns, but saw rather that they were living a moment. The feelgood spirit of one season which peaked in Kiev didn't fall in trajectory like expected, but sustained itself into a period of opium. There was no rebuilding or re-evaluation like in most pre-seasons, no jealousy of other clubs, but just Chester away in a friendly after Kiev.

England were playing Sweden that afternoon in a fixture of national importance, but Kopites who headed on a Merseyrail journey west stated that they didn't need England FC for big-club validation. A month earlier, Harry had wedded Meghan. Both stories - the wedding and the World Cup - overwhelmed media coverage. 'Sound' bar on Duke Street held a 'Fuck the Royals' party, with money given to foodbanks on the day. For many Reds it was nice to enjoy a day of solitude in Chester. New-boy Fabinho played and did *alright*, and Andy Robertson had a laugh in the sunshine with fans when they told him Celtic were beating Shamrock Rovers 7-0. He helped Liverpool win 7-0, too.

Fabinho had never played in his home country of Brazil. He was so talented that agents smuggled him into Europe as soon as he was old enough, firstly on loan to Real Madrid where he played one game, then to Monaco where he was signed after winning the league. Liverpool, for the first time in their recent history, were spending big money and keeping hold of their talents.

Fabinho cost £39m and his fellow countryman Alisson Becker, a goalkeeper, was bought one week later for £65m. Loris Karius, the wrongdoer of Kiev, had made another howler at Tranmere Rovers away. He was being assessed at the time - his mental state under scrutiny following his performance in Ukraine - but when he fumbled a ball from an easy free-kick and allowed Tranmere score, their Scouse winger Ben Tollitt told him: *'You're fucking shit!'*. Liverpool's decision was made for them.

Alisson settled into the squad immediately, taking out his guitar and serenading his teammates during his initiation in Spain. He'd go on to win the Golden Glove with 21 clean sheets during the season, beginning with West Ham at home on August 12th - the first game of an epic campaign.

Anfield was the same as always beforehand. Foreign tongues met around the ground and queued up for merchandise out of pop-up containers. In the line, they were given fliers saying 'No Fascism' and 'Don't Buy the Sun' by locals. They ate in Homebaked, a community asset that had been a bread shop (Kelly's) since 1926, before settling into their first-time seats to watch the game.

It was a mergence of new and old together with outsiders welcomed in. After a 4-0 victory, the new fans went to nearby pubs and drank together, like the famous Arkles and Sandon.

Local

A body of Liverpool's traditional support, however, went beyond Anfield's immediate circumference and headed to the Halfway House – a cramped old-fashioned setting with velvet seats and wooden stools with floral wallpaper and a smoke-aged vibe. It was standing room only with Scals wearing Porto, Dortmund and Sevilla caps, waiting for Jamie Webster to play. When the league table came on the television with one game played, they sang *'Liverpool Liverpool, top of the league'*. They'd sing it time and again that year.

Regulars straight away were enjoying home matches at Anfield like they were away games, and enjoyed away matches like children at Christmas. A win away at Crystal Palace on the 25th was followed up by a 1-0 home victory against Brighton. When Chris Hudson, between sips of Guinness, said 'There's a feeling isn't there?' his brother Andrew lowered his glass and backed him up: 'You can tell we're on the brink of it, you can tell it's close.' Chris then added: 'You're actually getting excited to get up and go to home games,' and Andrew replied that, from what he could tell, it all came from Klopp, but that now: 'Even the whole hierarchy of the club is run uniquely. They get it. There's a local heartbeat there which is important. It feels a bit different.'

The brothers are similar, but by this point *all* Liverpool fans were thinking the same. The indecision, undermining and pessimism of bygone years had been replaced with a unity and a conviction to win. Away at Leicester City, with its bordered-up shops and streams of fans in replica shirts, Scousers were in great voice. They equalised, Leicester, and their fans started waving £5 notes from their wallets at travelling Liverpudlians, who'd campaigned tirelessly for them and indeed all other fans to enjoy the benefits of a £30 away ticket cap. But Liverpool won 2-1 – the last laugh always the sweetest sounding.

At Tottenham in mid-September they won 2-1 again, despite their tireless striker Firmino getting his eyeball fingered and going off injured. He was supposed to miss the next game against Paris Saint-Germain, but was made of tough stuff and came off the bench to score the winner in a 3-2 victory. It was still early in the season but Liverpool were already defying themselves with emotional points gained and rescued.

The match against Southampton three days later would be more poignant because of the attendees. Jeremy Corbyn and John McDonnell came to Anfield, welcomed by Dan Carden, and gave donations to FSF's food collection before laying a wreath at the Hillsborough flame. McDonnell had a Guinness upstairs in the Solly pub with the Spirit of Shankly lads and said of modern football: 'There are class issues at play here; it's not just about making profits, it's a sport for everyone.'

Liverpool FC was a club born out of controversy that had secured its position as a community asset over the course of a century. The two leftist politicians were warmly welcomed by fans. Ian Byrne said: 'This club has to be steeped in politics. I'm all for advocating more politicised symbols on the Kop,' and Dan Carden concurred: 'You can't sanitise football and politics, it goes against this city's working-class heritage.'

Daniel Sturridge scored a spectacular equaliser late on against Chelsea in Liverpool's next match, causing a fan (Mick) to tumble onto the pitch and join in the celebrations, embraced by van Dijk in the process. Prior to that game on the 29th September, Callum Smith from Bootle became the WBA super middleweight World Champion. Peter Carney made a banner for him and the rest of the Smith brothers that was taken down on his bus. There was also a banner that read 'Justice for Greenfall'. It was clapped by the Chelsea fans, before ignorance returned and they (most) chanted about poverty to travelling Reds.

Since 2003, the Kensington club had been gentrified to such an extent that, for many in attendance, the gesture probably meant little. But the people affected by the disaster appreciated it, which'd present itself as the perfect olive branch for the future. Greenfall was an avoidable disaster, enabled by a lack of care afforded to working-class people. Liverpudlians empathised.

On the 3rd October Liverpool lost away to Napoli – a town of blind alleys, *Partenopei* and knives. There was no violence this time, not like there had been nine years earlier when Reds were stabbed, but the visit was still eerie. Back in 2010, when Neapolitans came to Anfield for the return leg, they were chased down Anfield Road and hid in turnstiles for safety.

There had been an inventive banner in the Kop that night. It was Elmo the Grouch in a bin saying 'Ciao Napoli' – a dig proposed by Inter Milan fans, allies of the Spion Kop. This time, the only real pain Reds felt in Naples was the disappointment of having lost the game, making it more difficult for Liverpool to progress from the group.

The biggest game so far came on 7th October 2018 against Manchester City. A banner was sneaked into the ground: a Kopparberg bottle with the words 'Stop Crying Your Heart Out' written on the top and bottom. The reference was there for those who knew to enjoy. Late in the game, City's winger Mahrez skied a penalty to keep the title race exciting. It finished 0-0.

Local

*

Liverpool's civic identity remained a complex subject. It appeared all the more confusing for any outsiders on the coach to Huddersfield on the 20th October. Accompanying the Reds that day was a group of lads from Glasgow Celtic. The Green Brigade had welcomed Liverpudlians down a few months earlier to look at their safe standing section and they travelled to Yorkshire to reaffirm the link. The friendship had been longstanding.

Back in 1994 Celtic raised money for the Hillsborough families. Since then there had been a constant flow of Celtic supporters visiting Anfield and Kopites travelling to Parkhead.

Andy MacKenzie is part of that contingent, who is taken by the shared politics, the Clyde and lust for Europe, as well as the antipathy to the establishment that defines both city and club. 'There is a feeling of enjoying life and not taking it too seriously. There is no pretence to either city because of the underlying working-class attitude,' he says.

The Liverpool – Celtic link had been enhanced by Shankly's friendship with Jock Stein, and by Kenny Dalglish too who was a legend at both clubs, but Nicky Allt thinks it's more geographical: 'Both have got strong working-class ethics. They're hard-edged cities on the river the people don't suffer fools.'

On the way to Huddersfield, despite the friendship, one Red put £2 in a Paddock pub jukebox and requested both 'Penny Arcade' and 'Simply the Best' – Rangers songs – to wind up the Glaswegians.

Joe McDonald of Dovecot (a member of the magnificent seven) plays it all down by saying: 'Some of the lads go and see Celtic but I keep away from all of that,' Liverpool is his team and nobody else. Chris Hudson concurs: 'I'd pick Celtic over Rangers but Liverpool is the one, I don't support anybody else.' The clubs - Liverpool and Celtic - are mates, but they aren't married.

Next, at home, Liverpool beat Red Star Belgrade 4-0 on the 24th October. Their fans had been banned from attending matches because of racist chanting, which made it the biggest official attendance of just Liverpool supporters at Anfield in years. Unofficially, however, there were hundreds of Serbians in the Anfield Road end with Liverpool tickets, secretly supporting their team.

There had been something refreshing about Anfield being an echo chamber. Cardiff City came to town next and brought the whole repertoire with them – including classics *'Always the victim'*, *'Sign on'*, *'Demba Ba'* and the favourite: *'Your support is fucking shit'*. Evidently they'd forgotten the backing their mining community had been given in the 1980s by Scousers who'd raised funds for them to eat. Nevertheless, Liverpool won 4-0.

In many senses it was a typical season. The Reds drew with Arsenal away early in November, then lost to Red Star Belgrade after spending what felt like 25-minutes walking down their tunnel before the game. They got back to winning ways against Fulham on the 11th November and then beat Watford on the 24th. But Paris Saint-Germain was to be another loss, against the most expensive assembled side in football history.

Back in 1978, PSG fans created the 'Kop of Boulogne' in tribute to the mythical Anfield legend. They were in awe of Kopites in 1981, too, when Liverpool used their home ground and city as a canvass to win another European Cup on. When the sides first met in 1997, *Virage Auteuil* presented a banner that read: 'Welcome to the Legendary Fans'.

Parisians must have thought the tribute was returned in late November 2018 when, in Liverpool's section, there were more fans in PSG caps than there was in the rest of the ground. It wasn't a unique gesture though: hats were a part of Liverpool fan culture, collected to pinpoint where in Europe they'd been.

On the Eurostar over, an older lady in a 'Five Times' t-shirt had walked up and down giving out mince pies to recognisable fans. The Firmino chant made another appearance outside Boss (it was first heard in Belgrade), but was sang with too many words and with too few pauses that it became indiscernible. Paul McCartney – who was playing to 35,000 people across town – would not have approved.

The conflict on the pitch was between the theatrics of Neymar who rolled around a lot and posed to the crowd, and Andy Robertson who, with his Caledonian values, seemed like a Shankly signing. Was he born to play for Liverpool? Afterwards PSG celebrated their victory as if they had won the cup. But the real story of the fixture came much later when a coach full of Liverpool fans discovered they had been harbouring two asylum seekers underneath the engine for 12 hours.

The 'Football Travel Limited' group of supporters first heard a rumbling when they crossed the border into England. Then, out popped two men. At a time of Brexit-inspired national xenophobia, the stowaways were given drinks, food, hugs, money and clothes by the Scouse contingent. 'It's about the way Scousers are so welcoming,' the coach owner told the Echo.

The fans and the two men got a group photograph together. It provided an unmistakably 'Liverpool' image: 'You can easily identify a Scouser,' says Kevin Sampson. 'That now-famous photograph of the lads coming back from Paris, they are clearly not from Leicester or Edinburgh: they're Scouse. It's visible and easily identifiable to us, the *je ne sais quoi* which marks them out. It was there in the late-70s and I can still recognise it now from 100 paces away.' Fashion had evolved again but still had a local flavour.

*

At Dover, the lads were either wearing adidas flip-flops or 110s, dark jeans or outdoor shorts, simple t-shirts, football caps and bubble jackets. It was a look that had grown through necessity, through comfort and economic dictation. Because there were no youth clubs or extra-curriculum activities in the early-2000s, a lot of youngsters took to wandering the streets in outdoor clothing, whatever the weather.

Their attire was functional and took on a street corner vibe, somewhat American, as if it was out of Baltimore or Detroit. But it was mixed together by geography, with the accessibility to climbing/walking routes so close to Liverpool: 'The last five years all the Scallies started going up Snowdon,' says Joe McDonald. 'It's all outdoor gear now. You've got the lads on the street, the lads at the match and the lads on the mountains, all in outdoor gear.'

'Berghaus was big in the '90s as well as other outdoor jackets like Helly Hansen,' remembers Andrew Hudson. 'Then it got taken over by Scals who were wearing North Face tracky bottoms and Rab. It's all about the mountaineering look.'

Hoodies came and went in the mid-2000s, like the Nike Athletic West and GAP designs, simply because they weren't waterproof and didn't serve a streetwear purpose, and were replaced, eventually, by black bubble coats that had been clocked for the first time when Fiorentina came to Anfield in 2009.

When people elsewhere started wearing The North Face for fashion, locals moved on to Mountain Equipment, Patagonia and Columbia. In the summer, the look became sunglasses on a cord, a jacket around the waist (just in case), a simple t-shirt or Under Armour and khaki shorts. 'Liverpool is a mad place,' reflects Brendan Wyatt. 'It's the only city where you'd see a kid wearing Jacob Cohen jeans and Valenciaga shoes standing at the bus stop going to his mums. You see everything on a large scale here. It's like everything else, once the rest of the country start to adopt them styles then Scousers stop.'

Tapping into that, Wyatt had opened his resurrected Transalpino shop on Bolt Street in 2015. He sees the value of fashion in Liverpool as an identity trait. 'If you're in, say, Winchester in the summer and a feller comes walking down the street you can instantly recognise him if he's a Scouser, just by how he's dressed, and you'll let on to each other. Can you say that about any other city? You can spot a Scouser anywhere in the world. We're quite unique, we've been oppressed by the government and it's a fight back. Rivals call us 'bin dippers' but we're better dressed than anyone else. That goes back to the seamen going over to New York.'

At matches in 2018/19, locals were able to walk around Anfield and distinguish instantly who was from the city and who was not. On derby day, however, with neither group wearing club colours, it was almost impossible to tell who was a local Red or Blue.

December was supposed to be the month when Liverpool's campaign ended. They were set to play 8 games in 4 weeks, starting with Everton. Like most derbies, it had its superficial displays. The day before, a charity 5k Santa Dash in town saw Evertonians wearing blue Father Christmas suits to run in, displaying their intolerance to all things red. Surface level tensions were stoked up later that evening when the Liver buildings were lit up in blue neon lights because, well, Moshiri owned them and could.

This was meant to be Everton's best team in a decade, with former Barcelona players and Brazil internationals in their ranks. But the game hadn't materialised into anything like fans expected. With 90 minutes played, it was in danger of being a handsomely-played bore draw.

In the 91st minute coins were thrown at Joe Gomez after Richarlison tried to headbutt him. Evertonians in the Anfield Road sensed a famous point was coming and threw a blue flare onto the pitch in the 95th minute in celebration. But as they rejoiced, waiting for the whistle to blow, van Dijk sliced a shot up high which Jordan Pickford fumbled onto Divock Origi's head. The Belgium nodded it into the net and Anfield went berserk. Klopp ran on the pitch punching out at invisible men. Liverpool won 1-0. There were scenes of delirium. In the Halfway House afterwards fans sang *'He's only got little arms'* – in reference to Jordan Pickford - all night long.

They, with so little in common, in a continuous battle for moral superiority, had together donated some 2.2 tonnes of perishables that evening for Fans Supporting Foodbanks – a record. Cut through the chants and tension, Liverpool and Everton fans had come together again to support the city.

Local

Away to Burnley on a cold wet night which would prove to be the end of Joe Gomez's season, Liverpool won 3-1. It had been, overall, the best start to a campaign in Liverpool's history, but they were still only 2nd in the league. Three days later they beat Bournemouth 4-0 and then defeated Napoli 1-0 on an evening that was supposed to end their season.

Napoli required just one point to go through. Their pintsized attacker Dries Mertens said to the Times beforehand that he'd been underwhelmed by Anfield's atmosphere when he visited in 2010 with FC Utrecht. "I looked at the sign and thought, 'is this so special?'" he said. Napoli supporters had gathered in Williamson Square that afternoon to drink in the Shakespeare. They shouted *'Fuck you Liverpool, fuck you Liverpool'* at old ladies shopping for fruit, and then went back Italy afterwards with their tails between their legs and only the Europa League to look forward to. Thanks in part to a last-gasp save by Alisson, Liverpool marched into the last-sixteen of the Champions League.

Jose Mourinho had been a villain at Chelsea for many Liverpool fans, but for Manchester United he was unworthy of any scorn – they were a tame enemy. On December 16th his passionless side were 6th in the league, 11 points away from Chelsea in 4th. Liverpool had to win to go top of the league.

United fans got into the festive spirit of goodwill to all men by singing *'Feed the Scousers, let them know it's Christmas time'* early on. The Reds responded by winning 3-1. Mourinho got the sack afterwards and George Sephton played a Paul McCartney hit as grinning Kopites rubbed their gloves together and headed into the warmth of Anfield's ale houses. *'Simply, having, a wonderful Christmas time'.*

If December was supposed to be a difficult month, it was proving to be anything but. Liverpool had won 5 matches already when they headed down to Wolverhampton for a Friday night fixture on the 21st. On the coach, Kopites handed out Christmas crackers, hats and mince pies. All of the old songs returned for their favourite time of year: *'Come and behold them, they're the kings of Europe'* ... *'Oh what fun it is to ride when Liverpool win away, hey!'* ... *'Everyone wants to know, Alonso Alonso Alonso.'* Trent Alexander-Arnold stood in the Liverpool end amongst the fans and was mobbed, hugged and kissed. The Reds won 2-0 and sang the Pogues for Virgil van Dijk, who scored in the 68th minute.

It was all shaping up well. A 4-0 win against Newcastle on the 26th kept Liverpool top, followed by a 5-1 spanking of Arsenal who took the lead early on. Klopp had done his usual and stood watching Arsenal warm-up before the game, shaking hands with his opposite numbers and patting rival players on the back. Was he the most popular manager in football?

Daniel Fieldsend

He had faith in his ritual and his players showed their 'champion' mentality, overcoming a good Arsenal side with ease. Robbie Fowler's silhouette banner had waved from the Kop before the game, which somehow channelled 'God' into Roberto Firmino: the Brazilian scoring an impressive hattrick. There was a new way of thinking for Reds who quite stoically began shrinking the off-field value of every opponent down into just a number – 3 more points acquired, that's all Arsenal were.

*

On New Year's day, Henry Winter of the Times penned an article that expressed his opinion that, because of what Liverpool were doing off the pitch, with foodbanks and charitable causes, and because of the way in which FSG had invested in the squad patiently, then neutrals should be prompted to support them instead of Manchester City in the run in for the title.

He received a massive backlash for his stance, from Carlisle to Croydon. Liverpool, their players and fans were called for all kinds by an angry Twitter mob. If supporters in general were typified by their clouded views, then Liverpool were in the eye of a storm.

They lost 2-1 to Manchester City in the next game – their first loss in the league – with the result being celebrated by, what seemed like, every neutral in the country (although such things are immeasurable and probably feel the same for every fan of every club). What was true, however, was how pleased Manchester United fans were to see Manchester City, their historic rivals, win against Liverpool – having decided that they were the lesser of both evils.

'Space' sang 'It's me and you against the world now' in 1996 and that's how it began to feel for Liverpool fans. The club lost again on the 7th January in the FA Cup to Wolverhampton Wanderers. Klopp fielded a team of youngsters (a 16, 17 and 18-year old started) which signalled his intention to reduce fixtures. He was putting all of Liverpool's eggs into the two most difficult baskets imaginable: the league and the Champions League. All Reds could do was hold faith in his ability.

Before he joined the club, Liverpool, as a squad, had never been very good at the dark arts of the game. If they tried to waste time, the other team would score. If they had a skilful rival, they'd treat him with sporting respect. Brighton on the 12th showed ways in which this Liverpool team was getting streetwise (Trent Alexander-Arnold would admit at the end of the season that they'd learnt from Real Madrid and Sergio Ramos in Kiev). Late in the game against Brighton there was a carnival of cute incidents. Gini Wijnaldum pointed out where Lewis Dunk had handled the ball, as if to antagonise him. Milner came on to waste time, and when Salah heard that he was about to be substituted, he jogged over to the other side of the pitch to kill more seconds. It was a welcome addition to Liverpool's game and the Reds won 1-0.

On the 19th they beat Palace 4-3, another game they'd have lost in the past. When news rang around Old Trafford earlier in the afternoon that Liverpool were losing, the Mancs cheered, because they had little else to cheer about in 2019.

Trent Alexander-Arnold signed a new deal that day and said 'I hope we can achieve a lot of success in the upcoming years.' Little did he realise... But Liverpool as a fanbase were starting to struggle with the pressures of competing for the league, even if the players were not.

Against Leicester at home the crowd were on edge, blanketing Anfield in nerves. Virgil van Dijk addressed supporters after the draw: 'Everyone wants to win so bad and that's what we want as well, but sometimes you need to be patient.' Another draw away to West Ham plunged Liverpudlians into further despair until a message from the Spion Kop 1906 members got Whatsapp'ed out midweek:

"Everyone going on Saturday, no matter what stand you're in, get in as early as possible. It needs to be loud for when the players come out to warm up. Get the momentum going again and get behind them: flags, rattles, scarves and voices. We've got a title to win."

There needed to be some realisation. Liverpool were top of the league and were competing in Europe. That Saturday they swept Bournemouth aside, winning 3-0. Alisson clapped his new banner, Mane sprinted 20 yards to stop Liverpool conceding a throw-in (showing McMahon-esque determination), and Firmino's chant was sang at a good pace for half-an-hour.

Afterwards, Jurgen Klopp referenced Liverpool's 'Unity Is Strength' banner taken to Labour party meetings and to home games. 'I can think of no better line at this time,' he said. Kenny Dalglish then came forward to build on van Dijk's plea: 'We've never won a trophy in my time here without the help of the fans. When it gets towards the finishing line that's when you need them most of all. If we can all stick together collectively that will give us a chance.' From this point on, it was total unity again – everybody enjoying the experience together, willing the team on.

That night at Hinterlands there was a Boss Night for Sean Cox. Fans raised £1500 out of their own pockets and Jamie Carragher donated an incredible

£11,000 in support. It all reinforced the idea that being a Liverpool supporter was more than simply partaking in the events on the pitch: it was about backing the team at all costs and supporting the community of fans worldwide, whenever they were in need.

It came out later that month that Liverpool had achieved the highest net profit for a football club in one season in history, some £95.7m. Only seven years earlier the club had struggled to find an additional £1m to buy a teenage Danny Wilson from Rangers. Now they had more money than ever before. But fans would only allow the club make such profits if they were being pulled along. FSG realised this and backed the 'More Than a Stadium' campaign, stating: "The club has committed to working in the local area to help improve street cleanliness and reduce anti-social behaviour and is working with Liverpool City Council to assist with parking enforcement and other prominent issues." It didn't take much, but it was the type of recognition than had never been afforded to local councillors in the past.

*

Keen to further the image of being entwined to the fanbase, the club got Alisson Becker to play his guitar down at District with Jamie Webster. The electrician from Croxteth played 'We love you Liverpool' while the Brazilian smiled and tapped along: *'Alisson's our goalie the best there is around, and Robbo is the greatest that Jurgen ever found. Virgil is our hero, a master of the game. And here's the mighty Salah, to do it once again!'* - Alisson was taught 'allez allez allez' for the first time but was a little bit rusty with the lyrics. By the end of the season he'd be on an open-top bus conducting thousands of fans word for word.

The Becker/Webster duet came before Bayern Munich at home on the 19th February. Pre-match, Klopp called Liverpool 'the most emotional club' in Europe, and he was right. As if to prove that fact, the famous 20-foot *'Joey Ate the Frogs Legs'* banner made by Phil Downey, his mum and his mate Jimmy Cummings forty years earlier was on the Kop for the first time in a long time.

4,000 Bayern fans, having been patrolled into Anfield by police, unfurled a message for UEFA: *'GR$$D KNOWS NO LIMITS £20 IS PL$NTY'*. All sides of the stadium applauded it. There was never any danger of violence, just mutual respect between two clubs who'd both won five European Cups. The match ended 0-0.

After Mourinho's sacking, Manchester United hired a manager who had, by all accounts, been a member of a Liverpool supporters' group in Norway until

1994. Ole Gunnar Solskjær instantly rejuvenated them and they'd not lost in six games. Their former defender, Nemanja Vidic, stated before the game that he wouldn't have any of Liverpool's defenders over Manchester United's, not even the flawless Virgil van Dijk. Inside the ground, Mancs shouted 'bin dippers' at Liverpool fans; Scousers shouted 'bin sniffers' back at them and, for all the build-up, that was that, a boring draw.

Liverpool went back top of the league but wanted more. They let their frustrations out on Watford on the 27th February, beating them 5-0. This was the sole emotionless fixture between two heated games. Everton, next, wanted more than anything to be the team to beat Liverpool and end their title challenge. Their fans campaigned on Twitter all week to turn Goodison Park into 'Besitkas' for Liverpool. Social media had always possessed an ability to be a vehicle for negativity, even at the best of times, and this was no truer than during derby week. Fans of both clubs woke up on the day of the game to find that Tony Bellew, the champion boxer and Evertonian, had been arguing all night with a fake Titi Camara account.

The conflicted tribalism of the derby was on display before the game as a collection of Blues poured out of the Albany singing *'And we'll hang the Kopites one by one,'* before they spotted a couple of Liverpool fans in scarves and chanted *'Murderers, murderers'* at them, blurring their moral stance somewhat. But there was a lot to admire about Everton that day. It was angry, it was working-class, it was hard and Scouse. It was a demographic largely outpriced and excluded from Anfield (for Reds) but still welcome over Stanley Park, where they could create a hostile Goodison - another stadium, like Anfield, that appeared out terraced houses in an era of metal, middle-of-nowhere stadia.

Everton had their moment when they sang Blue Moon and Liverpool fans had theirs when *'England's Number 1'* came on a big screen for Jordan Pickford, but everything was forgotten when both sets of fans applauded in the 17th minute for Sonny Chambers, a local lad who'd passed away on Valentine's Day.

It was back to winning ways against Burnley on the 10th, before the Reds flew out to Munich for their next Champions League tie. Bayern had won their past 8 matches to go clear at the top of the Bundesliga table, but that didn't really matter to Scousers who were unusually confident. The German club retained a certain purity – a beautiful city that saw itself as Bavarian first; a club hated within its own nation but admired on the continent, with fans who preferred to make mates and who demanded good football.

Daniel Fieldsend

There were many parallels with Liverpool, except at that present moment LFC were better than them. Nobody had been thinking about the Champions League too much before this point, hoping more that Liverpool would win the league and end their 30-year wait. But when Sadio Mane turned Manuel Neuer and scored the goal of the season thus far, securing qualification to the next round, fans started dreaming.

'We can beat anyone' became the rhetoric, something the players had known all along. Inside the Hofbräuhaus' in the centre of Munich, Reds did their own thing, went where they wanted and enjoyed the occasion in their own way – a contrast to typical European aways where they'd been herded together and monitored.

The ale was clean on Marienplatz and the songs were traditional – *'My Liverpool, the Kop will always rule'*. After the match, Sami Hyypia was mobbed outside the ground like Trent had been a month earlier.

Bayern had for so long been a barometer of elitism, but now it was clear that Andy Robertson was a better left-back than David Alaba, and Roberto Firmino was better than Lewandowski, and so on. Liverpool was becoming a 'Super-club' through patient architecture. Focus turned to the draw. *Who do we want?* Ajax, Porto, Barcelona, Tottenham, Manchester City, Manchester United or Juventus?

On an overcast Merseyside day, fans found out it was going to be Porto again, which'd do for them. It signalled clear passage to the next round. On the coach to Fulham, fans sorted out numbers for who'd be going over to Portugal: a familiar second home. It was March 17th - Paddy's Day - and the Dubliners songs being played as the coach arrived in London couldn't have been more out of place against the millionaire cherry blossomed streets of Hammersmith, where children and their mothers in rosettes sold cookies for local causes and practiced their manners. Ryan Babel equalised for Fulham at the banks of the Thames that afternoon before James Milner scored the winner in another emotional win.

Anfield seemed to be having 'game of the season' after 'game of the season' by this point. There had been a collection of tremendous atmospheres already, more than in recent years, and there'd be more to come. It was Tottenham's turn to hear an inspired Anfield on the 31st March, albeit through fortunate circumstances. Liverpool needed to win every game and were drawing in the 90th minute, watching the seconds tick away as all hope of a league title faded. Then. A cross came in from the left and Salah nodded it down onto Toby Alderweireld, who poked it past his own goalkeeper. Somehow, thanks to an own goal, the 'devil's club' had won again with seconds remaining.

Local

Reds began checking other teams' fixtures, weighing up the balance of aspirations between each club. *Barcelona have shipped in 4 past Villareal...we'll play them if we beat Porto... and if they beat Manchester United... and if United lose to Wolves they'll need to get something against City ...*

The old heads of the city rubbished such thinking: 'Just focus on us winning,' they said. But the flutters of excitement were tough to vanquish. On the 5th April (Ladies Day), Liverpool supporters setting off to Southampton from Dale Street at 11am joked that Reds had title races while the Blues had Aintree Races. That wasn't strictly true however, because Reds had both.

Jordan Henderson, who had for so long that season been asked to play in a holding role, was let off the leash at St Mary's and inspired the Reds to victory, snapping into tackles and barking at his teammates. For most of the season, Henderson had played a supporting act as van Dijk and the rest of the team took the plaudits. He was happy to do so, telling Klopp that he'd play wherever the team needed him. But with Fabinho's gradual adaption to Premier League football, Henderson was allowed to play further forward once more. It would be a turning point for him in his battle to secure the affections of Liverpudlians.

At home against Porto, Henderson had his name sung by the Kop for the first time since the title run-in of 2014. In a reflection of how far Liverpool had come, the quarter-final felt like a trivial game for them as they won 2-0 with ease. To further reflect upon the development of the club and their captain, just five years earlier Henderson had been subbed off before the hour as Liverpool were knocked out of the Europa League last-32 by Zenit St Petersburg without much fuss. Now, fans were praising him as Liverpool reached the semi-finals of the biggest competition in football.

A video emerged two days before their next match against Chelsea of a number of their supporters in Prague singing about Salah being a 'bomber'. It was an Islamophobic hate crime and Liverpool FC called it out for what it was, issuing a statement before anybody else: "This behaviour is unadulterated bigotry. There is no place for it in football, there is no place for it in society." Chelsea had throughout the course of the season been hosts to numerous racist incidents and were still smouldering from the abuse Raheem Sterling had received a few months earlier. It was the latest example of London-based bigotry overall, after Salah had been racially abused at West Ham, and Everton fans had been taunted with chants at Millwall.

The Egyptian responded in the best possible way, scoring from 32 yards with his left foot against Kepa, the most expensive goalkeeper in the world. For their part, the travelling Chelsea fans on the day had been respectful throughout the recognition for Hillsborough. 30 long years had passed without any accountability. Liverpool won 2-0 and afterwards Graeme Souness commented that it was the loudest he'd ever heard Anfield, even during his time as a player. Indeed, things were reaching ear-piercing levels of excitement.

Recognition for Mo Salah's geniality and impact for Muslims across the world came on the 17th April when TIME magazine named him as one of the 100 most influential people on earth. He was named alongside Mark Zuckerberg, Michelle Obama and Imran Khan, and he used the platform to campaign for Middle Eastern men to respect women better. John Oliver told TIME: "Mo Salah is a better human being than he is a football player, and he's one of the best football players in the world."

That day, Salah scored away in Portugal as Liverpool overcame Porto 4-1. The only real point of interest from a sociological standing was the introduction of Dom and Liam, filmed in a video that became viral, singing the updated 'Rotterdam or anywhere' chant for the campaign. To look at, they were Scouse in attire and attitude, but they had Manc accents and were born and bred in Manchester, adding weight to the opinion that 'Scouse' is as much a mentality as anything else. When the result of Tottenham vs Manchester City was announced over the tannoy at full-time, Dom and Liam were as loud as anyone in chanting *'Oh Manchester is full of shit'* - one can only imagine the abuse they'd received during their upbringing. Yet they remained loyal to the Reds, because their dads were Scouse and it was a part of their identity. Dom and Liam, on that matter, had travelled to more European aways in their time than a great number of Scouse lads had cared to.

If they 'got it' and what localism meant to Scousers, then the Cardiff fans who sang about England's disappointing World Cup campaign to them fans on the 21st certainly did not. Kopites laughed and joined in, before singing their own songs. It was a baking hot day and a fine occasion. That afternoon Everton hosted Manchester United at Goodison Park. Liverpool fans had left a reminder on the M57 for the incoming Mancs, tying a banner over a motorway bridge - draped over 'The Pies' - that read: 'Liverpool FC: Cream of Europe'. The Reds had an impending semi-final against Barcelona to look forward to, while United had a battle for 5th place to contend.

It was Easter Sunday, the Cardiff game, and everybody was in shorts as Liverpool won 2-0. After the match, with either a double league and cup victory or absolutely nothing to play for, Jurgen Klopp told reporters (but was speaking to the masses): 'If you are only motivated by winning the holy grail then something is wrong with you. We are motivated because we play for this club, because we want to win football games, because we enjoy the ride together with our fans, that's the truth.' In that spirit, Liverpool hammered Huddersfield in their next game 5-0.

By this point Manchester City had all but secured the league, winning their game-in-hand against rivals (or friends, it was hard to tell nowadays) Manchester United, going 1-point top of the table. Even for the most hopeful of Liverpool fans, it was clear they were not going to win it. Pep Guardiola and his unfortunate grey hooded jumper had inspired City to win 15 matches on the bounce. Reds were dejected, but they still had Barcelona to play in the semi-finals, Pep's Catalan hometown.

Any optimism before the game was quickly gone: Barcelona won on the 1st of May 3-0. Messi rolled around and smiled at cameras, Luis Suarez ruined whatever affection fans retained for him with his theatrics, and the public afforded a video of a man being pushed into a fountain – as unacceptable as it was – the same disdain they'd afford a double homicide.

With 'European away' etiquette diluted and in jeopardy, and with codes of practice under scrutiny, it looked as if the season was over. The league was gone and there was no way Liverpool could overturn the result. *'Next season we'll improve,'* said some fans. But the lyrics to the club's hymn had always been either the truth or clichéd depending on the time of year. Now it was the summer with trophies still to play for, so most kept hope in their hearts and continued to support and believe, because they saw no other alternative.

On the Friday night before their game against Burnley, stalls outside Goodison Park sold scarves with Lionel Messi's name on. Inside, hanging over the side of an advertisement board in the Lower Bullens, a fan had draped a Barcelona flag, framing his or her contemporary view of fandom and what it meant to be an Evertonian. In recent years, according to several Reds, the greatest joy many Blues had felt had been whenever Liverpool came close to winning a trophy and then lost. As Rookwood points out, that's part of tribalism (Liverpool fans had backed Bayern Munich in 1999), but it stung the nuanced on either side.

It mattered not however (or was not admitted to) that the Reds were more than 40 points ahead of Everton by this point. They were 26 points ahead of Manchester United and some 21 points ahead of Tottenham in 3rd. But crucially, with only a number of games left, Manchester City had 92 points and Liverpool had 91. In a hard-fought game against Newcastle in which Salah and Chamberlain picked up knocks (and with Firmino already injured), Liverpool somehow won 3-2, courtesy of a late goal from Divock Origi, taking the league campaign right down to the final day.

The young Belgian had been considered for years by many in football to be too conscientious to ever be a truly prolific finisher. He'd been third choice behind Daniel Sturridge for over a year and was loaned out to Wolfsburg in 2017 to regain some confidence. But Klopp had always admired Origi and had tried to sign him for Dortmund in his final year there. In 2015, not long after having joined Liverpool, Klopp smiled and told reporters: 'We're going to have fun with Origi.'

On the 7th May, he was proved correct. Vincent Kompany, in one of his last ever games, scored late on to secure the league for Manchester City against Leicester. With Liverpool 3-0 down in the first leg of the Champions League against the greatest football team in modern history, they were dubbed 'beautiful failures' by the press. Then, at the lowest possible point, the rumours began.

Back in 2014 when the Reds had last competed for the league title, there had been whispers of Liverpool fans congregating outside Manchester City's residence at Formby Hall, causing disruptions and keeping them awake. It wasn't true, but it planted a seed.

On the Monday evening before the Barça game, around 7pm, rumours began to spread again on social media, that the Barcelona team bus had been stolen by a group of Scallys outside the Hilton Liverpool One and was being driven down Long Lane. People gossiped that its windows had been bricked outside the Leg Iron pub and that it was later on its side behind the Showcase Cinema. The reports, again, were little more than fibs.

The following morning people whispered once more that, at 2am, somebody had sneaked quietly beneath the windows of the Hilton Hotel and, with everybody sleeping, set off fireworks to wake up the Barcelona team, disrupting their preparations for that evenings' match. This time, the rumour was true. It probably had little impact on the result and was certainly nowhere near as influential as Liverpool's meticulous analytic preparation for the game, which sought to find weaknesses in Barça's reactions to set-pieces, but the fireworks ignited an excitement for fans and provided a nugget of belief going into Anfield.

Nobody before the match had given Liverpool a chance. Jurgen Klopp gathered his squad together and asked them whether they wanted to talk about Manchester City's win over Leicester, whether anybody had anything to say? Not really, they responded, they just wanted to win their remaining matches. So they focussed on Barça. Before he spoke about the finer points of Liverpool's preparation, Klopp told the players that whatever people believed, that the season was finished and they wouldn't progress, it was nonsense: 'Because it's you,' he said, 'it might be possible. You are all giants.'

Klopp reinforced that sense of belief to the optimistic fans before the game in his programme notes, writing: "There is one thing everyone inside Anfield knows, including our opponents. This Liverpool never stops. This Liverpool never quits. This Liverpool gives everything at all times. Whatever happens this Liverpool leaves it all on the pitch. We don't do 'If only'."

Having lost to Roma in incredible circumstances the season before, Lionel Messi, in his first season as captain – a role he was born to occupy – had taken a microphone and told the *socios* in Camp Nou at the start of the season that Barcelona would do everything in their power to bring the European Cup back home. He was the greatest footballer to ever play the game in the eyes of many, but in the first half at Anfield he was anonymous, and his promise to the *socios'* looked unlikely.

Andy Robertson – a lad whose origins could not have been humbler – had dominated Messi and at had one point clipped him on the back of the head when nobody was looking. There had been a personal feud between the two of them ever since the Nou Camp tie. In that first leg, Jordan Henderson ran some 30 yards to intervene when the Scotsman and the Argentine were arguing before a corner. Liverpool had rattled Barcelona then, despite losing the game, with Messi calling Milner a 'donkey', and with Mane putting his hands on Vidal's face, prompting Suarez to shout in Robertson direction after Messi's first goal.

In that first half, Robertson and Lionel Messi, and Robertson and Suarez, were two different stories altogether. The Glaswegian called Suarez a fat so-and-so off camera and the three players pulled and kicked each other whenever possible. The Catalans weren't used to teams getting at them, in both respects of the term, and their inability to lose matches with grace became evident early on at Anfield when Divock Origi tapped in Henderson's shot.

The stadium had been sizzling beforehand but now it caught fire. Every newspaper in the world was about to cover the happenings, with reporters in disbelief: Origi scored first – Wijnaldum hit one in after coming off the bench – Wijnaldum again with a header – Trent's corner – Origi again – had it been given? – *yes!*

Daniel Fieldsend

When the Belgian scored in the box with nobody marking him, Kopites fell everywhere, running forwards in a state of ecstasy. Had Anfield ever heard such noise? There had been Internazionale in '65, Saint Etienne in '77, Chelsea in '05 and now this. Some fortunate souls had felt all three; some had experienced one or two. A lot of them, though, when the final whistle blew, credited this as the mountaintop of emotion. It had been a night on par with the very best.

At the sound of the whistle people lost all restraint. A ball boy – an academy prospect – ran onto the pitch and gave Messi the middle finger, chased awkwardly by two confused stewards. In those scenes of uncontrolled elation, with headlocks and limbs and backs twatted on rows of chairs – few people noticed him, but he was a portrait of the exuberance that probably allowed for such occasions to happen, an example of fans who bought into the mythology of Anfield, who kept the wheel turning.

There had been a symbolic moment just after the whistle when Luis Suarez – the old hero with a dubious nature – walked off the pitch, passing Mohamed Salah – the new hero – on the way, who beamed positivity wearing a t-shirt with the words 'Never Give Up' printed on. Its symbolism reflected the direction Liverpool were heading in as a club, or rather had already reached.

But the hero on the night was, again, Divock Origi. He'd scored the decisive goal that would forever be shown again and again.

If, at the end of it all, a career is not actually judged on numbers, like games played and goals scored, but is rather judged on the amount of 'moments' fans were able to enjoy, then the quiet young Belgian was already on his way to having a fabled career.

George Sephton in the corner of the Upper Centenary seldom received the credit he deserved for the job he did. Less pop, more local artists played. But at full-time he was applauded for playing the city's greatest ever musical talent, with his greatest song, at the most fitting of times. Just like the old days, Kopites sang along, swaying arm in arm: *'You may say I'm a dreamer, but I'm not the only one'.* Liverpool were in another European Cup final, imagine that?

In an evening of fine journalism, Rory Smith of the New York Times penned the best piece, writing:

> *"Liverpool's players stood in front of the Kop, those who had played and those who had watched, their heads shaking in disbelief, their arms draped over one another's shoulders, as if they needed to hold on to something, anything, to make sure it was real. In front of them, all around them, flags*

Local

fluttered and scarves waved and spines tingled as Anfield sang its hymnal. The stands were still full. Barely a soul had moved. Nobody wanted to break the spell, to head out into the night. Nobody wanted the feeling to end."

In the studio, Gary Lineker said to Robbie Fowler, 'you're quite emotional, aren't you?' To which the old, old hero replied 'I am. It means so much to everybody. And we did it. I'm so proud and so delighted to be a part of Liverpool.' Which perhaps was one of the most telling parts of Klopp's tenure. Everybody felt a greater connection to the club than they had in recent years, and those who were once on the periphery of it all were, in their minds, a part of New Liverpool.

The following afternoon Jeremy Corbyn stood up in PMQs and teased the Prime Minister Theresa May: 'Perhaps she could take some tips from Jurgen Klopp on how to get a good win in Europe?' he said. What was happening? Liverpool, the city of solidarity, had showed again that success was about teamwork and not individualism. Salah's 'Never Give Up' t-shirt had condensed the club's hymn into an equally fine message, which somehow explained the spirit that had, against all odds, gotten Liverpool to Madrid.

*

'Everybody keeps talking about Liverpool,' moaned Pep Guardiola. He'd bought in to the project at Manchester City when he agreed to become their manager three years earlier, believing the club could expand into a huge European name. But many at City became envious of the attention Liverpool were sustaining from the press – drawing from an affection that the club had secured over a fifty-year period. Despite his side having just won an historic domestic treble, Pep felt ignored.

People continued to talk and sing about Liverpool, including Guardiola's own players who chanted '*the Scousers won fuck all*' in a mock-up of Liverpool's '*allez allez allez*' song on a flight back to Manchester from London.

The lyrics referenced the injuring of a fellow professional, Mo Salah, as well as Liverpool fans having been 'battered in the streets'. Sean Cox's brother Martin told the Echo: "I feel like the players themselves have let their club down and the majority of their fans." City defended them, saying that the chant was about Liverpool fans being attacked in Kiev – as if that validated its use – and not Cox, at a final they themselves had failed to reach, having lost to Liverpool.

There was only one thing to do now for Liverpool, one way of silencing everybody who'd chipped away at the club throughout the year, who'd fuelled the republicanism of fan identity that had become synonymous with the club's supporters: Liverpool had to win the European Cup against Tottenham Hotspur in June.

Local

YOU'LL NEVER WALK ALONE

Gary, a homeless gentleman, who had been on the streets for two years, based himself halfway down Church Street and found an old Liverpool shirt from the '90s. Throughout May he wore it with pride. He got a piece of red fabric for his dog, too, and all of a sudden, the percentage of people who acknowledged him rose. Indeed, the most demoralising thing for homeless people is sitting by the publics' feet all day, being ignored as they spend their money. In May, Gary was no longer a nobody. He was a Red, always had been and always would be. And as a Red, he was on par with everybody else.

The whole city had been swept up again like it had eight times before. What would Liverpool be without Liverpool FC? Were it not for the industry of a handful of men, of Fagan and Moran and Evans et al, then what would the city look like now?

Peter Moore's lofty office stares out over the Three Graces and the Mersey. It is glassy and modern and is contrasted by its décor: specifically, a custom 'Joey Ate the Frogs Legs' banner that hangs in its corner. 20 Chapel Street was buzzing as workers prepared for Madrid; the chief executive's phone rang throughout.

Moore's career had taken him to the States, but he came back. Of the city he returned to he says: 'The raw ingredients of Liverpool were, and are, far superior than that of any other city. The river, the people, the Albert Dock, the Pier Head... This string of docks that Melville referred to; what an unbelievable city this is, it just needed polishing. When I was a lad the Liver building and St George's Hall were black. They sparkle now.'

Fenway Sports Group had been dazzled by Liverpool when they invested and they saw a bit of Boston in the Albert Dock, resurrected by Heseltine in the '80s. But not everybody in football recognised the city's 'raw ingredients' and in recent years a number of players, namely the American Clint Dempsey and the Icelandic midfielder Gylfi Sigurðsson, as well as Diego Costa from Spain and Willian from Brazil, had chosen to transfer to London clubs instead of Liverpool.

Jurgen Klopp wasn't fussed by that. He zoomed out, saw the bigger picture like FSG and had told players, essentially: 'If you don't want to sign for Liverpool, it's your loss'. This was a big club as far as he was concerned, and he continued to believe that with great stoicism, even when many fans forgot it.

A banner taken to Madrid summed up his era. It read: 'Jurgen Klopp – making us all skint since 2015'. Before he arrived, the club was in a limbo of irrelevance, but now thanks to his craft Liverpool was in another European final. The city reacted in its usual way (it'd had much recent practice). Posters covered windows, banners draped wherever possible and bunting joined houses together. The nans of the city, so blessed in the art of conversation, collected newspaper cuttings for their grandchildren and chatted to one other at bus stops. They'd mention Matalan, relatives and Mo Salah (*"isn't he lovely?"*).

Transit vans popped up in car parks as makeshift shops. T-shirts carried the words 'Never Give Up' – a message so poignant that a Speke boulevard resident mowed it onto the grass in 50-foot letters outside the airport, so the players and fans taking off could be reminded of it as they flew to Spain. By the weekend of the final, there was not one single Merseyside street without a piece of red fluttering outside one of its houses.

In the previous decade, Liverpool and Everton supporters had jostled for the ownership of locality, or at least the idea of it, and both had chants that began with: *'The city's all ours, fuck off to Norway / Kirkby'*. Each summer, Liverpool fans displayed their ownership credentials both visually and through song, taking over Liverpool's streets. Outside the Echo Arena (as it would forever be known) on the Monday before the final, thousands of supporters had congregated at the banks of a royal blue Mersey and sang the Roberto Firmino song. They'd been to Boss Night – an idea now watched all over the world but still not copied.

Evertonians going on holiday at the start of June to escape it all were greeted at Speke Airport by two massive banners: one reading 'YNWA' and one reading 'We'll Fight the Fight for Liverpool'. Travelling Reds dominated the roads to Madrid, barring the occasional Hackney cab full of Spurs fans. They ventured over by plane, train and boat. On the ferry from Dover to Calais, Kopites banged on their car roofs to a beat that echoed up and down: *'There's something that the Kop wants you to know...'*

Local

On Friday, Jurgen Klopp settled down to speak to the world's press, flanked by his two loyal icons: Alexander-Arnold and Robertson. The young Scouser in particular had grown to embody this new era, schooled in *Kloppian* football at the Academy. He was professional and articulate and dressed and acted like the modern Scouse male.

Speaking to Melissa Reddy of ESPN before the showcase final, he said: "There's a difference to Liverpool. People who aren't from [here] probably think we're over the top, but that's because we're really passionate about the things we love. We stand united on important issues and we fight for what we believe in with everything we've got." The youngest ever player to start in consecutive Champions League finals, Trent told the press that he'd give everything to bring the trophy back home.

Things were calm because people *knew* deep down that Liverpool were going to win this time. Klopp's desire for everybody to pull in the same direction was tangibly evident. Before the final, Jay McKenna reflected upon everything that had happened in recent years: 'Under Benitez everybody loved the team but hated the club ownership. Then in Hodgson's era everybody hated the team and hated the owners. We've been on a journey since then and I think people now like both Liverpool's owners and the team.' Tom Fairclough agreed with him: 'For the first time in my life it seems everyone is happy; nobody wants the owners to sell. When I took it seriously from '98, everyone wanted Moores and Parry out. Now it's as harmonious as it's ever been.'

Less than ten years earlier, Liverpool had been in the bottom three of the league, with Paul Konchesky's mother calling fans "Scouse scum" on Facebook. It now seemed like a distant memory. Joel Rookwood, on the final day of the 2019 season, brunching outside Neighbourhood in Woolton, said that if he saw John Henry walking down the street, he wouldn't shake his hand, he'd hug him: 'There were times when they've just done what they needed to do – we all remember the walk out – but the response gave me heart and I think that was one of the best things to have happened for the relationship between the club and us. It has opened a door for all of the positive, progressive and Scouse involvement that has been seen.'

And of Klopp, the man central to Liverpool's revival, Rookwood said with more sincerity: 'There are no superlatives in my vocabulary that could even begin to do justice to the impact of he has had on Liverpool, as a city and a club. I just don't have the diction.' That, speechlessness, from a university lecturer, perhaps said the most.

Daniel Fieldsend

The German was not Shankly; Shanks' lived in West Derby and welcomed visitors to his door, like having a Messiah within reach, whereas Klopp described that situation of walking through the city as being like a 'fire' that ignited when people saw him, such was the camera phone era, so he stayed in.

But for supporters, the man from the green village of Glatten had a bit of Shankly about him. They couldn't discern exactly what it was, but he'd whipped them into a frenzy like the Glenbuck native had done generations earlier, convincing them all that they were a part of the success of the club.

What's more, they believed him. *Marca*, the Spanish football daily, estimated that 70,000 Kopites had travelled over to Madrid for the final – a record number. They formed a never-ending river of red shirts from the main stage put on by the club all the way down *Felipe II*, outnumbering Tottenham fans in the city some 5 to 1.

For their worth, despite the media building it up to be an occasion of likely hooliganism, the Spurs fans were gracious and good natured and seemed just happy to be there. There was a mutual respect between the two sets of supporters, governed in their behaviour by the occasion itself.

As had been the case at every European final to date, in Madrid continental images were covered over by local interpretations. At *La Castellana*, beneath the world's largest Spanish flag, 'Plaza Margaret Thatcher' was redecorated with paper renaming it 'Jeremy Corbyn Square'. In 2014 when the Reds had last been in town it had been graffitied, but this was more tactful. There was a banner, too, held beneath its entrance that read: 'UEFA are as horrible as Boris Johnson' – a fitting comparison.

On *Calle Gran Via* the adidas shop, forever used as a billboard to display the images of Real's *Galactico* stars, like Beckham and Zidane, now had the faces of Roberto Firmino and Mohamed Salah plastered 15-feet high. Both were set to start that night's game.

With kick-off approaching, Tottenham fans inside the Wanda Metropolitano – right out at the very edge of Europe's highest capital – waved the plastic flags given to them by the club. Liverpool however had arranged for the Spion Kop 1906 to bring over a number of their famous wavers, including the 'Don't Buy the Sun' and 'Anne Williams: Iron Lady' ones for the whole world to see. Spurs had their St George's flags while Liverpool's end had homemade red banners draped over the sides. It looked so organic by comparison and showed the way things ought to be done (to inevitably be copied).

Locāl

The match itself was a dull affair, which mattered not afterwards. 22 seconds in with Kopites still singing YNWA, Sadio Mane – who'd watched Liverpool win the cup as a boy in 2005, in a remote Senegalese village – won Liverpool a penalty. Salah scored it and the Reds defended for 87 minutes before Origi – the moment man – scored the second.

At the final whistle it seemed as though the entire world started celebrating at once. Outside Carra's Bar in New York the streets filled with Reds and came to a complete standstill, forcing NYPD to tun up and watch the commotion. Neither the New York Red Bulls nor NYCFC would ever witness such fandom.

At Gladsaxe Stadium in Denmark, 5,000 people took to the pitch in celebration. In Indonesia there were fireworks and pyrotechnics as locals celebrated deliriously. Pubs in Montreal bounced, and in Ghana and Melbourne too – everybody in red shirts singing and dancing.

Mumbai and Dubai were the same, while videos came in from Saudi Arabia, Morocco, Algeria and Singapore. In Egypt, naturally, locals reacted as if they themselves had won the cup. Baghdad, Mauritius, Kuala Lumper... Had there ever been such collective scenes of global celebration in the history of the game?

In Lebanon outside *University Antoine* thousands of people gathered and lit more flares. In Thailand, on a road leading into Bangkok, there was a convoy of six vans decorated to resemble a homecoming parade, filled with fans who shouted '*We are Liverpool*' at nonplussed locals. And they were Liverpool, every single one of them.

Before carrying Klopp over and throwing him in the air, the players in Madrid stood together arm in arm, singing the clubs hymn. They were from dictatorships in Africa and from walled cities in the Netherlands. They were Belgian and Brazilian, Croatian and Cameroonian, and they all knew the song word for word, because Liverpool, so the press said afterwards, was the biggest and most mythical sporting institution in the whole world. Like Bill Shankly said once upon a time, 'if they didn't believe me before, they believe me now'.

LeBron James Tweeted 'YNWA' to 42.6m people as the club grew in stature in an instant, but more importantly Juventus sent their congratulations and Sean Cox watched from home with his family. His wife said: 'He was overjoyed when the final whistle blew and Liverpool were crowned champions.'

Within those scenes of global triumph and celebration was a kid from West Derby. 'I'm just a normal lad from Liverpool whose dreams just came true,' Trent Alexander-Arnold said on the pitch. In the studio, Jose Mourinho and Arsene

Wenger, two rivals of the past, smiled down at the scenes of jubilation. With fans singing YNWA beneath them, Mourinho declared 'This is more beautiful than anything we can say,' before Wenger – a cultured man – added: 'Liverpool is the city of music, of the working-class and of football. They always go together. Anybody who has managed in England knows that it is a special place and that's why they can always make miracles. Their strength is their solidarity and fighting spirit.'

The Reds were now 6 times champions of Europe, more than all of their domestic rivals combined: Manchester City, Manchester United, Chelsea, Everton and Arsenal.

At home, Concert Square overflowed with people from outside the city who climbed atop scaffolding and tables. The Radio City 96.7 tower turned off all of its letters from 100-feet up but kept just one number glowing, in red for all of Merseyside, West Lancashire and North Wales to see: '6'. Dan Carden began writing a motion for Parliament. The next day he tabled:

> "That this House congratulates Liverpool Football Club on its sixth European Cup title victory; further applauds the club's manager Jürgen Klopp, staff, and dedicated supporters on this magnificent and historic achievement, extending the City of Liverpool's proud footballing tradition; commends both sets of supporters and the people of the host city Madrid for a well-spirited final."

As a boy Carden never imagined the day would come when he'd be tabling such a motion. It was signed by members of every party, including the SNP. Joe Anderson congratulated the team and explained that the victory would be worth some £150m to the city. Afterwards, Arcadis, a finance consultancy, rated Liverpool as the fourth most invested in city in the UK, ahead of London, Birmingham and Manchester.

Forbes estimated that Liverpool had 580 million supporters across the world. The next morning, some 750,000 of them took to the streets of the city to welcome the team back home.

*

They walked down Upper Parliament Street where once there had been an uprising. They passed through Scotland Road where at one time the Irish had settled. Past Town Hall, where Shankly in the '60s, and then Militant in the '80s stood and addressed crowds, they continued – thousands of people from across the world swarmed through the streets of Liverpool as the past, marked by the very fabric of the buildings, met a bright and optimistic present.

They began gathering on Strand Road at 11am, waiting to secure a spot that would give a good view of the cup. The players, coming into the city from Speke, sang songs about each other all along Allerton Road and Childwall Fiveways. '*Saturday night and I like the way you move, Divock Origi*' serenaded Andy Robertson.

Early on in the parade James Milner, a natural leader whom many older fans believe could have played for any great Liverpool side, who at 33 was apparently 'getting better with age', got the bus driver to stop outside the home of wheelchair-bound Andrew Devine – the Hillsborough survivor who came out of a coma in 1997. Liverpool's players leaned over the edge of the bus and clapped back at Devine, nourishing the tether that made the club unique.

Gini Wijnladum, in an interview with his friend van Dijk, said of the scenes: 'You see grandmas, grandpas, babies and all ages – you see how much it means to the city. It's amazing.' His manager Klopp added to the description: 'I cried because it's overwhelming; when you make direct eye contact you see how much it means.'

Fans had waited at the Three Graces for almost 8 hours before the bus arrived, swept back and forth by the Mersey wind. They climbed wherever possible for a unique vantage point, just like they always had. This time, with everything happening on a greater magnitude, Scallies risked their lives to jump a wall and scale to the top of a 50-story building site. It was unfinished, had no windows or walls and was held up by its mere foundations, yet they swarmed to its edges, hundreds of them, and shouted through the wind to the crowds below.

An unused crane (Liverpool seemed to be forever decorated with cranes) standing some 200-feet high was ascended by Scals who treated it all as a playground.

As 6pm ticked into 7, the white sun started to sink behind Birkenhead like it had done for eternity. It stopped behind the Liver buildings and created a silhouette for the victorious Liverpool bus, which crept in slowly from the distance, savouring every wave, smile and tear. The wind caught hold of the pyro smoke that fans had set off throughout, whipping the crowds with soft red clouds, creating an image for the ages.

Time seemed to stop when fireworks suddenly erupted, causing tens of thousands of people to jump and cheer at once. Others were silent and crying.

Daniel Fieldsend

750,000 people, a record number, coloured the scene. They gazed in awe when pyro smoke came out of the clock beneath the Liverbird's tail. Those buildings, the symbol of Liverpool, once acknowledged by sailors who expanded an empire, whose clockface had been dined upon by proud local businessmen before they hoisted it into infamy, now had red pyro smoke coming out of them. The battle for the ownership of the city between Red and Blue was over in a moment: <u>We</u> are Liverpool.

If the ghost of Lord Erskine was looking down on it all from the top of Everton Brow, if he were finally capable of painting in words the impression the scene made, he'd have echoed in that moment Allen Ginsberg's declaration: that Liverpool "is the centre of the known universe". No longer the Venice of the North, nor the Belfast, Dublin, New York or Marseille – no other port would have harboured such a moment – Liverpool was out on its own in the most positive of senses. All of this, with 'riches overflowing' and a great community, painted by the industry of a handful of local men, just like Erskine saw. All of this was the place that the people sang of with pride, and if time ended there and then, they'd have drawn a degree of comfort from the place they'd always cherished. Victorious and glorious: 'My Liverpool home'.

Locāl

[i] 'The Problem With Scouse Exceptionalism' – Laura Brown – Liverpool Long Reads.

[ii] 'Get yer Scouse in order' – Tony Evans – The Anfield Wrap.

[iii] 'The Beatles Anthology' – Windspan . ru.

[iv] 'Jimmy Melia recalls Shankly's impact and discusses his own love of coaching' – Soccer Schools Liverpool.

[v] 'Gerry Marsden: Why YNWA is special to me' – Steve Hunter – Liverpool FC

[vi] 'Liverpool Everyman: 'the theatre was as rough as our performances'' – Chris Wiegand – The Guardian.

[vii] 'Anfield's 50 years of Never Walking Alone' – Simon Hart – The Independent.

[viii] 'Was Liverpool the home of the singing sixties?' – Simon Hart – The Independent.

[ix] 'Did the 1966 World Cup change England?' – The BBC

ibid

[xi] 'Phil Thompson - Kirkby lad who gave his all' – LFC History.

[xii] 'The Spirit of Scouse' – New Statesman.

[xiii] 'Liverpool FC: the Pink Floyd connection' – Jamie Rainbow - World Soccer.

[xiv] 'Toxteth riots, 1981' – Jamie Kenny – Big Issue North

[xv] 'Almost Famous: The Chris Pile story' – The Set Pieces.

[xvi] ''History broke Liverpool, and it broke my heart' – Linda Grand – The Guardian.

[xvii] 'I was wrong about the Self-Pity City; Ten years ago, Jonathan Margolis made a blistering attack on Liverpool. Today he recants.' - Liverpool Daily Post – 2003.

[xviii] 'Steven Gerrard story' – the Liverpool Echo – 2013.

[xix] 'Carragher: My early memories of Gerrard' – Liverpool FC .com – 2014.

[xx] 'Stop whingeing' – the Liverpool Echo – 2004.